Harry Binswanger

HOW WE KNOW

Epistemology on an Objectivist Foundation

TOF Publications

2014 New York

How We Know

Epistemology on
an Objectivist
Foundation

KLAUS NORDBY'S COVER ILLUSTRATION
capitalizes upon an analogy mentioned in the book:
gaining conceptual knowledge is like assembling
a jigsaw puzzle; both involve integrating particular
items, according to relationships among
their features, to form an intelligible whole.
In the cover illustration, the puzzle pieces
are analogs of the perceptual concretes integrated by a concept.
Each puzzle piece has a surface pattern; when the pieces are fitted together
correctly, the patterns join to form subtle circles.

Nordby has taken the analogy further: as indicated by the pieces already joined,
the completely assembled puzzle would show that the individual circles form
a grid — a higher-level pattern, in analogy to the all-important higher-level
integrations of conceptual cognition.

Note that the topmost, loose piece does not fit into the nearby slot.
Placing it there would contradict, not complete, the partial circles
showing on the pieces that are already in place. But if one inspects
further, one will find the place where that piece does fit:
the waiting space in which appears the author's name.

EDITION 1.5

Updates and ongoing discussion: www.how-we-know.com

Copyright © 2014 TOF Publications, Inc. All rights reserved.
ISBN-13: 978-1493753147

Cover design, book design & typesetting by Klaus Nordby.

Produced with Adobe InDesign CS6. Typeset in Adobe Minion Pro
& Adobe Brioso Pro, both designed by Robert Slimbach.

CONTENTS

2

3

4

5

6

7

8

9

10

11

ACKNOWLEDGEMENTS

M y unique and overriding acknowledgment is to Ayn Rand. Her achievements, and the inspiration provided in her novels, made possible not only this book but also my career in philosophy, and have shaped the course of my life.

My education in Objectivism, in philosophy in general, and in the art of objective writing, was aided immensely over decades by Leonard Peikoff. He, however, has seen no drafts of this work beyond a first draft of Chapter 1, many years ago, and he may well disagree with several of the positions I defend herein.

I am very happy to thank Gregory Salmieri for several extremely helpful conversations on epistemology, John Ridpath for his insightful comments on a draft of the book, and Tara Smith for organizing and leading a highly productive workshop on writing projects. Allan Gotthelf, now painfully lost to us, was always encouraging and enlightening.

Lee Pierson has earned my enduring gratitude for prodding me to study J. J. Gibson's invaluable work on perception and for calling to my attention elements of sensationalism and representationalism infecting my prior views. Travis Norsen responded patiently and astutely to my questions on physics.

A very special acknowledgment goes to Shrikant Rangnekar, who met with me weekly for more than *two years*, becoming my de facto coach on this project. He read over each section that I drafted, made very perceptive and philosophically informed comments on each page, and in many other ways acted to shepherd the work, which had been stalled out, to its completion.

Finding a good subtitle was an especially difficult task because it needed to convey that I am writing as an Objectivist, but not writing *on* Objectivism, while also avoiding any suggestion that the book's content forms part of Objectivism (Objectivism, being specifically Ayn Rand's philosophy, is limited to what she wrote or endorsed). It was Tore Boeckmann who came up with "Epistemology on an Objectivist Foundation," a subtitle which is both smoothly professional and as accurate as a short phrase can be. (The longer story is that ideas originated by Ayn Rand supply far more than the foundations of this work, as the many passages quoted from her should make clear.) He also asked me penetrating questions at a very early stage in the writing, questions that helped me recognize a wrong premise I had accepted, which was trapping me in a false alternative.

In like manner, I profited greatly from a question that Dina Federman asked in a graduate seminar I taught in 2002 at the University of Texas. After I had presented to the class my view of how cognition works, Dr. Federman raised her hand to ask me: "How is that different from Plato?" The question startled me, but over time I came to realize that I had indeed fallen prey to a Platonic error, which led me to get back on the proper, Aristotelian, path.

Several volunteers generously acted as "beta-testers" by reading through a late draft. They caught many errors and asked for clarification of more than a few badly written sentences. The book is thus much improved thanks to the efforts of: Michael Berliner, Tore Boeckmann, Tom Bowden, Chuck Butler, Bobby Sandler, Dan Sullivan, and Edwin Thompson.

Tym Parsons gave the book a superb, professional line-editing. Stephanie Bond did a no-holds-barred proofreading of two late iterations of the book, plus she generously reviewed the virtually final version, as did Richard Witt.

Allison Kunze, in an amazing display of tenacity, skillfully met the arduous challenge of indexing this densely interwoven material.

Klaus Nordby designed and composed the book, applying his exacting standards to every esthetic and typographical issue, large and small. He prepared the photographs and graphics, conceived and produced the ingenious cover design (about which, see the copyright page). And on the side, he provided some philosophically astute copy-editing, repeatedly finding passages that were unclear or misleading; rewriting these passages always paid dividends.

Finally, to my wife, Jean, I owe more, intellectually and emotionally, than I know how to express.

PREFACE

M ANKIND HAS EXISTED FOR 400,000 YEARS. BUT 395,000 OF those years were consumed by the Stone Age. The factor that freed men from endless toil and early death, the root cause of the elevated level of existence we now take for granted, is one precious value: *knowledge.* The painfully acquired knowledge of how to master nature, how to organize social existence, and how to understand himself is what enabled man to rise from the cave to the skyscraper, from warring clans to a global economy, from an average lifespan of less than 30 years to one approaching 80.

Though mankind has risen from the cave, things have not been going well for us lately. The serene confidence of the Age of Reason has given way to a cultural atmosphere of depression and anxiety — especially among the intellectuals, who have become convinced that life is "fear and trembling, sickness unto death." The art that speaks to modern intellectuals is typified by Edvard Munch's painting *The Scream* and by literature that trumpets the futility of all human endeavor and celebrates unintelligibility. In 1998, a panel of literary scholars and authors was asked to pick the top one hundred English-language novels of the twentieth century. Here is a small taste of the novel they rated as number one, James Joyce's *Ulysses*:

Im sure thats the way down the monkeys go under the sea to
Africa when they die the ships out far like chips that was the Malta
boat passing yes the sea and the sky you could do what you liked

What explains the critical acclaim for this puerile, subjectivistic chaos
— in an era when technology's disciplined, structured logic is putting
smartphones into the hands of people around the globe and landing remote-
controlled vehicles on Mars? What explains the wider malaise of our culture?

The two-word answer is: *bad epistemology.* Epistemology, the theory of
knowledge, is the branch of philosophy that defines the nature, means, and
standards of knowledge. Epistemology deals with the crucial questions:
What is knowledge? How is it acquired? How is it validated? Since knowledge
is man's means of dealing with reality, a man attempting to function on an
irrational epistemology is unequipped to deal with reality, dooming himself to doubt, confusion, and failure. Post-Renaissance philosophers, from
Descartes to Hume to Kant, have spun out ever worse theories of knowledge, and the intellectuals are the social group most directly and intensely
affected by philosophical theory. No effective antidote to the epistemological
poison has appeared, so the paradoxical situation described by Ayn Rand half
a century ago rings true today:

> If we look at modern intellectuals, we are confronted with the
> grotesque spectacle of such characteristics as militant uncer-
> tainty, crusading cynicism, dogmatic agnosticism, boastful self-
> abasement and self-righteous depravity — in an atmosphere
> of guilt, of panic, of despair, of boredom and of all-pervasive
> evasion. [FNI, 11]

Our technological success has come from a dedication to reason and logic,
but reason and logic have been distorted or openly attacked by mainstream
epistemologists for the last 200 years, ever since Kant's theory of knowledge
gained dominance in the intellectual world. Establishment epistemology has
carried to its logical conclusion Kant's claim that reason cannot know reality.
The result has been two schools of thought, one that accepts reason while
ignoring reality, and one that accepts reality while denying reason.

Rationalism is the school that scorns sensory perception and constructs intellectual castles in the air. Empiricism is the school that scorns
abstractions and demands that men hold their minds down to the animal
level of unconceptualized, unintegrated sensing. Rationalism ultimately

degenerates into mysticism, as in its ancient father: Plato. Empiricism ultimately degenerates into skepticism, as in its modern father: Hume.

The mystics hold that knowledge can be acquired without any sensory or rational means; knowledge is said to come from "intuition" or "revelation," which washes over us and to which we need only surrender. The skeptics, observing that men disagree — even about allegedly "revealed truth" — throw up their hands and announce that there is no truth, that any claim to knowledge is proof of dogmatism, and that we are doomed to perpetual doubt.[1] In the words of a former chairman of the UCLA philosophy department, "There are no answers. Be brave and face up to it."[2]

Both the mystic and skeptic schools fly in the face of human history. In the one thousand years ruled by the mystical view, from the fall of Rome to the end of the medieval era, reliance on alleged revelations and religious authorities led not to cognitive progress but to stagnation. On the other hand, since the rebirth of reason in the Renaissance, fueled by the rediscovery of Aristotle's works, a vast body of painfully won scientific knowledge — knowledge, not mere opinion — has produced our magnificent technological achievements. The broad record of human history shows that knowledge *is* achievable, but only by *reason*, applied to observational data.

Nonetheless, mysticism and skepticism have lived on, zombie-like, due to the success of the Kantian attack on reason. That attack has drawn its power from the errors and concessions in the theories of reason's defenders (e.g., John Locke). Lacking a clear, uncompromised understanding of what reason is and how it operates, epistemology has succumbed to the Kantian onslaught, leaving men to face the lethal false alternative of mysticism versus skepticism.

The advocates of reason have been unable to answer the crucial question: what makes a cognitive choice valid or invalid? Since God or nature doesn't tell us how to proceed in our thinking, what standard can we use to guide our thought processes?

Contrary to the foggy notions of a non-judgmental age, there is a *right* and a *wrong* direction to take — if grasping the facts of reality is one's goal. The *right* direction means the one suited to cognitive success; any deviation

---

1   In colloquial usage, "skepticism" often means merely a cautious, "show me" attitude, but in philosophy, "skepticism" means the idea that knowledge is impossible, that man knows nothing. Of course, that would mean that no one could know that skepticism itself was true. On the self-refuting nature of skepticism, see CHAPTER 1, CHAPTER 5, and CHAPTER 10.

2   Donald Kalish, *Time Magazine*, Jan. 7, 1966, p. 24.

from that direction is *wrong* — wrong in relation to that goal, wrong in terms of the unwaivable requirements of acquiring knowledge of objective reality.

Whether a man wants to know the sum of two plus three, the method of forging metals, or the principles of a proper political system, to reach the correct answer he must follow a definite series of steps. But the steps one takes in pursuing knowledge are not set by instinct, genes, or culture. The course of a thought-process is up to the thinker to choose (see CHAPTER 10).

Understanding *how* knowledge is acquired and validated enables one to bring the cognitive quest under one's conscious control and direction, equipping him to succeed in acquiring knowledge, to avoid whole categories of error, and to reach objective certainty in his conclusions.

On a wider, cultural scale, the need for a rational epistemology could not be more urgent. Western civilization itself is now under attack by the revived mysticism of Christian and Islamic fundamentalism and by the new skepticism of multiculturalism and postmodernism. The mystics say that science is wrong — false in its conclusions and blasphemous in its contravention of the Bible or the Koran. The skeptics say that science is neither right nor wrong — that truth, falsehood, good, and evil are baseless "constructs" imposed by a "patriarchal power-structure."

An open, progressing, benevolent future requires a theory of knowledge that rejects the false dichotomy that sustains both mysticism and skepticism: the dichotomy of Empiricism vs. Rationalism. What is required is a theory that upholds *both* sensory perception *and* logic, a theory that shows how abstract, conceptual knowledge derives in a logical fashion from perceptual observation.

That theory has been provided by Ayn Rand, especially in her work *Introduction to Objectivist Epistemology*. Rand's definition of "reason" sets the context for integrating perception and logic: "Reason is the faculty that identifies and integrates the material provided by man's senses." [VOS, 22] At the base of Rand's view of reason is her new theory of how abstractions, i.e., *concepts*, are formed from perceptual observation. Concepts are the tools of reason, and it is by means of concepts that man stores and accesses his knowledge.

The present work makes extensive use of Rand's Objectivist epistemology, as I understand it after fifty years of professional study and teaching. To a modest degree, I elaborate on and build upon Rand's system, but my extensions, even if valid, do not constitute part of the Objectivist philosophy, which is limited to what Rand wrote, plus those articles by others that were published under her editorship. (The definitive secondary source on Objectivism is Leonard Peikoff's consummate work, *Objectivism: The Philosophy of Ayn Rand*.)

In this book I do not assume any prior familiarity with the details of philosophy nor with Objectivism. This book is addressed to the intelligent layman, assuming he has a definite interest in understanding how we know.

The organization of this book follows one of the cardinal principles of Objectivist epistemology: knowledge is hierarchical. Chapter by chapter, I trace the development of progressively more advanced forms of knowledge, from its base in the axioms of all knowledge, through the fundamental role of sensory perception, to the formation and use of concepts, through more abstract concepts, to propositions, and inference — first from the standpoint of what knowledge is, then from the standpoint of the means of validating it. After this hierarchical progression, I devote a chapter to Rand's revolutionary identification that "man is a being of volitional consciousness" — i.e., that free will consists in one's sovereign control over the operation of his own mind. A concluding overview contrasts the right ("bottom-up") and wrong ("top-down") theories of how we know.

My perspective is causal and biological. Knowledge is an achievement, one reached by employing certain necessary means, and its purpose is to aid men in the task of survival.

Knowledge is a product of the wider faculty: *consciousness*. If one adopts the causal-biological perspective on consciousness, and applies it to each of the different functions and levels of awareness, one can gain a crucial, even life-altering, understanding of the mind and its cognitive needs.

The misunderstandings of consciousness that have wreaked havoc on the history of philosophy, making philosophy appear irrelevant to daily life, all stem from taking consciousness to be non-causal and non-biological — or even, in the latest aberration, non-existent. But consciousness exists, and it functions according to its nature. Refusing to recognize its existence and its identity makes men mysterious to themselves. It turns men, in Rand's graphic phrase, into "prisoners inside their own skulls."

To gain self-understanding, one must understand the essence of the self: one's mind.

ABBREVIATIONS

1

FOUNDATIONS

AWARE - having knowlege

CONSIDER SOME EXAMPLES OF KNOWLEDGE, FROM THE PRIMITIVE to the highly advanced. A dog knows where it buried a bone; a baby knows its mother; a savage knows how to hunt; a student knows the multiplication table; a physicist knows the laws of motion.

What do all these examples of knowing have in common? A retained awareness of some fact of reality. From the dog that retains its awareness of the bone's location, to the physicist who has a retained awareness of the laws of motion, information is stored and can be reactivated — whether the reactivation is automatic, triggered by sensory cues, as it is for the dog, or is volitional, as it is when a man asks himself questions in order to bring stored material back to mind.

Knowledge is not a transient state of awareness, as in viewing the passing scene from the window of an automobile, but a stable and enduring mental product — information that you possess, facts that you have gotten hold of, grasped.

Ayn Rand's characterization of knowledge summarizes this, and states the basic means by which knowledge is acquired: Knowledge is "a mental grasp of a fact(s) of reality, reached either by perceptual observation or by a process of reason based on perceptual observation." [ITOE, 35]

Def knowlege

mental grasp.

[handwritten margin note, top left: A statement neccessary contained in all others]

[handwritten margin note, top: cannot be proved (self-evident) — base for facts]

The First Axiom: Existence

Knowledge is of facts of reality, i.e., aspects of existence. The basis and starting point of all knowledge is the fact that there is a world to be known. Or, in Rand's indelible statement, "Existence exists." [AS, 1015]

The existence of things is perceived directly: we see things, hear things, feel them, smell them, and taste them. That *there is something* is perceptually given; it is not learned by inference from other facts (which themselves would have to exist). "Existence exists" is a formulation of what is self-evident. "Self-evident" means: available to direct awareness.

All knowledge, whether perceptual or intellectual, is of something, something that exists. Any claim to knowledge is a claim to know that something is the case, that some state of affairs *exists*.

Accordingly, "Existence exists" is not a derivative or restricted truth but an *axiom*: a fundamental, primary, self-evident truth implicitly contained in all knowledge.

Axioms cannot be proved. This is not a weakness or subjectivity lurking in them. Axioms are better than proved: they are self-evident. "Existence exists" does not need to be proved; it is directly perceived. Just open your eyes, and you know all there is to know about the reality of reality. There is an unlimited amount to be learned about what exists, the forms and varieties and aspects of existents, but nothing further to be learned about the fact that existence exists, nothing beyond what is contained in your first awareness at the start of your life: "it is."

Some people demand that axioms be proved. But such a demand fails to grasp what proof is. "Proof" is an advanced, not a primary, concept. It depends upon the prior concept of "existence," and on an immense body of other knowledge. Young children and savages have no concept of proof.

All ideas do have to be shown to be valid. But "validation" is a wider idea than "proof." There are, broadly, two forms of validation: by proof and by direct perception.

Proof is a process of inference — deductive or inductive inference. In either form, inference is a process of moving in thought from something known to something else logically related to it. An inference is made from something, not from nothing. Consequently, there must be a starting point. The starting point of any valid chain of proofs, however long, is the information given in direct awareness — i.e., the self-evident.

If you see footprints in the sand and conclude that someone has walked by, that conclusion is reached by inference. But your seeing of the footprints

[handwritten note: Def. forming a conclusion from premises.]

constitutes direct, non-inferential perception; the presence of those shapes in the sand is self-evident to you.

As Aristotle observed, it is illogical to hold that absolutely everything has to be proved. Proof is indispensable when direct observation is not available. But proof is neither necessary nor possible in regard to the basic information on which all knowledge is based: perceptual data. As important as proof is, it is the secondary, not the primary, means of validating ideas. The primary means is direct awareness.

Self-evidencies, directly perceived facts, are what make proof possible. To state the point in an extreme form: proof is what we resort to when something is not self-evident.

And let us ask: why does proof prove? What makes it "work"? Proof establishes an idea by connecting it to the directly perceived, the self-evident. To demand, therefore, a proof of the self-evident is an absurd reversal.

Many philosophers dismiss the idea of self-evidency as arbitrary or subjective. Since I will argue that consciousness and many facts about consciousness are self-evident, it is important to establish firmly the idea of self-evidency from the outset.

Although many things have been falsely claimed to be self-evident, in all such cases, the error lies with what has been taken to be self-evident, not with self-evidency as such. Again, "self-evident" means: available to direct awareness. The self-evident is that which makes itself evident by being directly observed, rather than by being inferred from something else.

"Self-evident" is not a synonym for "obvious." To one who has learned arithmetic, it is obvious that two plus two is four, but that truth is not self-evident; it is inferred by a process of comparison and counting. But that the page you are reading exists is not an inference: it is self-evident.

The data of sensory perception are self-evident, but the conceptual interpretation of that data, and inferences drawn from it, are not self-evident. They must be validated by reducing them back to the self-evident.

The opponents of self-evidency will tell you that in the medieval era it was self-evident that the world is flat, but we now know it is round. But the medievals were not able to perceive the shape of the planet. What is given in perception is a very small portion of the Earth's surface, and all one can say about what is given in perception is that the curvature is less than the eye can detect. The expanse of ocean or prairie one can see is indeed flat — to the standard of precision given in visual perception. To take a position on what the shape of the Earth is beyond what perception can reveal is to engage in either inference or blind guessing. Only astronauts in space are able to see

enough of the world to have a perceptual experience of its shape, and of course they see it as round.

Another stock example falls just as easily: the revolution of the Earth around the sun. It is not self-evident that the sun goes around the Earth, nor that the Earth goes around the sun. What is self-evident is that the sun and the Earth are in *relative* motion. It is not self-evident which frame of reference, that of the Earth or that of the sun, is the proper one to use in science.

Such alleged counterexamples to self-evidency have nothing in common with "Existence exists," which states a self-evident fact, a fact we confront in every waking moment, from our first acts of awareness to our last.

Although the truth of "Existence exists" does not have to be proved, one does have to prove that, within the class of truths, it has the special status of an axiom. Axioms are a special subclass of self-evident truths. Axioms are self-evidencies that express a primary fact at the base of all knowledge. Only a very few self-evident truths are axioms. A statement like "The grass in front of me is green," though self-evident, is not fundamental and is not contained in all subsequent claims to knowledge.

The axiomatic status of "Existence exists" has already been demonstrated by showing that it is an irreducible primary, presupposed by and implicitly contained in all knowledge. But there is also a specific test of axiomaticity. Because all knowledge depends on it, an axiom is cognitively inescapable. As Ayn Rand observes, an axiom is "a statement necessarily contained in all others, whether any particular speaker chooses to identify it or not." [AS, 1040] One cannot think at all without assuming the truth of a genuine axiom. An axiom is absolutely fundamental. Even the attempt to deny it tacitly counts on its truth.

For instance, in Ancient Greece, one Sophist announced: "Nothing exists." But if nothing exists, then his statement does not exist. He has to assume that his statement exists in the very act of denying that anything exists. And he has to assume the existence of much more: of himself, of his understanding of the meaning of the words he uttered, and of all the learning he had to accomplish from infancy onward in order to reach the day when he could make a fool of himself by uttering that self-refuting statement.

This test for axiomaticity is called "re-affirmation through denial,"[3] because the speaker has to implicitly re-affirm the axiom in his attempt to deny it. "An axiom is a proposition that defeats its opponents by the fact that they have to accept it and use it in the process of any attempt to deny it." [AS, 1040]

---

3   See, for instance, BLANSHARD, 1939, VOL. 2, 252.

Again, "re-affirmation through denial" does not prove an axiom to be true: axioms are perceptual self-evidencies, not something proved by anything else. "Re-affirmation through denial" tests only whether a given statement, already recognized to be true, is implicitly contained in all others, and thus has the status, within the class of truths, of an axiom. (In contrast, although a patch of grass is self-evidently green, saying "This grass is not green" does not in any way re-affirm its greenness.)

We must be very clear on what "Existence exists" means. It does not mean that there is some state or property of things constituting their existence. It does not say, "Things have the property of being" — there is no such property. It says that there are existents — things that exist. To posit a property of "beinghood" characterizing existents is to imply that there are non-existents which lack this property. But there are no non-existents: what is, is; what is not, is not. As Leonard Peikoff puts it, " 'Existence' here is a collective noun, denoting the sum of existents." [OPAR, 4] "Existence exists" is equivalent to "All that which is, is."

In fact, "Existence exists" simply puts into the form of a proposition the axiomatic concept "existence." To state "Everything that is, is" is simply to understand the concept "is." Or, equivalently, it is to have grasped the concept "everything."

Just as one cannot make existence into a property of existents, one cannot analyze the fact of existence in any way. It is a primary, irreducible fact. One can analyze a non-axiomatic fact into its components or aspects. But that process presupposes that those components or aspects *exist*. One can analyze lightning into electric discharges, or plants and animals into cells, but then the electric discharges or cells have to exist. What would one analyze existence into? That which does not exist?

Thus the ponderous, pretentious silliness of those philosophers who try to ask: "Why is there something rather than nothing?" I say "try to ask," because there is no actual question here, only words having the linguistic form of a question. Whatever answer one would try to give to this pseudo-question — call it the X-factor — the X-factor would have to exist, leaving the pseudo-question unanswered.

A simpler form of the same error can be found in the theist's pseudo-question: "What caused the universe?" Here, again, there is no actual question, because to ask for a cause is to ask for a cause that exists, and the universe is: all that which exists. When the theist uses this pseudo-question to "prove" the existence of a God, it does not occur to him that, by his logic, he must then ask: "What caused God?"

We may ask for a causal explanation of any particular thing *within* existence, but it is nonsensical to ask for a cause of existence as such.

Existence, the universe, is a self-sufficient primary. There is nothing that causes there to be something rather than nothing; there is nothing prior to existence, beneath existence, or outside of existence. Existence exists, and only existence exists. What is not, is not.

Nor can there be an origin of the universe or an end to the universe. Particular arrangements of elements within the universe — arrangements constituting ourselves, planets, even galaxies — can come and go. But the universe — the entirety of that which is — neither came into being (from what?) nor can go out of existence. There was no time at which nothing existed; the universe is not in time or space; time and space are relationships among things within the universe.

In other words, existence exists. Period.

The Second Axiom: Consciousness

The axiom of existence is the base of all our knowledge. But it is not the only axiom. The second axiom, implied in one's awareness of existence, is that one is conscious.

Consciousness is the faculty of awareness. Since knowledge is a retained awareness, to set the context for investigating knowledge, I need to discuss the axiom of consciousness in considerable detail.

An axiom is a truth that is cognitively primary, self-evident, and stands at the basis of knowledge. It is easy to show that "I am conscious" possesses each of those four characteristics of axiomaticity.

1. The fact that one is conscious is a truth; indeed consciousness, like existence, is a foundation of truth: truth pertains to a certain relationship between consciousness and reality. External existents, apart from any relationship they have to consciousness, are not "true" or "false" — they just *are*; truth and falsehood pertain to something mental — an idea, statement, proposition — in its relation to the external world.

2. The fact that one is conscious is a cognitive primary: for newborns, or even in the womb, cognition begins with being conscious of something — of a pressure, a temperature, etc. — and there is no cognition prior to being conscious.

3. The fact that one is conscious is self-evident: it is directly experienced, not inferred. To be sure, one's direct awareness of one's consciousness is not sensory, as one's direct awareness of existence is. One does not see or touch or taste one's awareness. But, from a very young age, one is directly, non-inferentially aware that in sense-perception, and later in more complex mental activities, one is aware. Self-awareness is a given for man.

4. The fact that one is conscious is the base of all knowledge: knowledge is a phenomenon of consciousness. To know by means of unconsciousness is a contradiction in terms. Roses and rocks do not have knowledge.

"I am conscious" passes the test of axiomaticity: re-affirmation through denial. "I am not conscious" is a self-refuting statement. Non-conscious entities exist, but they are not conscious of being non-conscious. Any attempt to consider the possibility of one's not being conscious presupposes that one is conscious to consider it. Stones do not consider, question, believe, or doubt anything. There are no stone philosophers to assert or deny that they are conscious.

Again, passing the test of "re-affirmation through denial" does not prove that one is conscious — one already knows that (and proof itself is an action of consciousness). Rather, the implicit re-affirmation of consciousness in any attempt to deny it establishes the epistemological status of "I am conscious" — it shows that this is not a limited or derived truth, but an axiom.

Just as there are thinkers who, explicitly or implicitly, attempt to deny existence, so there are those who attempt to deny consciousness. Often the rejection of consciousness is explicit, as it was in the case of the Behaviorist psychologists (John Watson[4] and B. F. Skinner being the arch-examples). If Martian philosophers existed, there would be no self-contradiction in their denying that Earthlings are conscious; but any behaviorist who admits to membership in the human race is contradicting himself by claiming to be aware that man is unconscious. The fact that behaviorists consider themselves to be scientists merely compounds the contradiction: science is a highly advanced product of consciousness. (A comprehensive autopsy of all forms of materialism — the doctrine that consciousness does not exist — will come at the end of this chapter.)

Consciousness, unlike existence, is a property: "Consciousness is an attribute of certain living entities, but it is not an attribute of a given state of awareness, it is that state." [ITOE, 56] Just as existence is not something distinguishable from, added to, or underlying the various things that exist,

---

4   "[C]onsciousness is neither a definite nor a usable concept.... [B]elief in the existence of consciousness goes back to the ancient days of superstition and magic." [WATSON, 4]

so consciousness is not something distinguishable from, added to, or under-lying the various states of awareness. Just as a chair's existence is not some-thing distinguishable from, added to, or underlying the chair, so the aware-ness provided by seeing the chair is not something distinguishable from, added to, or underlying the seeing. To be a chair is to exist; to see a chair is to be aware of it.

One cannot analyze the state of awareness as such. It is a primary, irreducible fact. There are no "consciousness atoms" to analyze the state of consciousness into. (The belief that awareness can be analyzed into neural states or processes will be refuted a little later.)

It is the state, not the faculty, of consciousness that is irreducible and unanalyzable; the faculty of awareness has a physical side — the nervous system — which, of course, can be analyzed physically and physiologically. But what it is to be aware of something, rather than being unaware, is a primary fact that cannot be analyzed.

The varieties and forms of states of awareness can be distinguished — as can the varieties and forms of existence. One can distinguish pain from pleasure, and both from memory or imagination — just as one can distin-guish, in regard to existence, tables from rocks, and both from molecules or galaxies. But one cannot ask "what is it to exist?" nor "what is it to be aware of something?" Existence and consciousness are irreducible primaries.

Axiomatic Concepts

Ayn Rand discovered that beneath axiomatic propositions lie axiomatic concepts. "Axioms are usually considered to be propositions identifying a fundamental, self-evident truth. But explicit propositions as such are not primaries: they are made of concepts." [ITOE, 55]

A proposition is a statement, such as "Cats are animals." A proposition applies some predicate (e.g., "animal") to some subject (e.g., cats). Thus, the general formula for a proposition is "S is P." To form or grasp a proposition, one has to know what the S and the P refer to — i.e., one has to have the concept of "S" and the concept of "P." If a child does not have the concept "cat" and the concept "animal," he cannot form or understand the proposi-tion "Cats are animals." Propositions presuppose concepts. Axiomatic propositions presuppose axiomatic concepts, with the implication Rand draws: "The base of man's knowledge — of all other concepts, all axioms, propositions and thought — consists of axiomatic concepts." [ITOE, 55]

In particular, the base of the axiomatic proposition "Existence exists" is the axiomatic concept of "existence." The base of the axiomatic proposition, "I am conscious" is the axiomatic concept of "consciousness." *ABSTRACT IDEAS*

The identification that axiomatic concepts, not axiomatic propositions, are the base of all knowledge resolves a long-standing dilemma about axioms. This dilemma can be put as follows. On the one hand, an axiom is a primary — something that one must know before one knows anything else. On the other hand, knowledge of the axioms as propositions is in fact gained very late in one's development, if ever. Clearly, the infant in its crib is not thinking to itself: "Existence exists," or any such sentence, before it has language. So if axioms are propositions, sentences, or thoughts, they are not available to a beginning knower. And, in fact, the vast majority of men have lived their whole lives never having heard or thought such propositions. So, if we need the knowledge of axioms in order to go on to further knowledge, how can that be reconciled with the preceding?

This dilemma dissolves once one recognizes that the required knowledge is not propositional knowledge. Propositions connect two separate items, a subject and a predicate that is distinct from it, as in "Dogs have tails." But an axiomatic proposition, as Rand notes, merely restate the fact that its subject term refers to. "Existence exists" merely puts into propositional form a single, unanalyzable fact — the fact that something is there, it *exists*.[5]

The fact of existence is grasped not through a proposition but *perceptually*. In the infant's first perception and in every succeeding one, it is aware of something that exists. Later knowledge merely names what is grasped, wordlessly, from the beginning. As Rand puts it, the infant from the outset has the axiomatic concept *implicitly*. It knows exactly what the philosopher knows when he uses the sophisticated term "existence." There is nothing more to be learned about the basic fact that things *are*. As far as the fact of existence goes, once you've seen one existent, you've seen them all.

Axiomatic concepts, held implicitly, are thus the base of cognitive development. Rand writes:

> The building-block of man's knowledge is the concept of an "existent" — of something that exists, be it a thing, an attribute or

DEF.

---

5   Likewise, "Consciousness is conscious" and "A is A" are restatements of the (implicit) concepts of "consciousness" and "identity."

an action. Since it is a concept, man cannot grasp it *explicitly* until he has reached the conceptual stage. But it is implicit in every percept (to perceive a thing is to perceive that it exists) and man grasps it *implicitly* on the perceptual level — i.e., he grasps the constituents of the concept "existent," the data which are later to be integrated by that concept. It is this implicit knowledge that permits his consciousness to develop further.[6] [ITOE, 5–6]

I am aware of something.

CONSCIOUSNESS: FOUR FUNDAMENTALS

Of the properties of consciousness, four are fundamental and undeniable.[7]

1. Consciousness has an object and a subject.
2. Existence has primacy over consciousness.
3. Consciousness is an active process.
4. Consciousness is a biological faculty.

I will discuss each in turn.

1. *Consciousness has an object and a subject*

A state of consciousness is an awareness of something, by some organism. Consciousness is an activity involving a relation of a subject to an object.

Consciousness implies an object, that of which one is aware. One can't see without seeing something; one can't think without thinking about something. For one to be aware, there must be the *what*, the object that one is aware of.

> Some object, i.e., some *content*, is involved in every state of awareness. . . . Awareness is awareness of something. A contentless state of consciousness is a contradiction in terms. [ITOE, 29]

something.
content
must be what
(object)

---

6   There are other axiomatic concepts besides "existence" and "consciousness." Notably, the concept of "identity" is axiomatic, and is expressed propositionally in the statement: "A thing is what it is," or "*A is A*." Rand describes the concept of "identity" as a corollary of the concept of "existence."

7   The first three of these facts are self-evident; the biological nature of consciousness is a fact that is reached by inductive inference.

What if one imagines something that doesn't exist, such as a golden mountain? There is still *content*: one is imagining *something*, not nothing. One is imagining a golden mountain, not a nothing; to imagine a golden mountain is to imagine *that*, not something else.

The materials used in imagination come from one's past perception of reality, here of gold and of mountains. Imagination is the ability to mentally combine and rearrange such materials. Imagination, in stark contrast to perception, is under direct volitional control: you can visualize whatever you like, but you can see only what is there to be seen.

If we liken imagination to painting something in the mind, the pigments have to exist or else there can be no painting; the materials of imagination have to come from memory of things taken in from reality. One cannot construct a fantasy out of sensory qualities that one has never experienced. We cannot, for instance, visualize ultraviolet, since its wavelength is outside the range of human vision. Men blind from birth do not have a visual form of imagination; they do not even have visual dreams.[8]

As Rand states, "Directly or indirectly, every phenomenon of consciousness is derived from one's awareness of the external world." [ITOE, 29] All consciousness is consciousness *of something*.

Consciousness also involves a subject, which is the man or animal that is conscious.

Consider how one forms the concept "consciousness." One forms the concept by reflecting on one's own mental actions, to integrate *one's own* seeing, hearing, thinking, remembering, imagining, etc.; then one includes the similar conscious activities of other men and of the higher animals. (One cannot experience or directly apprehend any consciousness other than one's own.)

Philosophers sometimes ask, following David Hume, "How do I become aware of the self? Introspection gives me only concrete mental acts, not a self." The answer is: it is *you* introspecting, *you* observing your consciousness of something.[9] It is not the case that one discovers that consciousness in general exists and then wonders whether it is attached to a person. One first becomes

---

8   Imagined content is usually compared to perceptual content, but it would seem to be more closely related to the content of memory. Imagining an absent friend's face seems to have just the same inner quality or "feel" as remembering it, which is in line with the point that imagination is the ability to rearrange *stored* perceptual data.

9   In addition, a direct experience of the self comes with one's exercise of free will. The difference between what one *does* and what merely happens to one is an experience of the self, the ego, as the cause of one's actions. (See CHAPTER 10)

aware of one's own consciousness and then infers that other people and the higher animals are also conscious.[10]

Rand's summarizing statement is:

Def
object
subject

> Existence exists — and the act of grasping that statement implies two corollary axioms: that something exists [the object] which one perceives and that one exists [the subject] possessing consciousness, consciousness being the faculty of perceiving that which exists. If nothing exists, there can be no consciousness: a consciousness with nothing to be conscious of is a contradiction in terms. [AS, 1015]

independent

2. *Existence has primacy over consciousness*

The fact that consciousness has an object means that consciousness cannot be self-contained. Consciousness is inherently something that points outside itself, to something else: its object.[11]

This leads to the principle Ayn Rand named "the primacy of existence": existence has primacy over consciousness. Consciousness is a secondary phenomenon: in order for an organism to be conscious of something, that something first has to exist.

The primacy of existence is the recognition that existence is independent of consciousness; things exist, and are what they are, whether or not any organism is conscious of them. By the same token, consciousness is dependent on existence: consciousness has to have an object rather than being purely self-contained.

(The contrary position, "the primacy of consciousness," reverses this order, treating consciousness as the self-sufficient primary, relegating existence to the status of a derivative of consciousness — as in the idea that God wished the universe into being.)

1) Existence
2) conclusion

Epistemologically, the primacy of existence is the recognition that existence must be known before consciousness is known, and that existence is known by extrospection, not introspection. [See PWNI, 24–25]

---

10   The basis of inferring that other people and the higher animals are conscious is, obviously, their anatomical and behavioral similarities to oneself.

11   The case of introspection, which involves consciousness of consciousness, will be discussed shortly.

From one's first grasp in early childhood of any action of one's conscious-ness, one learns that existence, the object of awareness, is independent of that awareness. Peikoff writes:

> From the outset, consciousness presents itself as something specific — as a faculty of perceiving an object, not of creating or changing it. For instance, a child may hate the food set in front of him and refuse even to look at it. But his inner state does not erase his dinner. Leaving aside physical action, the food is impervious; it is unaffected by a process of consciousness as such. [OPAR, 18]

One must (implicitly) accept the primacy of existence in order to grasp any concept of consciousness — e.g., "seeing," or "thinking." Such concepts require distinguishing between one's awareness and the object of which one is aware — e.g., between the act of seeing and what is seen — and the only means of doing so is to notice what depends on us and what exists independently (e.g., by observing what happens on closing and re-opening one's eyes).

The primacy of existence is fully consistent with the fact that self-consciousness exists: a consciousness can turn back on itself to make its own activities into an object. One can certainly be conscious of one's conscious-ness, through introspection. But introspection presupposes extrospection.[12] One can introspect only *after* one has perceived things; until then, one is not conscious, so there is nothing to introspect. *Consciousness precedes self-consciousness.*

> A consciousness conscious of nothing but itself is a contradiction in terms: before it could identify itself as consciousness, it had to be conscious of something. [AS, 1015]

To "identify itself as consciousness" requires making the distinction between subject and object, between self and the world, which presupposes that there is a world.

The opposite view, the primacy of consciousness, was injected into post-Renaissance philosophy by Descartes. Although he recognized that

---

12   The introspected object, e.g., a thought, must have had its own object. A thought must be a thought of something. (The object of thought does not have to be an external existent: one can think about a dream one had; but any dream is of something, and its content is ultimately derived from perception of reality.) No matter how many levels of "conscious-ness of consciousness of . . ." one adds, the final "of" requires an object.

consciousness must have an object, he asserted the possibility that this object might itself be mental, not external. He took the existence of his consciousness to be axiomatic, but the existence of existence to be non-axiomatic, problematical. He asked, in effect, "How do I know that there is a world outside my mind? What if all that I am ever aware of are experiences inside my own mind, not external reality?"

But to identify something as "an experience in my mind," I have to contrast my mental experiences with something else. Without the contrast between the internal and the external, "internal" loses its meaning. "Everything is internal" is an incoherent statement, one that contains an implicit contradiction. "Everything is only in my mind" likewise renders "my mind" meaningless. It is only the contrast between existence and consciousness that makes the concept "consciousness" possible.

The logical fallacy exemplified here was first identified by Ayn Rand. She called it "the fallacy of the stolen concept." [AS, 1039] A thorough treatment of the stolen concept fallacy will have to wait until CHAPTER 7, but it is worth pausing here to give a preliminary account.

The stolen concept fallacy consists of a certain kind of violation of the hierarchy of concepts. Concepts have to be formed in a certain order, and their meaningful use depends on not violating that order. A child's first concepts, such as "dog," are formed from sense-perception; then more advanced concepts, such as "animal" and "pet," are formed on the basis of the prior concepts, creating a hierarchy, in which some concepts depend on others. For instance, a child cannot grasp "pet" before he grasps "animal." (I am referring to the grasp of a concept, not merely the uttering of a word.)

But suppose a demented philosopher announces: "Pets exist, but animals do not." In violating the necessary hierarchy of concepts, his statement wipes itself out. Obviously, if there are no animals, there are no pets, since a pet is "any domesticated or tamed animal that is kept as a favorite and cared for affectionately." [RANDOM HOUSE COLLEGE DICTIONARY, 1980]

On the other hand, if one says only: "There are no such things as pets," one has made a false statement but has not "stolen" any concept. The concept-stealing here occurs when one attempts to retain the concept "pet" while denying the hierarchically prior concept "animal." Doing that "steals" the concept "pet" — i.e., uses "pet" without any logical right to do so.

The uniquely perverse nature of the fallacy of the stolen concept, in the form it usually occurs, is its attempt to use a concept in the very act of negating that concept's own base — thereby sawing off the cognitive branch one is sitting on. Consider the statement: "It has been proved mathematically that there are no such things as numbers." If there are no numbers, there is no science of mathematics and no such thing as a mathematical proof: one can grasp "mathematics" only on the basis of first grasping "one," "two," and other numerical concepts.

All the versions of the primacy of consciousness that litter the history of philosophy "steal" the concept of "consciousness," or some particular concept pertaining to consciousness. For, as Rand observes, "It is only in relation to the external world that the various actions of a consciousness can be experienced, grasped, defined or communicated." [ITOE, 29] To grasp "consciousness," one must distinguish actions of consciousness from their objects — i.e., from things that exist independently. When a Cartesian says, "Maybe nothing exists outside my mind," he has "stolen" the concept "mind," depriving it of any meaning, just as if he had said, "Maybe the entire universe is indoors," an utterance that renders "indoors" meaningless.

The recognition that existence is independent of consciousness, and that consciousness is the faculty of perceiving it, is the base of all further discussion of consciousness — in fact, of all further discussion, period.

3. Consciousness is an active process

So far, I have noted that consciousness is an organism's awareness of something that exists. The next point is that consciousness is an *activity*, an ongoing, continuous process of interaction with the world. This marks a fundamental re-orientation, rejecting the static view of consciousness, the view of Plato and the mystics. Rand gives a clear statement of the right view:

> Awareness is not a passive state, but an active process. On the lower levels of awareness, a complex neurological process is required to enable man to experience a sensation and to integrate sensations into percepts; that process is automatic and non-volitional: man is aware of its results, but not of the process itself. On the higher, conceptual level, the process is psychological, conscious and volitional. In either case, awareness is achieved and maintained by continuous *action.* [ITOE, 29]

Let's look at this point on both the conceptual and the sensory levels. The briefest introspection shows that conceptual awareness involves action. Thinking is an activity, and it is not possible to freeze a thought and hold it still. Perform this experiment. Think, "Triangles have three sides," and try to hold your mind locked on that single thought. It cannot be done; your mind automatically starts moving, with an implicit "now what?" and "so what?" You can look more closely at what you mean by triangles having three sides, you can picture a succession of triangles, you can repeat the same words over and over (though doing that soon turns them into meaningless sounds). What you cannot do is stop "the stream of consciousness," as William James phrased it. In regard to the *conceptual* level of awareness, we are aware by direct introspection that consciousness is an activity. And, of course, neuro-physiological action underlies conceptual processes.

In contrast, sense-perception may seem static. As you look at the page you are reading, it is simply there, motionless, for as long as you look. From science, however, we know that your nervous system has to be engaged in constant physiological action in order for you to have the seemingly static perception. But even pre-scientifically, what is evident to anyone is that perception requires the active use of our senses to explore the world, gather information, and make discriminations. Perception is not the passive regis-tration of momentary input. In viewing this book page, or any other object, your relationship to it has to *change* if your awareness of it is to continue. A constant background odor ceases to be experienced after a while; a con-stant low-level hum in the background drops out of awareness (though one can introduce a change by an act of attention, in which case it pops back into awareness).

Consciousness requires contrast, change, difference. *Consciousness is a difference-detector.*[13] The primary function of consciousness is to differen-tiate, which is an active process.

The fact that consciousness is active does not contradict the primacy of existence (nor imply that consciousness is somehow invalid). Rand's impor-tant aphorism makes the necessary distinction: *"Consciousness is meta-physically passive, but epistemologically active."*[14] That is, consciousness does not create or alter its object (consciousness is passive, metaphysically), but awareness is achieved by an active process (consciousness is active, epistemologically).

---

13   This is not meant as a definition of consciousness, but as a statement about its biological function and terms of operation. "Detect" here means "have discriminated awareness of," so "detector" cannot be used to define consciousness. In fact, consciousness, as an axiomatic concept, can be defined only ostensively, by providing examples, such as: your seeing this page, your thinking about these ideas, your remembering what the previous paragraph said, your feelings toward your friends, and so on.

14   Reported by Leonard Peikoff (in personal conversation).

4. *Consciousness is a biological faculty*

Consciousness is not only an action but also a living action. Living action is goal-directed. [BINSWANGER, 1990 & 1992] An organism's actions are adapted to securing its survival. Consciousness, like the heartbeat, is a biological activity that evolved because it promotes survival. But few philosophers in history have regarded consciousness that way.

The Judeo-Christian thinkers regard "things of the spirit" and "things of the flesh" as opposites, as belonging to different realities. Consciousness is an implant of the supernatural in man, religionists proclaim, and consciousness offers man, in their view, nothing but an intractable conflict with his "all too human" body.

Even Plato was attracted to this view: he describes the body as the tomb of the soul. But to Aristotle, this was nonsense: he recognized that the body is a living body and that the soul (i.e., consciousness) is the "form" ("entelechy") of the body — i.e., an expression of bodily powers. Death, he recognized, ends the life of body *and* soul. Human consciousness is an activity of a person, involving his body's interaction with the external world. The living body is not the tomb of anything; it is the enabler of consciousness. And when a person dies, what had been his body becomes a corpse.

Where does the soul go when you die? To the same place as your heartbeat.

Conscious activities, whether sensory or conceptual, have, like the heartbeat, a biological function. Man has eyes for the same reason he has a heart: to sustain his life; vision is an adaptive, biological, life-sustaining capacity. The same is true for the other sense modalities: each provides a man with life-sustaining information about the world.

And the same is true of the faculty of reason. The mind, the reasoning intellect, is a vital organ. A biologist could not understand the heart if he did not know its biological function, and a philosopher cannot understand reason, or any other faculty of consciousness, if he ignores the biological function of that faculty.

The heart serves the organism's survival by circulating the blood. In what way does consciousness serve survival? What does sight, for example, do for sighted animals?

First, note what makes an animal an animal. In simplest terms, the distinguishing characteristics of animals are the faculties of locomotion and consciousness. In contrast to a plant, an animal perceives the world and moves itself through the world. But the deeper issue concerns how the animal makes its living — how it gets nourishment.

Locomotion ref: — the act, the fact, the ability, power of moving.

Plants synthesize their own nutrients; animals feed on plants or on other animals which, ultimately, have fed on plants. Animal life depends on plants having photosynthesized the basic nutrients that animals need.

Putting it as simply as possible: animals eat. If they eat plants, the food supply within reach is soon exhausted, so they must move around: they graze. If they eat other animals, they need to catch their prey, which again means they must move around: they hunt. Whether they graze or hunt, animals need to find their food. Consciousness is their means of doing so.

(There is an exception to animal motility, and a telling one: There are some sea-animals, such as oysters, that do not move themselves through their environments during most of their lifespans, since their food floats to them. And oysters have no eyes.)[15]

In general, animals have to move to get food; consciousness enables them to locate their food. It also enables them to avoid being eaten, but food is the fundamental: life is not fundamentally the avoidance of death but the gaining of the materials for self-sustenance. Consciousness does also enable animals to attain other goals, e.g., to find mates for reproduction, but getting food is the fundamental.

That's the simplified overview. Now let's look in more detail.

Consciousness does several things, each of which contributes to the organism's survival.

1. Consciousness enables the animal to integrate all the various parts of its body to pursue its overall goal in relation to the perceived environment as a whole. When the lion undertakes the chase, all its muscular activity is coordinated to that single effort. And the lion chases its prey through a terrain, not as a simple stimulus-response mechanism: A plant's parts react "locally" — the leaf may curl to preserve heat on a cold day, but a plant cannot pull up roots and move to a warmer locale.

2. Consciousness enables the animal to bridge space, in the sense that the animal can respond to distant objects. The lion sees and smells its distant prey, crouches down, and begins to stalk.

3. Consciousness enables the animal to bridge time, by responding now and over a span of time to a goal that it will not reach and utilize until later.

15 If you can imagine an oyster with eyes, an oyster that lies motionless on the sea bottom, passively watching the passing scene, year in and year out, you have the exact opposite of my view of consciousness. I am not merely saying that eyes would have no survival value for oysters (and so did not evolve); I am saying that vision without locomotion would not actually be vision. Vision is connected with and depends upon self-produced movement (see CHAPTER 2).

The lion beginning its stalk crouches down now in order to capture its prey some minutes later.

4. Consciousness enables the animal to guide its actions according to the continuing changes in its goal and the requirements of reaching it. The lion uses an integrated perceptual awareness, involving sight, smell, and hearing, to adjust to the changing position of its prey in the perceived terrain.

5. Consciousness enables the animal to expand the range of its action: the organism as a whole is sensitive to minute changes in its environment. The lion's prey (switching here to its point of view) sees the rustle of a few stalks of grass, catches the lion's scent, feels fear, and bolts away. Perceptual awareness enables the animal to respond not just to separate stimuli but to the whole situation in the whole environment.

6. Consciousness enables the animal to *learn* — i.e., to acquire new knowledge. The ability to learn greatly reduces the time required for the adaptation of the organism to its environment. Instead of this adaptation requiring natural selection over hundreds or thousands of generations, an animal can learn in seconds what is the survival-significance of a novel stimulus and can adjust its behavior accordingly. The adjustment is also swiftly reversible: what formerly meant danger but now is safe can be treated accordingly.

Here, on the simple animal level, we see that consciousness involves cognition, evaluation, and the initiation of bodily action. Consciousness is distinguishable into these three functions (and others), but the three occur together, as parts of an inseparable whole: the faculty of consciousness. As philosopher Hans Jonas writes:

> Three characteristics distinguish animal from plant life: motility, perception, emotion. . . .
>
> Fulfillment not yet at hand is the essential condition of desire, and deferred fulfillment is what desire in turn makes possible. Thus desire represents the time-aspect of the same situation of which perception represents the space-aspect. Distance in both respects is disclosed and bridged: perception presents the object "not here but over there"; desire presents the goal "not yet but to come"; motility guided by perception and driven by desire turns *there* into *here* and *not yet* into *now*. [JONAS, 101]

Most philosophers in the history of philosophy have downplayed or even denied one or more of these three functions of consciousness. Even the pro-consciousness philosophers have typically regarded consciousness as nothing but cognition, as if values and action were incidental or dispensable. But if we are to understand consciousness, we must never lose sight of the biological fact that consciousness informs the organism about its environment for the sake of motivating, sustaining, and directing *action*, the action its survival requires.

> Knowledge, for any conscious organism, is the means of survival; to a living consciousness, every *is* implies an *ought.* [VOS, 24]

And if we are to understand *man's* consciousness, we must bring the same biological perspective to our consideration of his distinctive attribute: his rational faculty. Man's capacity of abstraction and thought is the product of natural selection. Each genetic variation in the makeup of our anthropoid ancestors that enhanced their brain-power gave them a survival advantage. Man's reasoning mind is a survival instrument, just as his heart and liver are. The ability to abstract, conceptualize, and think is not only pro-survival, it is *man's basic means of survival.*

Whether devoted to building a hut or measuring the speed of light, human thought is, in its biological origin and essential function, a tool of survival. Yes, man can misuse his mind — he can sever the connection of his mind to reality and drift among imaginary "constructs" of his own devising; but he can misuse any part of his body, too. The mind, like the body, is an instrument of survival, despite the fact that man does not automatically treat it as such.

The failure to adopt this biological perspective has crippled philosophy, preventing man from properly understanding his most vital organ: his mind. Philosophers have spun out theories that treat the mind as a self-contained phenomenon, ignoring its roots in and dependence on perception, emotion, and action in the world. The disasters that stem from ignoring the biological role of reason will become apparent as this book proceeds.

The nonbiological perspective stands markedly revealed in the common question: is it possible to develop a computer that can think? My answer is: before a computer could think, it would have to be able to understand ideas (concepts); before it could understand ideas, it would have to be able to perceive the world and to feel emotions, such as pleasure and pain, desire and fear; before it could perceive and feel emotions, it would have to be alive — i.e., be engaged in action to sustain itself. We can dismiss notions about a thinking computer until one is built that is alive — and then it wouldn't be a computer but a living organism, a man-made one.

Biologically, seeing is for moving, ideas are for doing, theory is for practice.

A word of caution is needed here. The philosophy known as "Pragmatism" is merely the other side of the same false alternative: cognition vs. action. In pseudo-rebellion against divorcing ideas from action, Pragmatists divorce action from ideas. An idea, they say, is nothing but "a plan of action." This is wrong. An idea is *for the sake of* planning action, but an idea is cognition, an awareness of some fact of reality. (Pragmatists are primacy-of-consciousness philosophers; they award primacy not to existence, but to some undefined jumble of existence and consciousness, which they call "experience.")

To make a plan of action, you must *know* something. For instance, to plan a plane trip to Detroit, you must know that there are planes, that Detroit exists, that there are airports, plane tickets, money to buy them with — and all the facts that newborn infants don't know — which is why they cannot form a "plan of action" regarding plane trips, or anything else.

Awareness of reality — cognition — is what makes possible any plans of action. We have to know the world in order to act successfully in the world.

It in no way denigrates ideas, in no way reduces them to "expedients," to remember that they are for the sake of guiding action. It is not that, as the Pragmatists say, we have to "play it by ear," "go with the flow," and engage in blind groping. We act on the basis of *knowledge.* And we do so even when we act on the basis of probability rather than certainty — knowledge of what is more probable vs. less probable is still knowledge, a very sophisticated form of knowledge. Those who lack this knowledge are ill-advised to invest in the stock market.

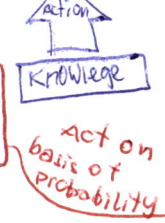

Much later in the book, we will see that conceptual knowledge builds in a hierarchy, ascending from the concrete to the abstract. We will see that, in contrast to conventional wisdom, the more abstract the knowledge, the more potent it is. At this point, I will only assert that a very abstract form of know-ledge — knowledge of *principles* — is the most powerful of all. Principles are, of course, exactly what Pragmatism rejects. Pragmatism opposes principles on principle.

Contrary to the claims of Pragmatism, abstract principles, including the principles of morality, are man's indispensable guide to coping with the demands of life and acting successfully in the world.

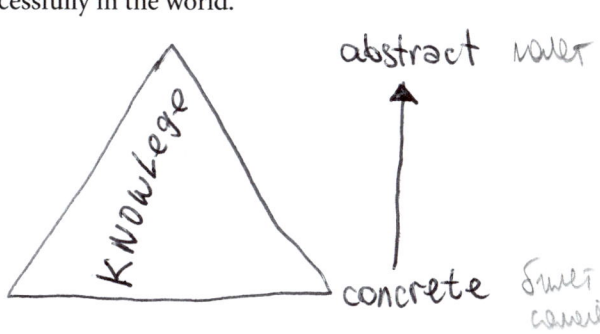

CONSCIOUSNESS AS IRREDUCIBLE

[handwritten: that can't be reduced or simplified.]
[handwritten: can not be analysed]

Like existence, consciousness is an irreducible primary. One can subdivide conscious actions, separating different kinds: seeing, for example, is one kind of conscious activity and hearing is another. Analogously, one can subdivide existents — e.g., into living and non-living things. But just as one cannot get beneath the fundamental fact of existence, so one cannot get beneath the fundamental fact of consciousness. One cannot reduce conscious action, qua conscious, to something else.

To ask: "What kind of action is consciousness?" is to ask: "What do all conscious processes have in common that makes them actions of consciousness rather than physical actions?" The only answer is: all these actions are actions of consciousness; they all involve awareness of something. And "awareness" is a synonym for "consciousness."

This irreducibility of consciousness is one reason why "consciousness" (like "existence") qualifies as an axiomatic concept.

> An axiomatic concept is the identification of a primary fact of reality, which cannot be analyzed, i.e., reduced to other facts or broken into component parts. It is implicit in all facts and in all knowledge. It is the fundamentally given and directly perceived or experienced, which requires no proof or explanation, but on which all proofs and explanations rest.
>
> The first and primary axiomatic concepts are "existence," "identity" (which is a corollary of "existence") and "consciousness." One can study what exists and how consciousness functions; but one cannot analyze (or "prove") existence as such, or consciousness as such. These are irreducible primaries. [ITOE, 55]

"Irreducible" here means: "cannot be analyzed." If you try to analyze what it is to be aware, you will soon discover that no analysis is possible. Aside from giving synonyms, the only terms that are available for your analysis are much too general. For instance, you might say that to be conscious of something is to be "in contact" with it. But chairs are in contact with the floor without awareness — so, what kind of contact is *conscious* contact? Or, you might try saying that awareness is a causal response. But the Earth is causally responding to the sun. So, what makes something a *conscious* causal response? Consciousness. That's all we can say. There is no further analysis.

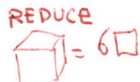

Consider, by contrast, some phenomena that *are* reducible.

We can <u>reduce</u> a whole entity to its parts — e.g., a box consists of its six sides. That reduction is possible because a physical whole is the sum of its parts. Or, we can reduce a physical object to the materials out of which it is made — e.g., the box is made of wood and nails. Again, the reduction is possible because the object is the materials out of which it is made.

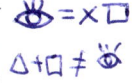

Consciousness is not a candidate for either of these kinds of reduction. The state or action of awareness does not have parts. Awareness does have aspects; e.g., your present state of awareness consists of seeing things, hearing things, feeling things, etc. But, unlike parts, such aspects cannot be physically separated, as the box can be taken apart. The seeing, hearing, etc. can be separated only mentally, by a selective focus or abstraction, from the organic whole that is consciousness.

The state or action of awareness is not composed of some stuff, as the box is composed of wood and nails. There are no spiritual components that get put together to form the field of awareness. Nor can consciousness be analyzed into physical components. An overall conscious activity — e.g., a thought process — can be analyzed into its stages or aspects, but not into any physical events, not even brain events.

Consider a conscious action in as much detail as you can. Do you find that it is composed of physical constituents? No. Take your reading of these words. You first see a word or phrase, then process it and "hear" the words in your mind, and you understand the meaning of those words. There are, indeed, non-conscious components, such as eye movements and the physical page-turnings, but there is no way to reduce the seeing, or the internal "hearing," or the understanding to one or more physical sub-actions — not without leaving out the essential, conscious aspect. Seeing the words involves physical and physiological processes but is not *reducible* to just the physical processes.

There are indeed unconscious sub-processes occurring — notably, the brain processes that underlie reading. Neurons fire in this brain center, then in that one. But what do these individual brain processes add up to? A larger-scale *brain process.* Not to a state of consciousness, not to the *seeing* or the *understanding.* The sum of small-scale physical processes is merely a large-scale physical process. The state of consciousness is left out.

This raises the question: If consciousness is an action, what is the entity that acts? There are two possible answers, but neither one will allow for a reduction of conscious actions to physical actions, existential or neural.

One can say that the entity that is conscious is the mental entity, the self. But, clearly, one cannot reduce the self to little sub-selves. The self, the ego, the "I," is an indivisible whole. Awareness is an organic unity; it has aspects, but no component parts. (In this regard, the relation of the aspects of a state of awareness to the whole awareness is similar to the relation of the attributes of an entity to the whole entity; an entity *is* its attributes and a state of awareness *is* its aspects.)

On a deeper level, one can say that the entity that is conscious is the man, as a total organism. And the man has parts, physical parts. But the physical parts are not the components of his state of awareness. We may assume that when a man is engaged in conscious activity, the physical organ that acts is his brain.[16] However, the parts of the brain and their individual actions are not parts of his *awareness*. If you want to describe the aspects of an action of consciousness as "parts," it remains true that the "parts" of an action of consciousness are mental parts, not physical parts — where "mental" means: pertaining to consciousness.

Again, parts of a brain process add up to a whole brain process, not to consciousness.

Brain actions are a necessary condition of consciousness. Brain actions underlie and are involved in the operation of consciousness. But brain actions are still something different from what they underlie: awareness. Peikoff writes:

> Even if, someday, consciousness were to be explained scientifically as a product of physical conditions, this would not alter any observed fact. It would not alter the fact that, given those conditions, the attributes and functions of consciousness are what they are. [OPAR, 35]

To discover that matter in certain combinations gives rise to the existence of consciousness would not permit us to *equate* consciousness with those combinations of matter or their physical actions. Mental actions are manifestly different from brain actions.

(The nearest analogy to the mind-brain relation in this respect might be the magnetic field produced by an electric current moving in a wire.

---

16 The tendency to over-isolate the brain from the total organism is plausibly challenged in Alva Noë's *Action in Perception* [NoË, 2004]; I am not committing myself to the position that the brain alone, rather than the total organism, is sufficient for consciousness; I am only saying that even on the view that it is, consciousness remains irreducible.

The electric current and the resulting magnetic field are two different, though causally related, phenomena. The current produces the magnetic field, but is not identical with the field. In a similar way, brain actions may produce awareness, but they are not identical with awareness. Nothing can be exactly analogous to consciousness, of course, precisely because consciousness *is* sui generis. So, we may dismiss the following objection: "How can consciousness, if not physical, be an exception to everything else in the universe?" The same objection would apply to whatever distinctions one made — e.g., "How can spoons have a distinct nature, since spoons would then be an exception to everything else in the universe?")

Consciousness exists and matter exists. Each is what it is, and neither is a form of the other. To be sure, matter is primary; without matter, there would be no physical world to be conscious of, no organism to be conscious of it, and no physiological means of being conscious. Nevertheless, matter and consciousness are two irreducibly different phenomena. And knowledge, the specific subject of this book, is a phenomenon of consciousness.

[margin note: no matter no objects to be conscious]

Despite this fact, however, most of those writing on consciousness today assume that consciousness can be reduced to matter. Materialism, the denial of the existence or causal efficacy of consciousness, holds a virtual monopoly in philosophy and allied disciplines. Even those few authors who state that consciousness is irreducible rarely expunge all their materialist premises.

It is worth looking at examples of how materialist premises can linger undetected in one's thinking. One contemporary author claims to reject materialism but then raises what he calls "the hard question" concerning consciousness: "the question of how and why cognitive functioning is accompanied by conscious experience." [CHALMERS, 25] But what else could cognitive functioning be "accompanied by," other than cognition, in other words, consciousness? And why does he say "accompanied" — as if when one learns something, being conscious were incidental to the process? This represents implicit materialism left over in that author's thinking.

Impressed by what computers can do, these implicit materialists ask, in effect, "Why do man's actions, such as playing chess, happen to be accompanied by conscious experiences? When computers play chess, they do so by purely physical means, so why is human chess-playing 'accompanied by' consciousness?"

But there is a mistake in the question: computers do not play chess; they do not perform *any* cognitive task. *Computers do not even add.* A computer is a physical mechanism in which the flow of electrical current flips switches.

A computer is essentially a switching device: it turns switches on or off, and it charges or discharges capacitors.

Strictly speaking, computers do not play games, check spelling, or process information. All these actions involve consciousness and are performed only by conscious human beings, even if aided in the task by physical devices such as a pen, a typewriter, or a computer.

As to the simplest case — addition — one need only realize that mathematical truths, such as that one plus one equals two, do not exist for computers and have no effect on them. Nothing is changed if the addition is formulated in binary: $01 + 01 = 10$. This mathematical principle does not exist for the computer: there are no ones or zeros inside the machine. There are not even any bits or bytes inside the machine, only high and low voltages.

Men can use a computer to help them add by using the physical state of the switches to control screen pixels to form patterns that, to us, represent numbers. Computers themselves no more add than do the old-fashioned, mechanical adding machines. The adding machines merely turn gears to rotate wheels with numbers painted on them. Gears and wheels do not add. Nor do computers. Addition is an action of consciousness.

You can count on your fingers, but fingers cannot count.

Computers cannot "process information," because information is not a physical phenomenon. Computers can only combine and shunt electrical currents. Only electricity, not information, has causal impact on the workings of the computer; information does not exist for the computer.

Of course, there is nothing wrong with saying colloquially that computers add, process information, and play chess. But in philosophy we have to be exact: in the strict sense computers only combine currents, throw switches, charge and discharge capacitors. Computers don't follow programs, they simply obey the laws of physics. That's all that goes on inside them.

If all human beings suddenly vanished from the face of the earth, but their computers remained running, there would be no information processing: the computers would merely be combining electric currents and lighting different pixels on their screens, not processing information or performing calculations.

Some materialists, relishing the man-as-computer model, have advanced the slogan: "The brain is the hardware, the mind is the software." Here, "software" is a stolen concept: something can be identified as software only in relation to the mind. Software, information, symbols, mathematics — none of these things exist per se in the physical world, apart from a relation to consciousness. Just as books contain only patterns of ink, so apart from man's mind, software exists only in the form of some *physical* patterns, such as the patterns of magnetized iron particles on a hard drive's disk. Patterns of ink qualify as *words* and patterns of iron particles qualify as *programs* only in relation to man's mind.

None of this is to denigrate computers, which are magnificent inventions — inventions of conscious human beings. When the IBM computer "Deep Blue" beat the world's top chess player, Garry Kasparov, that was not a defeat of the human mind but its triumph: it was a victory for the minds of the men who created and programmed the Deep Blue computer.

There *is* a similarity between a computer and the *brain*. The brain, like the computer, combines and switches electric pulses. But brain processes can correctly be described as dealing with ideas or information only in relation to the *mind* of the person whose brain it is. Apart from the mind that operates that brain, there are only physical states and physical changes.

Thus, there is simply no such puzzle as: "How is it that man's calculations are conscious, but the computer's calculations aren't?" One might as well ask: "Since my television can talk without being conscious, why do men happen to be conscious when they talk to each other?" Televisions cannot literally talk and computers cannot literally make computations.

Why do I say that this confusion represents implicit materialism? Shouldn't one say, instead, that this school of thought is actually too pro-consciousness, wrongly importing consciousness into what is purely physical? However, the belief that is actually operative is not that computers are conscious, but that human addition, chess-playing, etc. are purely physical processes. It is not that the materialists believe that computers have minds (despite the fact that they usually like to state their view in just that way); rather it is that they eliminate mind altogether. Their inability to see the difference between man and machine is not an elevation of the machine but a degradation of man.[17]

The better of these authors have come far enough from materialism to accept the existence of consciousness. They recognize that we see, think, and feel. But, clinging to the materialist definition of cognitive activities, they see consciousness as "epiphenomenal," as the proverbial ghost in the machine, and can find no causal role for it. Most of them even hold that everything that human beings do could be done by unconscious "zombies,"

---

17   For an excellent source on this degradation, see Tallis, 2011.

their science-fiction projection of beings that resemble us exactly in every physical and behavioral way, but are non-conscious.

Whether the materialism is explicit or implicit, it steals concepts in profusion — not blushing at statements such as, "What people believe to be mental is really non-mental" — ignoring that "believe" is a concept of consciousness. They make pronouncements like, "Consciousness is a myth"; "Consciousness is an illusion"; "The concept of 'consciousness' is invalid" — ignoring that "myth," "illusion," "concept," and "invalid" are concepts of consciousness.

One philosopher even titled an essay: "A Reason to Doubt the Existence of Consciousness." In that title, "reason" and "doubt" leap out as stolen concepts.

The very definition of "materialism" exhibits the stolen concept fallacy. "Materialism" is the theory that consciousness does not exist. But "theory" is itself a concept of consciousness, so the definition relies on that which it claims does not exist.

Materialism is the idea that there are no ideas.

Consciousness is an axiom, and there is no denying axioms: they have to be used and accepted in any attempt to deny them. "I deny consciousness"? — *denial* is an action of consciousness. Stones, plants, and computers cannot engage in denials.

Ironically, materialists — who see themselves as scientific, hard-headed realists — take their basic premise from the spiritualists. It is the spiritualists' notion of consciousness as supernatural, not of this earth, "spooky," that the materialists adopt as their concept of consciousness. On that basis, they decide, logically enough, that such a phenomenon does not exist. Materialists are blind to any view of consciousness other than that of the spiritualists. But this book asserts a third alternative: a naturalistic, causal, biological conception of consciousness.

When materialists (properly) reject the spiritualist, mystical conception of consciousness as "a fragment torn from God," they assume they have rejected consciousness. But they have rejected only a straw man.

Supernaturalism must not dictate the terms of this, or any other, question. The rational, scientific, realistic question is not: "Is there a ghostly tendril from another world in me?" but rather: "Am I aware of something? Do I see, hear, think, remember, feel pleasure and pain?"

But then the question answers itself.

second phenomen accomp othr

THE CAUSAL EFFICACY OF CONSCIOUSNESS

Biologically, consciousness is not a passive spectator; an organism's consciousness controls the actions of its body. It is the efficacy of consciousness in guiding such actions that explains the selection-pressure that favored its evolutionary development.

The contrary position, the claim that consciousness has no causal efficacy, holds that consciousness is an "epiphenomenon": an effect produced by the brain that does not itself have any effects, does not *do* anything. The standard analogy given by epiphenomenalists is that awareness is like the smoke that comes out of a locomotive: the smoke is an effect, a by-product, which does not act on the locomotive. In the same way, the actions of your consciousness — your pleasures, pains, fears, hopes, thoughts, plans — are supposed to be mere by-products of the brain's action, by-products that are causal dead ends, impotent to affect anything.

Epiphenomenalists are so opposed to consciousness that they exempt it from the causality that governs the rest of the universe: consciousness allegedly has causes but no effects. Note that their own illustrative analogy fails: the smoke leaving a locomotive does have an effect, however small, on the locomotive — as it does on the lungs of anyone who breathes it in. Nothing in the universe acts without having effects, and only a mystical view of consciousness would allow for making it an exception.

lungs

Epiphenomenalism is another case of a self-refuting idea. Anyone who asserts epiphenomenalism is contradicting himself: in asserting his view, he assumes that his *thoughts* are the cause of the sounds coming out of his mouth. Even asserting epiphenomenalism internally, as an unspoken thought, contains a contradiction: to think requires memory, and memory requires retrieving what consciousness has stored physically in the brain. The conscious storage and retrieval of memories evidences the mind's ability to interact with the physical brain.

contrad.
thoughts-sounds

Epiphenomenalism is actually a form of materialism. Whether one maintains that consciousness does not exist or that it does exist but cannot affect anything, including oneself, the significance is the same.

•MATERIALISM
• conc. not affect
not it, not out

From a biological perspective, epiphenomenalism represents a denial of the adaptive value of consciousness. If consciousness has no bodily effects, then it confers no survival advantage for organisms possessing it. But if so, how are we to account for the observed facts? How are we to explain the evolutionary fine-tuning of conscious experiences to fit survival needs? An epiphenomenalist must assume that it is just a cosmic coincidence that

if conc. no eff. then why have it

STANDOUT

the conditions that fulfill bodily needs — eating nutritious food, gaining shelter and warmth, drinking when dehydrated — happen to produce *pleasure*, while damaging physical conditions — a wound, starvation, breaking a limb — happen to bring *pain*. If the conscious experiences of pleasure and pain have no motivational power for the conscious animals, if the actions of the conscious animals are not affected by their experience of pleasure or pain, why are pleasure and pain correlated in this fashion with survival needs?

Clearly, there has been a selection-pressure acting in evolution to align pleasure and pain with actions that promote or impair survival, respectively. But that selection can occur only if pleasure and pain have effects on the animal's (or man's) behavior. Were pleasure and pain epiphenomena, there could be no selection operating to prevent animals and men from being so constituted as to feel excruciating pain when eating and ecstasy upon breaking a limb.

(People unschooled in evolutionary biology sometimes point to the rare cases in which pleasure and pain do not correlate with survival. E.g., some people like the taste of alcohol, which is unhealthy if over-used. But alcohol is not part of the environment to which man became adapted. And finding a few exceptions would not help the epiphenomenalist explain the general correlation of these allegedly impotent conscious experiences with survival.)

This evolutionary explanation of pleasure and pain in terms of their effects on survival is merely an illustration from science of what we know by direct introspection: consciousness *does* something; it has causal efficacy.

Since your consciousness causes your voluntary action, and since the physiological cause of your action is a process in the brain, it follows that your consciousness has the power to change the physical state of your brain.

This conclusion may appear to contradict the primacy of existence, since it means that consciousness alters the state of something in the physical world — the brain. But that worry is unfounded. The primacy of existence holds that a state of awareness neither creates nor alters its *object*. A pencil, for instance, is not affected by being seen or thought about. But the causal efficacy of consciousness does not imply otherwise.

When you raise your arm, you don't do it by somehow making your brain into the object of your awareness. When you reach for a pencil, the object of your awareness is the pencil, not your brain. And, of course, seeing and desiring the pencil does not alter it in the least. Awareness affects not the *object* but the *subject* — i.e., you.

Your inner decision to reach for the pencil is an act of your consciousness, based on your awareness of the pencil and your desire to use it. But there is no effect of your consciousness itself on *the pencil*. The instrumental value of the pencil to your purpose is also an objective fact, one not alterable by consciousness. There is never a case in which awareness alters its object.

What about the effects of self-observation? When one focuses inwardly on a feeling, doesn't that alter the feeling in some cases? No, not in any primacy-of-consciousness way; the inward focus changes what one is attending to; one's consciousness is then responding to a somewhat different object or changed context. This is not a case of consciousness molding the feeling: the feeling is a process, not an entity. Thus, when one speaks, informally, of "changing" a feeling, the actual meaning is that one process has ceased and a different one has begun. Even a seemingly static feeling is a dynamic state, like a waterfall, fed by ever new "waters" flowing in "the stream of consciousness." The fact that selecting a different object of attention produces different feelings in response is an expression of the primacy of existence: the object attended to causes the response in consciousness.[18]

The same is true of the effect of introspection on a thought process: one's critical scrutiny of a thought process will certainly influence the subsequent train of thought. But that is not a case of awareness altering the introspected thought, as if the thought were a static entity: it is a case of awareness altering the person, the subject, in a way that results in his having new and different thoughts.

The emotions one has and the thoughts that occur to one are generated by the brain (i.e., the subconscious). One's brain is what it is, independent of one's awareness of it. The brain is certainly not a creation of consciousness. The state of your brain can be altered, within definite limits, by your awareness of something in the world. The current state of your brain can even be altered by recognizing something about your consciousness, as when self-understanding causes a gradual change in your psychology. But it is not the case that wishing one had a different type of brain makes one's brain change, or that one can escape the effects on one's brain of what one does with one's consciousness. Yes, one's mind affects one's brain — in the only way that the nature of one's brain permits, given its independent identity.

---

18   If emotions could be changed by a wish or merely by looking at them, the profession of psychotherapy would be unnecessary. In reality, to cease feeling a certain way about a given kind of object, one must change the feeling's cause: the operative beliefs and automatized value-judgments. Sometimes simply learning the true nature of the object is enough to change the emotion ("Oh, that's only a toy gun"); other times one has to work over a long period of time to come to grips with and change an automatized evaluation, as is done in the better systems of psychotherapy.

For instance, if one wants to return a tennis serve, one has to put forth the mental effort required to get one's body in motion in the proper way. Even here, mere wishing doesn't make it so. Wanting to perform the proper actions to return the serve doesn't mean one will perform them: one has to focus one's attention on the right factors and give the right "orders" to oneself.

ignorance of conseq does not changes them

Nor is ignorance bliss, as the primacy of consciousness would have it. Ignorance of the consequences on the brain of making a certain choice does not affect those consequences. A policy of giving in to one's whims, for example, has long-term, inescapable consequences on one's motivational system — notably, in producing what we call a weak-willed psychology.

clarity Defining Logic

Or, on the positive side, a policy of seeking mental clarity, defining one's terms, and adhering strictly to logic develops a brain that is efficient, well-organized, and disciplined.

The point here is that the causal efficacy of a consciousness in regard to its own brain does not erase the brain's independent identity nor that of the object of which one is aware. Thus, the mind's causal efficacy is actually an instance of, not an exception to, the primacy of existence.

There is no alternative to accepting the fact that consciousness can causally affect the physical state of brain processes. For how else are we to describe the fact that it is my current conscious thoughts and perceptions that are *causing* the movements of my fingers on the computer keyboard? (See Schwartz and Begley, 2003.)

In confronting the causal efficacy of consciousness, materialists raise several artificial objections and threaten us with straw men. They claim that there is some problem with a causal interaction between the mental and the physical, because the two are radically different types of phenomena. But there is no principle requiring interacting existents to be similar. This is merely picture-thinking — which means non-thinking. The image evoked is that of two objects interacting; to interact, they must have a surface at which they can meet; if they don't contact each other, if they "miss" each other, there is no collision, no interface, no interaction. But in fact there is no requirement that interacting things be similar. "Similarity" is not a place where two existents meet, and "difference" is not a failure to make contact.

In actual fact, different things — even radically different things — interact. Rivers interact with rocks, plants interact with sunlight, man interacts with rainbows, and biotech corporations interact with DNA molecules.

All that is required for *A* to interact causally with *B* is that both *A* and *B* be part of the universe — i.e., that both *exist*, have a definite nature, and act accordingly. Both my thoughts and my body exist and have a definite nature; action follows accordingly. The fact that mind and body are different types of phenomena provides no grounds for making a puzzle out of their interaction.

As to the materialist's straw man, he is Descartes. "Cartesian dualism" is the accusation hurled at anyone who recognizes that consciousness is real and has real effects. But the error in Cartesian dualism lies in its reification of consciousness — in making it into a substance, *res cogitans*, rather than in merely acknowledging the existence of consciousness and its causal efficacy.

Consciousness is not an entity, not in the sense that a stone or an organism is. Consciousness is a faculty of an entity, a man or animal; the operation of consciousness is a process of that entity.

Actually, Descartes' mistake here lies, ironically, in his being too affected by materialism: he attempts to apply to consciousness a category derived from the physical world: the category of substance or entity. In dividing reality into *res cogitans* and *res extensa*, he forgets that *res* means "thing," a concept that derives from perceiving solid, *physical* objects. Nothing but confusion and contradictions can result from likening consciousness to physical objects.

The materialists are right to reject Descartes' reification of consciousness, and they are right to reject the related notion of a free-floating "soul." But they are wrong to reject the self-evident fact that man is conscious. Contra materialism, consciousness is undeniable. Contra spiritualism, consciousness depends on the physical body or nervous system. (Or, more accurately, consciousness depends on the organism — the person or animal, as a whole.) Such organisms have two aspects, a body and a consciousness, a physical aspect and a mental one. There is a sense in which one's consciousness depends on his physical body, but there is also a sense in which one's body depends on his consciousness: a completely unconscious body, a body in which the faculty has been destroyed or never developed, is *not* a functioning body in the sense applicable to that kind of organism.

Aristotle pointed out that it is an equivocation to call a severed human hand a "hand," because its essential function is absent. In the same way, a corpse is not a *human* body; it is the remains of what was a human body when there was a *person*. A person's *body* is an abstraction from what is given: the person. Likewise, a person's consciousness is an aspect of the whole person, abstracted out for separate consideration. The entity is the person, an integrated whole.

The Validity of Introspection

Implicit in being able to discuss all the preceding is the fact that we, as human beings, are aware of the actions and products of consciousness — i.e., we are each self-aware and can introspectively identify our own conscious processes.

> Introspection is a process of cognition directed inward — a process of apprehending one's own psychological actions in regard to some existent(s) of the external world, such actions as thinking, feeling, reminiscing, etc. [ITOE, 29]

The points I have made about consciousness are based on introspection. It is by reflecting on, conceptualizing, and identifying one's own mental actions that one comes to understand the general nature of consciousness.

The denial that we are self-aware is self-refuting: the denial maintains, in one form or another, that concepts of consciousness are invalid, that they do not represent an awareness of anything real. Since this claim presupposes knowledge of the distinction between contents of consciousness and external facts, it is just another form of denying the axiom of consciousness and commits the same stolen concept fallacy: the concept "invalid" presupposes, implicitly or explicitly, the concept "consciousness." "Invalid" refers to the status of an idea, a status that is differentiated from that of a valid awareness of fact. But making that distinction presupposes that we have recognized what it is to be aware of facts, which implies an act of self-awareness. The denial of introspective self-awareness presupposes what is being denied.

I have covered several undeniable facts about the nature of consciousness as such: consciousness has an object and a subject; existence has primacy over consciousness; consciousness is an active process, enabled by specific means; consciousness is a biological faculty; and, the state of awareness is both irreducible and causally efficacious. (There are also self-evident facts, covered in later chapters, that pertain specifically to man's consciousness, which is conceptual.)

The one-sentence, highly condensed overview is: consciousness is a living organism's active process of perceiving reality to acquire the information required for its survival.

We must reject the all-too-common practice of making arbitrary assumptions about what consciousness "ought to be" or how it "ought to function," and instead acknowledge these undeniable facts about what consciousness actually is. On that basis, we can go on to develop a proper understanding of the crucial product of consciousness: *knowledge*.

The beginning of knowledge, and the ultimate source of all knowledge, is sensory perception, which is the subject of the next chapter.

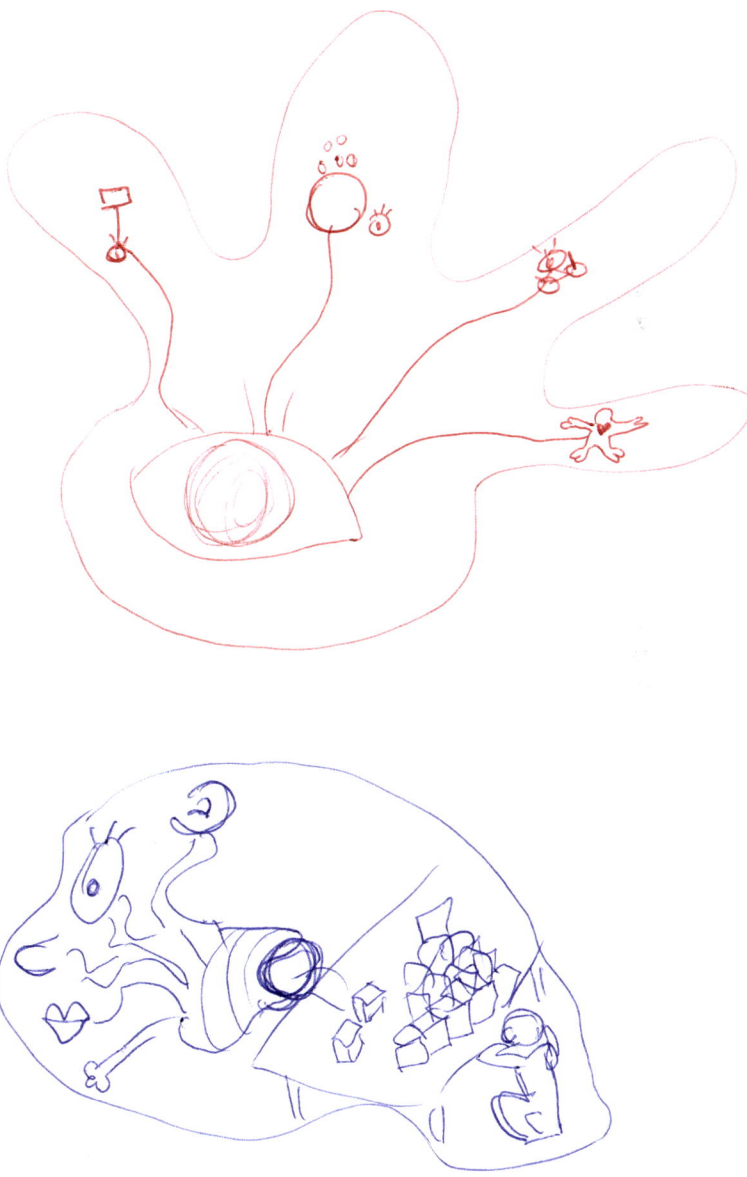

Fear = REACTION to content
(handwritten: Russian) восприятие
освед... о сущностях в соотв. и ...
получ... через сигналы чувств человек.
(boxed handwritten: Are / iD)

2

PERCEPTION

THE BIOLOGICAL FUNCTION OF CONSCIOUSNESS IS TO GUIDE ACTION, and the basic source of guidance is *cognition*. A cognitive process is one devoted to gaining information about reality. Cognitive activities range from an animal's perception of the entities in its immediate environment to man's complex processes of scientific investigation. However primitive or advanced, the cognitive functions of consciousness are directed toward providing awareness of what things *are*, of their *identities*.

(Some phenomena of consciousness, such as emotion and imagination, are not cognitive. E.g., to feel fear is to have an *experience*,[19] not to acquire information. Fear is a reaction to content acquired by other means. Cognitive acts — acts of awareness — are the faculty's base, making possible the rest.)

Sensory perception is an animal's or man's primary form of cognitive contact with the world. Knowledge begins with, develops out of, and is tested against sensory observation. This point is not self-evident, nor is it the view of cognition with which mankind began. Perception's fundamentality was

(handwritten margin note: tested against sensory observ.)

---

19   To Gregory Salmieri I owe the idea of using the term "experiences" to cover both cognitive and noncognitive mental states — e.g., seeing, fearing, and dreaming are all *experiences*, but fearing and dreaming are not acts of *awareness*. In the same vein, it is generally better to use the term "content" instead of "object" in discussing certain noncognitive states. Dreams have contents, but it is misleading to say they have objects (see pp. 282–83).

(handwritten: DReams)

first identified by Aristotle, but that identification did not become widely accepted until almost 1500 years later, after the long night of the anti-senses Dark and Medieval ages. Even at the dawn of the scientific era, perceptual observation was attacked and derided. How could men like Copernicus and Galileo cast aside the revealed word of God? How could they trust "observations" that were the product of debased bodily senses, or imagine that their limited, finite intellects, without aid from God, could produce anything other than confused, conflicting opinions?

Over a span of centuries, through the writings of Thomas Aquinas (c. 1250), Francis Bacon (1620), and John Locke (1690), the Aristotelian view won out, and mankind entered the Enlightenment era, the Age of Reason. But a counter-attack was soon launched by — of all people — philosophers. Starting with Descartes and bottoming out with Kant, a prominent line of philosophers peddled a secularized version of the old religious notions. "I have therefore found it necessary to deny *knowledge* in order to make room for *faith*," Kant wrote. [CRITIQUE, B, XXXI, Kant's emphasis]

For the open mysticism of the medievals, these philosophers substituted Rationalism — the idea that the intellect can spin out truths on its own, without needing sensory data. For the authority of sacred texts, they substituted the equally baseless notion of innate ideas or innate "categories." Instead of attacking the senses as "of the flesh," they attacked the senses on other grounds, to be discussed below.

Fully liberating the intellect requires rejecting both open mysticism and the secularized form of it, which is Rationalism. One must uphold the efficacy of the unaided individual mind. This means defending both the senses and reason. The remainder of this book is devoted to doing just that. I establish two fundamental points: 1) perception is the base of all knowledge; 2) valid concepts are formed from perception by an *objective* process. The present chapter presents a thoroughly naturalistic, biological view of sensory perception; the remaining chapters present the equivalent for conceptual activities.

PERCEPTION AS AXIOMATIC

Sensory perception is the primary and basic form of cognitive contact with the world. An organism born entirely without sense organs would be unconscious. Accordingly, the fact that the senses provide awareness of reality is axiomatic. The issue of the "validity" of the senses does not even arise: sensory awareness is *awareness* — which means that it has the status of a corollary of the axiom of consciousness.

The axiomatic nature of sensory awareness is confirmed by the argument of re-affirmation through denial, the test of axiomaticity. To make any statement denying the senses, one has to understand the terms the statement uses — "senses," "invalid," etc. But the meaning of these terms is learned, directly or indirectly, on the basis of perception. Without the senses' basic cognitive contact with reality, we could not have any concepts, including those used to claim that the senses are invalid. Thus, the attack on the senses constitutes concept-stealing on an unparalleled scale. Without perception, we would be unconscious, like vegetables; vegetables cannot ponder the validity of perception.

Because sensory awareness is axiomatic, philosophy, as distinguished from science, has very little of a positive nature to say about it. Much, however, has to be said to correct misunderstandings created by wrong philosophic theories of sense-perception, theories that have led philosophers down innumerable blind alleys.

The major source of error in this regard comes from confusing perception with lower or higher levels of awareness — i.e., confusing perception with sensation or with conceptual cognition.

PERCEPTION VS. SENSATION

Surveying the range of animal life on the planet, one cannot say with any confidence where on the evolutionary scale consciousness first appears. We know that we ourselves are conscious, and it would be bizarre to question the existence of consciousness in the higher animals, such as dogs and cats. But what about jellyfish, which have a "neural net," or flatworms, which have a primitive brain?[20] Perhaps neuroscience will someday provide a better understanding of the physical factors that give rise to consciousness, and that understanding will settle the question of which of the lower organisms are conscious and which are not. But for now such questions remain open and are for science, not philosophy, to investigate.

---

20   On what distinguishes a brain from a less developed group of neurons, see Sarnat, 2002. In another article, Sarnat notes that the flatworm, *planaria*, is "the simplest living animal having a body plan of bilateral symmetry and cephalization." [SARNAT, 1985]

As intriguing as these scientific questions are, they have zero import for and impact upon philosophy, which is concerned with *man's* consciousness. Non-human consciousness has philosophic significance only insofar as it illuminates, by contrast, the nature of man's consciousness.

(The scientist does, however, need the right philosophic base from which to proceed in studying sensory awareness and for investigating the mind-brain relationship. Scientists work from a philosophic base, and much of the research that scientists have done on sense-perception has been distorted by wrong philosophic premises. For example, the premise of materialism has led researchers to attempt to reduce perception to brain events and overt behavior, as if *awareness* did not exist. Yet these scientists claim to be aware of the people they study, the data they collect, and the content of their own theories.)

Among animals with sensory awareness, the simplest possess only the faculty of sensation.

A "sensation," as I use that term, is the most primitive form of conscious response, the response to energy impinging on receptors, not to objects in a perceived world.

The crayfish, for example, has light-sensitive cells near the end of its tail. Crayfish need to hide themselves from predators by moving into crevices or under rocks. By detecting light hitting the end of its tail, the animal can ensure that not just its head but its whole body is hidden: when its head is in darkness but its tail is still receiving light, the crayfish will crawl forward. The crayfish does not *see* any objects with its tail receptors — the sensory equipment is too primitive for that — but it responds to light vs. darkness, and if that response is a conscious one, it is as sensations not percepts that it experiences the illumination level.

A sensation is a conscious response to stimulation at the receptors, and that response lasts only as long as the stimulus is applied. A sensation is thus stimulus-bound: it is a sense or feeling, in response to what is currently stimulating the receptors.

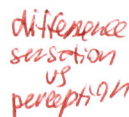

The higher animals have evolved a much more potent form of awareness: *perception*. There are a number of features that distinguish perception from mere sensations.

1. Perception is awareness of entities — of things (including their characteristics). Whereas the crayfish's tail-spot only discriminates brightness from darkness, human vision provides man with awareness not of stimuli but of the objects in the world, the objects that are responsible for the patterns

in the light received by the eye. We see trees, dogs, books, clouds — rather than just discriminating a general level of illumination. Human eyes, like the crayfish's tail spot, respond to light, but the human visual system is able to detect and exploit patterns in the light. The nature of these patterns is determined by the layout of the objects that reflected the light. Detecting these patterns enables the visual system to discriminate entities from each other. Thus, the content of visual perception is a world of entities. Vision contrasts not light with darkness but a lighter and/or differently colored *thing* against the other things in its background.

The same is true of hearing and touch. We hear the actions of *things*. Despite some marginal cases, as when one is aware of a background hum whose location and source are not apprehended, the normal case is hearing things that make sounds, not just the sounds: a slamming door, a barking dog, the click of keys on the computer keyboard.

Touch also discriminates entities, unless the conditions of perception are impoverished. We feel the table, the spoon in our hands, the keyboard under our fingers — all of which is quite different from simply feeling pressure on our skin. Even with eyes closed, we can explore by touch the objects within reach. Touch perception, as opposed to mere feelings on the skin, is an active, exploratory process, one that presents us with *entities*.

Taste and smell are more primitive, closer to the level of sensations. But they occur in a *perceptual context*: when we bite into a peach and taste it, we are already aware by sight and touch of the peach as an entity in the world and of the peach morsel as an entity in our mouth. Similarly, when we smell something, it is part of a perception of things emitting odors in a perceptual-level world. (Animals with a keen sense of smell, such as dogs, seem to have not just smell sensations but some form of perceptual awareness of a scent trail as an entity.) What perception provides is awareness of *entities*.

2. A point essential to understanding perception is that *perception is spatial*; it presents a world of entities *arrayed in space* — i.e., in their relative positions. We do not perceive one isolated entity at a time, but *a spread-out world of entities*, each entity being discriminated from the others that are next to it. Philosophers are apt to take as their example the perception of a single object: we see "an apple," for example. But apples do not float in a void; perception is of a world of spatially arrayed entities (see the two photographs on the next page, but bear in mind that perception is an ongoing process, not a snapshot)

The three-dimensional spatial array given in perception is what fundamentally distinguishes perception from sensation. It is not merely that perception (especially vision) gives entities, but also that perception provides the co-presence of all the entities that the animal can act on or be affected by. We see in one spread the entire scene of entities.

Contrast discriminating spatially arrayed entities with discriminating the

РАЗВЕЛЕНИЕ
ОТ ОПЫТА
А НЕ; ОТ
ОБЪЕКТА.

taste of one flavor element, say cinnamon, from others in what one is tasting. Such discrimination does not rise to the level of *perceiving* the cinnamon, precisely because the cinnamon is not given as *spatially* discriminated from the other flavors that one is also tasting. The perceptual world is spatially arrayed.

The space given in perception is not the abstract space of the geometer, with its three Cartesian axes, but the *relative position of entities.* As psychologist J. J. Gibson stresses, "visual space, unlike abstract geometrical space, is perceived only by virtue of what fills it." [GIBSON 1950, 5]

sensory qualities

3. Perception gives us awareness of a world of entities extending out in all directions from "here," i.e., from oneself. As one moves around in the perceived world, one's vantage point, and hence "here," moves, giving one a sense of one's current place in the world. Thus, perception includes at least some sense of self. And, of course, one perceives one's own limbs and trunk, and their spatial relation to the other things in the surroundings.

Additionally, a form of self-awareness is implicit in how the movement of one's head affects the scene's limits at any given moment. Gibson writes:

> The head and body of the observer hide the surfaces of the world that are outside the occluding edges of the field of view. . . . An observer perceives the position of here relative to the environment and also his body as being here. His limbs protrude into the field of view, and even his nose is a sort of protuberance into the field. [GIBSON 1986, 206, 208]

4. Perception is not a momentary, static impression but a continuous process over time. In the process of perceiving the world, the animal or man is an active, exploring observer. He scans his environment, moves through it, acts on it, and perceives the changes in the world that result.

Psychologists have learned that an animal needs *self-produced* motion in order to develop perception. In a classic experiment, Richard Held and Alan Hein reared kittens under conditions in which their only visual experience of their environment occurred while they were being passively transported through it. They did not develop normal perception; kittens raised in the same conditions but who moved themselves through the same environment did develop normal perception.[21]

Perception is both *for* action and *by* action: it is an active process, an ongoing awareness of the entities in the world, achieved by self-moving animals exploring their environment.

To summarize in a preliminary definition: "Perception" is the ongoing awareness of entities in their relative positions, gained from actively acquired sensory inputs.

---

21   "[V]isual stimulation of the active member (A) of each of 10 pairs of neonatal kittens was allowed to vary with its locomotory movements while equivalent stimulation of the second member (P) resulted from passive motion. Subsequent tests of visually guided paw placement, discrimination on a visual cliff, and the blink response were normal for A but failing in P." [HELD AND HEIN, 1963]

SENSATIONALISM

The preceding understanding of perception is radically at odds with most traditional views. According to most philosophers and psychologists, perceptions are constructed out of "sensations." This approach, known as "sensationalism," holds that when looking at an apple, we have now, or had in infancy, separate sensations of color, brightness, roundness, etc; the mind or brain supposedly puts together those separate sensations into the sight of the apple.

This notion is completely mistaken. Perception is a unitary phenomenon; it does not have sensations or anything else as *components*. It is not the case that sensations are cognitive "atoms" out of which perception is built up, whether by the brain or the intellect.[22]

Do not confuse *sensations*, which would be states of consciousness, with *physical* events at the sensory receptors. E.g., light-absorption by the rods and cones of the retina is a physical event, not a sensation. Though the incoming light interacts physically with a whole array of rods and cones in the retina, the resulting visual perception is continuous, global, unified. Whatever it is that the brain does in combining, decomposing, or shuffling the electrochemical outputs from the rods and cones, what results is your seeing a whole scene. The fact that the physical process begins with light hitting an array of discrete receptors does not mean that the ensuing state *of awareness* has parts. Note the parallel in the case of touch: when you grasp an object with several fingers, your touch-awareness, prior to any analysis, is unified, not broken into separate responses from each finger, let alone from each microscopic receptor in the skin.

A physical object *is* an organization of atoms. A table *is* a combination of atoms. And a certain combination of atoms *is* a table. But consciousness is not matter. There are no consciousness "atoms," no particles of awareness.

---

22   This marks one of the very rare occasions on which I differ with Ayn Rand; she wrote: "A percept is a group of sensations automatically retained and integrated by the brain of a living organism." Possibly she meant a group not of sensations but of *sensory inputs*, since it is hard to see how bits of *awareness* (sensations) could be integrated by the brain, which is physical. In the same passage, she speaks of "sensations as components of percepts." As explained in the text, I definitely disagree. However, this is not a *philosophic* issue, as she notes in the same article: "The knowledge of sensations as components of percepts is not direct, it is acquired by man much later: it is a scientific, *conceptual* discovery." [ITOE, 5] Gibsonians also, with some justification, oppose using the term "percept," which connotes snapshots rather than an ongoing, continuous process. (In a few places I do use the term "percept," but simply for linguistic grace to go with "concept.") I am indebted to Lee Pierson for both of these points and for encouraging me to study Gibson's works.

Consequently, it is a mistake to treat sensations as the "atoms" of awareness. More generally, it is wrong to treat consciousness on the model of matter by looking for *any* such "atoms" of awareness.

Perception is not *composed* of anything; perception is a global, seamless phenomenon. Even sensory modalities, though distinguishable, are not given as *parts* of awareness — not now, and not in earliest infancy. The newborn infant simply is aware — awake, conscious. Over time, it learns to *differentiate* each sense modality from the others — hearing from touch from smell, etc. But its awareness did not begin with separate or discriminated modalities that it then had to assemble. Its awareness began as, and remains, a single whole.

Consciousness is not put together from separate experiences. Rather, what we call "an experience" or (colloquially) "a sensation" is the product of analysis, something isolated out from one, unified "stream of consciousness."

Like "sensation," the term "stimulus" should not be construed on the atomic model, as if each stimulus caused its own particle of awareness.[23] A stimulus does not create an awareness where there was no awareness before. Rather, when there is a particular change in the ongoing sea of stimulation that the organism is immersed in, the organism becomes aware of that change, in addition to the things it was previously aware of. A particular stimulus causes a modification in the *field* of one's awareness, not the genesis of an "atom" of awareness; there are no such "atoms."

The sensationalist model is one of isolated zings of energy at the receptors resulting in corresponding pings of sensation in consciousness. But the zing-ping model contradicts what we plainly experience in perception: a unified, dynamic, seamless field of awareness.

The zing-ping model takes quiescent non-awareness as the norm, the default state — as if awareness were a *disturbance* interrupting nirvana. In fact, however, our perceptual systems operate in an ever-present, churning sea of stimulation — variations in light, sound, pressure, force, torque, etc. What we isolate as "a stimulus" is simply one wavelet singled out mentally from that choppy, roiling sea.

From the total perceptual experience, it is possible to abstract out a single *dimension* of response, such as brightness or softness. The products of such abstraction are often, but confusingly, referred to as "sensations." The better term is "sensory qualities." In some cases, when authors refer to "sensations," they mean these sensory qualities. The danger in using the term "sensations" is that it suggests that the infant starts life with an experience of disembodied

---

23 Nor is "stimulus" a good term to use in describing perception, since it suggests passivity on the part of the perceiving organism.

qualities, which he (or his nervous system) then has to join together to reach awareness of entities. This is a pervasive and seductive error. Brightness and the like are abstractions, not the "original stuff" of awareness, not material that gets assembled into a constructed whole. In fact, perception of entities is the given; individual qualities, such as brightness, are what we later analyze out as a single dimension or variable.

By analogy: we can analyze a force into its vector "components," but these are not actual constituents of the force. When a wind is blowing to the northeast, physics finds it helpful in calculations to analyze that force into two "components," a north component and an east component. But in reality, the northeast wind has no components — it is not a combination of a north-ward wind with an eastward one. In the same way, your perception of an apple is not a combination of sensations of color, brightness, texture, etc.

The error in sensationalism is reification: the fallacy of taking an aspect of a thing, grasped by mental analysis, as if it were an entity capable of separate existence. The simplest example would be thinking that a coin is a combination of heads and tails, rather than realizing that heads and tails are not entities put together to form a coin, but are aspects of the actual entity, the coin — aspects that we mentally isolate. Likewise, sensory qualities, like brightness and softness, are aspects of the perceptual whole, which we mentally isolate but which never existed as separate phenomena.

Analysis is indispensable to cognition, but analysis consists of breaking down what is given as a whole in perception. Thus, it is a complete inversion to treat the perceptually given as being a compound of sensory qualities or sensations — which are, in fact, aspects separated out by analysis.

Take another example: color perception. Although color seems at first to be a single quality, analysis identifies three factors: hue, saturation, and brightness. But we do not begin by having separate sensations of each factor. Nor does our experience of color require that we put together any such hue-sensations, saturation-sensations, and brightness-sensations. Only a minuscule percentage of the human race even knows about these three aspects of color.

Brightness, loudness, pressure, warmth, and the like are the simplest, irreducible dimensions of a global, multi-modality field of perceptual awareness, but these dimensions are not elements, components, or "atoms" of aware-ness put together by either the brain or the mind into a perceptual whole. Sensationalism must be rejected.

The term "sensation," apart from its colloquial use, should be restricted to the non-perceptual form of awareness experienced by the lower animals, such as earthworms.[24]

For the higher animals, those capable of perceiving entities, sensory qualities are given as inseparable *aspects* of whole entities, not as their *parts*. To isolate in awareness a given color from the entity possessing it, such as the fire truck's red color from the fire truck, is a relatively sophisticated feat, requiring an act of abstraction. In perceiving the fire truck, one sensory quality, such as its color, is not set off against its other qualities, such as its size or shape. What perception isolates are not qualities but *entities*. The fire truck is automatically *discriminated* from the other cars and trucks, the road, the buildings, etc. The spatial discrimination of entities from each other is *given in the perception*; it is not the outcome of some higher act of cognition. Perception presents us with an array of entities, each set off against the others in a three-dimensional world.

Even the idea that human beings in earliest infancy go through a sensation stage, during which they are aware not of entities but only of unintegrated sensory qualities, is a very dubious scientific hypothesis. There can be no *philosophic* argument to show that a sensation stage is required in order to reach the perceptual level, since many animals give every indication of being at the perceptual level from birth. E.g., a colt will begin running around only two or three hours after birth, a feat impossible without perception of entities.

For each sense modality — seeing, hearing, touching, smelling, tasting — there are sensory receptors that respond to stimulation from the environment. The *means* of this awareness is the impingement of energy upon sensory receptors. But we do not perceive the energy or the action of the receptors; we perceive entities, things. We do not see light; light enables us to see the objects that reflect or emit it. We do not hear air-vibrations; the impact of those air-vibrations on structures in the ear enables us to hear events in the world. And although we do feel the pressure of objects upon the body, touch *perception* is not the experience of pressure but of objects pressing, an awareness enabled by the force of that pressure. Taste and smell involve the detection of chemicals; however, the perceptual element is the tasting and smelling of *objects*, e.g., of a peach.

What are the sensory structures that make the higher animals capable of perceptual awareness? This is, of course, a scientific question rather than

---

24 The term "sensation" is used in as many as seven different senses [EFRON 1966, 149]. The failure to distinguish among them has led to widespread confusion.

a philosophic one. But a reference to some recent scientific work will be helpful in concretizing the nature of perception.

Direct Realism

The science I present here is based on the achievements of one researcher and
theorist: J. J. Gibson. Gibson revolutionized the scientific study of perception
by developing and building upon a proper philosophic base, which he aptly
termed "direct realism"[25] — an understanding of perception that explicitly
and thoroughly rejects the error of sensationalism. Gibson's direct realism
is the base for what follows.[26]

Gibson found that perceptual awareness stems from the ability of the
nervous system to detect relationships in the incoming stimulation, especially
higher-order relationships. This requires some explanation.

Consciousness is a difference-detector. One soon loses awareness of a
constant odor, pressure, or background hum. Even the seemingly static
vision of a changeless vista is accomplished and maintained only by constant
micro-movements of the eye, movements of which we are introspectively
unaware. In experiments that stabilize the retinal image, it is found that
visual awareness soon vanishes. [Riggs and Ratliff, 1950]

Further evidence: in the so-called *Ganzfeld* experiments, subjects' eye
sockets are fitted with half ping-pong balls, making their visual field
entirely uniform, deprived of all optical structure.[27] In the absence of any
differences in the incoming visual stimulation, the subjects soon report not
that they see a spread of white, but that they have stopped seeing altogether.
Sometimes they fear that they have gone blind. Even when the ping-pong
balls are dyed a uniform color, the color soon stops being seen. The same
type of phenomenon occurs in snowblindness.[28] Change not stasis, difference not sameness, is what consciousness is adapted to detect.

25 "Indirect realism" is the invalid notion that what we perceive are not objects in the world
    but internal products, such as images or "sense data" that "represent" external objects.
    This "representationalist" view, a recurrent error, will be discussed in detail near the end
    of this chapter.

26 Gibson's final and best treatment of perception is in *The Ecological Approach to Visual
    Perception* [Gibson, 1986]. Also quite valuable is his earlier work, *The Senses Considered
    as Perceptual Systems*. [Gibson, 1966]

27 I am indebted to Klaus Nordby for stressing the absence of optical structure.

28 *Cf.* Gibson's thought-experiment of a man standing in a uniform fog [Gibson, 1986, 53].

Animals capable of perception, as opposed to mere sensation, can detect *higher-order differences* — in particular, the difference between what changes and what does not. This higher-order difference enables a perceiver to use difference-detection to apprehend constancy, sameness, invariance — things that consciousness, as a difference-detector, is not otherwise sensitive to or does not highlight. Constancy per se is not normally detected, but *constancy amid change* is detected, because it is actually a (higher-order) difference: the difference between what is changing and what is not. Perception works precisely by what Gibson calls "extracting the invariants" — i.e., detecting *constant patterns* in the stimulation, patterns that stand out because their constancy makes them different from the items that change.

One of Gibson's examples of constancy amid change is the flow of the visual field resulting from moving forward. All points in the visual field flow radially outward, towards the periphery — except *one point*, the point toward which one is moving. The object that one is directly approaching does not move to either side in the visual field, as do all other objects. The straight-ahead object enlarges, but stays where it is in the visual field.[29]

No static images can capture the moving flow, but the three frames above, created from the photograph on page 62, are to illustrate how moving straight toward the middle apple causes an outward flow of all *other* points, blurred here to indicate their movement. The edges of the bowl move successively to the frames' borders, as do all the apples *except* the apple one is approaching.

29   I am careful to speak of "in the visual field," because it is also crucial to realize that the objects moving across one's visual field (due to one's own movements) may be stationary in reality. In that case, the objects are *perceived* as being stationary. (The term "visual field" is an imperfect one, but is the best available: it denotes the psychologist's perspective on a subject's means of perception, not the first-person, phenomenological perspective.)

The incoming light contains patterns, and, at a higher level, patterns of changes in the patterns. The organism's ability to detect and capitalize upon these patterns, including higher-level patterns, is what enables the organism to discriminate entities. The perception of a spatial array of entities requires multiple levels of pattern-detection in a complex neural process involving neural integration at multiple levels (retinal, ganglial, and cerebral).[30] The resulting conscious response is not the "ping" of a solitary receptor reacting to a zing of energy, but the enduring awareness of entities in the world.

In the visual discrimination of entities, a crucial element is the detection of *edges*. Edges produce discontinuities in the pattern of stimulation, a jump from one color to another or from one brightness level to another.

But edges do not maintain a fixed angular relationship with each other: as one moves around the object (or, as the object moves), there is a shift in perspective that changes the visual angles among the object's edges.

Take the case of viewing the top surface of a rectangular table. When one moves to a closer vantage point, that changes the angles of the light entering the eye and that changes the top's shape in the "visual field" (to borrow a dubious term): the shape begins as trapezoidal and becomes more so, if one approaches the table from a low viewing angle. When one moves in relation to a table, one is normally unaware of the perspectival changes, but these drawings, since they are two-dimensional projections, make the perspectival differences quite clear.

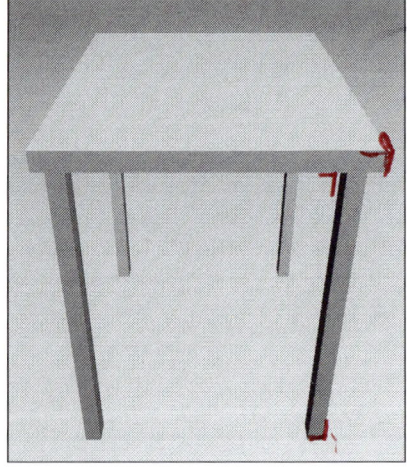

30   On the role of pattern-detection in cognition, see Hawkins & Blakeslee, 2005.

However, there is an invariant order to these perspectival changes; they are regular, lawful, and continuous. In approaching the table, at no point does one find the edge-pattern becoming, say, elliptical. Nor does an edge disappear (unless there is an intervening object, which is then itself seen). The regular succession of changes in the visual angles is what causes us to perceive the table's shape as being *constant*, not undergoing the kind of changes shown two-dimensionally in the drawings on the facing page.

It is often asked: "Why don't we see the table's shape change as we approach it, since the image projected on the retina changes shape with the perspective?" The question assumes that what we perceive is a rendition of the image on the retina. But perception is not of an image, nor is perception a passive transmission of receptor events. Perception is an *integrated* form of awareness, one that responds to patterns automatically extracted by the brain from the ongoing flow of sensory input. As a result, we experience the table shape as being constant.

In the human eye, there is indeed a retinal image, but the eye is not a camera. The image on the retina is upside down, perhaps fuzzy, constantly moving, changing; and there are two eyes with two slightly different images. Instead of using the camera as a model of vision, we should liken it to a radar dish sweeping the skies.

Moreover, human eyes respond not to points of light, but to patterns. These patterns exist in space and in time: there is the pattern of adjacent elements in a scene and there is a pattern over time regarding how those patterns move and flow, as the eyes move, the head moves, and the person walks around.

Gibson writes: "We look around, walk up to something interesting and move around it so as to see it from all sides, and go from one vista to another.... [A] moving point of observation is necessary for any adequate acquaintance with the environment." [GIBSON, 1986]

Much more could be said about the detection of higher-order spatial and temporal patterns, but the preceding should be sufficient to indicate how the perceptual level operates. The philosophic point is this: by detecting higher-order relationships, the nervous system is able to present us in perception with a three-dimensional world of entities discriminated from each other. No assembling of "awareness atoms" is involved or required. Perception results from the neurophysiological processing of physical inputs, not from an experience of "sensations," or of sensory qualities that somehow get combined. Sensationalism is wrong; direct realism is right.

PERCEPTION AS INERRANT *(not being able to be wrong)*

can direct to explore.
can not control that order

The means of perceiving and the means of conceiving are radically different. In contrast to the conscious and volitional nature of conceptual activity, the processes producing perception are physical and deterministic. With eyes open, you see; if a door slams, you hear it; if an object bumps against your body, you feel it. The automatic nature of perception is not contravened by your control over your senses and over the focus of your attention. You indeed can direct your senses to explore this object instead of that, and you can control, within a given field of perception, what you attend to. But in either case, you have no control over what you will perceive in consequence. The content of perception is dictated by what is there to perceive and attend to, given the physical conditions obtaining.

no judge
so no higher standard

Since perception is automatic and deterministic, the information provided by the senses is an absolute. It cannot be evaluated or judged — neither as correct nor incorrect, neither as valid nor invalid. The content of perception is necessitated by the objects stimulating one's senses, the external conditions obtaining (e.g., the level of illumination, for vision), and the automatic physiological processing done by the nervous system. Moreover, there is no "higher" standard against which to judge the deliverances of sense. Perceptual data is the self-evidently given, against which all conceptual and inferential processes are judged — not the reverse.

To properly describe perception, I call on Ayn Rand's distinction between "the metaphysically given" and "the man-made":

> To grasp the axiom that existence exists, means to grasp the fact that nature, i.e., the universe as a whole, cannot be created or annihilated, that it cannot come into or go out of existence. Whether its basic constituent elements are atoms, or subatomic particles, or some yet undiscovered forms of energy, it is not ruled by a consciousness or by will or by chance, but by the Law of Identity. All the countless forms, motions, combinations and dissolutions of elements within the universe — from a floating speck of dust to the formation of a galaxy to the emergence of life — are caused and determined by the identities of the elements involved. Nature is the *metaphysically given* — i.e., the nature of nature is outside the power of any volition.... The metaphysically given cannot be true or false, it *simply is.* ... [PWNI, 25, 27]

The content of perception is metaphysically given. As such, perception is unjudgeable. Just as it makes no sense to evaluate a natural occurrence like rainfall, it makes no sense to evaluate the content of perception. Rainfall is neither "valid" nor "invalid" — it just *is*. In exactly the same way, *hearing* the rainfall is neither valid nor invalid — it just *is*.

Questions of validity or invalidity arise only where there is volitional control of the cognitive process, culminating in a conceptual judgment — as when you *think* to yourself: "the pitter-patter I'm now hearing is rain." That thought may be true or false, valid or invalid, correct or mistaken. But none of these things applies to the *hearing*, as such. The hearing is the physically necessitated result of the action of sound waves on one's ears and what one's brain, as a physical organ, does with that input.

You control your thinking, your judgments, your reasoning, your interpretation of sensory experiences, but the experiences themselves are produced automatically, independent of your volition, which means that they are neither valid nor invalid, but "metaphysically given" facts.

Again quoting Rand: "[man's] organs of perception are physical and have no volition, no power to invent or to distort . . . the evidence they give him is an absolute." [AS, 1041]

There is indeed a polemical value to saying "Perception is valid," and such a statement is unobjectionable, if one means "Perception is of reality." But the deeper point is that perception is, if I may put it this way, beyond valid: as metaphysically given, perceptual data are the standard for judging what is valid or invalid.

The technical way of putting the conclusion is that perception is "inerrant." The content of perception cannot be erroneous or mistaken. More simply, the point to be affirmed is: "I see things, I hear things. I touch things and feel them. I am aware, in various forms, of things."

You cannot mis-see, mis-hear, mis-taste, etc. There is no such thing as "mis-perceiving." The very term is a contradiction: to perceive something is to be aware of it. And there is no such thing as awareness of what doesn't exist. We come back to perception as a corollary of the axiom of consciousness: perceivers perceive.

Perception vs. Conceptual Identification

There is, however, a familiar objection to the idea that perception is inerrant: the Argument from Illusion. This argument claims that optical illusions, and illusions involving other senses, show that the senses can be in error.

The millennia-old example is that of the straight object that appears as if it were bent when semi-submerged in water:

The stick looks bent, but it is actually straight. Isn't this, then, a case of mistaken perception? No, for we must distinguish between the act of *seeing* and the use of *concepts* to describe what is seen. There is nothing erroneous about the stick's appearance; one's eyes and brain are functioning as their nature demands. The perceptual data are not wrong or mistaken — but they can be *misleading*: a naïve observer is likely to conclude: "This stick is bent." If he does, it is that *conceptual judgment*, not the seeing, that is mistaken.

The water's refraction of light makes the stick look bent (i.e., resemble actually bent sticks), and one expects it to still look that way out of water:

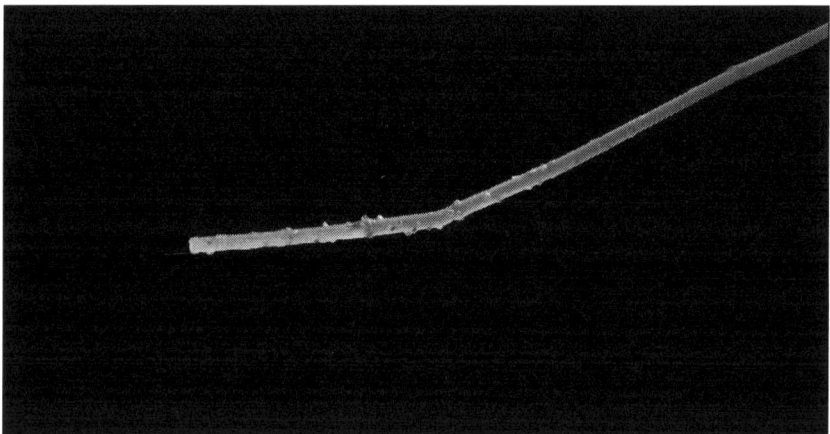

But seeing is seeing, not predicting. The sheer sight of the stick is not a prediction as to how it will look out of water, or in other conditions of perception; perception does not transcend time in that way, reaching into the future. (There are indeed perceptual-level associations and expectations about the immediate future formed pre-conceptually, as when a kitten learns to associate a match flame with a painful burn and subsequently to avoid it. This is perceptual association, not conceptual judgment.)

Expectations based on perceptual association sometimes fail to be fulfilled. For instance, a pet cat may associate hearing a certain sound in the kitchen with being fed but not be fed. Such frustrated expectations are not errors in cognition. Only states of awareness, not things like forming and using associations or expectations, count as acts of perception.[31]

In the bent-stick "illusion," what we see is the way a straight stick looks when semi-submerged in water. The image on the left is, after all, a photograph. The camera does not lie, and neither do the eyes.

Vision gives us an awareness of things in a certain form — how things look. Hearing gives us how things sound. Touch gives us how things feel. There is not and could not be a perception of things the way they do *not* look, sound, feel, etc. Things look, sound, and feel the way they must, given the sensory inputs and the brain's automatic processing of them. (Here, the water refracts the light waves, as it must.)

There are countless other illusions, involving shape, color, lightness and darkness, motion — you name it. But they all have the same form:

> Our senses tell us so and so.
> But so and so is not the case.
> _____
> Our senses have erred.

The error is in the first premise. Our senses do not talk to us. The senses do not form propositions. They do not make judgments. Perception is only perception, not perception plus a proposition. Your sight of the stick does not even include the simple proposition: "That is a stick."

It is crucial to be absolutely clear on what is perception and what is more advanced than perception.

---

31   Cf. Gregory Salmieri's distinction between perception and "post-perceptual processing." [SALMIERI, 2006]

"Perception" includes: seeing, hearing, touch, smelling, tasting, and awareness of things going on in our bodies (proprioception). "Perception" does *not*
include: association, expectation, prediction, classification, inference, propositions, intellect, reason, interpretation, judgment, thought.

There is a linguistic signal in English for the difference between the
perceptual and the conceptual: the locution "seeing that" always indicates
a judgment, never just perception. You see a tree. But to see *that* it is a tree
is "seeing" in only a metaphorical sense. To see *that* something is a tree is to
go beyond the perception to subsume what is perceived under the concept
"tree." Likewise, we are not dealing just with perception if we see *that* the tree
is big, *that* the tree is old, *that* its leaves are green. Perception includes only
seeing the big, old, green-leafed tree.

Earlier, I discussed the error of reducing perception to "sensations."
The Argument from Illusion makes the inverse error: reading the *conceptual*
level of awareness into perception. Where the doctrine of sensationalism dis-
integrates the perceptual level, implying that man does not directly perceive
entities, the other side of the same false coin intellectualizes the perceptual
level, claiming that perception involves the use of concepts, inference — even
theories. But perception is neither less than it is nor more than it is.
Perception is neither sensations nor ideas. Perception is an integrated, but
pre-conceptual, awareness of entities — a level of awareness not possible to
an earthworm but one enjoyed by such non-theorizers as frogs and fish.[32]

If we eliminate from the Argument from Illusion the confusion of perception with conceptual judgment, we have:

> Under these conditions, this looks a certain way.
> Under other conditions, this looks a different way.
> _____
> Therefore ... ?

No anti-senses conclusion follows.
In the stick case in particular, the actual situation is this:

---

32 Even Gibson succumbs to error here, holding that perception includes awareness of what
he calls the "affordances" of things — i.e., their potential benefit or harm for the agent.
Though some of things' simple causal powers are indeed given perceptually, the learning
of many of them is either by association (which is not direct perception) or, for man,
by reasoning. Gibson goes so far as to hold that we perceive that a mailbox "affords"
mailing a letter. In other respects as well, Gibson seems to be unclear on the perceptual-
conceptual distinction.

When semi-submerged in water, this stick looks similar in
  shape to things I have classified as "bent."
But when taken out of water, this stick looks different in shape
  from those things.

Therefore ... ?

The senses have made no "error" in responding as they do, and there is
no philosophic problem concerning the fact that some things, under certain
conditions, look like other things. One man from a certain angle resembles
another. A fox seen from a distance resembles a dog. The fact that one thing
can resemble another does not threaten the inerrancy of the senses.

There is nothing in the perception — the sheer *seeing* — capable of being
either correct or mistaken. Any misclassification prompted by the perceptual
appearance is an error not of perception but of conceptual classification.

A thing's appearance depends upon both its own nature and the conditions
of perception. The green hills, viewed from a distance, look blue — i.e., they
look the way blueberries look from close up. But no error occurs — until and
unless one makes a conceptual judgment: "Those hills are blue."

The same analysis applies to the Müller-Lyer illusion, shown below.

The two lines look the way lines unequal in length look, but they are of
equal length. But no error occurs — until and unless one makes a conceptual
judgment: "Those lines are of unequal length."

The looks of things do not interpret themselves, or tell us how to classify
them, or how the things perceived would look in other conditions — under
different lighting, from close up, or with the two lines moved close together.

This analysis resolves all cases of illusion. They all confuse the perceptual
with the conceptual. They all attempt to make philosophical hay out of
a perceptual similarity that tempts one to make an erroneous *judgment*.
Animals are not perplexed by perceptual "illusions" because they do not have
concepts and therefore do not make classifications. A given "illusion" may
cause an animal to act in ways inappropriate to the actual facts — as when
a cat sees itself in the mirror and reacts as if another cat were present — but
the animal is not "making a mistake." To call it a "mistake" is to project

our human perspective onto the animal. The actions of the intellect in interpreting, describing, or classifying perceptual information can be mistaken; the perceiving cannot be. Perception is awareness, and there is no such thing as "mis-awareness."

Often confused with illusions is a different type of case, that of color blindness. "Who is right," it is asked, "the man who sees red and green or the color-blind man who sees two patches of the same color?"

The answer is: neither is right and neither is wrong. The color-blind person lacks the power to make certain discriminations. It is not correct to say that he sees red as being green; rather, where we see a color-difference, he does not. Due to a physiological defect, he cannot detect certain differences that a normal person can detect. The issue, then, is not that one man sees red where the other sees green; rather, one man is sensitive to the red-green difference and the other is not. There is no more a contradiction here than between a sighted man and one completely blind.

The color-blind man gets *less* information — but not "misinformation": whatever information he gets is an unevaluable, inerrant absolute. One can make comparisons regarding the *quantity* of information gained, but not about the *quality* of that information. Any information acquired *is* information.

Different species, having different sensory physiology, pick up different kinds of information. Dogs are able to hear frequencies too high for us to hear; bees respond to ultraviolet light that we cannot see; bats perceive quasi-visually by means of echo-location; migratory birds are sensitive to the polarization of light. But whatever an organism is aware of, it is aware of. Perception is perception.

Form vs. Object

The dependency of perception upon its causal means has deeper implications: the content of perception is shaped by the nature of the organism's sensory physiology. Skeptics have used this fact to argue that perception is subjective — holding that we perceive not the world as it is, but only the world as it is relative to us — not the real world, but only a world of appearances.

It is in that kind of woozy language that this attack on perception is made. But recasting it in a clear form will not only lay bare its error but also highlight an important truth. Here is the better statement of this argument:

The content of perception depends on our nature.
Objects in the external world do not depend on our nature.

The content of perception is not objects in the external world
(but something in us).

The above may be called The Argument from the Relativity of Perception. The error in the argument is an insidious equivocation on "the content of perception." That phrase equivocates between the *object* perceived and the *form* in which we perceive it.

Perception, like all conscious activities, has two aspects: the form of awareness and the object of awareness. Distinguishing form and object is essential to understanding consciousness on both the perceptual and conceptual levels.[33] The object is *what* you perceive — e.g., a table. The form is *how* you perceive the object — e.g., as large, brown, rectangular, smooth, and so on. We perceive the object in the form of its sensory qualities.

If we make the form-object distinction, The Argument from the Relativity of Perception becomes quite different:

The form in which we perceive depends on our nature.
Objects in the external world do not depend on our nature.

The form in which we perceive is not objects in the external
world.

Thus, if we use the proper first premise, we reach a harmless (and fairly meaningless) conclusion.

To accomplish its skeptical purpose, the argument would have to have as its first premise: "The *objects* we perceive depend on our nature."

But that is manifestly false. The table we perceive exists and is what it is independently of us. The skeptic's argument needs to equivocate — to switch from a premise about *form* to a conclusion about *object*.

The form of perception is indeed "observer-relative." But that does not mean the form in which we perceive reality is subjective or distorted. The nature of one's perceptual systems is what it is and acts as it has to act,

---

33   The form-object distinction traces back to Aquinas, who has a brief, almost in-passing, identification of the same distinction as the *id quod* vs. the *id quo* — or the "that which" vs. the "that by means of which" [SUMMA THEOLOGICA, I, Q. 85, 2]. This distinction is emphasized in both Thomistic philosophy and Objectivism.

given the conditions. The resulting *form* of perception also is as it has to be, given the nature of the object, the perceiver's nature, and the current conditions of perception.

In perception, *both* form and object are metaphysically given facts. Both are unjudgeable. We cannot evaluate *what* we perceive — the object — as true or false, valid or invalid. If what you perceive is a tree, you cannot judge the tree as a valid or invalid object. It is simply the object, the tree. Similarly, you perceive the tree *somehow* — i.e., in a certain form, as looking like *this*, with this color, shape, size, texture, etc. That specific form of perceiving the tree results from the automatic, physiologically determined processes of your nervous system. You do not make it up, and you cannot change how you perceive the tree by ordering yourself to perceive it differently. Nor can you perceive the tree in the form that, say, a bat does — by the tree's echoes of high-frequency sound waves. That simply isn't the human means of perception.

It is nonsensical to maintain that one ought to be able to perceive the tree in a different form — as, say, vibrating atoms. There is no more basis for that "ought" than for the idea that rain ought to fall upwards. Attacking the senses for providing information in the form that they do amounts to what Ayn Rand called the fallacy of "re-writing reality": one is implicitly maintaining, "If I had written the script for reality, I would have had rain falling upwards and trees being perceived as collections of atoms." But reality is what it is — and one's physical means of perception is part of reality; the form of perception resulting from those means is metaphysically given.

There is no "right" or "wrong" way for things to look or sound or feel. There is only the way that they *do* look, sound, and feel — as they must, given their nature, the conditions, and the nature of our perceptual apparatus.

Things have an appearance — but the appearance is the *form* of perception, not the *object* of perception. The visual appearance of a tree is how the tree looks — how (form), the tree (object), looks.

The form of perception is partly dependent on our human physiology. But, the object of perception is not. The form is the form of *awareness of objects*. It is *how* we perceive, not *what* we perceive. What we perceive is the object — that is what is meant in this context by "object."

I want to emphasize that the form-object distinction is not some minor point trotted out to answer skeptics. The distinction between the what and the how of cognition is essential to the whole approach to consciousness I am presenting here, the approach developed by Ayn Rand. I will give a series of examples to concretize and clarify this crucial distinction.

Consider what happens when you change the tint control on a color TV, so that what looked green before, now looks bluer; what looked blue before, now looks redder, etc. You still see the same objects, but in a different form. You have not changed the channel, which would result in your seeing a different set of objects. Changing the tint changes only the form, while leaving the same object and the same information content.

No matter how bizarrely you set the tint control, you cannot see colors that are wrong — merely colors that are different from the ones you are accustomed to seeing. It is not the case that the normal form is the *right* way for objects to look and the other is the *wrong* way; what you call the "right" tint-setting is simply the one that makes the televised world match the way you perceive the natural world. That is a comparison of the form of perceiving the screen images with the form of perceiving actual objects — a comparison of form to form. But what you cannot do is compare form to object; you cannot compare a banana's seen color with its "real color." Color is a form of perception; the "real color" of the banana *is* the color it is seen to have.

Suppose that, from birth, your nervous system had been peculiarly different, so that you always saw things in a shifted spectrum. Suppose that grass looked blue, the sky looked red, etc. If so, then those would be the normal colors, for you. And in learning language, you would learn to use the word "blue," not "red," to denote the color of the sky, even though *your* form of perceiving the sky was like *my* form of perceiving a fire truck. Neither your spectrum nor mine would be "right" or "wrong," "truer" or "less true" — just as neither the Fahrenheit scale nor the Celsius scale is the "right" scale, and neither English nor French is the "true" language. There is no such thing as "the way things look to God" — no standard of how things "should" look in contrast to how things do look, as a necessary result of one's perceptual physiology. There is no look apart from a looker.

One's senses are like physical instruments, which respond to physical stimulation in the form that physical causality dictates.

Consider an actual physical instrument: a standard mercury thermometer. The height of mercury in a thermometer does not reproduce or resemble or copy temperature; it registers it. The senses do not reproduce reality, they register reality. They register, ultimately, the information contained in the patterns of energy that strike them.[34]

In a mercury thermometer, sometimes a gap appears in the column of mercury. But this does not mean that the thermometer then gives a "false" result. It still registers the temperature, but now the person reading the thermometer must re-calibrate the scale in order to interpret the results correctly. The thermometer still gives a causally necessitated result that accurately reflects the temperature. Even if a defect in the thermometer makes it respond non-linearly, the instrument remains an accurate and useful source of information as long as there is a one-to-one correspondence between each temperature and each position of the mercury. To use this "defective" thermometer, one need only mark it with the appropriate non-linear scale.

In general, as long as each state of the instrument correlates with a single state of what it is to detect, the instrument is functional, and capable of giving an informative reading. The same is true of the senses, with the "calibration" (i.e., determination of conceptual meaning) being done by the intellect. The senses, like measuring instruments, can fail to function, but if they function at all, they cannot function *erroneously*. Every state of a thermometer, a voltmeter, a Geiger counter, is causally necessitated, and so is every state of a perceptual system.

Today, modern technology makes it easy for us to understand that information can be displayed in various ways, and that the form in which we display information does not alter the content of that information. For instance, a sonogram uses sound echoes to make a visual display of shape. The display on a radar screen presents information extracted from reflected radio waves.

Consider the fax machine. A photosensitive element scans across the document, registering each tiny dark or light patch as a high or low voltage. Then these patterns of voltage are transformed into tones that are sent across the phone wires. At the other end, the tones are turned back into voltage patterns that cause a printer to reproduce the black and white patches, giving the same dark-and-white pattern as in the original. That is an example of how information can be changed in form without losing any of its information content.

---

34 It is proper to use the term "information" here, but not in regard to the contents of a computer (see CHAPTER 1) precisely because we are discussing the relation of physical facts to a *consciousness*.

A particularly dramatic example of different forms of perceiving the same object is provided by a prosthetic device developed to enable blind people to acquire visual information. The device is a video camera mounted on the patient's forehead. The information from that camera is processed and transformed into presses on the patient's back by an array of blunt pins that he wears. By the pattern of the pins' pressure, the blind person feels, in the *form* of pressure on his back, the pattern of light, including how that pattern changes as he moves around. As a result, the blind person effectively "sees" objects in his environment by means of feeling touches on his skin. He picks up the same kind of information, though with less resolution, that a sighted individual does, but in a different form — as touch rather than as sight. [BACH-Y-RITA, 1969]

Perhaps the most decisive example of form vs. object occurs when the same facts are perceived through different sense modalities. We become aware of an object's shape both by sight and by touch — two different forms of perceiving the same fact. Likewise, the texture of sandpaper is perceived both by sight and by touch: same fact, different perceptual forms.

The form-object distinction makes short work of an old philosophical chestnut: adapting one's left hand to cold water, one's right hand to hot water, then plunging both hands into the same pail of lukewarm water, which then feels warm to one's left hand and cool to one's right hand. The difference in the state of the two hands results in two different forms of response to the same water-temperature. There is no contradiction between the two forms of awareness, and neither is in error.

Next, consider an example that switches sense modalities. If you push on the lower outside corner of your bottom eyelid, the pressure should stimulate some of the receptors in your retina. If done properly, a circle of light will appear in the opposite part of your visual field (by your nose and near the top of your visual field). Here, you are mechanically stimulating retinal receptors, which are normally stimulated by light. The result is a neural discharge sent to the brain which produces the experience of a circle of light. You have a visual form of response to the pressure of your finger. It is an unusual form of being aware of pressure, but the content is the same as when you feel pressure by means of receptors in your skin. The object — and the information — is the same.

As a final example, consider your awareness of heat, in the form of warmth, when something contacts your skin. Physically, the heat is the vibratory motion of the molecules in the object touched. Now, imagine a race of humanoids on another planet who experience that heat in the form of vibrations, not warmth. The difference in the two forms of perception would have no philosophic significance. Neither form could be declared to be the "right" or "wrong" way to perceive heat. Both forms of perception would be metaphysically given, and both forms would provide information about the object.[35]

Perception vs. Hallucination

What about delusions or hallucinations? For instance, there is the following common experience. When in quiet surroundings, perhaps lying down in bed before falling asleep, one sometimes hears for a couple of seconds a pure high tone. The sound is caused by something internal to the ear. But it is physically caused, not the result of the mischief of some intervening spirit, like Descartes' evil demon. One is hearing *something*, something real, only it is a state of one's body rather than something in the external world.

Take the extreme case. Suppose someone swallows LSD and "sees" ants crawling on his arm. But there are no ants. Isn't he mis-perceiving? No, because what he is doing is not "perceiving" — not in regard to the phantom ants. He is hallucinating. *Hallucination is not a kind of perception.* It is an experience in consciousness, but the hallucinatory content does not represent awareness. The LSD-ingester is not "seeing ants" — because there are no ants there to be seen.

It must be noted that the hallucination, though not a perception, is nonetheless causal and deterministic. What the LSD-ingester is experiencing is the chemical action of the LSD on his nervous system. If he concludes from the experience that ants are present, it is the conclusion that is wrong. The experience — even though not a cognitive one, not a case of perception (insofar as the ants part of it is concerned) — is neither erroneous nor correct; it is just an experience.

The experience, though not perception, still has a form. (It has no object but it does have a content.) The form is the colors and shapes (the colors and shapes of ants); the cause of that content is the action of the drug on the nervous system. One might think that the experience represents a perception of the LSD, or of its action on the nervous system. But the experience fails to qualify as a *perception* of the LSD because the experience does not include any *discrimination* of the drug or its action from other things; one is not

35 This example was given by Ayn Rand in the second lecture of the series "Basic Principles of Objectivism."

aware of a spatial array of co-present entities within which the LSD is located. Contrast experiencing LSD in the form of ants on one's arm with actually *perceiving* LSD — looking at it in a test tube or, using some sort of brain scan to follow its path through another person's brain. The delusory experience has a form and a content but does not locate a discriminated existent among others in the world. Thus, the experience is not a *perception* — neither of the LSD nor of (non-existent) ants.

There can be cases in which one experiences a hallucination due to other bodily disturbances, such as extreme hunger, thirst, or prolonged sleep deprivation. Such hallucinations are not acts of perception and are not produced by external objects stimulating the senses. Even when the person having such hallucinations cannot distinguish them from perception, that fact casts no doubt on the cognitive value of perception. The remedy called for is not epistemological — not some process of "checking" — but medical. If he mistakes the content of his hallucinations for perceptual awareness of the world, the error lies in that judgment.

Thus, what may be called "The Argument from Delusion" fails: hallucination and the like are not instances of perception, and neither is any erroneous judgment one makes in response.

Dreams are not hallucinations, but obviously they are not cases of perception. There is no way to get from "With my eyes shut, I dreamed something unreal" to "What I see with my eyes open is unreal" (an idea that steals the concept "unreal"). Nor is there any philosophic significance to the fact that while asleep one is not in a condition that permits distinguishing dreams from wakeful perception: while asleep, a person is not able to make any cognitive judgments. A person asleep cannot "think he's awake and perceiving," because he cannot think at all. (And the question: "How do you know you are not dreaming right now?" already presupposes that the person one is addressing is awake and not dreaming.)

The Argument from Delusion, like the Arguments from Illusion and from the Relativity of Perception, fails to undermine the inerrancy of perception. It had to fail; otherwise we would know nothing, including these arguments.

A FINAL DEFINITION OF PERCEPTION

On the basis of all the preceding discussion, I offer the following, more advanced, definition of "perception":

"Perception" is the direct awareness of reality, in the form of spatially arrayed entities, that results from the automatic neural processing of actively acquired sensory inputs.

(It is taken as understood that the awareness is ongoing, not momentary or episodic, and that perception is "metaphysically given," and hence inerrant.)

THREE GENERAL CONCEPTIONS OF CONSCIOUSNESS

1. Objectivism: consciousness as identification

As I said at the start of this chapter, the biological approach to understanding consciousness recognizes that its function is to guide action, and that its essential means of fulfilling that function is by discovering the identity of things in the world — in Rand's statement: "consciousness is identification." [AS, 1015] Identification is an active process, with definite stages or steps.

But it takes a certain sophistication to appreciate the active nature of consciousness and much more sophistication to make the distinction between the form of perception and the object of perception. The unsophisticated attitude toward perception tends to be that known as "Naïve Realism."

2. Naïve Realism: consciousness as reproduction

Naïve Realism is a form of realism in that it implicitly accepts the primacy of existence: Naïve Realism recognizes that consciousness is awareness of what exists. But the naïve part of Naïve Realism is that it construes perception on the model of mirror reflection. Just as a mirror passively reproduces an image of an object, so consciousness, on this conception, creates internal replicas of objects in the world.[36] Naïve Realism holds that consciousness is not identification but *reproduction*.

This view is captured in a phrase often used by the Ancient Greeks: "Like knows like." The meaning is: to know is to become like the thing known. Seeing a tree, for the Naïve Realist, consists of forming a copy of the tree inside one's mind.

---

36 I use the mirror analogy despite the fact that flat mirrors do not actually produce an image, just reflect light. A parabolic mirror properly set up, however, can produce such an image of an object.

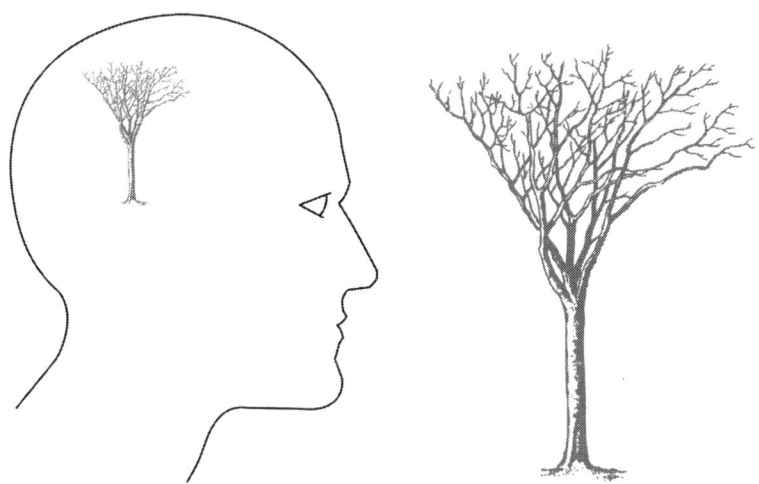

(When made concretely real, as in this diagram, Naïve Realism may well appear to be childishly silly. Nonetheless, it is the implicit premise shaping most people's initial approach to understanding perception, and eradicating all traces of Naïve Realism from one's thinking often takes some vigilance.)

The internal replica of the tree is held to be mental, not physical: what is reproduced inside one's mind is said to be the form of the tree without its matter. Aristotle seems to take this view when he analogizes seeing to the pressing of a signet ring into wax.[37] The wax is like one's consciousness and the signet ring is like the external object perceived. The idea is that in perception, as with impressing the signet ring, the form (here shape) is duplicated — in the one case it is reproduced in consciousness and in the other reproduced in wax.

What drives the idea that "like knows like"? I believe it is the desire to get underneath consciousness, to reduce it to something else. Likeness is a familiar relationship, so it is taken as the model.[38] But, as I argued in the first chapter, consciousness is irreducible. The attempt to get "beneath" awareness, the attempt to say what awareness consists of, is fundamentally mistaken. Awareness is a primary relation of a subject to an object and is not to be construed on the model of any other relation.

---

37   *De Anima*, II, 12, 424a17–24. Cf. ibid., II, 5 and III, 2, 425b27–426a26.

38   In the modern era, the same motivation applies, I believe, to the "new realists" who seek to reduce consciousness to "the intentional relation of identity." See, e.g., Parker, 1953.

The Naïve Realist view has important implications for how one regards the identity and activity of consciousness. If consciousness is reproduction, then accuracy in reproducing the external object requires that consciousness be static and featureless, rather than active and possessed of its own identity. For a pond's surface to clearly reflect things, it must have no motion, no waves or ripples to alter or destroy the image. Naïve Realists assume that consciousness must likewise be still and "pure" if it is to accurately reproduce objects. But in fact consciousness is active, and this activity is essential to its achieving awareness.

Naïve Realism has insuperable problems. The most obvious problem is that it conflicts with the fact that perception does involve physiological processing, and that this processing does determine the form of the resulting perception. Differing means of perception result in different forms of perception of the same object, a fact exploited by skeptics in their Argument from the Relativity of Perception. E.g., fatal to Naïve Realism is the example of the two pails of water: if the same water is warm to one hand and cool to the other, how can one believe that perception is reproducing the state of the object?

But the reaction against Naïve Realism was directed at the wrong target — the Realism instead of the naïveté. The fact of sensory processing was taken to mean that we do not perceive the external world but only the product of the processing. The processing was taken to create an internal object — an image in consciousness — with that mental image, not reality, being the direct object of our awareness.

3. Representationalism: consciousness as self-consciousness

Naïve Realism held that consciousness is reproduction (the perceiver taking on the form of the external object). The subsequent, utterly disastrous view held that *consciousness is representation*. To perceive, according to Representationalism, is to be aware of an *internal* object — an image, an impression, an appearance — which may represent the external object.

According to Representationalism, what we know directly are appearances, images in our minds, not the external world. We get the report of the senses, as interpreted by the processing, and we are aware of that report, not things — or not "things as they are in themselves," in Kant's phrase.

Representationalism unwittingly accepts the Naïve Realist assumption that consciousness, to be valid, would have to be a causeless revelation. Then, in response to the recognition that perception is causal, these theorists move "true consciousness" inside the mind. What results is a kind of interior Naïve Realism: one directly (and causelessly) perceives only contents inside of one's mind. Perception is then construed as the observation — in effect, by a "little man in the head" — of these internal images. Reality recedes behind a "veil of appearances," never itself to be perceived, but figuring only as the hidden cause of the images.

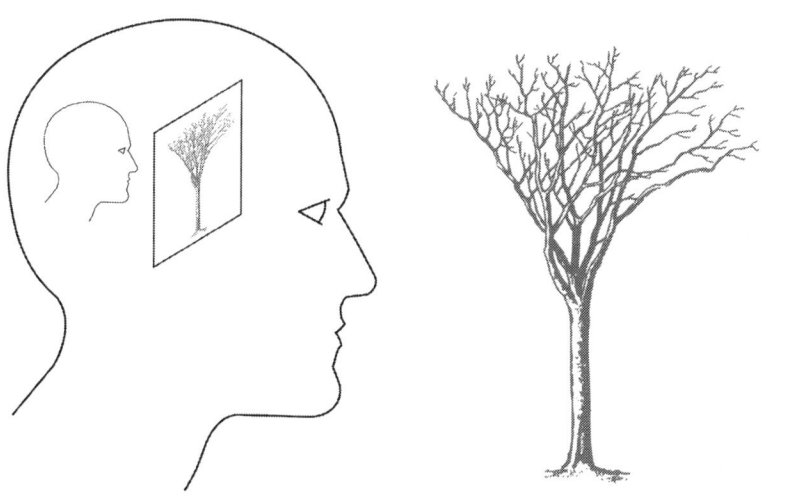

Representationalism is rarely advocated openly and explicitly. It lives in the shadows, as an unidentified assumption warping theories of perception and subverting our understanding of consciousness as such. When the representationalist model is made explicit, as Gibson does in the following passage, its insoluble problems and hopeless circularity become unmistakable.

> [It is] tempting to believe that the image on the retina falls on a kind of screen and is itself intended to be looked at, that is, a picture. It leads to one of the most seductive fallacies in the history of psychology — that the retinal image is something to be seen. I call this the "little man in the brain" theory of the retinal image, which conceives the eye as a camera at the end of a nerve cable that transmits the image to the brain. Then there has to

be a little man, a homunculus, seated in the brain who looks at this physiological image. The little man would have to have an eye to see it with, of course, a little eye with a little retinal image connected to a little brain, and so we have explained nothing by this theory. We are in fact worse off than before, since we are confronted with the paradox of an infinite series of little men, each within the other and each looking at the brain of the next bigger man. [GIBSON 1986, 60]

Representationalism's unstated credo is: consciousness is self-consciousness: we perceive our perceptions, observe our observations, and thus are aware only of what our minds create in us, not the external world.

But in perception, there is no internal image (which would then itself have to be perceived, leading to Gibson's infinite regress). The way things appear is not *what* we perceive but the *form* in which we perceive them. We perceive objects in the world, as they appear — i.e., in the form necessitated by our means of awareness. The appearance of the tree is the appearance of *the tree*, the manner in which the tree is given in perception.

Moreover, lacking the distinction between the metaphysically given and the man-made, Representationalists treat neural processing as if it were volitional and conceptual, as if perception were an *interpretation* of the world made by an internal journalist. Still worse, the objectivity of the internal journalist is not ascertainable, since we cannot get out from behind our eyes to see, without eyes, how things "really are."

Representationalism begins with Descartes and culminates in Kant. Descartes held that we could be deceived about everything — except our having internal states. Descartes retained the primacy of existence to the extent of taking the correspondence of these states to the external world as the standard of validity. Kant went whole hog on the primacy of consciousness, rejecting the standard of correspondence to reality. Reality, he held, is unknowable (which it would be, if Representationalism were true), so we cannot talk about such a thing as correspondence to reality, and we cannot take that correspondence as any kind of standard. Instead, Kant held that all standards have to be consciousness-based — i.e., subjective (which he calls a new form of objectivity.)[39]

---

39 "Hitherto it has been assumed that all knowledge must conform to objects. But all our attempts . . . have, on this assumption, ended in failure. We must therefore make trial whether we may not have more success in the tasks of metaphysics, if we suppose that objects must conform to our knowledge." [CRITIQUE, B, xvi]

Among psychologists studying perception today, Representationalism is the near-universal model. Seeking to avoid using terms like "consciousness" and "awareness," psychologists substitute the term "representation." They assume that "veridical" perception consists of the resemblance of the internal representations to external objects.

This assumption, though utterly without foundation, can be hard to dislodge. The assumption appears in a welter of absurd questions, such as: "Since the retinal image is upside down, how does the brain turn it right side up?" "Since the retinal image of a distant object is small, how does the brain compensate for that to interpret it as representing a larger object at a distance?" "Since the retinal image is moving around due to both tiny and gross movements of the eye, how does the brain stabilize the image?" — and so on. All of these questions assume that the job of the sensory system is to produce an image in the mind, an image that looks like the object in reality. Since the object is right side up, large, and at rest, an accurate internal image of it must be as well.

But the actual job of the sensory system is not to produce an internal image that "looks like" the object. The perceptual system's job is to detect and make us aware of things, in a specific form. Note that the level of mercury in a thermometer does not "resemble" temperature — whatever that would even mean.

Representationalists respond to the skeptics' attacks on the senses by beating a retreat back inside consciousness. "Okay," the Representationalist concedes, "I can doubt that my experiences accurately copy things out there; I can even doubt the existence of the external world; but at least I know that I'm having experiences, and I hope that they at least roughly correspond to external things." But as the history of thought following Descartes shows, this retreat provides no refuge from the all-consuming skepticism to which Representationalism inevitably leads.[40]

Naïve Realism holds that perception is internal effigy-making ("like knows like"). Representationalism's "advance" is to add effigy-viewing to effigy-making. Both Naïve Realism and Representationalism hold, arbitrarily, that valid awareness can involve no processing. The Representationalist tries to uphold the validity of consciousness by positing an unprocessed awareness that takes place between the "little man in the head" and the internal image.

---

40 Descartes attempted to escape from this skepticism by arguing that God's goodness guarantees the general validity of our perceptions, an argument riddled with arbitrary assumptions. In principle, there is no way to "prove" existence from consciousness: the concept of "proof" presupposes that one has grasped that existence exists.

But, in fact, *processing is inherent in the nature of consciousness.* Consciousness is not mirroring but identification — identification achieved by specific means. The false assumption of both Naïve Realism and Representationalism is: if consciousness has an identity, if it is something that works by a specific causal means, it cannot be conscious of the identity of things in the world. The Law of Identity can apply to the world or to consciousness, but not both, they assume. If the world is something definite, then to know it, the mind must be a nothing. If the mind is something, then the world is unidentifiable, which means that consciousness is not conscious. Accordingly, epistemology collapses into the impossible alternative of mysticism or skepticism. Rand neatly summarizes all this in her work on epistemology:

> The hallmark of a mystic is the savagely stubborn refusal to accept the fact that consciousness, like any other existent, possesses identity, that it is a faculty of a specific nature, functioning through specific means. . . . [T]he last stand of the believers in the miraculous consists of their frantic attempts to regard identity as the disqualifying element of consciousness.
>
> The implicit, but unadmitted premise of the neo-mystics of modern philosophy, is the notion that only an ineffable consciousness can acquire a valid knowledge of reality, that "true knowledge" has to be causeless, i.e., acquired without any means of cognition. . . .
>
> All knowledge *is* processed knowledge — whether on the sensory, perceptual or conceptual level. An "unprocessed" knowledge would be a knowledge acquired without means of cognition. [ITOE, 79–80, 81]

The sensory qualities — e.g., redness, loudness, and sweetness — are actually perceptual forms. Taking these qualities as our examples will bring the basic issue into sharp focus. Naïve Realism holds that redness and sweetness exist in the apple alone, apart from any relation it has to consciousness. Representationalism holds that redness, sweetness, and all of the sensory qualities exist in the mind of the perceiver alone, not in the object. On a proper understanding, the sensory qualities are *not locatable* in this manner — they are neither in the object alone nor in the perceiver's mind alone but are the product of the interaction of the perceiver with the object.[41]

---

41 See the section headed "Sensory Qualities as Real," in OPAR, ch. 2.

The apple has certain inherent properties such that when it interacts with our specific sensory system, the result is an awareness of the apple in a particular (red) form. The point is more easily grasped in regard to sweetness, which resides neither in the mind alone nor in the apple alone, neither "in here" nor "out there" but rather as the product of the interaction between the perceiver and the perceived. To clarify this point, Rand gave the analogy of a collision between a car and a truck.[42] The collision is in neither the car alone nor the truck alone, but in both — i.e., constitutes their interaction. We perceive every object in a certain form, resulting from the interaction of its identity with the identity of our sensory system.

APPEARANCE AND REALITY

The understanding of perception given in the last two sections points the way to gaining a proper understanding of the traditional distinction between appearance and reality. We use this distinction to contrast what a thing appears to be versus what it really is. When does this contrast exist? When there are potentially *misleading* similarities: "The man appeared to be Jim, but it was really Bob." Or, "The stick appears to be bent but in reality it is straight." But the "really" or "in reality" here does not refer to something beyond or independent of perception. Rather, "in reality" refers to what is disclosed in *other* acts of perception. It is further *perceptual* information that shows us the need to correct the *judgment*, by concluding: "That is not Jim, but Bob" and "The stick is not bent, but straight."

Nor does the new judgment throw out as "mistaken" the original perceptual data: one does not say "My eyes were deceiving me when I looked at Jim." Jim *does* have an appearance similar to Bob's; a photograph of the two of them would also display that similarity. The semi-submerged stick *does* look similar to the way bent objects look out of water. What gets revised in such cases is the *conceptual judgment* of what is perceived.

None of the perceptual data itself can be rejected or treated as invalid. The later judgment includes the initial perceptual appearance, rather than contradicting it or wiping it out. To be Jim *includes* the fact that he looks like Bob. To be a straight stick *includes* the fact that it will look like a bent stick when semi-submerged in water. To be yellow *includes* looking black under a blue light. How something appears under a given condition of perception (and of the perceiver) is a matter of ineluctable cause and effect (as studied

---

42 Rand in personal conversation with Leonard Peikoff, circa 1972.

by the science of psychophysics). The judgment "This is X" integrates the thing's perceived qualities here and now with its perceived qualities across all other conditions of perception.

Accordingly, there are two perfectly proper ways that we use the concept of "appearance." The first expresses uncertainty, as when one says, "This appears to be gold, but I'm not sure." (Or, when put into the past tense, it expresses a revision of one's judgment: "It appeared to be gold, but it turned out to be iron pyrite.")

The other correct use of "appearance" is one that is more relevant to the issue of perception. This use occurs when one distinguishes a thing's sensory qualities — how it looks, feels, tastes — from its constituent physical properties. For instance, a surface will *appear* smooth to the touch when it has only very small irregularities. In this case, we are not saying that the surface isn't "really" smooth; that idea makes no sense. Rather, we are saying that a certain physical state of affairs produces a certain sensory quality.

The wrong view of the distinction between appearance and reality occurs when philosophers claim that perception as such gives us "only" appearance, not reality. This is a disastrous error. Do I know only the appearance of the pen in my hand, not how the pen really is? One cannot make *that kind* of distinction between appearance and reality.

The claim that perception does not provide awareness of reality (or of reality "as it really is") represents a massive stolen concept. If we perceived only appearances, never reality, we could not have the concept of "reality" (nor the concept of "appearance").

Every appearance is the appearance of reality.

Reality appears to us in a certain form, and no form of perception can be treated as either invalid or privileged.

The form-object distinction puts an end to all these confusions and sophistries. It enables one to reject the hopeless attempt to *compare* appearance to reality — i.e., to compare form to object. One can compare forms of perception to each other, as in comparing how a house looks from here to how it looks from over there. Or, one can compare objects of perception to each other, as in comparing one house to another. What makes no sense, however, is trying to compare a form of perception to the object of perception, as if we could wonder whether the house's appearance looks like the house, or whether sugar is *really* as sweet as it tastes.

Of course, it makes sense to wonder whether the house is as big as it looks ("Would that house measure as large as I would estimate it to measure, judging by how it looks from here?"). As noted earlier, that can be a valid question to raise, because it concerns the relation of perceptual data to conceptual judgment, not the relation of the form of perception to the object of perception — i.e., not the nonsensical comparison of "things as they appear" to "things as they really are."

The root of the notion that we can compare form and object is the Representationalist model of the little man in the head perceiving images, as in the drawing on page 89. That model sets us up to ask whether or not the internal tree looks like the external one. But the model is utterly wrong and the question is nonsensical; it amounts to asking "Does the look of the tree look like the tree?" But looks don't have looks. Appearances don't have appearances. A look or an appearance is a *form* of perception, and we don't have a form of perceiving our forms of perceiving.

A form of perception is *how* a thing looks, and that is not something that can either match or mismatch *what* we are looking at. Analogously, the manner in which a thermometer responds to a temperature (by its mercury-level) is not something that can either match or mismatch a temperature. The relation here is not similarity-difference but cause-effect. The senses do not copy the object, they respond to it. Like physical instruments, the senses respond to the operative causes in the only way they can; how they respond is metaphysically given, and thus not subject to judgment.[43]

Perception is an active process of detecting and grasping the identity of objects, an automatic, inerrant process of awareness. Questions about perception's "fidelity" in "corresponding" to the object stem from the false assumption that perception copies something. As Gibson states:

> The information for the perception of an object is not its image. The information in light to specify something does not have to resemble it, or copy it, or be a simulacrum or even an exact projection. *Nothing* is copied in the light to the eye of an observer, not the shape of a thing, not the surface of it, not its substance, not its color, and certainly not its motion. But all these things are specified in the light. [GIBSON 1986, 304–305]

The Naïve Realist says: "Rubies look red because they are red." The Representationalist says: "Rubies look red but maybe they are really some other color."

---

43 To gain value from a thermometer requires calibrating it and establishing its scale; likewise to gain the cognitive value of the senses requires a similar process of interpreting and integrating the material they provide. But in neither case is there such a thing as "checking for validity." Thus, the slogan here could be: Calibration sí, validation no.

The proper view of perception holds: "Rubies looks red because the human visual system produces that form of response to rubies under standard lighting and viewing conditions."

I gave drawings that illustrate the Naïve Realist and Representationalist models of perception. But I cannot do the equivalent for the proper theory of perception, because the proper theory relies on the form-object distinction and there is no way to separate form and object in a drawing. I cannot draw a tree apart from how it looks (form), and I cannot draw the form in which the tree is seen except by drawing the tree.

I could, of course, draw a man who is facing a tree with his eyes open. But I cannot draw his form of seeing the tree. The form in which he sees the tree is not a second object; it is not an image inside his head. But to draw is to draw *objects*, objects *in* a form. Perspective is an example of a perceptual form; I cannot make a drawing *of* perspective; I can only draw things *in* perspective. The *way* things appear is not an object and thus cannot be depicted apart from objects.

Perceptual awareness is of some object, by some means, and in some form. Perceptual awareness is not image-making, image-viewing, hypothesizing, or judging: it is *perceptual* awareness. And perceptual awareness is not misperceiving, dreaming or hallucinating: it is perceptual *awareness*.

3

CONCEPT-FORMATION

LIKE PERCEPTION, REASON HAS A BIOLOGICAL FUNCTION. Man needs knowledge, knowledge that extends beyond the perceptual. He needs to know how to obtain food and shelter, forge tools, and satisfy all the needs of his survival, material and mental. Reason enables man to gain the conceptual knowledge his survival requires.

> For man, the basic means of survival is *reason.* Man cannot survive, as animals do, by the guidance of mere percepts. A sensation of hunger will tell him that he needs food (if he has learned to identify it as "hunger"), but it will not tell him how to obtain his food and it will not tell him what food is good for him or poisonous. He cannot provide for his simplest physical needs without a process of thought. He needs a process of thought to discover how to plant and grow his food or how to make weapons for hunting. His percepts might lead him to a cave, if one is available — but to build the simplest shelter, he needs

a process of thought. No percepts and no "instincts" will tell him how to light a fire, how to weave cloth, how to forge tools, how to make a wheel, how to make an airplane, how to perform an appendectomy, how to produce an electric light bulb or an electronic tube or a cyclotron or a box of matches. Yet his life depends on such knowledge . . . [VOS, 22–23]

But the biological function of reason has not been widely understood or appreciated. The long Platonic tradition, still gripping the intellectual world, holds that reason is concerned with "higher," "spiritual" matters, not the allegedly "materialistic" issues of life on this earth.

Platonism pits the perceptual and conceptual levels against each other, opposing spirit to matter, mind to body, intellectuality to worldly concerns, theory to practice. For Platonists, man's consciousness is split between mind and body — between a faculty directed toward a "World of Forms" (heaven, in effect) and a faculty dealing with this earth. Man is caught in an internal war between his "higher" and "lower" nature; Christianity took over and intensified this Platonic dichotomy, damning outright all things earthly.

The mind-body dichotomy is not only indefensible philosophically, in the light of modern biology, it represents an archaic embarrassment. We know that man evolved from pre-conceptual primates, and that our present intellectual capacity developed gradually, as the brain evolved. Man's conceptual faculty arises from the nature of his brain, and the human brain is an elaboration of the primate brain. The conceptual faculty, reason, is an enhancement of perceptual consciousness, not an alien element wrenching man's soul away from perceptual concretes.

After the work of Darwin, Mendel, Fisher, Watson and Crick, we know with full certainty that man's conceptual faculty evolved due to natural selection — which means: *man's conceptual faculty has survival value.*

The preeminent evolutionary biologist Theodosius Dobzhansky puts it eloquently:

> The adaptive value of forethought or foresight is too evident to need demonstration. It has raised man to the status of the lord of creation. [DOBZHANSKY, 1967, 468]

The root of the mind-body dichotomy is a wrong answer to the crucial question of epistemology, a question that remains even after rejecting any "higher reality." That question is: by what means are abstractions connected to perceptual concretes?

There are no *directly perceivable* referents for higher abstractions. For instance, when we say "Honesty is a virtue," the words "honesty" and "virtue" do not designate perceptual objects — they stand for abstract relationships. One cannot commune with Plato's Form of Virtue in some world of pure abstractions to learn or validate this moral principle. What then is the actual relation of abstractions, *concepts*, to the concretes we perceive by our senses? And, more basically, by what specific means does one, in late infancy, advance from percepts to concepts? How are concepts formed from perceptual concretes? And how do we go from those concepts to more abstract ones, then to conceptual judgments, then to principles? In other words: "How do we know?" — when the knowing is conceptual?

The *validity* of concepts and reason is not in doubt. If the conceptual level were not valid, you could not be reading this book; you could not know anything beyond what you could, like an animal, see, smell, hear, taste, and touch. In an age of computers, cell phones, and space exploration, we are not waiting to find out whether or not reason works. Rather, the issue is discovering *how* reason works. And the purpose of discovering that is to be able to define standards of cognition, standards to use in steering and evaluating our mental processes.

The operation of our perceptual equipment is automatic and infallible; the exercise of the faculty of reason is not automatic but volitional, and therefore can be misused, leading to error. We consciously control how we think, making constant choices regarding what to think about, how to proceed, what counts as evidence, and what constitutes sufficient evidence to be certain of a conclusion.

> Man is neither infallible nor omniscient; if he were, a discipline such as epistemology — the theory of knowledge — would not be necessary nor possible: his knowledge would be automatic, unquestionable and total. But such is not man's nature. Man is a being of volitional consciousness: beyond the level of percepts — a level inadequate to the cognitive requirements of his survival — man has to acquire knowledge by his own effort, which he may exercise or not, and by a process of reason, which he may apply correctly or not. Nature gives him no auto-matic guarantee of his mental efficacy; he is capable of error, of evasion, of psychological distortion. He needs a *method*

of cognition, which he himself has to discover: he must discover how to use his rational faculty, how to validate his conclusions, how to distinguish truth from falsehood, how to set the criteria of *what* he may accept as knowledge. [ITOE, 78–79]

A man's survival, well-being, and happiness depend on his knowing what to do (and how to do it). He needs to know that fire can be tamed and that striking together two rocks of a certain kind can make sparks that will start a fire. He needs to know that seeds can be planted, that a keystone will hold an arch together, that 2 + 2 = 4, that a certain stock is (or is not) a good investment, that the ratio of HDL to LDL cholesterol is important for his vascular health, that a certain person *is* "Mr. (or Miss) Right," that political candidate X is most likely to preserve his freedom.

Each item of knowledge he needs represents a thought, a proposition. ("A keystone will hold an arch together.") Propositions are composed of concepts (e.g., "keystone," "hold," "arch"). The mere fact that a proposition pops into a man's mind ("XYZ Co. stock is a good investment") — even when it "feels right" — is not the least assurance that it is true.

The truth of a proposition depends on the validity and precision of the concepts of which it is composed. Will candidate X support freedom? That depends on what the concept "freedom" means. Is abortion murder? That, in turn, depends on what "murder," "human," and "life" mean. Is it immoral to be selfish? That depends on what "moral" and "selfish" mean.

Are there objective standards for determining the proper meaning of the terms we use? Such standards would depend upon knowing what the cognitive purpose of concepts is, what role they play in cognition.

Concepts are the tools of thought; if the tools are useless, malformed, or otherwise defective, the thought cannot achieve its goal: knowledge of reality. The validity of one's thinking depends upon the validity of the concepts one uses.

To gain proper guidance in conceptualization, we must first know what concepts *are*. And to know that, we must understand how concepts are formed.

THREE THEORIES OF CONCEPT-FORMATION

What *exactly* does one do, starting at about age one, to advance from sensory perception to the possession and subsequent use of concepts? The child certainly can direct his senses to look at this or that object; he can selectively focus his attention on a given aspect of a thing — its size or its shape. What happens next?

Concepts are abstract, but the world we perceive is concrete. How do we come to have abstract ideas? What is the relationship of abstractions to perceptual concretes?

A concept is held by means of a word — e.g., "man," "furniture," "justice." The simplest words are proper names. The word "Tom" names Tom. Likewise, the earliest theorists assumed, when we say "Tom is a man," we must be using "man" as a name for some one, perceivable existent: man, or manness. Manness is the "one in the many," as the Ancient Greeks put it; manness is the one "universal" found in Tom, then in Dick, then in Harry. We can call each of them a "man," they held, because "man" refers to this one "universal": manness. The unstated assumption was: for a concept to be valid, it must be like a percept: an awareness of a perceivable existent, out there in reality, independent of consciousness.

The Realist Theory

This assumption is the defining characteristic of the theory of concepts known (somewhat misleadingly) as "Conceptual Realism," which is usually shortened to "Realism." According to Realism, a concept is a term that designates a *metaphysical universal*: a special kind of non-specific element present in all the members of a class, an element that is grasped directly by some sort of non-sensory "intuition" or "insight."

Realism began with Plato. Plato went far beyond the mere acceptance of metaphysical universals; he concocted another, "higher," reality for universals to inhabit — his "World of Forms." In that unperceivable, transcendent realm, there is one perfect, unchanging Form corresponding to each of our concepts. There is the "Form of Man," the "Form of Triangle," the "Form of Justice," etc. Each Form is supposed to be a non-material entity that is the perfect exemplar of the corresponding concept. The differing, changing, imperfect concretes in this world are rendered intelligible only to the extent of their imperfect "reflection" of the pure Forms. Tom, Dick, and Harry, for example, count as *men* only insofar as they, however imperfectly, reflect the eternal Form of Man. (Plato regards Forms as *more* real than the concrete particulars of the physical world, calling the World of Forms "the really real reality.")

The Sophist Antisthenes is reported to have said, "I have seen many men, but never have I seen Man." Plato responded: Antisthenes is not looking with the eyes of his intellect. The Form of Man, Plato maintained, is available to man through intellectual vision — a kind of (ultimately) mystical insight into the World of Forms wherein Man resides. The direct object of conceptual awareness, Plato held, is a Form in another dimension.

Aristotle, though he was Plato's student, rejected this whole metaphysics. Aristotle recognized that there is only one reality, the world of concrete entities, the world that we perceive. But in his theory of concepts, Aristotle did not fully break free from Platonic assumptions. (Here, I give the traditional interpretation of Aristotle, but gratefully acknowledge recent scholarship indicating that Aristotle's actual view of concepts is quite close to the one I defend in this chapter. [LENNOX, 2000, chs. 1, 2, 7, 8])

Aristotelians (if not Aristotle himself) hold a theory known as "Moderate Realism." Moderate Realists count as Realists because they hold that abstractions refer to metaphysical universals; the theory is "moderate" in holding that these universals exist as aspects of perceptual concretes, not as separate entities dwelling in another world.

In effect, Moderate Realism shatters the Platonic Form and puts a fragment of it inside each concrete. Rejecting Plato's separation of Forms and particulars, the Moderate Realists hold that concretes in this world are a compound of particular and universal elements, of matter and form (with a small "f"). Tom, Dick, and Harry each have their own "manness" (which is held to be natural, not supernatural). "Manness" is what is taken to be the same in each of them, which is why they can all be called "men." Men differ in their matter: I have my body, which is somewhat different from yours. Considered qua man — i.e., in terms of their manness — all men are identical. But because that manness is found in different "stuff," we are many and differing: one man is short, another tall; one has pale skin, another dark skin. The differences are differences in matter.

Centuries later, John Locke took the further step of jettisoning the form-matter apparatus, treating universals as *attributes* of things. For Locke, there is no such thing as either "manness" or "essence." Rather, men all have the rational faculty and other attributes in common. In these attributes, men "agree" — i.e., are the same — however much their other attributes may differ.

In all its variants, Realism holds that concepts reflect an awareness of a metaphysical universal — i.e., a *non-specific* existent found in the external world. Plato's version of Realism holds that by turning away from the physical senses, the "mind's eye" can apprehend the universal existing in a separate dimension. The Moderate Realists hold that we mentally separate the universal from the concrete by narrowing our focus to ignore what is specific and varying, in order to zero in on the universal element lying within that concrete. Here, for instance, is a Thomist text's statement of the process, with the author's own emphasis:

> We confine our attention to certain elements of the [single concrete] under consideration, shutting out all the other elements, and *stripping them of all particularizing determinations*. Abstraction consists precisely in this function and in nothing else.... [Abstraction is] a special spiritual power within me, which "shines upon the sense data, and makes them capable and ready to produce a knowledge in which reality is deprived of all its concrete and individual features." [De Wulf, 13, 25]

Locke's version of Moderate Realism tries to avoid positing non-specific universals, but implies them nonetheless:

> ... the same colour being observed to-day in chalk or snow, which the mind yesterday received from milk, it considers that appearance alone, makes it a representative of all of that kind; and having given it the name *whiteness*, it by that sound signifies the same quality wheresoever to be imagined or met with; and thus universals, whether ideas or terms, are made. [Locke, II, XI, 9]

Here, "whiteness" is the universal. It has to be a *non-specific* attribute, since it is found in the slightly different shades of white characterizing chalk, snow, and milk. With regard to the concept "man," Locke implies that man's rational faculty is a non-specific attribute, even though men clearly have differences in their intelligence, their degree of rationality, the things they think about, the language in which they think, etc.

On any Moderate Realist theory, we grasp the non-specific attribute by abstraction, which is conceived as a *subtractive* process, as a process of disregarding differences. Locke, for instance, writes that "the mind, to make general ideas comprehending several particulars, *leaves out* . . . those qualities that distinguish them . . ." [LOCKE, III, VI, 32 (my emphasis)]

In summary, the three tenets of Moderate Realism are:

1. Non-specific properties exist.
2. Abstraction is subtraction.
3. Concepts are an awareness of the non-specific property.

Moderate Realism takes from Plato its basic assumption: concepts name a pre-existent universal, which is a "one" in each of the "many." Moderate Realists diverge from Plato only in regard to where that universal is to be found: not in a world of Forms but locked inside the things of this world. For instance, "blueness" is held to be something lying beneath the various shades of blue; we can grasp blueness in isolation by mentally stripping away what varies in the different shades.

The Failure of Realism

The Realist theory fails at the outset, at its first and fundamental premise: the assumption that non-specific properties exist. In fact, nothing outside the mind is general, "blurry," non-specific. There are no universals "out there" in the external world. Locke's example of "whiteness" disguises this problem, since chalk, snow, and milk differ little in color. But white and black are special cases; if we consider any other color, such as blue, the shade differences are dramatic. Where is the one universal "blueness" in a blueberry, the sky, and a robin's egg? The difficulty becomes more obvious as we get more abstract — e.g., when we form the more abstract concept "color." All the colors that we perceive are specific, such as this shade of red or that shade of blue. There is no "coloredness" to be perceived or "intuited." Likewise, "shape" is always found as this shape or that different shape, not as some non-specific "shape-as-such."

The same is true for concepts of entities. When we focus perceptual attention on an entity, what we see is always something specific: *this* tree, *this* table, *this* dog — which differ from *that* tree, table, or dog, respectively. How does one reach the *concept* "tree," "table," and "dog," each of which refers to an unlimited number of *differing* individual entities?

To be sure, the differing concretes are in some sense "the same when viewed abstractly." All dogs are dogs, however much they differ in particular respects. All shades of blue are still shades of blue. But what does "the same when viewed abstractly" mean? That is a serious and profound question that cannot be bypassed by a hand-waving reference to "having something in common" or "finding the same whiteness" in chalk and milk.

The "problem of universals" is actually the question of the basis of concepts. The issue can be stated as follows. The concretes to which a given concept refers are neither identical to each other nor possessed of any non-specific properties. What then warrants our treating them as the same, as being interchangeable units, when viewed abstractly?

As Rand puts the question:

> To exemplify the issue as it is usually presented: When we refer to three persons as "men," what do we designate by that term? The three persons are three individuals who differ in every particular respect and may not possess a single *identical* characteristic (not even their fingerprints). If you list all their particular characteristics, you will not find one representing "manness." Where is the "manness" in men? What, in reality, corresponds to the concept "man" in our mind? [ITOE, 2]

The Realist notion of a "universal" — an existent that is non-specific — represents the improper separation of two axiomatic concepts: "existence" and "identity." To *be* is to be *something*, to have a specific identity. To be nothing in particular is to be nothing at all — i.e., not to be. In Rand's statement: "Existence is Identity." [AS, 1016] But the Realist theory posits the existence of non-specific, generalized, "blurry" universals. (The only alternative for a Realist is to maintain, in defiance of plain fact, that the concretes referred to by a concept have to be *identical* in some respect, as if all shades of blue were identical, all lengths were identical, etc.)

The Realists' separation of existence and identity reaches its clearest expression in Locke. His concept of a "substratum" in which a thing's qualities supposedly inhere is a "something I know not what" — i.e., an existent without any identity (since the identity pertains to the qualities not to the substratum). But a thing *is* its attributes.

It is an error to take attributes to inhere in something else, like pins in a pincushion. Each attribute is an aspect of the whole, separated mentally but not capable of physical separation from the whole. Plato, too, separates the concepts of existence and identity, as in his concept of formless "space," in the *Timaeus*. Unfortunately, the Aristotelians are guilty of the same error, which surfaces in their position that "prime matter" is identity-less, with the identity of any concrete belonging to it only in virtue of its form.

The Moderate Realists' notion of abstraction as a subtractive process follows from their metaphysics. Abstraction for them is simply selective perceptual attention to the universal element in concretes — a stripping away mentally of whatever differs among them. But since every feature may differ, the abstraction-as-subtraction process leaves us with . . . nothing. The concept of "number" is the purest illustration of Realism's conundrum: 6 and 17 differ *in quantity*; if we abstract away the differing quantity of each, we are left with nothing.

Because Realism fails in its analysis of the basis of concepts, it collapses into subjectivism: Realism provides no objective way to resolve disputes. Is a fetus a human being? On Realist premises, there is no way to settle this question because we don't know how to determine if "manness" is present in the fetus. We don't know which differences to subtract away and which to leave in. Should we include or strip away such differences as: whether the entity is inside the mother's body or outside it, whether it breathes or doesn't, whether it eats food or absorbs nutriments from the mother's bloodstream? Some people "intuit" one "essence," others "intuit" the opposite one.

Realists are deprived of the means of settling such disputes because their theory comes down to: either you "intuit" the universal or you don't — which turns concepts into subjective "constructs."

Consider now a second way the Realist theory lands in subjectivism: of the many features characterizing concretes, *which* ones should we use to form our concepts? The Realist theory can have no answer to this crucial question. Realism implies that there is a nature-given set of criteria to use in forming concepts, as if it were self-evident how we should divide up and classify the things we perceive. There is a certain plausibility to this idea on the lower levels of abstraction, for such concepts as "table" and "triangle." But more abstract concepts, like "momentum," "freedom," and "murder" are more obviously made by us. What are the proper characteristics for us to use in forming such abstractions? No guidance can be given on Realist premises. Realists can only say "Just look with your mind's eye" — advice that is manifestly hopeless.

Realist theories reify abstractions: they take the generality that exists only in man's mind and make it into a "universal" existing in the external world, either in a separate dimension (Plato) or as non-specific characteristics in the concretes of this world (Aristotle and Locke). Concepts are indeed general: they do apply universally to a range of concretes. But in reading that *mental* generality back into *things*, Realists are endorsing that epitome of *un*realism: the primacy of consciousness. As Rand observes, the Realists are "assuming that reality must conform to the content of consciousness, not the other way around — on the premise that the presence of any notion in man's mind proves the existence of a corresponding referent in reality." [ITOE, 53]

Realists hold that reality contains "universals," and that these can be grasped passively by the intellect, as if they were perceptually given. This, as we shall see, totally misconstrues what concepts are and do.

The Nominalist Pseudo-Theory

Realism's problems spawned the Nominalist reaction. Accepting the Realist claim that concepts would require pre-packaged universals, Nominalists bite the bullet and conclude that concepts have no objective basis, that concepts are nothing but *words*. Ludwig Wittgenstein, for example, writes: "To say that we use the word 'blue' to mean 'what all these shades of color have in common' by itself says nothing more than that we use the word 'blue' in all these cases." [WITTGENSTEIN 1958, II, 3][44]

This is Extreme Nominalism, a truly lunatic theory. It flatly contradicts every aspect of our actual usage of concepts. For instance, Extreme Nominalism implies that it is an inexplicable miracle when two people independently apply the word "blue" to the next blueberry they see. Since the blueberry and the other things previously called "blue" have *nothing* in common, according to Wittgenstein, the two people should be equally prepared, on the Nominalist theory, to say "yellow" or "pink" — or, for that matter, "railroad."

Just as there is Moderate Realism, so there is Moderate Nominalism. The Moderate Nominalists hold that the referents of a given concept, though they share no "universal," are still *similar*, and that their similarity makes it "convenient" to refer to them by the same word. Moderate Nominalism,

---

44 Some would argue that Wittgenstein here is not committing himself to this position, merely proposing it for consideration, or to point out the vacuity of the phrase "have in common." That point of historical interpretation is not important for my purposes: whether or not Wittgenstein finally endorses this extreme position, it expresses one possible response to the failure of Realism.

however, treats similarity as an unanalyzable, primary fact. Things just resemble each other, Nominalists say, and that's the end of the matter.[45]

The failure to analyze what similarity (or "resemblance") consists of makes it impossible to defend the objective validity of concepts and lands in rank subjectivism. Nominalists, of any variety, are unable to answer the two crucial questions: 1) *How similar?* and 2) *Similar how?* That is, 1) how similar must concretes be to warrant inclusion in the same class? and 2) which similarities should we use in forming our conceptual classifications?

The Nominalists' inability to answer these questions does not trouble them. How similar do the conceptualized concretes have to be? No one can say, they tell us, and then they trot out examples of "borderline cases" to argue that the boundaries of a concept's application are set arbitrarily. How white does a thing have to be to be called "white"? Does cream have "whiteness"? Is a stool a kind of chair without a back, or does it have its own "essence"? In the continuous development of the human fetus, when does "rationality" or "manness" appear, and why then? The Nominalists complain that "nature doesn't tell us" the answers to these questions, and conclude that the boundaries of concepts are set arbitrarily, by blind tradition or by "stipulation."

When we raise the question: "Similar, how?" Nominalism's utter collapse into subjectivism becomes dramatically evident. The arch-example here is Wittgenstein's theory of "family resemblances." Take a hypothetical family: the Kowalskis. Bill and Bob Kowalski have similar noses. Bob and Jane Kowalski have noses that look rather different but have very similar chins. Jane and Lewis Kowalski have different noses and chins, but have similar eyes. And so on. No one characteristic runs through all members of the Kowalski family. The same is true of all concepts, Wittgenstein claims: there is no one respect in which the things subsumed are even similar. Accordingly, Wittgenstein could have no objection to the following example. A pumpkin is similar to a basketball (in shape); a basketball is similar to a hockey puck (in purpose); a hockey puck is similar to a hockey stick (in the sport involved); a hockey stick is similar to a broom (in how one moves it). We can go on indefinitely. This conceptual stew is what one ends up with on the Nominalist theory.

---

45   Consider this passage from *The Stanford Encyclopedia of Philosophy* entry on Nominalism: "A final version of Nominalism is Resemblance Nominalism. According to this theory . . . what makes square things square is that they resemble one another, and so what makes something square is that it resembles the square things. Resemblance is fundamental and primitive . . . ."

As Ayn Rand remarks, "Wittgenstein's theory that a concept refers to a conglomeration of things vaguely tied together by a 'family resemblance' is a perfect description of the state of a mind out of focus." [ITOE, 78]

The result is that, for the Nominalist, how concepts are to be formed and used becomes a matter of feeling. This subjectivism has a devastating impact upon higher-level abstractions. One man feels that aborting a fetus and killing an innocent adult "resemble" each other, so he calls both "murder"; another man feels differently and maintains that abortion is a right. One man feels that a free lunch and free speech are similar, another man disagrees. One man feels that Al Capone and John D. Rockefeller were similar enough to be classified together, as being "rapacious" and "predatory." But are they? How similar and in what way? Nominalism not only has no answer, it regards all such questions as in principle unanswerable.

Thus, the Nominalist theory deprives man of objective guidance in the crucial aspect of his life: how to form and use the concepts on which his control over the course of his life depends.

The Realist theory lands in subjectivism by implication, but Nominalists defiantly embrace subjectivism as a matter of principle. This is ironic, because Nominalism entails the rejection of all principles. For Nominalism, no statement of the form "All As are B" can be known to be true. After all, each A is unique, and so is each B. Under Nominalism, no generalization (induction) is valid. If there is no way to treat the concretes subsumed under a concept as interchangeable units, there can be no reasoning from one case to any other; we must face each new concrete in a cognitive vacuum. A scientist might spend a decade studying the characteristics, properties, and capacities of John, but then when he turns to consider Paul, he must begin all over again. None of his knowledge of John is necessarily applicable to Paul because, to paraphrase Wittgenstein, to say that John and Paul are both men is to say nothing more than that we apply the word "man" to each. Or, for Moderate Nominalists, though John and Paul resemble each other, we have no reason to think this resemblance is sufficient to warrant applying to Paul anything learned from studying John — just as we have no warrant to apply to a broom things learned from studying pumpkins.

Stepping back to get an overview, we can state the problem of concepts as follows. The concretes to which a given concept refers are *similar* but not *identical*. The blue of the sky is similar but not identical to the blue of a blueberry. A beagle and a collie are similar in some way, though not identical, and this similarity is what enables us to classify them as dogs. The question then is: *What is similarity?* How does the fact that observed concretes are *similar* warrant our treating them as the same, as interchangeable units, qua referents of a given concept?

The Objectivist Theory

Ayn Rand's theory of similarity grounds her Objectivist theory of concepts. She defines similarity as: "the relationship between two or more existents which possess the same characteristic(s), but in different measure or degree." [ITOE, 13]

Things that are similar differ *quantitatively*. The blue of a blueberry is not *identical* to the blue of the sky, but the two differ quantitatively, in measurable ways. A given blueberry is a darker blue than the sky; the hue of the blueberry has more red in it, shading towards purple; the sky's blue is brighter than the blueberry's. These are differences in degree along the three measurable axes: hue, saturation, and brightness. Modern computers usually provide a color-setting dialog box that uses numbers from 0 to 255 to specify the setting of each of these three parameters. Any of the colors that we can see can be specified by a trio of these three numbers. (On my monitor, blueberry blue is approximately 139, 142, 74; sky blue is 139, 200, 160.) Color differences are a matter of *measurements*.

Consider now the case of similar *entities*. The similarity of a particular beagle to a particular collie is more complex, but still one of measurable quantity. The beagle is smaller and stouter; the beagle's hair is shorter and straighter than the collie's; the collie's nose is longer and more tapering; the beagle's nose is shorter and blunter; the collie's bark is lower-pitched; etc. There is no non-specific "dogginess" lodged in the beagle and the collie. They differ in every respect, but the differences are in *how much* of each characteristic — size, straightness of hair, ratio of length to width of nose — they possess. The differences are differences in the measurements of commensurable characteristics.

In contrast, a very young child beginning to form concepts would not perceive a pig and a collie to be similar. Why not, if similarity is an issue of quantitative differences? After all, the pig's differences from the collie are also measurable — the pig is fatter, pinker, with a measurably different shape, etc.

The answer to this question lies in a cognitive process neglected by traditional theorists: *differentiation*. Similarity is inherently perceived against a background of difference. As I have stressed, consciousness is a difference-detector. When a naïve, pre-conceptual child attends to two items, it is their differences, not their similarities, that will be prominent. Although a beagle and a collie are similar, putting them side by side serves to focus attention on their differences (for a pre-conceptual child). But sensitivity to difference can be turned to advantage here. When the child observes a beagle, a collie, and a pig, the huge differences between the pig and the dogs leap to the foreground of awareness, making the two dogs appear similar. The pig appears to be different in kind from the two dogs, while the dogs appear to differ from each other only in degree — i.e., similar in contrast to the pig. Even though a conceptually advanced adult observer could say that *all three* animals have commensurable characteristics (color, shape, weight), for the beginning conceptualizer, the difference that dominates his attention is the difference between the two dogs and the pig.

In the same manner, two shades of blue put side by side will simply be perceived as different, but when a contrasting color, such as green, is added to the comparison, the two shades of blue appear similar, appear to go together, as opposed to the particular green that they are being contrasted to. Hue is the commensurable characteristic possessed by all three colors, so hue serves as the background that pushes into the foreground the marked difference between the blues and the green.

The grasp of similarity requires a minimum of three concretes having a commensurable characteristic(s): two whose measurements differ slightly and one that differs greatly in measurement from both.

The arch example is location. Is the Empire State Building near to or far from the Chrysler Building? That depends — it depends on what we are comparing them to. If the comparison is to a location across the street from the Empire State Building, the Chrysler Building is far. If the comparison is to the Sears Tower in Chicago, the two Manhattan buildings are near to each other. And if the comparison is to the location of a mountain on Mars, all three buildings are near to each other.

This can be represented graphically:

Considered by themselves, A and B are in different places. Considered in contrast to C, A and B, though not in the *identical* place, are seen as falling in the same general region — i.e., at the left end of the line.

"Near" and "far" are the stand-ins for "similar" and "different." *Similarity is measurement-proximity.*

"Proximity" is a relative term, depending on a contrast with something that is more distant, which we can call "the foil." Similarity is thus contextual, a matter of *relative* proximity of measurements in contrast to the *relatively* distant measurement of a foil. In such a set-up, the bigger difference swamps the smaller difference, making the smaller difference appear as similarity. What is experienced as similarity is, at root, lesser difference.

For this mechanism of contrast to work, *all three* items, the two similars and the foil, must be compared along the same axis. They must share a commensurable characteristic, as in the diagram above, where horizontal position is the commensurable characteristic. If the position of A and B were to be considered in the same frame of awareness with, say, the smell of a peach, no similarity would be established, as there is no commensurable characteristic uniting those three items: no single unit of measurement can be applied to them. They are not *different* but *disparate.* Differentiation requires a commensurable characteristic to serve as the axis along which the things can be compared.

Rand refers to this commensurable characteristic as the "Conceptual Common Denominator" (CCD):

> A commensurable characteristic (such as shape in the case of tables, or hue in the case of colors) is an essential element in the process of concept-formation. I shall designate it as the "Conceptual Common Denominator" and define it as "The characteristic(s) reducible to a unit of measurement, by means of which man differentiates two or more existents from other existents possessing it." [ITOE, 15]

It may be helpful to connect Rand's terminology with the traditional terms "genus" and "differentia." A *genus* is the wider category to which a given concept's referents belong. E.g., the genus of "triangle" is "polygon." What is the relation of "genus" to Rand's "CCD"? The CCD is not a category but a measurable characteristic, one possessed by all the things in the genus, as "having a certain number of sides" is a characteristic of all polygons.

The *differentia* is the referents' distinguishing characteristic, the one that isolates them from all the other things within the genus. For triangle, the differentia is "three-sided." So, we form "triangle" by differentiating shapes according to the number of their sides (CCD), triangles having three.

Though the CCD plays a crucial role in conceptualization, neither the CCD nor its function is explicit in the mind of the beginning conceptualizer. The CCD's role is precisely to serve as the unnoticed background — not to call attention to *itself* but to something else: the difference between the similars and the foil, whose measurements lie noticeably farther away on the same CCD. When a child differentiates two blues from green, the CCD is hue; but the child's attention is drawn not to hue as such (the sameness among all three items) but to blue vs. green (the difference in hue).

Thus, the CCD plays an indispensable role, but (at the beginning levels) an unnoticed one. The CCD serves to draw attention to the difference between the similars and foil, a difference which is so striking that it appears as a difference in kind ("These are blue, that is green"). Analogously, I can draw a figure on a blackboard with white chalk because the black slate contrasts with the white, yet what draws your attention is the white figure, not the black slate which, though essential, serves only as background.

Later in a child's development, he will grasp "color," but he can do so only by contrasting "color" with something further afield, say shape, within a wider (implicit) category: visual attribute. On either level, one uses the CCD, but only as background.

Now we are in a position to find the "one in the many." Or, rather, to see that the one in the many, the "universal," is man-made, not given in nature, yet not created subjectively. A concept classifies together *concretes whose measurements fall within the same category of measurements within the CCD.*

To be perceived as similar, and be grouped together, concretes need not have identical measurements in any respect, but they each must have measurements that fall within the same range or category. "Blueness" does not exist *per se* in the sky, the robin's egg, or the blueberry. But, contra Wittgenstein, "blueness" does name an observed fact about each: the fact that each shade's specific measurement falls within a certain range of measurements within the CCD *hue*. Crucially, this range is graspable only by *differentiation* from the very different measurements of one or more foils whose own hue-measurements fall outside that range.

Although a child makes color comparisons by simply perceiving the degree-differences (bluer, less blue), today we know the exact measurements responsible for hue differences: the wavelength of the reflected light.[46] The blue range is: approximately 450–485 nanometers. The neighboring green range is approximately 500–565 nanometers. These numbers represent real lengths: the actual, physical distance between successive peaks in the light waves. A particular hue of, say, 462 nanometers in wavelength falls squarely within the blue range, even though there is no non-specific "blueness" lodged within it. And that *specific* hue, will be perceived as similar to one of, say, 475 nanometers, *when contrasted with one solidly within the green* range — say 535 nanometers. 462 and 475 seem close together when contrasted with 535.

Consider another, quite different, example. Suppose a teacher gives a multiple-choice exam to his class, with the usual result of a wide variation in scores. The teacher has established the familiar grading ranges: A: 90–100, B: 80–89, C: 70–79, and so on. If Frank scores 86 and gets a "B," that does *not* mean the teacher has "abstracted the B-ness" out of Frank's score. There is no such B-ness to be reached by discarding specific scores, as if selective attention would reveal some residue of B-ness. Rather, the teacher recognizes that the completely *specific* score of 86 falls within the range of 80 to 89. Patricia's score of 83 is categorized as "essentially" similar to Frank's, even though it is not identical to Frank's. For both students, the grade of "B" is reached by omitting the specific measurements of their scores and retaining only the fact that their scores fall somewhere within the B-range.

The same mechanism of classification lies behind all concept-formation. All concepts are formed by implicitly or explicitly omitting the intra-range measurements of similar concretes. The similarity results from the closeness of their measurements within a CCD — close when compared to a foil whose measurements lie markedly farther away along that same CCD.

The items classified together by a concept are the *same* in the following respect: their measurements all fall within the same range or category. E.g., the different shades of blue all fall within the *same* range on the spectrum; the "blueness" *is* that range. Or, in terms of test grades, the B-range of 80–89 is one thing, not many, and falling in that range is what is the same about all the tests graded B.

In general, the so-called "universal" characteristic that makes a concrete qualify as a member of class X is not some non-specific X-ness inside the concrete, per Realism, but is the category of measurements, the category that includes each concrete's *specific* degree of X. Rand's important summary

---

46 For simplicity, I am taking only monochromatic light here, to avoid the complexity of how different wavelengths combine (cf. the trichromatic theory of color vision).

statement is: "The distinguishing characteristic(s) of a concept represents a specified category of measurements within the 'Conceptual Common Denominator' involved." [ITOE, 15]

Each concrete possesses its own *specific* degree of the distinguishing characteristic, which may be different in quantity from the degree to which other similar existents possess it. There is no non-specific "blueness" in things, only specific shades of blue. In the case of concepts of entities, such as tables, the concretes share several characteristics that jointly distinguish them from other kinds of entities, but each of these distinguishing characteristics always exists in a specific amount. All tables, for example, have a horizontal surface and supports. But the number of supports may vary from having one pedestal to having many legs, and the geometrical measurements of the shape of the tabletop may vary rather widely.

In all cases, however, the similar concretes possess varying degrees of the distinguishing characteristic, and those degrees fall within the "specified category of measurements" — which is why they appear as similar.

The mental process of grasping the distinguishing characteristic is called by Rand "measurement-omission." Measurement-omission is the core of the Objectivist theory of concept-formation. Having identified that similar concretes possess the same characteristic, but vary in their measurements, Rand was able to identify the nature of abstraction. The process of abstraction consists in interrelating the concretes in a certain way: one grasps the range or category of measurements that embraces all their varying measurements.

Concepts, then, are formed by omitting measurements. But omitting measurements is not a process of deletion or excision, as if we could mentally strip away the specific measurement from the characteristic. Rand is very clear about the difference between "measurement-omission" and the narrowed, eliminative focus of the abstraction-as-subtraction view:

> Bear firmly in mind that the term "measurements omitted" does not mean, in this context, that measurements are regarded as non-existent; it means that *measurements exist, but are not specified.* That measurements *must* exist is an essential part of the process. The principle is: the relevant measurements must exist in *some* quantity, but may exist in *any* quantity. [ITOE, 12]

Measurement-omission does not consist in ignoring the specific and varying measurements of concretes (à la Locke). When we omit the measurements, we are not ignoring anything; we are grasping something more:

the relationship among the measurements, the fact that the similar concretes are "near" to each other, as contrasted with the "far away" measurements of the foil.

When Rand says "That measurements must exist is an essential part of the process," the process she is referring to is the process of measurement-omission. One *uses* the measurements to interrelate the similar concretes. One needs to focus one's attention *on the specific measurements,* in order to see "where they are" — i.e., to grasp the category of measurements within which the similar concretes fall. E.g., the child has to focus on the *specific* shapes of particular tables (and of the foil, e.g., a chair) in order to perceive the tables as being similar, and to establish the range of shape-variation.

The process of measurement-omission is one of grasping a segment of the CCD — the segment representing the range embracing the similar concretes. Thus, *measurement-omission is measurement-integration* — the establishment of a range or category of measurements.[47] This is illustrated in the diagram below, where part of the dotted line becomes a solid line.[48]

Although the diagram uses thin, sharp demarcation lines, in actual concept-formation such hyper-precision is rare; usually one establishes only a rough region, allowing for borderline cases, such as greenish-blue. (Borderline cases pose a problem for the Realist theory of a "universal," which must be either present or absent, but not for the Objectivist idea of an axis of continuously varying measurements.[49]

When one later encounters another similar concrete, D, it is seen to fall within the same range:

Thus, D is classified with A and B.

---

47   The term "measurement-integration" replaces the term I formerly used: "measurement-inclusion" [BINSWANGER, 1989], which I now use in regard to propositions (see CHAPTER 5).

48   I owe to Gregory Salmieri the idea of integrating the points into a line. [SALMIERI, 2006]

49   For more on borderline cases, see ITOE 72–74 and *infra* 222 and 238–39.

Within the established range, the particular measurements differ only quantitatively; the range accommodates those differences, because they are much smaller than the pronounced difference each has with the foil, C.

Thus, to grasp that things "have the same distinguishing characteristic" is to grasp that their measurements, though varying, all fall somewhere within the same range along the CCD that they share with the foil.

UNIT

Concepts are formed by treating existents as *units*. A "unit," in Rand's definition, is "an existent regarded as a separate member of a group of two or more similar members." [ITOE, 6]

Since similarity is a quantitative relationship, the term "unit" from mathematics is meant literally here. "Unit" means "one," and to regard an existent as *one* is to view it in relation to a group—e.g., as a (one) book. The group is formed by mentally isolating things that are similar in some way, even if only in location ("objects on my desk"). Each of the similar existents is a "one" that can be used as a standard for counting or for measuring degrees.[50]

When two things differ only in quantity, they can be readily integrated, because a larger one is reducible to the same units as a smaller one, plus more of the same units. For instance, a length of 3 inches is reducible to inch + inch + inch, and then a length of 4 inches is reducible to that plus another inch—i.e., another one of the units that compose the 3-inch length. Thus, "the more" is "the less" plus more of the less. (A child, before knowing of units and numbers, can easily become aware of this fact by seeing, for example, the change in length of a rubber band as it is stretched and released or by seeing the changes in shape he imposes on his modeling clay: rounder, less round.)

Understanding concept-formation in terms of establishing quantitative relationships is the opposite of the Realist idea that we form concepts by staring at one concrete in the attempt to achieve an "insight" into some non-specific feature of it. On the Objectivist theory, concepts are formed

---

50 Counting measures quantity. Counting consists in pairing items, one by one, with the members of a given group whose specific quantity is taken as a standard—e.g., pairing five cows with each of the five fingers on one hand. Later, numerals are introduced, to provide a uniform, systematic set of standards. Each number stands for the quantity of the group formed by the *sequence* of numerals terminating in that numeral. "3" stands for the quantity of the sequence: 1–2–3, a group consisting of three numerals.

by contrast and comparison among concretes — i.e., by the conceptualizer adopting a *wider* focus, not a narrower one. It is not a subtractive process, but an additive (integrative) one.

There is no "universal" present in a concrete, so looking harder or more selectively at one concrete will not find it. To grasp the common characteristic that isolates the similars from the foil requires shifting one's attention back and forth between a minimum of three concretes — the two similars and the foil — then omitting the measurements of the similar concretes by seeing their range or category of measurements within the (implicit) CCD.

Measurement-omission is done on the premise that "the relevant measurements must exist in *some* quantity, but may exist in *any* quantity" within that range or category of measurements.

In speaking of "measurements" I am referring to the subconscious mechanics of the concept-forming process, not to any consciously performed, explicit, process of measuring. A child beginning to conceptualize things is, of course, incapable of explicit measurement. On the conscious level, he is aware only of similarities and differences. But the *objective basis* of those similarities and differences is the quantitative variation of a commensurable characteristic. Where this commensurable characteristic is absent — i.e., where the items are disparate — no differentiation and no awareness of similarity can occur. Rand's example is: "No concept could be formed, for instance, by attempting to distinguish long objects from green objects." [ITOE, 13] To make a differentiation, one needs an *A* and a non-*A* — e.g., blue and non-blue, or long and non-long. The *disparate* must be firmly distinguished from the *different*. (This distinction will be important when we discuss concepts of characteristics in CHAPTER 4.)

To omit specific measurements is not to discard them, ignore them or put them aside. It is to see them as some specific amount of a characteristic which varies in quantity. Length "with measurements omitted" does not mean a length which is *neither* three inches *nor* twenty inches *nor* any other specific amount; it means a length which is *either* three inches *or* twenty inches *or* some other specific amount.

The Realist theory of concepts says just the opposite. Locke, for example, says that "triangle" is a concept of what is neither equilateral nor scalene, "but all and none of these at once." [LOCKE, IV, VII, 9] The Objectivist theory holds that the concept of a triangle includes those that are *either* equilateral, *or* isosceles, *or* scalene. The sides of a triangle must have some specific relation to each other but may have any.

Hegel took the "neither/nor" view to its ultimate extreme. Quoting from Hegel's premier interpreter, W. T. Stace:

> Being . . . is the highest possible abstraction. All character, all determinations of any kind, have been abstracted from. Hence being has no character and is utterly empty. Because being is thus utterly empty, it is therefore equivalent to nothing. . . . Being, then, is nothing. . . . [B]eing has no determinations whatsoever. Therefore, there can be no difference between being and nothing. The thought of being and the thought of nothing are the same, and pass into each other. [STACE, II, FIRST DIVISION, I, A-B]

This equation of existence and non-existence is a reductio ad absurdum of the abstraction-as-subtraction idea. Abstraction as measurement-omission, operating on the "some but any" principle, regards "being" or "existence" as the widest and fullest concept, embracing all differences. To exist is to have some but any determinate identity, to be *either* an entity *or* an attribute *or* an action, etc. Abstraction as measurement-omission means that the cognitive content of concepts is rich — and grows progressively richer as we form progressively higher abstractions (the subject of the next chapter).

MEASUREMENT

Since measurement is the core of the Objectivist theory, we need to look further at what measurement is. Rand writes:

> Measurement is the identification of a relationship — a quantitative relationship established by means of a standard that serves as a unit. Entities (and their actions) are measured by their attributes (length, weight, velocity, etc.) and the standard of measurement is a concretely specified unit representing the appropriate attribute. Thus, one measures length in inches, feet and miles — weight in pounds — velocity by means of a given distance traversed in a given time, etc. [ITOE, 7]

It is clear how simple, physical characteristics such as length, weight, and color are measurable. Complex shapes, such as the shape of a leaf, are also measurable, by separately measuring length-width ratios, part by part. In discussing why tables appear similar in shape, Rand notes:

> . . . a given shape represents a certain category or set of geo-metrical measurements. Shape is an attribute; differences of shape — whether cubes, spheres, cones or any complex combina-tions — are a matter of differing measurements; any shape can be reduced to or expressed by a set of figures in terms of *linear measurement*. . . . [A] vast part of higher mathematics, from geometry on up, is devoted to the task of discovering methods by which various shapes can be measured — complex methods which consist of reducing the problem to the terms of a simple, primitive method, the only one available to man in this field: linear measurement. (Integral calculus, used to measure the area of circles, is just one example.) [ITOE, 14]

At a given stage of scientific knowledge, some similarities may not be reducible to exact, numerical measurement. Before the invention of the thermometer, differences in hotness could not be reduced to numbers. Even today, differences of hardness are often measured on an *ordinal* scale, according to which substance can scratch which (as diamonds can scratch steel, steel can scratch iron, iron can scratch lead) — all of which establish rank order but not the numerical degree of hardness. To establish the rank order of things in an ordinal measurement, one changes the unit for each new comparison, always using the same characteristic for each of them (e.g., hotness or hardness).[51]

Establishing numerical measurements, whether ordinal or cardinal, is the most precise form of identifying quantitative relationships, but the grasp of quantitative relationships is what goes on anytime one sees that *this* is bigger or brighter than *that*. Approximate measurement is still mea-surement in the sense relevant to concept-formation. One is still aware of a commensurable characteristic, as opposed to the impossible attempt

---

51 A good example is the old classroom exercise of lining up students in order of height, which was done ordinally, not by using a yardstick. The teacher would begin by having two students stand next to each other, judge their heights, and have the taller student stand in front of the shorter. Then, each remaining student would be positioned in the line between the ones who were just shorter and just taller than he. This procedure meant that, each student in the line, one at a time, served as the unit of height against which the new student's height was measured. Thus, the unit varied, but the characteristic did not.

to quantitatively compare, say, a rock and Saturday, which lack a commensurable characteristic.

An interesting case of measurement is that of measuring materials qua materials, such as wood, copper, water. Obviously, one can measure the attributes of the objects formed out of various materials, but in what sense is the difference between copper and lead a difference in *measurement*? On the sensory level, one uses the difference in perceptible qualities — the colors differ, the densities differ, the hardness differs, etc. These are differences in degree and are measured only approximately.

Modern chemistry, however, goes to a deeper level: copper and lead differ in "atomic number." Atomic number is a measurement. It refers to the number of protons in the nucleus of the atom: copper has 29 protons, lead has 82. And in the case of molecules, the differences are differences in measurement: methane has one carbon and four hydrogens, ethane has two carbons and 6 hydrogens, etc.

Or, taking the case of food materials, bread and cake differ in the *amount* of sugar. Differences in the preparation process are also specified quantitatively, as in a recipe: "Add ¼ pound butter to ½ cup of flour and one cup of milk, stir slowly for two minutes, over a low heat . . ." Thus, even foods can be specified in terms of measurements.

Throughout my discussion, I have often used the phrase "range or category" of measurements. The reason for using two terms is that not all CCDs vary continuously. Some CCDs come already digitized, in effect. Triangles, for example, have exactly three sides; their number of sides is not a range from 2.4 to 3.3. The CCD for "triangle" is: number of sides of a polygon, but the distinguishing characteristic is not a range, but a category: three. Or, length is extension in exactly one dimension, area in exactly two, volume in exactly three. Length is "some but any" extension in exactly one dimension. The CCD of "length" is: number of dimensions of extension; the distinguishing characteristic is the category (not the range): one.

Whether the distinguishing characteristic represents a range or a single value within the CCD, if there are varying measurements within that range or category (as there normally are), then they are omitted on the "some but any" premise. For instance, length is extension in exactly one dimension, but within that category, all the different lengths are included by a process of measurement-omission.

If a child considers a match, a pencil and a stick, he observes that length is the attribute they have in common, but their specific lengths differ. The *difference is one of measurement*. In order to form the concept "length," the child's mind retains the attribute and omits its particular measurements. Or, more precisely, if the process were identified in words, it would consist of the following: "Length must exist in *some* quantity, but may exist in *any* quantity. I shall identify as 'length' that attribute of any existent possessing it which can be quantitatively related to a unit of length, without specifying the quantity." [ITOE, 11]

In a few cases, even the distinguishing characteristic does not vary in degree. Take the concept of "inch" for example. Inches do not vary in length. The CCD for "inch" is length, but within that CCD, the distinguishing characteristic is exactly *this* much of it. Or, if one defines the inch as one-twelfth of a foot of length, it is still exactly that ratio, not a range. A standard of measurement, like the inch, has to be an exactly determinate amount of the characteristic in question.

To form the concept of a standard of measurement, such as the inch, one must omit the measurements of other (non-distinguishing) characteristics.[52] In regard to measuring length, there used to be a concrete physical object that served as the standard meter: a platinum bar in Paris. Using that bar as the standard of length required omitting the measurements of all its other characteristics — for instance, its specific width, thickness, hardness, material, location, etc. The meter-bar was given the particular width, thickness, etc. that best suited it to be used as a standard of length.

The first concepts a child forms are concepts of entities, since entities are what perceptual awareness discriminates for him. As a summary of her theory, here is Rand's description of the process of forming the concept "table."

> The child's mind isolates two or more tables from other objects, by focusing on their distinctive characteristic: their shape. He observes that their shapes vary, but have one characteristic

---

52   The omission of non-distinguishing characteristics, however, is simpler: at the first stages of forming a concept, one can simply disregard these differences, as when a child ignores a table's color. Sooner or later, however, the child will attend to these characteristics, notice that they too vary in degree, and treat these differences as omitted measurements: he realizes that a table must have some color but may have any.

in common: a flat, level surface and support(s). He forms the concept "table" by retaining that characteristic and omitting *all* particular measurements, not only the measurements of the shape, but of all the other characteristics of tables (many of which he is not aware of at the time).

An adult definition of "table" would be: "A man-made object consisting of a flat, level surface and support(s), intended to support other, smaller objects." Observe what is specified and what is omitted in this definition: the distinctive characteristic of the shape is specified and retained; the particular geometrical measurements of the shape (whether the surface is square, round, oblong or triangular, etc., the number and shape of supports, etc.) are omitted; the measurements of size or weight are omitted; the fact that it is a material object is specified, but the material of which it is made is omitted, thus omitting the measurements that differentiate one material from another; etc. Observe, however, that the utilitarian requirements of the table set certain limits on the omitted measurements, in the form of "no larger than and no smaller than" required by its purpose. This rules out a ten-foot tall or a two-inch tall table (though the latter may be sub-classified as a toy or a miniature table) and it rules out unsuitable materials, such as non-solids. [ITOE, 11–12]

INTEGRATION

I have discussed so far only the first stage of the concept-forming process: the isolation of two or more similar items from a foil. At this stage, the conceptualizer has mentally grouped things according to their similarities and differences, but has no firm, enduring mental product — i.e., no concept. To put it loosely, he has sorted but not yet conceptualized. To form a concept, he must perform the second basic process of consciousness: integration.[53] Having a concept requires integrating the similars into a new mental entity.

Integration is a process of mentally interconnecting a group of separate items to form a permanent, usable whole. In grasping the range or category of measurements that unites the similar items, the conceptualizer is connecting them together in his mind, but what he has at this point

---

53   Measurement-omission is itself a kind of integration, as discussed above, but now I'm talking about the enduring, open-ended integration that follows.

is a transient state of awareness, not a permanent product that he can store, carry forward, and use in the future. To achieve that, an act of full integration is required. Such integration is achieved by the use of a *word*.

The word, as a sensuous symbol, has a crucial function in conceptual cognition. The word completes the integration, binding the units into a single, new mental entity. Although Nominalism is wrong in reducing everything to words, we cannot overreact by throwing out the word with the bath water. The use of a word is indispensable (though a visual image of a representative concrete may play the same role for the first few concepts formed).

Contra Nominalists like Wittgenstein, the word is not what the units have in common; what they have in common is the distinguishing characteristic(s) — i.e., the range or category embracing their individual, varying measurements. Thus, the word is not "the one in the many"; rather, it is the means of retaining one's grasp of the one in the many — i.e., the means of retaining the awareness that *these* things, when contrasted to *those* markedly different things, can be viewed as distinguishable members of a group. The word is not the *object* of cognition, but its *form*, not the *what* but the *how*.

Rand illustrated her theory of concepts by drawing an analogy between a concept and a file folder.[54] This analogy is extremely valuable, and I will make repeated use of it. Picture a sloppy office clerk accumulating a lot of paperwork strewn across his desk. Soon there are hundreds of separate pieces of paper pertaining to all sorts of different subjects. To bring order to his workspace, his first step would be to put related pieces of paper together into separate piles. Suppose that he makes one pile for employees' expense accounts, another for bills that have been paid, another for correspondence with suppliers, another for résumés from job-applicants, and so on.

This rudimentary system brings certain advantages, but it will soon turn into a mess, with overlapping piles scattered all over the desk, the chair seats, the floor. Any passing breeze wreaks havoc with the piles. And after he has formed a few dozen piles, it will become increasingly difficult to remember where he placed a given pile or, when looking at a given pile, to remember what it is about and why he formed it. Clearly, what he needs to do is to introduce file folders to keep the papers in each pile together,

---

54 Rand drew this analogy in 1966, long before computers were common, so the analogy
    is to physical file folders, not computer "file folders" (which would make less forceful
    and less exact analogs to concepts). It is the old-fashioned, manila file folders,
    with sheets of paper tucked inside them, that I ask the reader to bring to mind wherever
    I use this analogy.

so each can be handled as a single entity, and to begin systematizing them by labeling the folders as to their contents, placing them in file-drawers, etc.

We can now cash out the analogy: the piles are analogous to the perceptual groupings that one establishes on the basis of observed similarities and differences. The file folders are analogous to words in their conceptual function. *Words transform the piles into files.* Assigning a word thus completes the concept-formation process by linking the units together into a single, new unit, thus forming a many-to-one network of connections.[55]

Speaking extemporaneously about the role of the word in this respect, Rand noted:

> ... the word comes at the end of a process of conceptualization, not at the beginning. One's mind first has to grasp the isolation and the integration which represents the formation of a concept; but to complete that process — and particularly to retain it, and later to automatize it — a man needs a verbal symbol. But as far as the process of concept-formation is concerned, the word is the result of the process.

Rand was then asked if that meant that the concept is formed prior to introducing the word, with the word being used as a means of retaining the concept. She replied:

> That is a word's main function, but its function is not merely that. I meant exactly what I said: to *complete* the process. Let me make this a little clearer. Suppose a child is forming the concept "table." First, he has to isolate a table from the rest of his perceptual concretes, then integrate it with other tables. Now, in this process words are not present yet, because he is merely observing, and performing a certain mental process. It is after he has fully grasped that these particular objects (tables) are special and different in some way from all the other objects he perceives ... that he has to firm up, in effect, his mental activity in his own mind by designating that special status of these particular objects in some sensory form [i.e., by means of a word].

---

55   In describing the mechanics of the process, "linking" or "connecting" are better terms to use than "associating," which suggests a coincidental, non-logical connection. The concept, in contrast to the word, is the logical structure and functioning of the set-up, which remains the same whether one is linking dogs to "dog" or to "chien."

It is for the purpose not only of retaining the concept but also of making and completing the process of concept-formation that he has to designate the tables by some kind of sensory symbol. The main function of doing so is to enable him to retain the concept and be able to use it subsequently. But even apart from the future, in the process of forming that concept, in order for it not to remain a momentary impression or observation which then vanishes — in order to make it a *concept-forming* process — he has to identify what he has just observed in some one, concrete, specific, sensory form....

Now, it has to be a specific unit; and it cannot be specific, it cannot be concrete, unless it is sensuous. Because reality is concrete, and we perceive by means of our senses. Suppose we attempted to have a concept which was symbolized by a certain feeling. Let's say that I have a feeling of combined pleasure and disgust at the concept "table" — suppose I tried to hold that concept by means of such a feeling. Needless to say, that would not be a concept. It would not last beyond the mood of the moment. And I would not have performed the most important part of the process — namely, the substitution of one handleable, perceivable, firm, objective unit for the enormity which I want to subsume under this concept. [ITOE, 164–165, 166–167]

Mentally linking similar existents to a word ("I'll call these things *tables*") makes the grouping permanently accessible as a store of knowledge about its units. Words' information-handling power makes possible an exponential growth in knowledge, the growth observable in a child's cognitive development from infancy to adulthood, as well as in the historical progression of mankind's knowledge.

It is a commonplace to observe that words — whose full implementation is language — permit the communication of knowledge and thus the transmission of knowledge across generations. But Rand makes a deeper point: beyond a certain level, language is essential to the acquisition of knowledge in a single, private mind.

Concepts and, therefore, language are *primarily* a tool of cognition — *not* of communication, as is usually assumed. Communication is merely the consequence, not the cause nor the primary purpose of concept-formation — a crucial consequence, of invaluable importance to men, but still only a consequence. *Cognition precedes communication*; the necessary precondition of communication is that one have something to communicate. ... The primary purpose of concepts and of language is to provide man with a system of cognitive classification and organization, which enables him to acquire knowledge on an unlimited scale; this means: to keep order in man's mind and enable him to think. [ITOE, 69]

Consider man's predicament if he lacked words. Assume that he could observe similarities and could form and remember perceptual groups. Without words, his connections would be associational, rather than logical. He would be caught in the Wittgensteinian chaos of forming not concepts but a hodge-podge of associational clusters, as in my earlier example of pumpkin — basketball — hockey puck — hockey stick — broom.

If we lacked words, one consequence would be the inability to form generalizations. In order to move from observations of two or three concretes to a generalization about all concretes of a kind, there must *be* a kind — rather than a random series of associationally linked images. No generalization could be formed from the pumpkin-to-broom cluster of associations.

Assigning a word completes the process of integration, producing a new mental entity — a concept.

Summarizing and condensing all the preceding is Ayn Rand's definition of "concept": "A concept is a mental integration of two or more units possessing the same distinguishing characteristic(s), with their particular measurements omitted." [ITOE, 13]

By analyzing how concepts are formed, Rand has solved the age-old "problem of universals." She has shown what concepts refer to in reality. Concepts do not refer to some Platonic "Form" in another dimension, nor to an Aristotelian "essence" in things, nor to a Lockean non-specific attribute, nor to Nominalist vague "resemblances." Concepts refer to existents that have, within a range or category, "some but any" degree of the same characteristic(s). As Rand puts it:

Now we can answer the question: To what precisely do we refer when we designate three persons as "men"? We refer to the fact that they are living beings who possess the *same* characteristic distinguishing them from all other living species: a rational faculty — though the specific measurements of their distinguishing characteristic *qua* men, as well as of all their other characteristics *qua* living beings, are different. (As living beings of a certain kind, they possess innumerable characteristics in common: the same shape, the same range of size, the same facial features, the same vital organs, the same fingerprints, etc., and all these characteristics differ only in their measurements.) [ITOE, 17]

The Realist error is not merely that it assumes the existence in external reality of pre-packaged universals, but also that it models concepts on perception, as if a concept were a high-powered percept (of the "universal").

Although a concept derives from perceptual observation, to form a concept is to *interrelate* concretes rather than engage in some kind of "insight" into one of them. As the genus of Rand's definition indicates, the concept is an integration, an act that creates "a single, new mental entity which is used thereafter as a single unit of thought." [ITOE, 10]

When used in a proposition, to make a conceptual identification, concepts do constitute awareness of the units to which they refer. But that awareness is something quite different from perceptual awareness. First, perception is automatic; conceptualizing is an active, conscious, and volitional process. Second, perception is a source of new, primary data, but concept-formation is not. Conception is not perception.

(Making logical connections among concepts does enable one to discover new factual relationships, as when a child learns that 2 plus 2 is 4. But such connections merely make explicit facts that were already implicit in the concepts — in this case, implicit in "4," "2," and "plus." The child is not connecting abstractions floating in the sky; he is tracing out the implications of the observed facts he has conceptualized. Perception is still the only originative source of the data used.)

The conceptual faculty, like consciousness in general, has a biological function. To understand concepts fully, we need to consider not only how they are formed and operate, but also the survival function they serve.

In the most general sense, it is clear that concepts serve the end of expanding one's range of knowledge. And the survival value of knowledge is manifest. But the crucial question remains: what exactly is the function of concepts in cognition? What does integrating similar concretes into a single new mental entity do to expand the range of our knowledge?

To answer these questions, I turn to a major new topic: the inherent limit on how much data the mind can deal with at once, and what that implies.

UNIT-ECONOMY

First some background. Everything that exists is finite. Whether it is an entity or an aspect of an entity, each existent is exactly what it is, and no more than that. This applies to the faculty of consciousness as well. The faculty has a specific identity, and that identity permits it to do certain specific things, but not more than that.

For instance, on the perceptual level, a given organism's range of hearing is limited to a certain range of sound intensities and frequencies. A dog can hear sounds too high-pitched for a man to hear. The audible range is set by the physical nature of the organism's auditory system. The same applies to all sense modalities; each has a specific means of operation, which determines what it can respond to, with what resolution, how rapidly, etc.

Man's conceptual faculty has its own specific, delimited identity. Accordingly, every aspect of conceptual processing has operational limits, or "specs" in computer-language. For instance, one cannot learn with infinite rapidity; it takes time to take in, absorb, digest, and fully integrate a body of new material.[56]

Another important operating limit pertains to intensity. The physical analogy here is to pressure; pressure is force per unit area. The same force applied to a smaller area produces a greater pressure, which is why a sharp knife edge will cut something that a blunter knife will not: a given force produces a more intense pressure when the area of contact is smaller. Likewise, the mental intensity one can bring to bear is limited, and it can be spread over a greater or lesser number of units. Thus, the power of concentration: the same intensity is applied to a smaller number of units, increasing the "mental pressure" applied to each unit.

---

56 In effect, there is some neural equivalent of the speed rating for a computer's CPU. The CPU rating, in cycles per second (hertz), refers to its basic "clock cycle," the unit of time required for its simplest operations. A computer has other rate-specifications — e.g., the various bit-per-second ratings for memory chips, bus speed, and disk access. There are doubtless analogs to this in limitations on the speed of brain functions, resulting in the span of time it takes to memorize something, to recall something, etc. There are other neural analogies to computer architecture, such as the number of CPU registers and the "word" length (e.g., 32-bit vs. 64-bit architecture).

A man cannot concentrate on everything presented to him at once. Giving more attention to one thing is achieved by giving less attention to other things. This is apparent even in vision: one's visual field is much wider than what is in clear, focal vision at any given moment. That limit applies not just to vision, but to every aspect of consciousness, including the conceptual faculty. In particular, *there is a limit on the number of distinct units one can hold in focal awareness at any given moment.*

This simple fact is the basis of the conceptual level's power and biological value. Everything that concepts do for man, everything that raises man above the animal levels, is traceable to the fact that concepts permit *economizing* on units. "Conceptualization is a *method* of expanding man's consciousness by reducing the number of its content's units." [ITOE, 64]

Rand introduces the principle of unit-economy by comparing man's cognitive capacity to that of animals. Since the following passage goes to the essence of the Objectivist theory of concepts, I quote it at length.

> The story of the following experiment was told in a university classroom by a professor of psychology. I cannot vouch for the validity of the specific numerical conclusions drawn from it, since I could not check it first-hand. But I shall cite it here, because it is the most illuminating way to illustrate a certain fundamental aspect of consciousness — of any consciousness, animal or human.
>
> The experiment was conducted to ascertain the extent of the ability of birds to deal with numbers. A hidden observer watched the behavior of a flock of crows gathered in a clearing of the woods. When a man came into the clearing and went on into the woods, the crows hid in the tree tops and would not come out until he returned and left the way he had come. When three men went into the woods and only two returned, the crows would not come out: they waited until the third one had left. But when five men went into the woods and only four returned, the crows came out of hiding. Apparently, their power of discrimination did not extend beyond three units — and their perceptual-mathematical ability consisted of a sequence such as: one-two-three-many.[57]

---

57 This story's source is an 18th-century work, *The Intelligence and Perfectibility of Animals*, by C. G. Leroy. His almost identical account concludes: "In fine, it was found necessary to send five or six men to the watch-house to put [the crow] out in her calculation. The crow, thinking that this number of men had passed by, lost no time in returning." [LEROY, 126]

Whether this particular experiment is accurate or not, the truth of the principle it illustrates can be ascertained *introspectively*: if we omit all conceptual knowledge, including the ability to count in terms of numbers, and attempt to see how many units (or existents of a given kind) we can discriminate, remember and deal with by purely perceptual means (e.g., visually or auditorially, but *without counting*), we will discover that the range of man's *perceptual* ability may be greater, but not much greater, than that of the crow: we may grasp and hold five or six units at most.

This fact is the best demonstration of the cognitive role of concepts.

Since consciousness is a specific faculty, it has a specific nature or identity and, therefore, its range is limited: it cannot perceive everything at once; since awareness, on all its levels, requires an active process, it cannot do everything at once. Whether the units with which one deals are percepts or concepts, the range of what man can hold in the focus of his conscious awareness at any given moment, is limited. The essence, therefore, of man's incomparable cognitive power is the ability to reduce a vast amount of information to a minimal number of units — which is the task performed by his conceptual faculty. And the principle of *unit-economy* is one of that faculty's essential guiding principles. [ITOE, 62–63]

There are two distinguishable points here:

1. There is a limit on the number of units man can simultaneously hold in focal awareness.

2. Concepts are man's means of overcoming that limit (by condensing many units into one).

The first point has become established in the literature of cognitive psychology, stemming from George A. Miller's classic article, "The Magical Number of Seven, Plus or Minus Two: Some Limits on Our Capacity for Processing Information." [MILLER, 1956]

In informal conversation, Rand often referred to this capacity-limit as "the crow epistemology," or just "the crow." That usage has become common in the Objectivist literature, and I will use it as a shorthand expression from this point on. (The value of the shorthand is itself an instance of "the crow epistemology.") A few more examples of "the crow epistemology" should nail down the point.

A quick glance suffices to distinguish two peas from three peas, but not 42 peas from 43. Counting the peas enables their quantity to be easily held as one unit ("42") and that quantity is easily distinguished from any other enumerated quantity.[58] An average person would begin to run into difficulty in trying to distinguish six peas from seven by sheer perception, and almost certainly could not reliably distinguish ten peas from eleven (without counting or forming subgroups).

Bear in mind that a *unit* is something held as a separately *discriminated* item. To hold in mind something as a unit requires that, while focusing on it, one retains awareness of its separate, distinct identity, as well as its similarity to the other members of the group. Merely viewing several dozen dandelions spread across a lawn does not count as holding in focal awareness dozens of *units* — i.e., holding in one frame of awareness their individual features in addition to their similarity. But doing that for three dandelions poses no problem.

The same need for unit-reduction applies, on a higher level, to the numerals. It is easy to distinguish the numerals "10" and "100," and hold in mind their distinct identities, but the case is quite different for "1000000000000000000000" and "1000000000000000000000." Commas are introduced into large numbers to form groups of threes, thus reducing the number of perceptual units by a factor of three.

For the same reason we introduce the new number-words "thousand," "million," "billion," and so on. Thus, we can think "four billion" rather than four thousand thousand thousand.

Science, which routinely works with very large numbers, introduces unit-economical notation that counts the decimal places (which are powers of 10). E.g., the mass of the Earth is: 5,980,000,000,000,000,000,000,000 kilograms. In the unit-economizing form of notation, that becomes: 5.98×10^{24} kilograms. If we then have to divide 5.98×10^{24} by 2.0×10^{21} it becomes quite easy: divide 5.98 by 2 and subtract the smaller exponent, giving 2.99×10^{3}.

Though quantities and numerals provide the simplest illustration of the need for unit-economy, the principle applies universally to cognition. In any field and on any issue, economizing on units magnifies the power of one's consciousness by concentrating a given intensity of thought on a small number of units. This increases the per-unit mental intensity, giving one mental leverage.

Concepts achieve an immensely greater degree of condensation than does counting or the use of commas to break up long numerals. The number

58   For more on counting as unit-reduction, see ITOE, 63–64.

of units that a concept retains by means of a single word is not fixed and finite, but unlimited. A concept, in Rand's term, is "open-ended": it applies to all the existents of a given kind — past, present, and future. "Man," for instance, does not apply to merely those men whom one has seen or considered; it applies to every man who has ever existed or will ever exist.

It is the substitution of one word for an open-ended number of similar units that gives concepts their cognitive power. If concepts were frozen after their formation, rather than being open-ended, they would be reduced to proper names for the small group of units from which they were formed. The open-ended nature of concepts permits inductive generalizations to be formed, so that we can apply the knowledge gained from study of some concretes to every concrete of that kind that we subsequently encounter.

Crucially, a concept is open-ended not only in regard to its application but also in regard to its content — i.e., the information about the units that it stores. All facts learned about the units qua units are to be added to one's conceptual file. When one learns that all men have kidneys, the concept "man" stores this new information.[59] Such updating is required if the conceptual file is to function as a file, rather than being frozen in place, like a set of papers stapled together.

How is the open-ending of a concept accomplished? What are the underlying mechanics? In his ongoing experience, the child comes to realize that he has discovered a recurring type of thing, and that leads him to form an intention (wordlessly, at this early stage) to apply the concept to all future instances. E.g., in forming the concept "table," the child repeatedly encounters new tables, motivating him to, in effect, set a "standing order" to identify every object of this type as "a table." The same applies to his discovery of new features of tables. (Simple identifications of this type become automatized; the open-ending of more advanced concepts requires an active, deliberate commitment to expanding one's knowledge and keeping one's mental files up to date.)

The issue of open-endedness brings to the surface a basic difference between the Objectivist and the Realist theories of concepts. For Realism, a concept refers to only the "universal" feature supposedly found inside the concretes.[60]

---

59   In fact, the explicit, conscious identification, "Men have kidneys" is what accomplishes the filing: focusing on (and valuing knowing) this fact tends to form a corresponding link in one's brain between (to oversimplify) the neural correlates of "man" and "kidneys." (See CHAPTER 5 on conceptual identifications.)

60   This closed-ended, frozen view of concepts is the error that generates the "analytic-synthetic" dichotomy (see CHAPTER 5).

For Objectivism, the concept refers to the units — the things out there in reality, with *all* their characteristics, *known and yet to be discovered.*

For instance, the concept "man" refers to men. Men have the characteristics that they have, whether or not these characteristics are yet known. Human beings had capillaries before William Harvey discovered the existence of capillaries. But when Socrates used the concept "man," he meant those entities — entities which *have* capillaries, even though Socrates was ignorant of that characteristic of the entities his concept designated. Since his concept of "man" denoted men, and since men have capillaries, the meaning of his concept included the capillaries.

Since our concepts mean and refer to existents, not just our present knowledge of those existents, in a sense we mean more than we know. By observing *some* of the characteristics, we are able to classify them. But we are classifying *them* — the existents *in toto* — not just our present knowledge of them.

Objectivism rejects the assumption that a concept equals its definition. The definition's specific function is to be a unit-economical way of *summarizing* a concept's meaning, but the meaning of a concept includes much more than just the characteristics that we use to conceptualize things. The distinguishing or defining characteristics are *how* we classify, not *what* we classify. *What* we classify are the existents, with *all* their characteristics. The concept "pea" refers to the peas, not to only those characteristics that, in a given context of knowledge, best distinguish peas from other legumes.

Indeed, since existence *is* identity, the existents *are* their characteristics. By the same token, a characteristic is one aspect of a thing's total identity. Characteristics do not exist as such, but only as characteristics of entities (or of an entity's attributes, actions, relationships, etc.) Characteristics can be isolated mentally but cannot be physically separated from the entities that possess them.[61]

Accordingly, the concept of an entity is the concept of the whole entity, not just of some characteristics of the entity. The concept of an action is the concept of the whole action, not just of some characteristics of the action. Even the concept of an attribute is the concept of the whole attribute, not just of some characteristics of the attribute.[62]

---

61   Sometimes one speaks of parts of entities as being "characteristics" of them, but a part of an entity is actually itself an entity, not a characteristic. (See ITOE, 264–274.)

62   Attributes can have characteristics, in the broad sense of that term. E.g., a man's attribute of being suntanned has such characteristics as: its degree of darkness, its recency, and its effects on his appearance and health.

Since a concept subsumes units as they actually exist, with all the characteristics that they possess, the information stored by the concept expands with every new discovery about the nature of the units. Rand uses the file-folder analogy to make the distinction between the knowledge stored in a concept, in a given person's mind at a given time, and what that concept refers to in reality:

> Since concepts represent a system of cognitive classification, a given concept serves (speaking metaphorically) as a file folder in which man's mind files his knowledge of the existents it subsumes. The content of such folders varies from individual to individual, according to the degree of his knowledge — it ranges from the primitive, generalized information in the mind of a child or an illiterate to the enormously detailed sum in the mind of a scientist — but it pertains to the same referents, to the same kind of existents, and is subsumed under the same concept. This filing system makes possible such activities as learning, education, research — the accumulation, transmission and expansion of knowledge. [ITOE, 66–67]

The cognitive function of concepts pertains to what Rand calls "psycho-epistemology" — the psychological mechanics of the cognitive process.[63] In regard to concepts, the "crow" limitation is a psychological fact about how consciousness works, a fact that explains what concepts accomplish for us in cognition. Since man can deal with only a few units at a time, he needs the condensation provided by concepts — including the automatization of the word which designates the concept. Thus, the cognitive value of concepts is psycho-epistemological: the conceptual condensation of "the many" into a "one" overcomes the limits of the "crow."

The full cognitive power provided by a concept's unit-economy and open-endedness will become apparent in the next chapter, when I discuss "abstraction from abstractions."

Rand provides a vivid and memorable summary of the Objectivist theory of concepts by means of a mathematical analogy:

---

63 Rand defines the field of "psycho-epistemology" as: "the study of man's cognitive processes from the aspect of the interaction between the conscious mind and the automatic functions of the subconscious." [RM, 18]

The basic principle of concept-formation (which states that the omitted measurements must exist in *some* quantity, but may exist in *any* quantity) is the equivalent of the basic principle of algebra, which states that algebraic symbols must be given *some* numerical value, but may be given *any* value. In this sense and respect, perceptual awareness is the arithmetic, but *conceptual awareness is the algebra of cognition.*

The relationship of concepts to their constituent particulars is the same as the relationship of algebraic symbols to numbers. In the equation $2a = a + a$, any number may be substituted for the symbol "a" without affecting the truth of the equation. For instance: 2 x 5 = 5 + 5, or: 2 x 5,000,000 = 5,000,000 + 5,000,000. In the same manner, by the same psycho-epistemological method, a concept is used as an algebraic symbol that stands for *any* of the arithmetical sequence of units it subsumes.

Let those who attempt to invalidate concepts by declaring that they cannot find "manness" in men, try to invalidate algebra by declaring that they cannot find "a-ness" in 5 or in 5,000,000. [ITOE, 18]

The Objectivist theory holds that concepts are formed by grasping similarity against difference; the measurement-relationships among existents result from their having a commensurable characteristic. Contra Realism, concepts are not formed by passively intuiting some metaphysical "universal." Concepts are not formed by zeroing in on one concrete, seeking an "insight" into its "essence," but by widening one's focus, interrelating several concretes through a process of contrast and comparison, then integrating them by means of a word.

Abstraction is not subtraction but integration.

4

HIGHER-LEVEL CONCEPTS

CONCEPTS OF CONCRETE ENTITIES, SUCH AS "TREE" AND "DOG," represent only the entrance to the conceptual level. At this beginning stage of conceptual development, a child can subsume the next tree under "tree," and the next dog under "dog," and children do generally delight in pointing to things and announcing their names. But there is little they learn from doing so: there is as yet no conceptual knowledge in their mental "file folders"; there are only perceptual memories of past trees or dogs plus a few associational links to other perceptual memories.

In order to gain the full power of the conceptual level, the child must be able to add explicit, conceptual content to his conceptual files. To get beyond "Here tree" and "There dog," he needs to be able to think such a thought as "Trees grow tall." But "grow" is an action, not an entity, and "tall" is an attribute. Similarly, he needs to be able to think "Dogs are animals," but "animal" is a higher-level concept, not one formed from direct perception, as "dog" is. Dogs are perceptually similar; animals, which range from flies to elephants, are not. How does a child form higher-level concepts, since they are too abstract to be formed directly from perception as first-level concepts are?

Higher-level concepts are formed by the process Rand calls "abstraction from abstractions." It consists of turning the concept-forming process back on its own products: the input to the process is not concretes but earlier-formed concepts. The input used to form the concept "animal" is the prior concepts of, say, "dog," "flea," and "elephant." The process is iterative: "animal" and "plant" will become the input for forming, years later, the still more abstract concept "organism."[64]

Abstraction from abstractions is also the process that enables the child to form concepts of the characteristics of entities — what the entities are and do — to identify not only "dog," but also "tail," "wagging," and "bushy," not only "tree" but also "tall," "growing," "evergreen," and "deciduous."

It is abstraction from abstractions that allows one to acquire the full human vocabulary, giving one the power of *thought*, the power that has enabled man to become, in Dobzhansky's phrase, "the lord of creation."

A child who has only first-level concepts is, metaphorically speaking, living hand-to-mouth, without any tools of production. The child's cognitive progress depends upon his acquiring the equivalent of baskets, nets, weapons, huts — all of which expand his efficacy, better his life, and save him time. Just as the development of basic tools, and then tools for making tools, made possible man's material progress, so the step-by-step formation of concepts at higher and higher levels of abstraction makes possible his intellectual progress (which is required for his material progress).

If somehow, overnight, we lost all higher-level concepts, industrial civilization would be wiped out, and we would be helpless — blinking uncomprehendingly at the machines, computers, automobiles, and factories we could neither value nor use. It takes higher-level concepts to understand that the oddly shaped box is not just a "box" but a computer, that the books on the shelf can be read to learn things, that two plus two is four — in other words, to recognize anything beyond the level of "dog," "berry," and "rain."

Higher-level concepts are essential to the human level of existence.

---

64 The earlier concepts are not the only input to the process; a growing body of related knowledge is also required. Abstraction from abstractions is not a mechanical, but a cognitive and contextual process.

THE FORMATION OF HIGHER-LEVEL CONCEPTS

Let's look more closely at the nature and genesis of higher-level concepts. At the opening of her chapter, "Abstraction from Abstractions," Rand identifies the two different directions the process can take:

> Starting from the base of conceptual development — from the concepts that identify perceptual concretes — the process of cognition moves in two interacting directions: ... toward wider integrations and more precise differentiations. [ITOE, 19]

Wider Integrations

Wider integrations are the simpler case. To form wider concepts, one applies the same processes of differentiation and integration that one used to form first-level concepts, but with earlier-formed concepts taken as the units to be integrated. A simple example is forming the concept "furniture" from the prior concepts "table," "bed," "couch," "dresser," etc. These first-level concepts are taken as units, which are then differentiated from architectural features, such as walls and doors, and/or from other objects in a room, such as plates, appliances, and rugs. Then one integrates the items of furniture according to their possession of a distinguishing characteristic, with their differing measurements omitted. Rand describes the process of forming the higher-level concept "furniture," as it starts from first-level concepts such as "table," "bed," "sofa," etc.

> The *distinguishing* characteristic of the new concept is determined by the nature of the objects from which its constituent units are being differentiated, i.e., by their "Conceptual Common Denominator," which, in this case, is: large objects inside a human habitation. The adult definition of "furniture" would be: "Movable man-made objects intended to be used in a human habitation, which can support the weight of the human body or support and/or store other, smaller objects." This differentiates "furniture" from architectural features, such as doors or windows, from ornamental objects, such as pictures or drapes, and from a variety of smaller objects that may be used inside a habitation, such as ashtrays, bric-a-brac, dishes, etc.

The distinguishing characteristics of "furniture" are a specified range of functions in a specified place (both are measurable characteristics): "furniture" must be no larger than can be placed inside a human habitation, no smaller than can perform the specified functions, etc. [ITOE, 22]

Thus, the process of integrating first-level concepts into wider ones follows the same pattern as that of forming first-level concepts: the grasp of similarities against a background of differences, the omission of measurements on the "some but any" principle, and the integration of the earlier-formed concepts, by means of a word, to create a new, open-ended, mental entity.

Note that the widening process treats the old concepts' distinguishing characteristics as measurements to be omitted. This is entirely appropriate, given that a distinguishing characteristic is a range (or category) of measurements. E.g., the distinguishing characteristic of green is the wavelength range of 500–565 nanometers, and we omit measurements within that range to grasp "green"; likewise, to get "hue," we omit the hue measurement-ranges, expanding to the entire visible spectrum of about 380–750 nanometers, on the premise that a hue must have some wavelength within that range, but may have any.[65]

Rand shows how this point applies in omitting measurements to form "furniture":

> The distinguishing characteristics of these units are specified categories of measurements of shape, such as "a flat, level surface and support(s)" in the case of tables. In relation to the new concept ["furniture"], these distinguishing characteristics are now regarded in the same manner as the measurements of individual table-shapes were regarded in forming the concept "table": they are omitted, on the principle that a piece of furniture must have *some* shape, but may have *any* of the shapes characterizing the various units subsumed under the new concept. [ITOE, 21–22]

In terms of the file-folder analogy, the wider concept, "furniture," is a larger file folder, such as a hanging folder, which holds other file folders.

---

65 "Color" is wider still, embracing measurement differences in saturation and luminosity. And, as mentioned in the previous chapter, it is somewhat an oversimplification to equate hue with wavelength, but the complexities of color vision are irrelevant to my purpose, which is to illustrate the concept-forming process.

The resulting view is vitally different from that of the Realists. The Realists' abstraction-as-subtraction model implies that wider concepts have less cognitive content than the narrower ones from which they are formed. For the Realists, "table" abstracts the "universal" from individual tables by mentally subtracting away and discarding everything that differs among tables. Then, "furniture" discards even more, retaining only that which all items of furniture have in common, discarding even the "universal" features of tables (and of beds, sofas, dressers, etc.). It was this abstraction-as-subtraction premise that led Hegel to conclude that the concept of "existence" has no content at all (see page 119).

Rand's theory recognizes that concept-formation is integrative, which means that the wider concept contains more cognitive content than any of the narrower ones from which it is formed. In forming the concept "table," one grasps relationships among tables (as against a foil, such as a chair). To form the concept "furniture," one must retain that fact plus grasp something more: the wider relationships among tables, chairs, beds, etc., in contrast to rugs, doors, and other items from which furniture is differentiated.

Thus, the resulting wider concept, "furniture," subsumes and includes all the information about the first-level concepts (plus their interrelationships). The hanging file folder contains the narrower file folders; a file drawer contains the hanging folders; a file cabinet contains several file drawers, and so on. And since the first-level concepts denote entities in reality, with all their characteristics, the wider concept does as well; the wider concept represents a wider perspective, as "furniture" does by virtue of integrating tables, chairs, etc.

For Realists, reaching a more abstract level means having a narrower "insight" into a universal embedded inside a given universal — the "furniturehood" lurking inside of "tableness" and "bedness." For Realists, the wider the concept, the emptier of cognitive content.

Realism cuts itself off from reality at the first level, since it holds that concepts like "table" do not refer to entities, but only to the supposed universal element in them; it then compounds the error by taking "furniture" to refer to an even more rarefied universal, leaving the concept with even less content. The Objectivist theory retains the link to reality: wider concepts refer, via the narrower concepts they integrate, to existents as they are in reality, with all their characteristics.

Subdivisions

The second type of higher-level concept consists of subdivisions or "narrowings" of existing concepts. Narrowings have virtually never been discussed in the history of epistemology — the discussion of higher-level concepts, scanty as it has been, has ignored narrowings to focus exclusively on widenings. Yet narrowings — conceptual subdivisions — are by far the more common type of higher-level concept.[66]

There are two ways of subdividing an earlier concept: 1) by narrowing the earlier concept's measurement-range, or 2) by adding a new characteristic, a characteristic not used in forming the earlier concept.

The simpler case is subdividing by narrowing an existing range of measurements, as "scarlet" narrows "red" or "toy poodle" narrows "poodle."

Consider the process of subdividing the concept "table" to form "coffee table" and "dining table." These two subdivisions are formed by narrowing the height measurements (coffee tables being lower than dining tables) and narrowing the function-measurements (to keep objects within easy reach while seated on a couch vs. while seated higher, in dining chairs). In the preceding chapter, I gave the example of a teacher grading students' tests. The introduction of plus and minus grades is a clear case of making subdivisions by narrowing the measurement-ranges: if the grade of B is assigned to 80–89, B+ is typically used for 87–89, and B- for 80–82.

In forming this type of subdivision, the old distinguishing characteristic serves as the CCD, within which a new, narrower range of measurements serves as the distinguishing characteristic for the new concept. Within the narrower range, the particular measurements are omitted.

The second type of narrowing is more complex and more interesting: cross-classification. An existing concept is narrowed according to the presence or absence of a new characteristic. Rand gives the example of forming "desk" as a narrowing of "table." The essential difference between desks and other tables consists in the presence of drawers for stationery supplies — a characteristic not specified in, and orthogonal to, the original concept "table."

---

66   Based on making random samples of words in the dictionary, I estimate that 90% of higher-level concepts are narrowings. The predominance of narrowings over widenings makes perfect sense: each narrowing divides one concept into several subsets, and each widening does the reverse, combining several concepts into one superset. By analogy if there are an average of 20 counties per U.S. state, then there are 1,000 counties (subdivisions) and only one nation (wider category).

The concept "man" can be subdivided in numerous ways by adding different characteristics to the distinguishing characteristic: "boy" (adding age and gender), "Negro" (adding race), "Republican" (adding political affiliation), "economist" (adding profession). To give an idea of the range of possibilities that cross-classifications open up, here are some further examples — each using a different basis of cross-classification: "cousin," "student," "criminal," "Baptist," "environmentalist," "theorist," "hero."

Cross-classifications range across a rich and interesting variety of cases, and they serve many different cognitive purposes. As with all conceptualization, the basic process remains the same: differentiation, measurement-omission, and integration.

Subdivision is a fairly easy process to perform, because the integration is already established, and one need only make finer differentiations within it. Differentiation is an easier task than integration.

Conceptual Hierarchy

The process of abstraction from abstractions gives rise to a phenomenon of immense importance for epistemology: hierarchy.

In its most general usage, a "hierarchy" is an ordered relationship among items: each item is located in a series according to its dependency upon the item below it.[67] Examples are military rank (private, sergeant, captain, etc.) and levels of courts (trial, appellate, supreme). The hierarchy terminates in (or begins with) a primary, or set of primaries. This primary is the fundamental item of the series, the one on which all the others depend. For instance, the military hierarchy terminates in the Commander-in-Chief, or each of the floors of a building depends on the one below it, terminating in the ground floor.

The hierarchy of *concepts* results from the iterative nature of abstraction from abstractions. Higher-level concepts depend upon the earlier ones that they integrate or subdivide. "Organism" (a widening) depends on "plant" and "animal," and these concepts, in turn, depend on earlier concepts formed from perception, such as "tree" and "bush," and "dog" and "pig." "Celebrity" (a narrowing) depends on "fame" and "man."

---

67   There is an unfortunate ambiguity in speaking of "above" and "below" here. I take the perspective that a hierarchy moves "up" from its base or foundation, though one could alternatively say that the hierarchy flows down from the top (e.g., the Commander-in-Chief is usually thought of as being at the "top" of the military chain of command).

This dependency is absolute: without lower-level concepts to link them back to perceptual reality, the higher-level concepts lose their meaning, becoming empty sounds.

The hierarchy of concepts concerns the necessary order of their formation. By virtue of the identity of man's consciousness, concepts have to be formed in a certain order. The concept of "stockholder" cannot be formed before the concept of "stock," which cannot be formed before the concept "corporation," which cannot be formed before the concept "business."[68]

It is the condensation afforded by the first-level concepts that permits the formation of wider concepts, because the wider concepts would not be graspable without that condensation. Take the formation of the wider concept "furniture." Tables, beds, and dressers have no *perceptual* features in common. A table does not look like a bed, and neither of them looks like a dresser. Nor do these objects look similar when contrasted to such non-furniture items as a kitchen cabinet or a refrigerator. The level on which items of furniture are in fact similar — which involves their movability plus their function — is too wide a level to be grasped directly from perception. In other words, the perceptual variety of items of furniture is too great for the "crow."

Likewise, consider the concept "organism" as denoting any living being, whether plant or animal. A child can *see* the similarity among dogs, or among horses, or among trees. But now picture the child, before he has any concepts, looking at a grassy field on which there are dogs, horses, trees, and rocks. Given the limits of the "crow," no child can grasp by just looking at the scene that the living organisms (dogs, grass, horses, trees) are similar as opposed to the rocks. In order to reach the required scale of aware-ness, the child must first condense the dogs into "dog," the horses into "horse," then "dog" and "horse" into "animal," and he must separately condense "tree" and "grass" into "plant." Only after these intermediate con-cepts have been formed and automatized can he then consider the two units "animal" and "plant" in opposition to "rock." (Even this is a simplification: one would have to form many more concepts — e.g., "growth," "repro-duction," and "action." In fact, one would have to make propositional identifications — e.g., "The animal and the plant act on their own, but the rock remains where it is unless pushed or pulled by an external force.")

To fully appreciate the hierarchy of concepts, one must firmly disting-uish between grasping concepts and merely uttering words. Just seeing

---

68   The overall order allows, in some cases, for options regarding the particular details of its implementation. See ITOE, 204–217.

a man wearing a uniform is not sufficient to form, from this perception, the concept "soldier." Other people who wear uniforms — nurses, policemen, prep school students — are not soldiers, and the concept "soldier" does not mean simply "people wearing this kind of clothing." (In contrast, the concept "man" can be, and is, formed directly from perception.) A given child may use the *word* "soldier" just on the basis of the uniform, by mimicking the language of adults, but this is imitation, not knowledge — not a grasp of the concept "soldier."

Even for adults, such non-conceptual imitation is all too possible, especially in the case of higher abstractions like "justice," "freedom," "romance," and "inflation." Many people use such words while having only a woozy, shifting idea of their meaning and their actual connection to the facts of reality. Rand describes the right and wrong choices one confronts in moving beyond first-level concepts:

> There are many different ways in which children proceed to learn new words thereafter. Some (a very small minority) proceed straight on, by the same method as before, i.e., by treating words as concepts, by requiring a clear, first-hand understanding (*within the context of their knowledge*) of the exact meaning of every word they learn, never allowing a break in the chain linking their concepts to the facts of reality. Some proceed by the road of approximations, where the fog deepens with every step, where the use of words is guided by the feeling: "I kinda know what I mean." Some switch from cognition to imitation, substituting memorizing for understanding, and adopt something as close to a parrot's psycho-epistemology as a human brain can come — learning, not concepts nor words, but strings of sounds whose referents are not the facts of reality, but the facial expressions and emotional vibrations of their elders. And some (the overwhelming majority) adopt a precarious mixture of different degrees of all three methods.
>
> But the question of how particular men happen to *learn* concepts and the question of what concepts *are*, are two different issues. In considering the nature of concepts and the process of abstracting from abstractions, we must assume a mind capable of performing (or of retracing and checking) that process.
> [ITOE, 20–21]

The hierarchy of concepts is the order required to grasp the concept, not merely to parrot the word. And "grasping" means "taking firm, secure hold of," not merely "having a faint, brushing encounter with." To grasp "soldier," one must first grasp "army" or "military," which in turn requires grasping "war," "nation," and so on, until one gets back to first-level concepts — i.e., those that can be formed from perception, without needing to use any previously formed concepts in the process.

Thus, the hierarchy of concepts is a logical hierarchy, not a chronological one. The specifics of the chronological order often vary with circumstances. For instance, an American child may not learn the concept "dingo" until many years after he has learned the concept "animal," but that does not mean that knowing "animal" is a prerequisite of forming "dingo," as shown by the fact that an Australian child might well form "dingo" before "animal." One can form "dingo" directly from perception, which means that "dingo" is a first-level concept, regardless of whether one forms it at age 1 or age 10. "Animal," in contrast, is inherently second-level. To grasp it, one needs to have conceptualized *some* types of animals, but which particular animals a child uses — whether dingos and kangaroos, or cats and pigs — depends merely on the order in which he happens to observe various animals.

(In the case of two widely-separated concepts, there may be no particular hierarchical order between them. For instance, nothing dictates the order in which one learns the concepts "arithmetic," and "divorce." But a prerequisite of forming the concept "arithmetic" is having the concept "number," and one cannot grasp "divorce" before having "marriage.")

It is easy to be insensitive to the hierarchical order and to squash concepts down to one level, because after a concept has been learned and automatized, it becomes so much "second nature" that it feels as if one always knew the concept, or as if it could be formed from perception — like "dog." "Retroactive self-evidency," one might call this error. Retroactive self-evidency is particularly pervasive in the computer field: using a new application passes quickly from the befuddling to the seemingly self-evident — one feels about such know-how, "it's just obvious." But in almost all cases, it is obvious only *after* it has been identified.[69]

The hierarchical view of concepts is not that of the typical man on the street — nor of most philosophers in their armchairs. Far more common is the assumption that concepts are not grasped consciously but absorbed passively from the social setting in which the use of language develops. But

---

69 Even natural selection was deemed "obvious" — once Darwin had discovered it. Biologist G. G. Simpson wrote: "Darwinian natural selection was based on a few concepts all obviously true once they had been pointed out. After Darwin had pointed them out, honest biologists agreed they had been extremely stupid not to see them before." [SIMPSON, 51]

concepts represent knowledge. To recognize that certain existents are similar to others is to know something about the world. In the case of the simple, first-level concepts with which a child begins, each concept is formed by recognizing a similarity against a background of differences, and that is the discovery of a fact. To see the similarity of dogs to each other, as against cats, is to learn a fact of biology, not to adopt a social convention, like learning to say "Gesundheit" upon hearing someone sneeze.

(For an infant or toddler, the knowledge condensed in a first-level concept is not yet explicit, propositional knowledge. Upon first entering the conceptual level, one is not yet able to form a sentence and make an assertion. But the child's later ability to form propositions is based upon his having previously stored knowledge in the concepts he uses to do so. For propositions to be cognitive, concepts must be cognitive.)

To illustrate the fact that a concept represents knowledge, not a social practice in the use of words, consider the case of words whose meaning one has forgotten. If one can no longer recall from high-school biology what "monocotyledon" means, one is unable to make meaningful statements about monocotyledons. What is gone is not the word, not a social practice, but knowledge: an understanding of which things in reality are similar in which respect. If one recalls that the term has something to do with plants, one can indeed express that in a proposition. But "something to do with plants" does not constitute a grasp of the concept, even though one had grasped it years ago. The knowledge can be regained, of course — in this case, by looking it up, in a source written by someone possessing the knowledge.

Neither the concept "monocotyledon" nor even the concept "dog" represents a gift granted by society. Grasping any concept is an achievement, one that requires effort, attention, and doing mental work. The product of that work, a concept, is a grasp of facts of reality — i.e., knowledge.

We need to bear in mind Rand's observation that "no matter how many men mouth a concept as a meaningless sound, *some* man had to originate it at some time." [ITOE, 21] To originate a new concept requires making fresh observations, and, for higher-level concepts, that origination also requires a sustained effort to relate things, in a quest to find common denominators.

A fairly simple example of the difference between origination and learning from others is provided by the concept "velocity." High school physics students today have little difficulty in integrating the concepts of "speed" and "direction" to form the concept "velocity," which denotes speed in a given direction. But consider the fact that the origination of this concept, which is the key to understanding the laws of motion, required the genius of a man like Galileo. The simple concept "speed," even precisely measurable speed, does not suffice to explain motion. For example, the basis of understanding planetary orbits lies in realizing that, though a planet's *speed* remains roughly constant, its *velocity* is continuously changing as it follows its curved path.

By using the Galilean concept of "velocity," Newton was able to explain how gravity is the force responsible for the changing velocity of the planets, and that the planets are constantly accelerating towards the sun, even though their distance from the sun remains almost constant. "Acceleration" is a still more abstract concept, defined not as a change in speed but as a change in velocity. Only this conceptual hierarchy makes it possible to understand such seemingly paradoxical facts as that a ball thrown upwards, though losing speed as it rises, is accelerating downward from the moment it leaves one's hand, in accordance with Newton's Second Law of motion ($F = ma$).

Newton's three laws of motion, as simple as they are, cannot be grasped until one has grasped, then related, the concepts of direction, speed, velocity, and acceleration. These concepts do not lie flat, in effect, on a plane; instead, they have a hierarchical structure: a necessary order of learning. "Velocity" is a cross-classification and cannot be grasped before "speed" and "direction." Likewise for "acceleration," which is a change in velocity. If one forgets the actual meaning of "velocity," and attempts to use it as a synonym for "speed," one's concept of "acceleration" will be sabotaged. A higher-level concept depends for its meaning on the prior concepts used in its formation. Deprived of that base, a concept becomes a meaningless sound. That is exactly the fate of "stolen concepts" — e.g., of "illegal" in "The U.S. Constitution is illegal."

The hierarchy of concepts is not metaphysical but epistemological. To be sure, a concept's place in the hierarchy is partly determined by metaphysically given facts — e.g., by the scope of differences that must be embraced — but what makes the scope of differences matter is "the crow epistemology." Certain differences are too big, or too subtle, to be taken in perceptually and register as perceptual similarities, even when juxtaposed with other things sharing a CCD. The differences between civilians and military men are real, but too wide-ranging to be taken in at the purely perceptual level. At the other end of the range, the subtle differences between two varieties of beetle can be recognized by the prepared mind of the naturalist, but not by a child of two who is just forming the concept "bug."

Earlier, I gave the example of "organism," which embraces differences too wide-ranging, in terms of perceptual features, for a child to grasp without the aid of the condensing power of prior concepts, such as "animal" and "plant." But metaphysically, apart from the cognitive requirements of man's mind, there are no "levels of existence." Apart from man's perspective, organisms exist, animals exist, and Lassie exists, period. The hierarchy of concepts is epistemological, not metaphysical.

The hierarchy of concepts has another source besides "the crow epistemology": the nature of man's senses. The concepts "ultraviolet" and "molecule" cannot be formed directly from perception — because neither can be perceived. Thus, this hierarchy stems from facts about the *identity* of man's consciousness, a factor that plays a crucial role throughout epistemology.

ABSTRACT VS. CONCRETE

The fact that there are conceptual subdivisions ("narrowings") alters our understanding of what "abstract" means. Previous philosophers, countenancing only widenings, equated "more abstract" with "more general." But concepts also become more abstract when they make subdivisions of an existing concept. Consider "crimson" and "red." Crimson is a specific shade of red, so "crimson" is less general than "red." But a child would have to learn "crimson" as a subdivision of "red." "Crimson" is thus both more abstract than "red" and *less* general.

This point is more obvious with narrowings that cross-classify, like "employee," which is a cross-classifying subdivision of "man" (a man who works for another). "Employee" is more abstract than "man," but less general. Grasping "employee" requires a host of prior conceptual knowledge — which is why a two-year-old is not prepared to grasp "employee."

Abstractness, then, does not equal generality. Generality is a matter of scope — the number of units encompassed by the concept. Abstractness is a matter of what has to be conceptualized on the basis of what. As Peikoff notes, "Concepts, therefore, differ from one another not only in their referents, but also in their *distance from the perceptual level.*" [OPAR, 91–92] One can move further away from the perceptual level in either direction — going "up" (widening) or "down" (narrowing). Starting from the first-level concept, "man," one gets more abstract both when one widens to form "animal," and when one narrows to form "employee."

The hierarchy of concepts soon becomes quite complex. Not only can one move "up" to a wider concept, or "down" to a narrower concept, one can, so to speak, reverse directions — moving "up" from a concept that one reached by moving "down," and vice-versa. A few examples will illustrate the rich complexity of conceptual development.

"Female" is an example of moving "up" on the basis of having previously moved "down." "Female" is a widening. It integrates such concepts as "woman," "mare," and "hen," to reach the idea of the female of some but any animal species. But "woman," "mare," "hen," etc. were each reached by narrowing. "Woman" is a narrowing of "human being," "mare" of "horse," and "hen" of "chicken." So, "female" is an integration (moving "up") from a set of narrowings (each reached by moving "down"). Adding to the complexity, the process of reaching "female" also depends on having as an automatized context the wider concept "animal," and, for the full concept "female," such concepts as "reproduction."

Conversely, here are some examples of moving "down" on the basis of having previously moved "up." From "animal," a widening, one moves "down" to make subdivisions, such as "predator." Or, from "number," a widening of "one," "two," "three," etc., one moves "down" to form "even" and "odd."

In forming cross-classifications, an earlier concept is narrowed by the addition of another characteristic; the added characteristic must have already been conceptualized.[70] The concept of the added characteristic may itself have been reached by either a widening or a narrowing. For instance, take the case of narrowing "man" to reach "artist." The concept "artist" narrows "man" by reference to "art," which is a concept reached by widening from the individual arts — painting, literature, music, etc. "Collie-owner" narrows "man" by reference to a certain subcategory within "dog" plus "ownership," a concept that depends upon many earlier widenings and narrowings.[71]

As a result, beyond the first, simple steps in the development of concepts, the hierarchy of concepts becomes an increasingly complex affair, involving "two interacting directions," in Rand's phrase quoted earlier. The hierarchy is not at all a linear progression, not even if we allow for proceeding in two directions — "up" and "down" — from the perceptual level. The hierarchical

---

70   The added characteristic may initially be grasped only perceptually, as when one notices a similarity among personality types or musical styles; but the completion of the concept-forming process requires a definition, and that, of course, requires an explicit, conceptual grasp of the characteristic.

71   Strictly speaking, a concept has to be one word, but in a few of the examples in this book I ignore this requirement — or fudge it with a hyphenated word, like "collie-owner." Interestingly, English is moving in the direction of eliminating hyphens and forming one longer word, as with "healthcare" and "website."

dependency of some concepts on others is real and unavoidable, but this hierarchy is not a simple sequence, like the number line, which extends in two directions (positive and negative).

Hierarchy has sometimes been analogized to structures — to skyscrapers or pyramids. But the most accurate analogy for the hierarchy of concepts is the suspension bridge. Some of the higher parts of a suspension bridge serve to hold up the structures below them; other parts do the opposite, supporting what lies on top of them. But every part of the suspension bridge is subject to and works in relation to the force of gravity, just as every concept in the hierarchy is subject to the necessary order of learning. Just as a given part of a suspension bridge has support but also supports other parts, so a concept in the hierarchy may have prior concepts that make it possible, while also making possible grasping other concepts that rest on it.

And just as any bridge part will fall unless it is supported, ultimately, by the ground, so any concept which does not reduce through intermediate concepts back to the perceptual level will fail to function cognitively. Ungrounded "concepts" are mere sounds, without a cognitive link to the facts of reality. Rand calls them "floating abstractions." (Methods of preventing floating abstractions will be discussed in CHAPTER 7.)

In the field of abstraction from abstractions, certain concepts require special attention: concepts of characteristics, concepts of consciousness, and axiomatic concepts.

Concepts of Characteristics

The first concepts a child forms are concepts of entities — e.g., "dog," "table," "cookie." These concepts are formed directly from perception, rather than requiring prior concepts, and perception is geared toward discriminating entities from each other. Though we also perceive the attributes and actions of entities, perception does not *discriminate* attributes or actions from entities. When we perceive a big dog barking, the dog is given as discriminated from the ground on which it is standing (and from every other entity in the scene), but we are not given any discrimination of the dog's size from the dog; nor are we given any discrimination of the dog's action of barking from the dog. Yet, after a period of development, we are of course able to form the concepts "big" and "barking." By what means do we do this? How do we form concepts not of entities but of their *characteristics*: their colors, shapes, locations, what they are doing, and what they can do?[72]

This is an important question, because concepts of characteristics are our means of identifying the nature of a thing, breaking down what is, perceptually, an unanalyzed whole. It is one thing to see a red ball rolling by, it is quite another to isolate its color, shape, or action and to name it. Concepts of characteristics offer this analysis and identification, enabling us to gain explicit, conceptual knowledge of what things are and do. Doing so enables us to connect the properties of a thing to its actions — i.e., we can identify causal factors.[73] E.g., the ball's round shape is necessary for it to roll, but its red color is not.

By breaking down perceived entities into separate characteristics and then identifying the action-consequences of each, man has been able to harness the power of wind, water, fire, sunlight, and petrochemicals.

For instance, man uses concepts of characteristics to grasp that wind *pushes* in a certain *direction*; he uses that analytical knowledge to develop the sailboat. Similarly, he observes that *flowing* water *pushes* things, and uses that analytical knowledge to invent the waterwheel. Even at a more primitive stage, in learning how to tame fire, he must recognize that fires are *hot*, that fire has *fuel*, that different fuels *burn* differently, that a fire can be *starting, steady, or dying*. This is the kind of analytical knowledge that

---

72   I include "actions" under "characteristics" to avoid having to repeat "characteristics and actions."

73   "The law of causality is the law of identity applied to action. All actions are caused by entities. The nature of an action is caused and determined by the nature of the entities that act; a thing cannot act in contradiction to its nature." [AS, 1037]

permits primitive man to progress from fearing fire to taming it, to making wood fires, inventing torches, then candles, then ovens and foundries. None of this would be possible if man were restricted to the pre-analytical concept of "fire" as being just "that kind of thing." Without concepts of characteristics, man would be restricted to "Here is wind" and "There is fire," which is in itself hardly any advance over the perceptual associations formed by animals. Concepts of characteristics make possible man's mastery of nature — and of himself.

In view of the inestimable value of causal knowledge, it is imperative to understand how characteristics are isolated and conceptualized.

Concepts of characteristics are formed by the same basic method used to form concepts of entities; the difference here pertains to what is being conceptualized, not directly to the means of doing so. Nevertheless, there are some wrinkles — and some questions — that arise regarding concepts of characteristics.

To form a concept of an *entity*, we contrast two or more instances of the entity with a foil — e.g., some tables vs. a chair. Likewise, to form the concept of an attribute, we contrast this and that instance of the attribute with a foil — e.g., two or more shades of blue vs. a shade of green. To form the concept of an action, we contrast this and that instance of an action with a foil — e.g., two or more instances of a thing moving vs. being at rest. And, as with entity-concepts, concepts of characteristics are formed by measurement-omission, on the "some but any" principle, and are integrated into a new mental unit by means of a word.

We form higher-level concepts of characteristics just as we do in the case of higher-level concepts of entities.[74] "Blue" is first-level, within attribute-concepts; "color" is a widening; "indigo," and "ultramarine" are narrowings. Narrowing by cross-classification is exemplified by "pastel blue," if we allow two words to count as a concept, since "pastel blue" stands for those shades

---

74 A technical issue arises regarding "levels," because the term has two senses. In one sense, only concepts of entities are "first-level": only entity-concepts presuppose no prior conceptualization. Since concepts of characteristics presuppose concepts of entities, concepts like "blue" are not "first-level" in this sense. But, in another sense, "first-level" denotes concepts that do not integrate or subdivide any prior concepts, and in this second sense "blue" is first-level: it conceptualizes what is directly perceivable. Accordingly, these concepts need no validation or checking (there's no such thing as getting "blue" wrong). Concepts like "blue," "round," and "moves" are part of the incontestable base to which more abstract concepts must be reduced and against which their validity is to be judged. As such, they could be called "reductively first-level."

that contain a considerable amount of white.[75] "Pastel" itself is a narrowing of a previous widening ("color").

Colors are attributes, but the mechanics of concept-formation are the same in the case of characteristics in categories other than "attribute." For concepts of actions, the first-level includes something surprisingly wide: "motion." The motion of things is given directly, in vision, hearing, and touch.

In conceptualizing "motion," the child has, in one way, an easier task than in conceptualizing attributes: he can observe one and the same entity when it is moving and then when it is not, as in observing his mother walking, then standing still. He also observes the same alternative with other entities: his ball rolls then stops; he waves his hand then holds it still; a car, a bug, a bird — all move and then don't move. By omitting the measurements of what moves — whether it is big like the car or small like the bug, whether it is round like his ball or shaped like his hand — and by omitting the measurements of the motion (fast, slow, toward him or away, rotating or translating), he forms the concept "move" — which, in English, is likely to be first captured as "go."

The concept "motion" has many, many narrowings. One narrows "motion" by narrowing one or more measurement-ranges that were left open in forming "motion." For example, "rising" is moving upwards, "slowing" is decreasing in speed, "walking" is a certain kind of movement of an animal with legs, "sinking" is falling in water.

And the narrowings can be further narrowed. An impressive array of English verbs use subtle differences to narrow "walking." Consulting several thesauruses, I found 20 different narrowings of "walking." Here are a few: ambling, striding, pacing, sashaying, strolling, limping, parading. All these different ways of walking differ in the measurements of the component aspects of walking. (Note that, hierarchically, it would be impossible to form the concept of, say, "strolling" before the concept "walking.") The concept "parading" is a cross-classification, narrowed not only by the features of the motion itself, but by the purpose of parading: to display oneself to others.

Concepts of relationships are the most complex type of concepts of characteristics, since these concepts involve not just relating things (as all concepts do) but also isolating the relationship itself. Spatial relationships are the simplest case, since they are given in visual perception. Examples of concepts

---

75   I do think there are some concepts which, in English, are held as two or even three words. "Black hole" and "stolen concept" are examples. German routinely combines words into one compound word.

that are first-level within this category are: "in," "on," "beneath," "near," "behind," etc. The words for these, as well as for temporal relationships, are prepositions:

> Prepositions are concepts of relationships, predominantly of spatial or temporal relationships, among existents; they are formed by specifying the relationship and omitting the measurements of the existents and of the space or time involved — e.g., "on," "in," "above," "after," etc. [ITOE, 17]

A widening of "on," "in," "beside," etc. would be "with" (in one sense). A narrowing of "on" would be "atop" (which excludes being on the side or bottom). Later come myriad cross-classifications, from the relatively simple "astride" to such complex (non-spatial) relationships as "marriage."

In regard to any concept of a characteristic, we must distinguish between an adjective and the abstract noun, which refers to the characteristic as such. "Small" is less abstract than "smallness." "Small" is an adjective, a word that *describes*; "smallness" is a noun, a word that *names* that attribute. Likewise, "sharp," "flexible," and "polite" describe, but "sharpness," "flexibility," and "politeness" name the attribute involved. (Verbs can also be nominalized, which creates gerunds, as in "Walking is good exercise.")

In English, a suffix, such as "ness," or "ity," is normally used to distinguish the nominalized adjective from the adjective. But we do not use such suffixes in the case of color-concepts: we do not say "greenness," just "green," when we are making that color the subject of our thought. The shrinking of "greenness" to "green" is exploited in the following equivocation, which helps concretize the difference between an adjective and the corresponding noun:

> Grass is green.
> Green is a color.
> ―――――――――
> Grass is a color.

— as if grass were an attribute. The equivocation becomes clear if we force the green-greenness distinction:

> Grass is green.
> Greenness is a color.

— which is not a syllogism, and no conclusion follows.

Note that the equivocation cannot be slipped by us when the language does make the noun-adjective distinction, as in the case of "long" and "length":

> This rope is long.
> Length is an attribute.

To produce a syllogism, the second premise would have to read: "Long is an attribute" — which is neither proper English nor meaningful.

Going from a verb (e.g., "move") to its nominalized form ("motion") offers certain advantages. The nominalized characteristic can be made the object of separate study, as if it were an entity — as in studying "motion" or "immigration" (from "immigrate"), or "happiness" — which is in one way the same as, and in another way quite different from, "happy."

Any characteristic that rewards specialized study gets its own nominalized form. Nominalized forms of characteristic-concepts enable us to direct attention to the characteristic and its sub-characteristics, rather than being distracted by its relations to the other attributes of its entity. Consider the difference between: "Whenever one object acts on a second object, the second object reacts equally and oppositely on the first object" and "For every action there is an equal and opposite reaction." The second statement is far more unit-economical, and it directs our attention to the action itself, in abstraction from the other characteristics of the objects that act and react.

Now let's confront the intriguing question of how we isolate a characteristic from the entity that possesses it, which we must do before we can conceptualize the characteristic (as, e.g., an adjective).

In forming concepts of entities, such as "table," we attend to characteristics, but we do so perceptually: we selectively focus on characteristics, e.g., shape, in order to classify *entities*. The child at this early stage is not conceptualizing "shape" as a characteristic. Rand writes:

> In the process of forming concepts of entities, a child's mind has to focus on a distinguishing characteristic — i.e., on an attribute — in order to isolate one group of entities from all others. He is, therefore, aware of attributes while forming his first concepts, but he is aware of them *perceptually, not* conceptually. It is only after he has grasped a number of concepts of entities that he can advance to the stage of abstracting attributes from entities and forming

separate concepts of attributes. The same is true of concepts of motion: a child is aware of motion *perceptually*, but cannot conceptualize "motion" until he has formed some concepts of that which moves, i.e., of entities.

(As far as can be ascertained, the perceptual level of a child's awareness is similar to the awareness of the higher animals: the higher animals are able to perceive entities, motions, attributes, and certain numbers of entities. But what an animal cannot perform is the process of abstraction — of mentally separating attributes, motions or numbers from entities. It has been said that an animal can perceive two oranges or two potatoes, but cannot grasp the concept "two.") [ITOE, 15–16]

In thinking about how we form concepts of characteristics, we must take care not to commit the fallacy of retroactive self-evidency. Having so long ago automatized concepts like "white" and "round," we might easily assume that these characteristics are given to us directly in the same way that entities are. But perception isolates entities from other entities, not characteristics from other characteristics. As adults, when we look at a white, round table, it is self-evident to us that the table has the color and the shape as *characteristics*; but that was not self-evident in early childhood, before we had ever performed the process of isolating those attributes from the entities that possess them. What is "obvious" to a modern adult is not necessarily a "given" for the beginning conceptualizer. What needs to be explained is the mechanics of the process of abstracting characteristics from the entities that possess them.

At the entrance to the conceptual level, awareness of attributes serves only as the means of distinguishing among entities; the perceptual focus on an attribute is not, per se, the isolation of one attribute from all the others that constitute the entity. But that isolation is precisely what is required for conceptualizing the attribute. How is this isolation performed?

In principle, an isolation of one existent from others can be achieved by one of several means. If the existent is an entity, it can be physically separated from surrounding entities, as a single piece of gravel in a pile can be picked up and inspected individually. Parts of entities can be physically separated from the whole entity, as when one pulls a leaf from a tree. (Parts of entities are themselves entities.)

Even without detaching it, a part can be isolated by attending to its spatial position — by tracing around its edges with one's eyes and fingers.

But attributes (and actions and relationships) are not *parts* of entities, and they cannot be isolated by separability, location, or any physical means. While physical means can be used to isolate a leaf from the tree it is part of, no physical means can isolate from the tree its height, its age, or its action of swaying.

To isolate a characteristic from the entity that possesses it, one must use not a physical but a mental means: differentiation. Consciousness is a difference-detector, and there are two basic types of differentiation that we can use to isolate a characteristic from the entity.

The simplest form of isolating a characteristic occurs when the characteristic in question may be present or absent in the same entity. The same entity — the child's mother — can be walking or still, standing or seated, happy or sad. The very same blossom that was white yesterday is brown today. In such cases, the child is aware that there is one entity that has changed, so he will not use the difference to make a conceptual subdivision (as if there were two types of entity: walking-mother vs. still-mother, white-blossom vs. brown-blossom). The difference of which the child is aware is a difference in a *characteristic*: his attention is drawn to the one factor that changes, against the background of those that do not. (This represents the application to concept-formation of Mill's Method of Difference, which he formulated as a technique for isolating causal factors.[76])

Next comes the stage of integration. When the child observes a similar change in other entities (bread in the toaster goes from white to brown), if he has already conceptualized the entity involved (bread), he is prepared to differentiate what changes (color) from what does not (the other attributes of the bread). Then he can omit measurement-variations within the brown range, while retaining that range.

How is the isolation of a characteristic accomplished in cases of characteristics that are permanent rather than sometimes present and sometimes absent? The child can isolate the characteristic by considering a wide range of entities having only one perceptual feature in common. For instance, a child can notice the same color, blue, in many far-flung cases: blue shirt, blue berry, blue hills, blue lake. What is the same and what is different across all these

---

76   In Mill's wordy statement: "If an instance in which the phenomenon under investigation occurs, and an instance in which it does not occur, have every circumstance in common save one, that one occurring only in the former, the circumstance in which alone the two instances differ, is the effect, or the cause, or an indispensable part of the cause, of the phenomenon." [MILL, III, VIII, 2]

cases? The sameness is in the one attribute, blue: it is constant while all the other attributes vary.

Here the child is making a *second-order differentiation*: he is distinguishing between what differs and what does not.[77] In a first-order differentiation, one distinguishes *A* from *B*; in a second-order differentiation, one distinguishes the differing from the non-differing. In a first-order differentiation, the characteristic is the *means*; in the second-order differentiation, it is the *object*, the thing being conceptualized. E.g., color is one means by which a child differentiates blueberries from other berries, but then he is forming "blueberry" not "blue." It is the second-order differentiation that makes the color into the *object* of his concept-forming process; it permits him to isolate the blue color from the other attributes of the concretes, such as their size, shape, solidity, and texture: these other attributes vary widely among the shirt, the lake, etc. while the attribute of color does not vary. The similar color stands out: it is the one thing that does *not* vary. The highlighted similarity is in color, not in the type of thing having the color.

This second-order differentiation constitutes the equivalent, for concept-formation, of Mill's Method of Agreement: "If two or more instances of the phenomenon under investigation have only one circumstance in common, the circumstance in which alone all the instances agree is the cause (or effect) of the given phenomenon." [MILL, III, VIII, 1]

A child at this early stage of forming concepts needs to have automatized the concepts of the various blue things — shirts, berries, etc. — to avoid being swamped by all the differences among them. If he has already classified shirts as one type of thing and berries as another, and so on for the other concretes, he is prepared to grasp that, among these familiar, conceptualized entities, there is one thing that is the same: they are all blue.

The second-order differentiation (the Method of Agreement) prevents one from using attribute-differences to subdivide *entities*, as when a child uses blue to subdivide berries into blueberries vs. others. Subdivision requires a Conceptual Common Denominator (CCD), but the shirt, the lake, and the berry are disparate things, which lack any obvious CCD. Consider the different axes along which these concretes vary: the berry is small, the lake is big; the lake is liquid, the berry and shirt are solid; the shirt is for wearing, the others are not, and so on. All the salient attributes — except color — vary.

---

77   See CHAPTER 2 for a discussion of how the same kind of second-order differences are
      exploited by the perceptual system.

Thus, among the characteristics that are differing, the child's attention is drawn to the one that does not differ: the blue color.

There is a further reason why entity-concepts must precede concepts of attributes, and of the other kinds of characteristics. To be a characteristic is to be something that *characterizes an entity*. Attributes are attributes of entities, actions are actions of entities, relationships are relationships among entities, etc. To grasp "blue" is to grasp it as something that *entities* can be. If a child has not yet learned that "blue" implies a blue *thing*, then whatever sounds he may utter, he does not yet have the concept "blue."

In fact, a child does not have the full concept of "blue" until he open-ends the classification. He needs to understand, implicitly not explicitly, the wide range of phenomena that can be blue: a physical object, like a shirt, a living thing, like a berry or a fish, a liquid, the sky, etc. He does not have the concept "blue" if he knows as "blue" only his shirt; he does not have "fast" if he knows only cars as things that move fast. This is another way in which concepts of characteristics require the prior formation of entity-concepts.

Once the child has mentally isolated the attribute of being blue, he can omit two categories of measurements: 1) the measurements pertaining to different shades of blue, and 2) the measurements of all the other varying characteristics of blue things (size, shape, solidity, etc.). The omission of the second category of measurements is what enables him to apply "blue" to each of the wide range of things that are blue.

An interesting variant of the Method of Agreement can be used to isolate a given characteristic, even in a primitive state of knowledge: the metaphorical use of entity-concepts as adjectives.

Imagine how a primitive man might form the concept "tiger lily." Suppose he is a jungle dweller of 50,000 years ago. Assume that he possesses many concepts of entities, such as "lion," "tiger," "flower" as well as subdivisions of "flower," such as "lily," "rose," etc. but has no concepts of characteristics. One day he notices a new flower that clearly is a lily but is orange with black stripes or spots. It reminds him of tigers. In a burst of inventiveness, he calls it a "tiger lily." Though "tiger lily" is still an entity-concept, his metaphor makes "tiger" into an implicit adjective, just as if he had called it a "tigerish" lily ("tigerish" being an adjective).

In creating the metaphor "tiger lily," he is regarding the coloring of these lilies as being similar to that of tigers, and he has incorporated that similarity into the name: "tiger lily." Because tigers and lilies are so different, he is not tempted to unite "tiger" and "lily" into a wider entity-concept (as he does when he integrates "tiger" and "lion" into "feline"). What he has done is to form a subdivision of "lily," but the means of doing so is by the metaphor that spotlights the characteristic shared by otherwise disparate things.

If he later encounters many things that are tiger-striped, the same kind of subdivision would be applied to other entity-concepts. Eventually, that would lead to the development of "tigerish," "tiger-like," or some other linguistic method of distinguishing nouns from adjectives.

Of course, not many things are in fact tiger-striped. So I now switch the example to "orange." "Orange" originally meant the fruit, not the color. When someone early on got the idea that his friend's hair was like the fruit, he probably called it "orange hair" — that being simply a clever metaphor, like "apple cheeks" or "hook nose." Later, as all sorts of things having that color began to be likened to the fruit, this use of "orange" died as a metaphor and became an adjective ("orange-like," in effect).

Note that many of the subtler shades of color are still named for entities: turquoise, aqua, burnt umber, amber, rose, pearl. Color-concepts derive from an awareness of the similarity between one entity with a distinctive color and another entity, already conceptualized as a different kind of entity, that has the same color.

Again, after many, many instances, in different contexts, of using a noun as an implicit adjective (rose lips, rose cloud, rose pebble), someone reached the level of differentiating "rose" used in this way from "rose" used in the literal sense, to denote the flower, and some linguistic differentiation was made — e.g., "rosy."

The noun used metaphorically (e.g., "rose" in "rose lips") could have served the function of adjectives before adjectives ("rosy") were devised. (As I noted earlier, one learns the adjective, "rosy," long before one learns its nominalized form, "rosiness.")

Thus, by this "tiger-lily" route, concepts of attributes can be formed without beginning by abstracting the attribute from the entity, but, instead, by initially combining one entity-concept with another entity-concept, as a metaphor. The metaphorical noun-combinations focus attention on characteristics, and, by their nature as words, provide the means of eventually denoting characteristics as such: the invention of adjectives.

Here's another example. The origin of "red" in English turns out to be blood — "rud" in Old English. Imagine primitive men continually using the blood metaphor: blood leaf, blood cloud, blood hair. Their repeated use over time of the same word, "blood" (or "rud"), focuses attention on the linguistic similarity, and eventually the same word is sensed to have two different functions: to refer to literal blood and to compare something else to blood. This sensed difference then gets expressed linguistically: "rud-ish" or "ruddy," which became "red."

One can also use the "tiger-lily" method to form concepts pertaining to other characteristics, for instance concepts of actions. In modern English, many action-concepts have been derived from entity-concepts — e.g., "to ski," "to roof" (a house), and most recently "to mouse" (move a cursor with a mouse). It is likely that more ancient concepts, like "to wave" were similarly derived from nouns (to act like a water wave).

I have outlined three ways to use differentiation to isolate a characteristic: by differentiating the same individual entity when it has or lacks the characteristic (the Method of Difference); by a second-order differentiation of those characteristics that vary and those that do not (the Method of Agreement); and by the tiger-lily method of combining entity-concepts metaphorically (another form of the Method of Agreement). The use of one or more of these means enables a beginning conceptualizer to isolate a characteristic, which then permits him to omit its varying measurements and form the appropriate concept.

CONCEPTS OF CONSCIOUSNESS

On this base, we are prepared to analyze a much more advanced — and more powerful — set of higher-level concepts: those pertaining to consciousness. Some examples are: "hear," "remember," "desire," "think," and "understand." Since consciousness, at root, is an activity, the primaries in this category are concepts of mental actions[78] — notably: "perception," "evaluation," "emotion," "thought," "reminiscence," and "imagination." [ITOE, 30]

The formation of concepts of consciousness requires introspection and is considerably more difficult than the formation of concepts of external existents. Mental phenomena do not have the stability and the observer-independence of physical objects. In investigating a physical object, say a bracelet, one can take hold of it, methodically scrutinize every part of it, manipulate it, turn it this way and that to observe it from different angles. In introspecting a thought or an emotion, one cannot use such tactics;

---

78   This is not to imply that these processes are "purely" mental in some Cartesian sense: though irreducible qua conscious, all conscious actions have a neural base (see CHAPTER 1), and emotions have a bodily component.

only some partial, rough substitutes are available. Mental actions and states are continuously changing; as soon as one begins to scrutinize a mental content, it changes, and it will fade out unless continually "refreshed." Moreover, conscious states are "transparent to the user," in computer jargon; it takes a special introspective act to make the means of awareness of the world into an object of awareness in its own right.[79]

In this difficult and largely uncharted territory, I will limit myself to explaining how concepts of consciousness fit the Objectivist theory of concept-formation.

The central question for the Objectivist theory here is how the formation of concepts of consciousness involves measurement-omission within a CCD.

Take a concept that is first-level within this category: "seeing." How does a child form the concept "seeing"? The concept "seeing" abstracts the action of consciousness from its varying contents, i.e., the objects seen. Contra the Realist theory, one cannot subtract the things seen from the seeing of them. As I now look out at the cityscape beyond my apartment window, I cannot, by any act of selective attention, separate the scene from my viewing of it. If I attempt to ignore the content — the buildings and sky that I see — I am not left with any residue to consider. Again, abstraction is not subtraction but differentiation: if I close my eyes, the action of seeing, the visual perception, ceases. By deliberately shutting and re-opening his eyes, even a toddler can differentiate the seeing from the things seen, the action of his consciousness from its content.[80] One can also differentiate the seeing of an object from the feeling of touching it, the hearing of the sounds it makes, etc., though these differentiations are more subtle than the dramatic difference resulting from closing and re-opening one's eyes.

As in isolating a characteristic from an entity, the child isolates the action of his consciousness from its content by differentiation, not by Realist

---

79   It is difficult to do much introspection "in real time," because that requires splitting one's focus between consciousness and self-consciousness, between the introspection and the extrospective activity being introspected. Most introspection is retrospection, but retrospection is also not as stable, manipulable, and repeatable as extrospection.

80   An interesting question is whether an animal, when it closes and opens its eyes, is aware, implicitly, of the difference between seeing and not seeing. I doubt that it is; probably, the animal simply sees, then does not see. The child, unlike the animal, can voluntarily, delib-erately shut and re-open his eyes, as an act of agency. The child's level of control over his body is of a different order from that of an animal's, and, I believe, gives the child a sense of self not possible to an animal. A child's sense that he caused the changed experience may be required for his isolation of the action of his consciousness from its content.

subtraction. As discussed above, the differentiation is, in effect, an implicit use of Mill's Methods.

But do acts of seeing differ quantitatively? When acts of seeing differ, do they differ in measurement? Regarding the measurable aspects of consciousness in general, Rand writes:

> In the realm of introspection, the concretes, the *units* which are integrated into a single concept, are the specific instances of a given psychological process. The measurable attributes of a psychological process are its object or *content* and its *intensity*.
>
> The content is some aspect of the external world (or is derived from some aspect of the external world) and is measurable by the various methods of measurement applicable to the external world. The intensity of a psychological process is the automatically summed up result of many factors: of its scope, its clarity, its cognitive and motivational context, the degree of mental energy or effort required, etc.
>
> There is no exact method of measuring the intensity of all psychological processes, but — as in the case of forming concepts of colors — conceptualization does not require the knowledge of exact measurements. Degrees of intensity can be and are measured approximately, on a comparative scale. For instance, the intensity of the emotion of joy in response to certain facts varies according to the importance of these facts in one's *hierarchy* of values; it varies in such cases as buying a new suit, or getting a raise in pay, or marrying the person one loves. The intensity of a process of thought and of the intellectual effort required varies according to the *scope* of its content; it varies when one grasps the concept "table" or the concept "justice," when one grasps that $2 + 2 = 4$ or that $e = mc^2$. [ITOE, 31]

Mental intensity is not a single attribute but a composite, an "automatically summed up result" of several, more specific attributes. The analogy from the external world is size: size is the product of a thing's length, width, and thickness. Just as a body gets bigger when it increases in any of these dimensions, so a conscious state is made more intense ("bigger" in internal, psychological terms) when it increases in clarity, scope, emotional impact, etc.

Let's concretize this by taking the case of seeing. The intensity of seeing varies in regard to: clarity, acuity, time, attention, and purpose (and probably with other factors). One sees a given object less *clearly* when one's eyes are focused on something closer than that object, when one is looking at it through fog or smoke, or when the object is seen with peripheral rather than foveal vision. *Acuity*, in the sense of the amount of detail seen, varies with distance, with the condition of one's eyes, and with lighting conditions. *Time* makes the difference between glancing, gazing, staring. More or less *attention* can be paid to what one sees, and to seeing vs. listening, feeling, tasting, etc., in accordance with one's *purpose* at the time.

Consider the wealth of conceptual subdivisions of "seeing" that have been formed to capture sub-ranges within the above axes of measurement. Here are some, listed in alphabetical order: descry, espy, gawk, gaze, glance, glimpse, look, ogle, peek, peer, scan, scrutinize, stare, watch. The measurements used in making these subdivisions are only approximate, but precision here is irrelevant: the child need observe only a variation in degree — in the more and the less. And these subdivisions do exhibit that kind of variation. Scrutinizing differs from glancing in being more intense in time, attention, and purposefulness. Ogling differs from gazing in being more emotionally involved and attentive. Descrying differs from gawking in being more purposeful, more discriminating, and far more acute. Scanning differs from merely looking by being more purposeful, more systematic, and less static (scanning involves a systematic movement of one's gaze).

The point of discussing all these types of seeing is to show that instances of seeing differ in their intensity along the various axes of measurement. To conceptualize "seeing," a child needs to become aware of the similarity among different acts of seeing, but he does not need to know explicitly how to measure them nor what the different elements of intensity are. Different instances of seeing, despite their variations in intensity, are experienced as similar when contrasted to what goes on in darkness or with eyes shut, or when contrasted to instances of hearing.

After one has separated the seeing from the thing seen, or more broadly has separated any action of consciousness from its content, one conceptualizes that action in the same way that one forms any other concept:

> The formation of introspective concepts follows the same principles as the formation of extrospective concepts. A concept pertaining to consciousness is a mental integration of two or more instances of a psychological process possessing the same distinguishing characteristics, with the particular contents and the measurements of the action's intensity omitted — on the

principle that these omitted measurements must exist in *some* quantity, but may exist in *any* quantity (i.e., a given psychological process must possess *some* content and *some* degree of intensity, but may possess *any* content or degree of the appropriate category). [ITOE, 31–32]

The widest categories — entity, action, attribute, relationship, etc. — apply to consciousness in much the same way that they apply to external existents.

In the external world, the basic category is "entity." While there are no actual entities residing in consciousness, the nearest mental counterparts to entities are *products of consciousness*. This category includes such things as concepts, knowledge, syllogisms, sciences, memories, decisions — each of which exists as a permanent, recallable unit. I do not regard particular sights or feelings as falling into the category of products of consciousness: although they do result from a process, they are transient states rather than stable, retained, usable, entity-like packages.

Conscious processes and states have *attributes* — for instance, they are clear or vague, pleasant or painful, general or specific — and there is the umbrella attribute of intensity. *Actions* of consciousness are, as mentioned earlier, the primaries in this field (products of consciousness are products of some mental action). There are *relationships* among aspects of consciousness — e.g., clearer than, more pleasant than, derivative of, contradictory to — and relationships to reality — e.g., truth and reference. There are *capacities* of consciousness — e.g., vision, intelligence, or any mental ability. There are *states* or *conditions* of consciousness — e.g., confusion, alertness, dejection, concentration.

In chapter 4 of ITOE, Rand discusses some of the complex ramifications of concepts of consciousness. She covers such higher-level concepts as "concepts of method" (e.g., "logic") and "composite concepts" (e.g., "marriage," "trial"), which integrate concepts of consciousness with existential concepts. She also provides a discussion of grammatical concepts, such as "but" (in my view, not necessarily hers, these concepts are instructions to consciousness, rather than being concepts that name conscious processes).

Concepts from the value-realm, such as "love," are subject to what Rand calls "teleological measurement." Teleological measurement involves using a standard of value to rank the degree to which things serve as means to an end, with one's life as the ultimate end, and the time devoted to that end as the CCD. The reader is directed to her chapter for more discussion on all these topics; here, my purpose has been limited to showing that concepts of consciousness are formed by the same type of processes — differentiation, integration, and measurement-omission — that is used to form existential concepts.

As we consider the wide range of things that are subject to measurement, it is perhaps necessary to observe that not every difference is a difference in measurement. For example, the difference between consciousness and external existents is not one of degree. It is not the case that "being" and "knowing" are two different amounts of something. Nor does an action differ quantitatively from an attribute. To hold otherwise would be to endorse some ludicrous form of Pythagoreanism, in which everything reduces to numbers. The Objectivist theory does not imply that there is one common unit of measurement, or CCD, in terms of which all existents have their place, as if "running" were 732 units and "big" 28.

The only common denominator among all existents is that they exist and are what they are; but neither existence nor identity is a characteristic, let alone a commensurable one.[81]

AXIOMATIC CONCEPTS

In the first chapter, I discussed the fact that axiomatic concepts are prior to axiomatic propositions. The primary axiomatic concepts are: "existence," "identity," and "consciousness." (There are a few other axiomatic concepts, the most noteworthy being "entity" and "action" or "change.") Axiomatic concepts warrant special discussion here: since they are in one sense first-level and in another sense higher-level, they constitute a special case.

The sense in which axiomatic concepts are first-level concepts is that the facts they integrate are given in perception. Indeed, these facts are present in every act of awareness, which is why they are axiomatic. Every act of awareness consists of being *conscious* of the *identity* of something that *exists*. From the newborn's first sensory impression, he is *aware*; he is aware of *something*; something that *exists*. There is no awareness that is of an identity-less nothing. Even a dream, which isn't awareness of the world, is a state of consciousness that has content; that content exists (as images or as a mental state) and is what it is (e.g., a dream that one is flying is something different from a dream that one is walking on the ground).

---

81 For a discussion of how one forms such basic concepts as "attribute" and "action," see ITOE, 274–276.

As aspects involved in every experience, the axioms are *implicit* from the start of a consciousness, which apparently begins even before birth, in the womb. And from the first sensory experience, there is nothing further to be learned about what it is to be conscious, or what it is for there to be something, or what it is for the something to be something. The concepts of existence, identity, and consciousness are first-level in this sense: the facts they designate are perceived or experienced directly.

However, axiomatic concepts are only *implicit* in experience. To identify them explicitly, to conceptualize them, requires a sophisticated development. Long before knowing the abstract terms "existence," "identity," and "consciousness," we use the simple words "is," "this," and "know." But to isolate these basic, omnipresent facts and name them abstractly, we must have a plethora of earlier concepts — plus extensive familiarity with the process of conceptualization. We saw above how forming the concept of "consciousness" requires differentiating action from content; it also requires omitting large sets of measurements: "Whatever the size, shape, color, etc. of *what* I see, I see it when my eyes are open but not when my eyes are shut."

By contrasting seeing with not seeing, hearing with not hearing, etc., one can generalize to reach the idea of consciousness as such. But what a man cannot do is project what total unconsciousness would *be like for him*. For in that condition, there is no mental content — and no him.

Just as a particular action of consciousness, seeing, can be contrasted to its cessation, so a particular thing's existence can be contrasted with its *absence*, when that particular thing no longer exists. For instance, George Washington no longer exists. Or, after a log is burned, though the ashes remain, the log is gone; it exists no more. From such examples, it is easy to form the idea of any particular thing's existence or non-existence.

But the axiomatic concept of "existence" goes much further: it refers to the totality of that which exists — just as the concept of "consciousness" refers to the totality of one's experience. The totality of one's consciousness does not cease when one shuts one's eyes, and the totality of existence — the universe — does not go out of existence when a log is burned or a particular man dies.

How, then, do we form the full concept of "existence," the concept that Rand uses in stating "Existence exists"? The full concept is reached as the final step in a series of progressive widenings. E.g., one goes from: all the dishes, to all the man-made objects, to all the objects — to all the *everything*. This final, unrestricted use of "all" is not based on any process of differentiation, but none is required. Existence has no contrary: there is no nothing;

what is not, is not. The process requires no differentiation because, after one can undertake a deliberate, self-conscious process of widening, the question naturally arises: "What is the widest category of all?"

By a process of progressive widening, one can, without any differentiation, arrive at the "integration of all existents" that Rand describes:

> Since axiomatic concepts are not formed by differentiating one group of existents from others, but represent an integration of all existents, they have no Conceptual Common Denominator with anything else. They have no contraries, no alternatives. The contrary of the concept "table" — a non-table — is every other kind of existent. The contrary of the concept "man" — a non-man — is every other kind of existent. "Existence," "identity" and "consciousness" have no contraries — only a void. [ITOE, 58]

What measurements are omitted in forming axiomatic concepts?

> The measurements omitted from axiomatic concepts are all the measurements of all the existents they subsume; what is retained, metaphysically, is only a fundamental fact; what is retained, epistemologically, is only one category of measurement, omitting its particulars: *time* — i.e., the fundamental fact is retained independent of any particular moment of awareness. [ITOE, 56]

For instance, one's awareness of a table occurs at some particular time, but the table exists across time, independent of one's consciousness of it. This is the primacy of existence (see CHAPTER 1). Consciousness perceives what exists; it does not create its objects. (The same is true of consciousness itself: introspection does not create the mental activities that one is introspecting; self-consciousness does not create consciousness.)[82]

In omitting what Rand calls "psychological time-measurements," axiomatic concepts serve an important function:

> Axiomatic concepts are the *constants* of man's consciousness, the *cognitive integrators* that identify and thus protect its continuity. They identify explicitly the omission of psychological time measurements, which is implicit in all other concepts.

---

82 Time and space are usually considered a pair, but phenomena of consciousness, such as thoughts, have no spatial location.

It must be remembered that conceptual awareness is the only type of awareness capable of integrating past, present and future. Sensations are merely an awareness of the present and cannot be retained beyond the immediate moment; percepts are retained and, through automatic memory, provide a certain rudimentary link to the past, but cannot project the future. It is only conceptual awareness that can grasp and hold the total of its experience — extrospectively, the continuity of existence; introspectively, the continuity of consciousness — and thus enable its possessor to project his course long-range. It is by means of axiomatic concepts that man grasps and holds this continuity, bringing it into his conscious awareness and *knowledge*. It is axiomatic concepts that identify the precondition of knowledge: the distinction between existence and consciousness, between reality and the awareness of reality, between the object and the subject of cognition. Axiomatic concepts are the foundation of *objectivity*. [ITOE, 56–57]

In order to form a judgment about a thing's objective nature — to judge what something *is*, not just how it looks now — one must have grasped the difference between existence and consciousness, at least implicitly. Every judgment asserts that its subject *exists* and does in fact have the *identity* ascribed to it. Even "I dreamed that I was flying" asserts that such a dream did occur and was of flying, not of something else. Even a statement about what *seems* to be the case or is wrongly believed to be the case assumes the existence of the appearance or the wrong belief. To judge is to seek to identify what something is. Thus, all judgments presuppose and use the (implicit) concepts "existence," "identity," and "consciousness."

CHAPTER 5 takes up the deeper question: what is the nature of a judgment? To answer that question, we must investigate the process by which we advance from forming concepts to forming *propositions*.

5

PROPOSITIONS

CONCEPTS ARE TOOLS. THE VALUE OF ANY TOOL LIES IN ITS USE. What concepts are used to do is to *identify*: to state in words what something is.

The form in which we make conceptual identifications is the *proposition*.[83] A proposition is the combination of two or more concepts into a single thought, as in "The table is brown," "Tops spin," or "Plants need water."

A proposition must be distinguished from the sentence used to express it. A sentence is a series of words; the proposition is the thought behind those words. A sentence is the concrete, sensuous form of a proposition in just the way that a word is the concrete, sensuous form of a concept. Just as the word "table" denotes the same concept as "Tisch" does in German, so "The table is brown" is the same proposition as that expressed by "Der Tisch ist braun." The linguistic symbols differ, the thought is the same. The proposition is the cognitive content of the sentence, as distinguished from its linguistic form. (More technically, a proposition represents the form of a judgment,

---

83 Ayn Rand said that she intended to write a "Volume II" of *Introduction to Objectivist Epistemology*, to explain propositions, but she died before undertaking it, and ITOE has only two or three sentences on conceptual identification. The present chapter is very largely my own theory.

in abstraction from whether one is asserting it, denying it, considering it, etc., but I am putting aside this subtlety.)

A given sentence may combine two or more propositions — i.e., make two or more identifications. "Plants need sunlight, and animals need food" is a single sentence, but two propositions. More complex sentences may express several propositions. But we are concerned here only with understanding the basic form of the proposition: the assertion that a predicate, P, applies in a specified way to a subject, S: "S is P."[84]

The first step to making such a conceptual identification is to have something to identify — i.e., to have isolated and observed some subject-matter, S. When one grasps some fact about that thing — a feature of it, what it is made of, what it is doing, etc. — one can name that fact explicitly by applying an appropriate predicate, P.

Suppose, for instance, that a child is concentrating on a green top as it spins. The ability to form propositions comes when he can use words — i.e., concepts — to name what he is aware of, as in: "That is a top." "The top is spinning." "The top is green." The propositions he forms identify facts in conceptual terms — i.e., he subsumes what he sees under a concept, in an act of classification. "That is a top" classifies the object he sees under the concept for that kind of entity ("top"). "The top is spinning" classifies its action. "The top is green" classifies one of its attributes, its color. (As will be discussed, the grammar specifies just how the concept functions in any given case.)

The essence of the proposition is the application of a concept to observed facts. Perceptual observation is the basic form of discovering what things are, their *identities*; propositions apply concepts to subjects known directly or indirectly by perception. By applying concepts, the proposition identifies the *kind* of fact one has observed — based on its similarity to other things known — enabling one to connect the observation to the whole network of one's knowledge.

Take "The top is spinning." A pre-conceptual child may enjoy watching the motion of the top, but he needs the concept "spin" in order to think the thought "The top is spinning," and thus to relate its motion to the similar motion of other things — a spinning coin, a revolving carousel, a twirling ice-skater. Or, suppose that during a drought the grass gets browner each day. The color of the grass is present in the visual fields of both the men

---

84   Propositions are not the only kind of locutions. Imperatives ("Sit up straight!") issue
      orders; interrogatives ("Where is she?") ask questions; conditional statements ("If it rains,
      we'll get wet.") make contingent judgments, etc. However, the base of all these is the
      "S is P" proposition.

and the animals in that area, but only the men can form the proposition "The grass is turning brown." An animal would not be able even to take the initial step of isolating the color of the grass as a separate fact, let alone take the subsequent steps of comparing the present color to that of previous days. Everything beyond viewing the current scene (which includes grass that happens to be browner than yesterday's grass) requires concepts and their use in propositional thought.

CLASSIFICATORY PROPOSITIONS

The simplest and earliest propositions are those that classify an entity under a first-level concept, e.g., "That is a dog." When a toddler points at a dog and exclaims, "Dog!" he is, in effect, making that kind of proposition: he is subsuming the dog he sees under his previously formed concept, "dog," just as if he had uttered the full sentence, "That thing is a dog."

To subsume something under a concept is to classify it — i.e., to grasp that it qualifies as a *unit* of an existing concept. What qualifies an existent as a unit is its essential similarity to the other existents already integrated by the concept. It is this dog's essential similarity to the animals already conceptualized as "dogs" that enables the child to classify it as a dog. The child says "Dog!" because he is aware, perceptually, of this similarity.[85]

Underwriting the similarity is measurement-proximity — i.e., the fact that this animal's shape, size, diet, keenness of smell and hearing, etc. have measurements falling within the "dog" range or category. The canine shape, though instantly recognizable, is a complex set of ratios, such as of maximum height to maximum length and thickness, head size to body size, eye separation to head size, etc. For simplicity in diagramming the role of measurements in classification, I take as the CCD the relatively unimportant characteristic of overall size (volume).

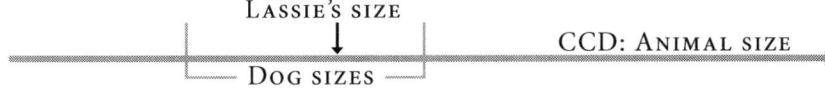

---

85   The proposition, however, is *about* its subject, not about the similarity involved. Grasping similarities is the *how*, not the *what*. A proposition *about* similarity would take that similarity as its subject-term, as in: "The similarity of A to B is …."

Thus, *measurement-relationships* underlie the two basic operations of the conceptual level: concept-formation and conceptual identification. Concept-formation operates by *measurement-omission* (to establish a range) and conceptual identification operates by *measurement-inclusion* (inclusion in an established range). Concept-formation creates the file folder; a classificatory proposition applies the information in the file folder to the subject.[86] The child, of course, is aware only of similarity and difference, not of the underlying measurement-relationships, which is a phenomenon identified by the epistemologist.

A further step in the same direction comes when the child forms higher-level concepts; these enable him to make wider classifications. Forming the wider concept "animal," allows him to make the wider classificatory identification: "Dogs are animals." Here, the subject is a class of thing, dogs, not a single concrete, Lassie. But the process is the same: "dog" represents a measurement-range that is, from a wider perspective, only a sub-range within the animal range of measurements, as distinguished from that of plants.[87] In effect, he places the "dog" file folder inside the "animal" folder. Or, more literally, he grasps the fact that the concept "dog" is a unit of the wider concept "animal."

Just as wider concepts, like "animal," make possible propositions having greater generality, so conceptual subdivisions, like "collie," make possible propositions having greater specificity. "Lassie is a collie" is more specific than "Lassie is a dog."

Many of our concepts represent "cross-classifications" (see CHAPTER 4), and these are frequently used as predicates. E.g., "Lassie is a pet." ("Pet" is a cross-classification.) From this array of quite simple higher-level concepts, one can already see the permutations start to proliferate: "Collies are animals," "Some collies are pets," "Pets are animals," etc.

---

86   All mental content, including concepts, is *stored* in the nervous system in *physical* form. Neuroscience has found that this storage involves changes in neurons and their synaptic connections. (For a well-written, popularized history of some very recent discoveries concerning how the brain stores memories, see McDERMOTT, 2011.)

87   In forming "animal" (as a category ranging from, say, fish through mammals) two broad CCDs are involved: "form of locomotion" and "type of consciousness," and each of those involve several axes of measurement. E.g., both a fish and a dog move themselves around and are conscious, in contrast to a tree or a bush, but there are many measurable differences in how they do so. Their different forms of locomotion and consciousness are adapted to their different means of survival in their distinct "ecological niches."

Descriptive Propositions

All propositions apply concepts to a subject, but only some propositions *classify* their subject as a whole. Classification occurs only when the predicate is a *noun*, in which case the predicate names a class of things. Since concepts start from perception, and since the content of perceptual awareness is entities, a child's earliest propositions have concepts of entities as their predicates. But soon thereafter, the child develops concepts of characteristics — of attributes, actions, relationships — as discussed in CHAPTER 4. (For ease of expression, I continue to refer to actions as "characteristics," even though actions are not attributes.)

Thus, there is a difference between propositions that classify and propositions that describe, a distinction first made by Aristotle. [CATEGORIES, II, 1a20–1b8] Where a classificatory proposition classifies its subject as a whole, a descriptive proposition *analyzes* out of the whole subject a part, an attribute, the material of which it is made, etc. In a descriptive proposition, the predicate can be an adjective ("Tom is *tall*"), a verb ("Tom *ran*"), or a prepositional phrase ("Tom is *in the kitchen*").[88]

One function of *classificatory* propositions is to connect concepts to other concepts, which organizes one's mental file folders into a network. Having one's concepts organized logically is of inestimable value; it means that identifying something as *P* carries with it or implies that it is also *Q, R, S, T* — and so on, for everything to which *P* is logically connected. Some of the most valuable of these connections are to the characteristics of *S*. "Man" stores all the characteristics of men: that they have a certain range of size and shape, that they walk, talk, think, learn, have parents, form societies, buy and sell things, create works of art. Having the concept "man" is cognitively valuable not because it "labels" men, but because it *stores knowledge of their characteristics*. Descriptive propositions are the means of identifying characteristics. And bear in mind that it is the analysis expressed in descriptive propositions that permits the identification of causal factors, the key to man's mastery of his environment and the progress of civilization.

How, then, do descriptive propositions work? What is the process of propositional judgment when the predicate is not a concept of an entity, but of an entity's characteristics? What are the underlying mechanics when a child thinks "Lassie barked," or "Lassie is big," or "Lassie is on the couch"?

---

88 Nouns may appear in the predicate of descriptive propositions, as shown by "Tom opened the *door*" and "Tom is the *winner*" — neither of which classify Tom.

Here, the child is not classifying Lassie under "barked," as he did when he classified her under "dog." We cannot say "Lassie is a barked," as we say "Lassie is a dog." Lassie is not an instance of barking (nor of bigness nor of on-the-couchness). But in applying such terms to Lassie, the child is still proceeding conceptually. He is not merely hearing Lassie's bark, but identifying it conceptually, by applying the concept "bark" to that particular sound he just heard her make.

The difference between classificatory and descriptive propositions is that classificatory propositions put the subject *as a whole* into a class of similar existents; descriptive propositions analyze the subject, isolating a characteristic of the subject, then identify that the measurements of that characteristic fall within the measurement-range denoted by the predicate. Thus, one first zooms in on one characteristic, isolating it from the subject's other characteristics, recalls the term for that characteristic, and then zooms back out to regard that characteristic as being part of the subject's overall identity.

In a descriptive proposition, there is indeed a classification made, but one that is implicit not explicit, and the predicate classifies a characteristic, not the subject as a whole.[89] When one says, "The rope is short," one is classifying its length, while retaining the fact that it is *the rope's* length. An adult with an advanced vocabulary could express the same thought as: "The rope's length is short." Likewise, "The frog jumped," is the same as "The action of the frog was to jump." But these expanded formulations use abstract terms ("length" and "action") that the young child does not yet know.

In a descriptive proposition, the predicate-term classifies a characteristic, but only as a means of describing the subject. In contrast, in a classificatory proposition, the classification is not the means but the end, i.e., the point of the statement.

In both types of proposition, the overall purpose is to bring to bear on the subject the knowledge stored in the predicate. The effect of classificatory propositions is to realize: "All that which is true of the *P*s is true of this *S*." (E.g., all that which is true of dogs is true of this thing.) The effect of descriptive propositions is to realize: "All that which is entailed in having characteristic *P* is true of this *S*." (All that which is entailed in being a short rope is true of this rope.)

The basis of the child's use of "short" is his recognition that the rope's length falls into a measurement-range, the measurement-range established earlier,

---

89 I am indebted to Gregory Salmieri (personal discussion) for defending this analysis, which I had considered, but prematurely rejected. See Salmieri, 2013.

when he formed the concept "short." Applying the adjective "short" relates the rope's length to the length of other things. "The rope is short" places its length within the "short" range within the implicit CCD: (relative) length. (But the CCD is only implicit; at this first stage, he does not have the concept "length," only "short" and "long.") In sum, descriptive propositions, like classificatory ones, work by *measurement-inclusion*.

The process of forming any proposition is essentially the same as the process of forming a concept. In concept-formation, one grasps certain similarities, based on measurement-proximity in contrast to the measure-ment-remoteness of a foil, and one establishes a range or category of measurements. In proposition-formation (i.e., conceptual identification), one also grasps a similarity, but the range of measurements has already been established, so that one recognizes that the subject's characteristics are included in that established range. Thus, the diagram given above, to show the mechanics of "Lassie is a dog," applies to descriptive propositions as well as to classificatory ones.

Both descriptive and classificatory judgments require awareness of char-acteristics. Descriptive propositions focus on characteristics individually, but classificatory propositions are based on *a connected set of character-istics*, those common to the members of the class. In classifying Lassie as a dog, we identify the kind of thing Lassie is. The point of doing so is to be able to apply to Lassie our knowledge of the set of canine characteris-tics she shares with other dogs. Contrary to the Realist theory of concepts, the proposition "Lassie is a dog" does not state her "being" or her total identity. It does not state, for instance, the fact that Lassie is a movie star, or even that she is a collie. The proposition "Lassie is a dog" identifies Lassie's possession of those canine characteristics that are universal to dogs, not her possession of those additional characteristics.[90]

In traditional logic, descriptive propositions are assimilated to classi-ficatory ones by making up artificial classes in which to place the subject. "This rope is short" is treated as if it subsumed the rope in the class of "short things." But there is no such class and no concept "short things." We should not attempt to reduce description to a kind of classification. Though classificatory propositions are chronologically prior to descriptive

---

90   This marks a difference between concepts and propositions. The *concept* "dog" subsumes all the characteristics of dogs, even those not known at any given stage of knowledge, and includes individual differences as potentialities (e.g., "a dog can be a movie star"). This point about concepts is the basis for rejecting the dichotomy between "analytic" and "synthetic" propositions, to be discussed below.

propositions, even the first classificatory propositions ("Dog!") depend upon perceiving the characteristics of the subject.

Thus, description is not a disguised classification. "Big" is an adjective, not a noun; nouns name, adjectives characterize. This takes us to the subject of grammar.

THE ROLE OF GRAMMAR

Grammar is essential to propositions. The different parts of speech are designed to indicate differences in metaphysical status: entity vs. attribute vs. action, etc. Nouns and pronouns stand for entities; the other parts of speech pertain to characteristics of entities. I say "pertain to" because the other parts of speech — adjectives, verbs, adverbs, etc. — do not *name* characteristics of entities; instead, the other parts of speech *use* concepts of characteristics to permit the formation of descriptive propositions. For instance, "soft" is an adjective. In contrast, the noun "softness" *names* the attribute in order to make it into a subject ("Softness is good in a pillow"). We say, "The pillow is soft," not "The pillow has a soft." Likewise, "jumped" uses our concept of the action to describe what an entity does — vs. saying: "The frog is (or has) a jumped."

Grammar provides the means for specifying the particular way the predicate applies to the subject. It is different, for instance, to say "He lied," and "He is a liar." The former describes his action; the latter classifies him as a certain kind of person. Since English grammar makes much use of word order, there is quite a difference in meaning between "He loves only her," and "Only he loves her." There is even a difference between "He loves her," and "She is loved by him." The first is about him; the second is about her, directing our attention to the effects on her of being the object of his love. (In inflected languages, such as Latin, the "case" of the terms does the work that in English is done by word-order.)

Grammar also provides the mechanism for combining concepts *within* the subject ("The proud, thin man is speaking") or *within* the predicate ("Joe is a proud, thin man"). Characteristics can be combined cumulatively ("proud, thin") or, by using adverbs, to make one characteristic modify another ("proudly thin"). "A proud, thin man" means a man who is proud and thin, but "a proudly thin man" means a man who takes pride in being thin — the grammar specifies which is meant.

As this brief foray into a vast field indicates, grammar is an essential part of the mechanics of the proposition. In Rand's words, "Grammar is a science dealing with the formulation of the proper methods of verbal expression and communication, i.e., the methods of organizing words (concepts) into sentences." [ITOE, 37]

In sum, a proposition identifies a subject by grasping that it, or a characteristic of it, is a unit of the predicate. The mechanics of the process reduce to grasping the measurement-relationships involved. The grammar keeps straight what is being related to what and precisely how. All this can be put into a definition: A "proposition" is a grammatically structured combination of concepts to identify a subject by a process of measurement-inclusion.

The grammatical structure of a proposition indicates whether it classifies or describes — i.e., whether it identifies the subject as a whole or a characteristic of it. In either case, a proposition uses one's awareness of a similarity, which means that one is aware, at least implicitly, that the measurements of a characteristic(s) of the subject fall within the category of measurements covered by the predicate concept. E.g., we classify a given figure as a pentagon because it has five sides, or describe a given man as tall, because his height exceeds six feet.

NEGATIVE PROPOSITIONS

Up to this point, I have been considering only affirmative propositions. Negative propositions are those having the form "*S* is *not P*" — e.g., "Lassie is not a beagle" or "Lassie is not small." Negative propositions are *differentiations*. Negative *classificatory* propositions assert that the subject is *different from* the existents subsumed by the predicate, and thus is to be excluded from the predicate-class (Lassie is excluded from the class of beagles). Negative descriptive propositions assert that, within the predicate's CCD, the subject's measurements fall outside the range covered by the predicate-concept (within the CCD "size of animal," Lassie's size-measurements fall outside the "small" range for dogs). Negative propositions work by measurement-*exclusion*.

Thus, negative propositions do not refer to some supposed "negative facts." Everything that exists is *something*. To be non-*P* is to have a positive identity, but one that is different from *P*. A thing that is red is non-green — by virtue of what it *is*: red.

(Outside of philosophy classes, negative propositions are used only when there is a CCD permitting a differentiation, not to make pseudo-assertions like "Saturday is not in bed," or "Man is not a triangle." To make a measurement-exclusion, there must be a CCD; the characteristic is excluded in the sense of being placed on the CCD, but outside a specified measurement-range. There is no CCD uniting man and triangle. In contemporary logic classes we are told that "non-P" includes every existent of which P cannot be truly asserted, but in actual cognition, "non-P" means that which is *differentiable* from P, not that which is *disparate* from P. The question "Is or isn't man a triangle?" is illogical.)

A special kind of negative statement is: "S does not exist." There are two different cases regarding this proposition. In the first case, we are talking about what did exist but has gone out of existence: "George Washington no longer exists." Here, we are not, contradictorily, saying "S exists as something different from what exists." We are saying, "George Washington died." The same principle applies in the case of inanimate things that go out of existence — they go out of existence qua the kind of thing they were, but their constituents remain. E.g., a drinking glass, when smashed, goes out of existence qua drinking glass, but the glass of which it was made remains, just in a new arrangement. Or, a newspaper is burned and goes out of existence qua newspaper, but the chemical constituents remain, although some are dispersed in the air.

But the interesting case is the one in which the subject never existed: "God does not exist," "Unicorns do not exist," "An integer square root of 17 does not exist." In these cases, the actual subject is not an existent, because there never was and never will be one. Instead, the actual subject is an idea — the idea of God, or of unicorns, or of an integer square root of 17. What the proposition is differentiating is not an existent from other existents but a valid idea from an invalid one. The proposition "S does not exist (and never has or will)" means one of two things: "The idea of S is false" (contradicts known facts) or "The idea of S is a fiction, one produced by imagination not cognition."

The corresponding reverse statement, "S exists" (in the sense of "S is real") means, in this usage, "The idea of S is valid: I perceive or infer something fitting the description of S." Normally, the point of saying "S exists" is to counter the idea that S does not exist — i.e., is mythical or fictitious, as when someone asserts "The Abominable Snowman exists." "S exists" cannot mean that S has the property of existence, since there is no such property. Nor does

"*S* exists" classify *S* among the existents; classifying *S* already presupposes that *S* exists to be classified. Also, "the existents" does not isolate one class among others. There are no others. Rather, "*S* exists" means: "I am aware of something that fits the description of *S*, so the idea of *S* is not a fiction."

The overall point is that negative propositions are about the *difference* between one existent (including ideas) and others. *All propositions are fundamentally positive*: they state facts of which one is aware, including the (positive) fact of differences. All propositions are about what is. There is nothing else to talk about. Existence exists; non-existence does not.[91]

THE ANALYTIC-SYNTHETIC DICHOTOMY

There are further ways of classifying propositions, but I will restrict myself to warning against one unwarranted and destructive division: the false dichotomy of "analytic propositions" vs. "synthetic propositions." According to the advocates of this widely accepted dichotomy, propositions like "Dogs are animals" are radically different from propositions like "Dogs need water." The first statement, philosophers have held, is an "analytic proposition," one known by analyzing the concept "dog." It is true "by definition," the proponents of the dichotomy say. But "Dogs need water" is supposed to be "synthetic," because we cannot arrive at this identification just by analyzing the concept "dog"; to learn it, we must observe the empirical facts. "Analytic" statements are held to be "truths of logic," which supposedly can be known without sensory observation. "Synthetic" statements, on the other hand, are held to be "empirical truths," as they add to the concept facts that are only "contingent" and, therefore, cannot be asserted until we see what "happens" to be the case (and which, it is claimed, might "happen" to be otherwise, tomorrow).

There are many, many errors and fallacies in this separation of logic from observation, and in the related notion of "contingent" facts, but rather than discussing them, I refer the reader to the comprehensive and devastating criticism of this dichotomy in Peikoff's "The Analytic-Synthetic Dichotomy" (an article that Rand edited and chose to include in her book *Introduction to Objectivist Epistemology*).

---

91 There is not even a *concept* of sheer "non-existence." On this, see ITOE, 149–150. (To apply the lesson of this section, the first sentence of this footnote means: " 'Non-existence' is not a valid concept"—i.e., it is different from a valid concept.)

The basic error behind the analytic-synthetic dichotomy is a wrong view of what a concept is. A concept is based on the observation of similarities and differences. Thus, both "Dogs are animals" and "Dogs need water" are facts learned on the basis of observing things in the world—in the one case, by observing dogs, animals, and plants, and in the other case by observing dogs and what happens to them when deprived of water (plus what happens to other animals when deprived of water).

The analytic-synthetic dichotomy treats a concept as if its content were limited to only those characteristics used to form it or define it. But the cognitive role of a concept is precisely to serve as an *open-ended* file folder—i.e., as a device for storing (and then applying) facts learned by observation, new facts being stored as they are learned. The dichotomy, in effect, staples the file shut right after it is started. The result is that new conceptual identifications are treated as either stipulations ("true by definition") or rank guesses about "contingent" matters.

The open-ended nature of a concept is essential to its cognitive (and action-guiding) function. The complaint "But this is new information about the referents of the concept" reveals, in Rand's description:

> . . . the unadmitted presupposition that concepts are not a cognitive device of man's type of consciousness, but a repository of closed, out-of-context omniscience—and that concepts refer, not to the existents of the external world, but to the frozen, arrested state of knowledge inside any given consciousness at any given moment. [ITOE, 67]

A concept refers to certain existents, and those existents have the characteristics that they have. All the units' characteristics, all the information in the conceptual "file," including the characteristics used to form the concept, are learned from perceptual observation, directly or indirectly. No characteristic is learned or validated by "analyzing the concept," if that means analyzing something other than the integration of observed facts. Observing reality is the only way to acquire knowledge, and all the so-called "analytic truths"—from "*A* is *A*" to "Bachelors are unmarried" to "Dogs are animals"—are based on perception. There is no other source of knowledge.

Peikoff summarizes:

> . . . concepts mean *existents*, not arbitrarily selected portions of existents. There is no basis whatever—neither metaphysical

nor epistemological, neither in the nature of reality nor of a conceptual consciousness — for a division of the characteristics of a concept's units into two groups, one of which is excluded from the concept's meaning.

Metaphysically, an entity is: all of the things which it is. Each of its characteristics has the same metaphysical status: each constitutes a part of the entity's identity.

Epistemologically, all the characteristics of the entities subsumed under a concept are discovered by the same basic method: by observation of these entities. . . . The fact that certain characteristics are, at a given time, *unknown* to man, does not indicate that these characteristics are excluded from the entity — *or from the concept*. [ITOE, 98–99]

CONCEPTS VS. PROPOSITIONS

To some extent, the analytic-synthetic dichotomy is due to ignoring the differences between concepts and propositions, as in the common belief that a concept is only a shorthand tag for its definition, which is a proposition. But there are crucial differences between concepts and propositions, and one cannot understand either until these differences are recognized.

To form a concept is to create a new file folder; to form a proposition is to use existing file folders. Concepts are information-handling tools, not (primarily) identifications. Propositions are the identifications. Concepts condense and store information discovered. Propositions make use of concepts to formulate explicit identifications. A concept is a cognitive device, a means not an end. Propositions are the end in relation to which concepts are the means. Concepts are the elements of thought; propositions *are* the thoughts.

Accordingly, a proposition does not have the kind of unity that a concept has. Propositions are not integrations — not in the sense that concepts are. A proposition is an organized *combination* of concepts (or proper names) not an *integration* of them: the parts of the proposition — the individual words — remain apparent as components.

In contrast, the unity of a concept is seamless. As Rand describes concept-formation: "The uniting involved is not a mere sum, but an *integration*, i.e., a blending of the units into a *single*, new mental entity . . ." [ITOE, 10] That kind of "blending" does not occur in a proposition.

A consequent difference between concepts and propositions concerns their permanence. A concept is a permanent file folder, but the majority of the propositions that one forms are about particular, transient circumstances — e.g., "There goes a fire truck," or "It's time to have lunch." Such propositions are used, but not stored. In contrast, any concept, e.g., "truck," represents an open-ended file carried forward to form a permanent part of one's cognitive equipment.

A concept is stored by a specific word, and one needs to store that word and be able to recall it. But the equivalent is not usually true for propositions. One does not need to memorize specific sentences, not even for general propositions expressing a truth that is to be carried forward. For example, there are many facts that I know about hammers — all hammers — but I have not memorized any sentences regarding that knowledge.[92]

A concept's function is to store an ever-growing body of information about its units; the proposition is the application of that stored information to a new unit — i.e., an act of conceptual identification.

Concepts function as file folders that store knowledge about their units, including all their common characteristics. "Dog" applies to all those four-footed, tail-wagging entities out there in reality. Those entities have all the characteristics that they have, including their need of water, whether or not one already knew that fact. The function of the concept is to store that knowledge, as it is learned, and to make it permanently accessible. But the function of a proposition is more limited: to make a specific connection. A proposition states only what it states. E.g., the proposition "Dogs are animals" states that dogs have the characteristics that are common to all animals; it does not state that dogs were domesticated from wolves, even though the *concept* "dog" does include that fact, because the concept stands for dogs, and dogs were domesticated from wolves.

A proposition says what it says, nothing more. A proposition does *imply* more than it says, but such implications are not necessarily recognized by the person asserting the proposition. If someone says, "Dogs that bite people should be kept muzzled," his statement has all sorts of implications, but he may not be aware of them. Grasping implications takes a separate mental act: inference. As grammarians remind us, "implied" does not mean "inferred." A given proposition does not in itself contain all its implications; nor does it

---

92   To be sure, there are the rare cases in which it is important to remember a specific linguistic formulation — e.g., for definitions and for statements of basic principles, such as scientific laws. In such cases, one normally names the formulation — "Ohm's Law," "The Golden Rule," "the definition of 'man,'" etc.

contain all its presuppositions or all its possible integrations with (or contradictions to) the rest of one's knowledge.

A concept, in contrast, is open-ended and gets continually updated to store newly learned facts. A typical proposition does not ever get updated. (The idea of updating a proposition makes no sense.) E.g., a child first forming the concept "man" does not know that man has a pancreas, but when he learns that fact, it takes its place in his mental file folder. But suppose that, at age three, he states, "Man has two hands." When, years later, he learns about the pancreas, that does not convert his earlier proposition into: "Man has two hands and a pancreas." A proposition states only what it states. The very nature of a proposition is to make something *explicit*, as opposed to leaving it implicit.

The purpose of a concept is to store whatever is learned about its units qua units. The purpose of a proposition is to bring to full, conscious awareness the specific, delimited fact(s) that it states.

Thus, concepts and propositions differ in open-endedness. A concept is open-ended in two ways: extensively and intensively. Extensively, a concept subsumes all the units: past, present, and future. Intensively, a concept subsumes all the units' characteristics: known and yet to be discovered. The situation is different for propositions. Only general propositions, such as "Dogs have tails," are, like concepts, open-ended extensively (true of all dogs, across time); most propositions concern particular facts and are *closed-ended*. The point is that even general propositions are not open-ended *intensively*: one does not add new information to them over time, with the growth of knowledge. (A given proposition can become richer in meaning over time, but that is a different issue: new data is not stored in them.)

The closed-endedness of propositions stating concrete facts ("It's time for lunch") does not make them inferior to generalizations. Just as concepts are for the sake of conceptual identification, so general propositions are for the sake of their concrete application. The ultimate purpose of all propositions is to guide one's actions in the world, and that means guiding particular actions dealing with particular concretes. Metaphysically, *only concretes exist.*[93] From the broadest perspective, the entire conceptual level — the sphere of science, philosophy, wisdom, the intellect — is for the sake of: "I should now do this, not that."

---

93   Even in the mind, only concretes exist: abstractions are concretes as mental existents, and
     it is only in regard to their use in cognition that they are abstract. See ITOE, 153–158.

Though "meaning" is a term used in more than one sense, the point can be put in the following way. The meaning of a concept is the existents it integrates, with all their characteristics. The meaning of a proposition is the limited fact it states: the subject's possession of a certain characteristic(s).

The Cognitive Function of a Proposition

In a tantalizingly brief lead to the cognitive function of propositions, Rand states:

> Since concepts, in the field of cognition, perform a function similar to that of numbers in the field of mathematics, the function of a proposition is similar to that of an equation: it applies conceptual abstractions to a specific problem. [ITOE, 75]

An analysis of propositions in terms of subject and characteristics suggests how to flesh out Rand's statement. First, her statement has to be understood correctly. Her point, as I read it, is not that a proposition equates subject and predicate — not, absurdly, that "Lassie is a dog" says that "Lassie = dog" — but, as she says, that there is a similarity in *function* between a proposition and an equation. The overall function of propositions and of equations is to advance our knowledge. "Lassie is a dog" advances our knowledge in a manner similar to the way "2 + 3 = 5" advances it.

But just how does the arithmetic equation advance our knowledge? What is the "specific problem" that "2 + 3 = 5" solves? The problem is to identify the overall quantity of a group, a group known to consist of a pair and a trio. But there are an unlimited number of other equations that would also identify the quantity of 2 + 3:

$$2 + 3 = 4 + 1$$
$$2 + 3 = 18 - (4 + 9)$$
$$2 + 3 = \text{the cube root of } 125$$

And so on. Every valid equation makes a connection between terms on the left side of the equal sign and terms on the right. Propositions, likewise, make a connection between subject and predicate. Establishing a connection between arithmetic terms or between subject and predicate means that knowledge can be applied: knowledge of what is on the right side of an equation, or knowledge stored by the predicate of a proposition.

Why, though, is "5" *the* answer to the question, "What is the quantity of a group composed of two units and three units?" What is wrong with giving as the sum "18 − (4 + 9)"? The answer is that "5" is the most unit-economical way of stating that group's quantity. Giving the sum as "5" makes available the greatest amount of other knowledge. "5" gives direct access to all the facts in the "5" file folder, such as that the quantity is 1 more than 4, that it is the same as the quantity of fingers on one hand, is odd, prime, has no integer square root, is the cube root of 125, etc. Identifying the sum of "2 + 3" as "5" implicitly relates that quantity to the whole integrated set of mathematical facts that we have stored, carry forward, and continue to learn more about. The one term "5" on the right-hand side of the equation relates the two terms on the left to a kind of "central repository" for information on this quantity.

Propositions perform a similar function. The proposition "Lassie is a dog" enables us to apply to Lassie all the knowledge of dogs stored in the "dog" file, which is the "central repository" for information on this kind of animal.

We can see the same point by approaching it from another direction. Since the source of all information is perceptual observation, the question arises: how can applying concepts in a proposition move us forward, cognitively? Since the Realist theory of concepts is false, since concepts are not an independent means of access to reality, revealing an "essence" that is hidden from perception, what does the application of concepts add to what we already know from perception?

The answer is: relationships. Identifying that Lassie is a dog relates her to other dogs, to other animals, to plants, and (going in the other direction) to other breeds of dogs, to kennels, leashes, dog-owners, dogfood, etc. To identify, in a descriptive proposition, that Lassie is friendly, relates her to other friendly dogs, unfriendly dogs, friendly and unfriendly people, stories of friendship, psychological causes of friendship, types of friendship (Aristotle distinguished three of them), friendships that turn into romances, issues of loyalty to friends, etc. Some of these relationships are perceptually available, others are graspable only through intermediate abstractions, but are reducible back to perception. The point is that the word or concept is not just "a label," but a file folder stocked with a growing wealth of knowledge about the units.

In this regard, the file-folder analogy can be misunderstood: some physical file folders store concretes. E.g., a file folder for bank statements contains all the individual bank statements one has received. One can pull out that file folder and open it to find any particular statement. But one's mental file folders (i.e., concepts) are not for storing the concept's units. Rather, the folders are for storing knowledge about the units.

When one makes a conceptual identification of a concrete, one is not (normally) doing the equivalent of placing the concrete into a folder; rather, the contents of the folder are applied to the concrete. The purpose of identifying Lassie as a dog is not to have another example of "dog," but to understand Lassie. The purpose of identifying that the U.S. government is deeply in debt is not to have another example of debt, but to understand the economic condition of the nation. And in every case, the purpose of identifying that *S* is *P* is not to add to some catalog of instances of *P*, but to recognize what *S* is — i.e., to recognize that S is characterized by being *P*.

Introspection supports the point that concepts do not agglomerate concretes: bringing a concept to mind does not pull up all or most of the things one has identified as instances of it. If I say "lunch" to you, that does not make it easy for you to recall the tens of thousands of lunches you have eaten (not even just those that you consciously identified as lunches). And there would be no purpose in doing that if one could. The purpose of a concept is to store not rafts of concretes but items of knowledge about any concrete of a given kind. This permits one to apply knowledge gained from the study of some concretes to new instances, as they arise.

The point of identifying, for instance, that Joe is a (college) sophomore is not to enlarge one's set of known instances of sophomores; the point is to understand *Joe*. The proposition "Joe is a sophomore" applies to Joe the knowledge stored in the "sophomore" file. Here again, any proposition is about its subject, not its predicate. The predicate is the means of identifying in conceptual terms what the subject *is*.

A concept has cognitive content, not just referents. The concept stores knowledge about its referents, knowledge acquired by observation or by inference from observation. To use a different metaphor, the concept is like a water reservoir, and the proposition is like a pipe that enables water to flow down from that reservoir to fill a particular basin.[94] *The flow of information is from the predicate to the subject.*

---

94 Treating the pipe and basin together as the proposition makes for a more accurate, though less neat, analogy. Overall, this metaphor for propositions is less apt than the file-folder metaphor for concepts. But it does capture the idea that the concept's contents exist for their use, as the water is stored in the reservoir so that it may be piped out.

How does information get added to the conceptual file? By means of a higher-order proposition: a proposition whose subject is the predicate of the original proposition.

In the higher-order proposition, one identifies something about that kind of thing — the kind denoted by the predicate of the lower-order proposition. In the "sophomore" example, the higher-order propositions would include, first a definition: "A college sophomore is a college student in his second year of study," and then such other information as: "Sophomores are typically 19 to 20 years of age," "Sophomores are qualified to take certain courses not offered to freshmen," "Sophomores are said to have an exaggerated sense of what they know," "Sophomores who have not yet picked a major are expected to do so in that year of study," and so on.

These higher-level identifications, which take "sophomores" as their subject, make it possible for that concept to store knowledge about all its units. Then we call upon this knowledge when we reason deductively: "Joe is a sophomore, therefore he is qualified to take certain courses that he was not qualified to take as a freshman."

The proposition "S is P" has its cognitive value in the fact that "P" is not merely a symbol for all the things similar to S in a given respect, but that "P" has itself been identified by means of higher-order propositions of the form "P is Q." The higher-order identifications permit us to apply that knowledge (with whatever qualifications are necessary) to S, by the simple deductive process:

S is P

P is Q
$$\overline{\phantom{S \text{ is } Q}}$$
S is Q

Because concepts store knowledge, once one learns that S is P, the fact that S is Q becomes *implicit in the structure* of one's conceptual filing system: since the P folder is stored "inside" the Q folder, placing S in P also means placing S in Q.

Accordingly, the purpose of deduction is to *make the implicit explicit* — to bring an item's implications into full, conscious awareness.

(The process of acquiring entirely new knowledge, as in learning that P is Q, is essentially inductive. One does not deduce that sophomores are in their second year of study; that fact is part of the knowledge used to form the concept "sophomore," which is, in pattern, an inductive process; the process is also inductive when one learns, e.g., that colleges expect a student to commit to a major by the end of their sophomore year.)

Thus, concepts and propositions interact. Concepts make propositions possible, but then higher-order propositions enable us to add content to those concepts. Propositions make thought itself possible; indeed, propositions are the form that thinking takes. And some of that thinking leads to the formation of new concepts, concepts that could not have been formed without propositions using earlier knowledge.

The concept of "furniture" provides a simple example. Items of furniture are not *perceptually* similar. A bed does not look like a chair. In order to grasp "furniture," one has to do some thinking, and that means forming such propositions as: "The tables, beds, and chairs can be moved around, but the built-in cabinets can't be; we put things inside both the stove and the desk drawers, but the stove is for heating things and the drawers are for storing things." The need for propositional thought is, of course, greatly multiplied in the case of scientists forming new concepts (e.g., "gene," "electron," "factorial.")

Adding to the complexity and richness of cognitive processes is the fact that new perceptual observation is also involved in this spiraling process. The hierarchical progression is: perception, conceptualization, propositional thought; but that of course does not mean that one ceases performing one stage when one begins performing the acts of a higher stage. Just as conceptualization does not replace but supplements perception, so propositional thought does not replace but supplements, and extends the possibilities of, conceptualization.

The proposition is a means of bringing to mind and applying to the subject the knowledge stored in concepts. The primary direction of information flow is from the predicate to the subject; the predicate illuminates the subject by bringing stored knowledge to bear upon it.

Propositions are knowledge-appliers.

6

LOGIC: THEORY

THE ABILITY TO FORM PROPOSITIONS GIVES RISE TO A CRUCIALLY important phenomenon: the ability to think about one's own thinking and thus to judge one's own judgments. Concepts of consciousness enable one to identify what one's mind is doing — whether one is perceiving, thinking, emoting, imagining, etc. Axiomatic concepts enable one to distinguish between what is only in one's mind and what is a fact of the external world, to distinguish between what merely *seems* to be and what really *is*, between one's wishes or fears and the facts of an independently existing reality.

The evaluation one makes of a mental process or product affects subsequent cognition; it affects what next comes to mind, and how what is in one's mind is filed in memory. Judging affects retrieval and storage. Different results ensue from judging "That stick is bent" and "Though that stick seems bent, in reality it is straight." The effects of passively spinning out a daydream are very different from those resulting from actively judging, "Though I wish things were otherwise, they are what they are."

In consequence, a man's ability to evaluate his mental processes gives him a power of self-control that liberates him from the reactive nature of the perceptual level. Perceptual cognition is *automatic*; perception is world-generated, hard-wired, and deterministic. Conceptual cognition, in contrast, is *volitional*: self-initiated, self-directed, and controllable.

Thus, man can use his mind to control the operation of his mind; he can use the ideas he has formed to steer the process by which he reaches further ideas; he can use axiomatic concepts to judge the relation of his mind's actions to reality and to direct his mind on that basis.

By using concepts of consciousness and axiomatic concepts to make introspective judgments, man becomes *cognitively self-determining*. He can decide by conscious, explicit choice what questions to ask, what issues to consider, what aspects to focus on, how to proceed.[95]

But conceptual functioning is *fallible*. Although perception is inerrant, conceptual processes, by virtue of being volitionally controlled, can be misperformed, resulting in conclusions that are false — i.e., that contradict perceived fact. To correctly identify reality on the conceptual level, man needs a method, with standards, to guide him. We give this method the name "logic."

Since the purpose of logic is to align one's thinking with the facts, logic requires that one start from and work with the only source of information about the facts: perceptual observation. In the conceptual use of that data — in concept-formation, propositional judgment, and inference — logic defines the kind of procedures one must follow in order to keep one's thinking connected to perceptual reality. (Logic is not only the method of proof but also the method required to gain knowledge.)

Man survives, progresses, and prospers by acquiring and using conceptual knowledge. Logic is the method of acquiring knowledge and of ensuring that it *is* knowledge.

THE THREE LAWS OF LOGIC

In dealing with perception-derived material, the guidance logic provides flows from a single imperative: *Be consistent*. Because contradictions do not exist in reality, a mental process that involves or implies a contradiction has departed from reality and is invalid; a conceptual product that contradicts any fact is false. Aristotle, "the father of logic," identified the Law of Non-Contradiction, stating that it is the basic principle of all knowledge. He gives this careful formulation of the Law:

---

95   In an interesting paper, Lee Pierson and Monroe Trout argue that all consciousness, even the perceptual level of animals, is volitional, not deterministic. [PIERSON, L. & TROUT, M., 2005]. The problem with this view is that the animal would be "choosing" blindly; concepts are required to project the future, evaluate alternatives, and direct one's actions.

The same characteristic cannot both belong and not belong to the same thing at the same time and in the same respect.[96]

A thing cannot be hot and not be hot at the same time. If it changes, over time, from being hot to being cool, that does not violate the Law of Non-Contradiction. In fact, change is embraced by the law: to be cooling down is not to be, at the same time, not cooling down. "In the same respect" is also essential: a thing may be hot in one part and not in another; it may be hot in relation to ice and not hot in relation to lava. But at a given time and in a given respect, it is what it is, and is not what it is not.

The corollary of the Law of Non-Contradiction is the Law of Excluded Middle: a given thing must either have or not have a given characteristic at a given time and in a given respect. It must either be A or not be A.

(Violations of Excluded Middle reduce to contradictions. A violation of Excluded Middle would be something that isn't A and isn't non-A. But, as explained in the preceding chapter, what isn't A is still *something*, just something different from A. Thus a violation of Excluded Middle would be something that is different from A and isn't different from A — a contradiction.[97])

Later Aristotelians recognized that both these laws stem from the axiom of identity: "A is A." A thing is what it is.

There are many ways of formulating these three laws. I suggest the following formulations are those that get to the fundamental: the metaphysical issue of what it is to *be*:

THE LAW OF IDENTITY: To be is to have a specific identity. (A is A.)

THE LAW OF NON-CONTRADICTION: To have a given identity is to have no other. (A isn't non-A.)

THE LAW OF EXCLUDED MIDDLE: Not to have a given identity is to have some other. (What isn't A is non-A).

---

96   *Metaphysics*, IV, 3, 1005b19; I added "characteristic" to what, in the Greek, is just "the same." Literally: "[For] the same simultaneously to belong and not to belong is impossible to the same and according to the same." τὸ γὰρ αὐτὸ ἅμα ὑπάρχειν τε καὶ μὴ ὑπάρχειν ἀδύνατον τῷ αὐτῷ καὶ κατὰ τὸ αὐτό.

97   As mentioned in CHAPTER 5, I presuppose the exclusion of such absurdities as, "The square root of two is red." Rather than saying, "The square root of two is neither red nor not red," the correct statement is: "The square root of two is not the kind of thing that can have one color or another." "Not" and "non-" express *difference* not *disparateness*.

The following formulations are more economical and more memorable, but they are consequences of what is stated in the more careful formulations:

Identity: Everything is something.
Non-Contradiction: A thing can't be everything.
Excluded Middle: A thing can't be nothing.

The Laws of Non-Contradiction and Excluded Middle are reformulations of the Law of Identity made for the purpose of guiding cognition. To think that a thing is *A* and non-*A* in the same respect, is implicitly to hold that the thing is everything in that respect. But to be everything in a given respect is to be nothing in particular in that respect — i.e., to lack identity.

For instance, if a ball simultaneously is and isn't all red, then it has no specific identity with respect to color. If the ball is simultaneously here and not here (or neither here nor not here), then it has no identity in regard to location. (Epistemologically, a concept represents a differentiation; to file a thing under the concept and simultaneously under that from which the concept is differentiated would wipe out the concept. If "table" and "non-table" have the same referents, then "table" becomes a meaningless sound.)

Knowledge is an awareness of the identity of things; logic enjoins us to use our conceptual faculty in ways that recognize that things are what they are, rather than being contradictory or identity-less. Thus, Ayn Rand's definition: "Logic is the art of non-contradictory identification." [AS, 1016][98]

Logic applies to every level of conceptual functioning: to concept-formation, to propositional judgment, and to inference. Inference, though the most advanced of these three processes, is the simplest one to analyze. Here, Aristotle's great discovery was the syllogism, which is the "atom" of deductive reasoning. The simplest type of syllogism has the following form:[99]

> Lassie is a dog.
> Dogs are animals.
> _____
> Lassie is an animal.

---

98   It is an "art" in the sense of a method; the corresponding science that identifies the required methods is epistemology. Epistemology is the theory of the method, logic the method.

99   I reverse the traditional order of major and minor premise, which, in my opinion, wrongly subordinates the progression of one's thought to the issue of which term has the wider scope. Also, I eschew "All" as both misrepresenting the terms in which one actually thinks and, in some instances, raising needless questions about special cases.

The "middle term" — "dog" — establishes the conclusion because of the law of identity. It is because a dog is a dog that the syllogism establishes the conclusion — i.e., identifies the fact that the subject term, "Lassie," is subsumed under the predicate term, "animal." The connection made depends upon the terms having the same referents with the same identity. Where the same word is used but with different meanings, the fallacy of equivocation is committed — e.g., switching between the metaphorical and literal meanings of "pig" in: "He is a pig, pigs have four legs, so he has four legs."

The cognitive mechanics of the syllogism are also based on the law of identity. To use the file-folder metaphor on this example, the premise "Lassie is a dog" represents recognizing that the file of information on dogs applies to Lassie. But that folder is connected to the wider "animal" folder, as stated in the second premise. If the information about animals applies to dogs, and the information about dogs applies to Lassie, that implies that the information about animals applies to Lassie. The deduction makes this implication explicit. To deny that Lassie is an animal would be to use the "dog" file inconsistently: both as a subfolder of "animal" and not as a subfolder thereof.

Aristotle identified not only the rules of syllogistic deduction and the Law of Non-Contradiction as the standard of logic but also the fact that sensory perception is the self-evident base and court of final appeal for all conceptual conclusions. His achievements in logic lay dormant for many centuries, but their recovery almost a millennium later led to the Renaissance and the Scientific Revolution. [RANDALL, 1940]

LOGIC AND THE IDENTITY OF CONSCIOUSNESS

As fundamental and pathbreaking as Aristotle's work was, it is incomplete. The principles of logic he formulated pertain to the *objects* of cognition. But logic must also take into account the nature of the *subject* of cognition: the nature of the thinker's mind. Identifying this fact and working out its implications for logic is the achievement of Ayn Rand. [ITOE, CH. 8] She stresses that man's cognitive equipment has a specific identity, with specific terms of operation, which the principles of logic must reflect: ". . . the rules of cognition must be derived from the nature of existence and the nature, the *identity*, of his cognitive faculty." [ITOE, 82]

Knowledge is a mental product. Any product is made by working up the proper materials, following a proper method. Automobiles cannot be made out of bricks; nor can they be made by combining the right materials

— steel, glass, plastic — in the wrong way. Likewise, one cannot make knowledge out of errors, vague approximations, wishes, or daydreams. Nor can one make knowledge out of truths improperly combined, as in combining "Men are human beings," and "Women are human beings," to conclude, "Men are women." Both the right input and the right method of production are required. Identifying the right method of production depends upon identifying the nature of the equipment; a given drill cannot penetrate faster than a certain rate, a given crane cannot lift more than a certain maximum weight. There are equivalent limits on the nature of man's mental equipment — notably the limit imposed by "the crow epistemology." (See CHAPTER 3)

A mental procedure is logical if it adheres to the identity of the materials supplied by reality (via perceptual observation) *and* accords with the identity of man's consciousness. Any mental procedure or product that contradicts either reality or the requirements of cognition is *illogical.*

The requirements of cognition are *requirements*, not merely matters of "convenience," as 20th century philosophers liked to say. Some conceptualizations are intelligible, usable, cognitively productive, others are not. The issue is wider than cognition: achieving any end has its necessary means. To achieve the end, it is necessary, not merely "convenient," to conform one's actions to those means. It is not "inconvenient" but *wrong* to travel (unnecessarily) north when one's goal lies to the south. It is not "inconvenient" but *wrong* to attempt to travel from Boston to London by swimming the Atlantic. Making mental choices that flout the requirements of cognition results not in "inconvenience," but in cognitive paralysis, confusion, and plain error.

Man's cognitive mechanism is what it is and cannot function in contradiction to its nature. The nature of man's consciousness includes two facts that are central to logic:

1. Perception is the base of all conceptual cognition (the primacy of perception).[100]
2. Only a few distinguishable units can be held in one frame of awareness ("the crow epistemology").

---

100 Although Aristotle grasped this point, it is more explicit and more developed in the Objectivist epistemology. The term "primacy of perception" is my own and is discussed in CHAPTER 11.

Knowledge is based on the data given in perception. From that base one builds new knowledge upon old, in an incremental, step-by-step process. Knowledge is not gained by revelation from on high and it is not gained in huge gulps. Knowledge is built up, in "crow-friendly" steps, from specific perceptual observations. We start somewhere: 1) where we are in the universe, and 2) with the kind of information our perceptual system is scaled to detecting. E.g., an infant lives in a specific location, with sense organs sensitive to a specific range of energy differentials and not others. He can perceive the people and furniture in the room, but not the atoms that compose them and not the ultrasonic frequencies that a dog can hear.

From his first perceptions, the child's knowledge grows step by step. His progress is made possible by further observation, observation of new things and of new aspects of old things. At a certain point in his development, he is able to form concepts. From then on, observation and conceptualization reinforce each other, in a spiraling process, as I discuss later in this chapter.

Now we are prepared to revisit the issue of fallibility. When a child forms his first concepts, the ones for perceived objects, though some mental effort of directed attention is required, the process is infallible; there is, for instance, no such thing as getting the concept "table" wrong. Even if a child forms a concept of "table" that differs somewhat from the concept that adults name by that word, the child is nonetheless aware of whatever similarities he is aware of, and his condensation of the similar concretes cannot be faulted.

The same is true of the application of simple concepts when a child forms his first propositions, such as "That is a table." All that is required is the minimal effort of attention to the thing before him and the recollection of what the word "table" means. Even though he may err in application, as when he thinks the distant hills are blue, the process is too simple to require *methodology*, nor could the child at such an early stage grasp rules to follow. But on the middle and (especially) the higher levels of conceptual cognition, conscious adherence to rules (logic) is required in order to identify facts objectively.

In accordance with the identity of reality and the identity of conceptual consciousness (especially, the two facts stated above), there are two overarching facts about the nature of knowledge that we must adhere to: knowledge is contextual and hierarchical. The two basic injunctions of the Objectivist conception of logic are: *hold context* and *obey hierarchy*. [OPAR, CH. 4] Though context and hierarchy are closely interconnected, let's look at each in turn.

CONTEXT

Knowledge is contextual: it consists not of isolated atoms of information but of a network, a fabric of interwoven connections.

The word "context" suggests by its structure ("con" + "text") the simplest meaning of "context": the surrounding text. In reading a given word or phrase, one needs to hold in mind the sentence of which it is a part. Likewise, the sentence is part of a paragraph, section, chapter, etc. Meaning is contextual: without a context, one does not know the right way to interpret an isolated term — e.g., the word "one," as used earlier in this sentence.

Peikoff defines "context" as: "the sum of cognitive elements conditioning an item of knowledge." [OPAR, 123]

The contextual nature of knowledge reflects a metaphysical fact and an epistemological one. Metaphysically, reality is an interconnected whole; not only are there no contradictions in reality but also each existent is part of the same, causally interconnected universe.[101] Epistemologically, consciousness works by relating things — i.e., by detecting differences and, in the case of human consciousness, by detecting similarities (based on differentiation from a foil).

On the perceptual level, integration occurs automatically: one's brain automatically combines sensory inputs to present one with an integrated, global field of awareness embracing all sense modalities. Perceptual awareness is automatically contextual. But on the conceptual level, in order to go beyond obvious things that occur to one automatically, one must actively choose to do the work of integrating new observations and ideas into the existing structure of one's knowledge.

Contextuality is inherent in man's conceptual activities at every level. The basic act of concept-formation is clearly contextual: concepts are formed by grasping relationships of similarity against a background of difference (see Chapters 3 and 4). Propositions are formed to relate subject and predicate (see CHAPTER 5), which allows the knowledge embodied in the predicate to be applied to the subject, and also to integrate into the wider context, since the predicate itself is connected to other conceptualized information (see the end of CHAPTER 5). Going still higher, principles, theories, and whole sciences are each formed in a context and apply in that context.

---

101 Hume's claim that every "event" is "loose and disconnected from every other" results from his wrong, sensationalist view of perception. Contra Hume, in perception we are aware of a world of entities, not of floating sensory qualities (see CHAPTER 2).

The network of knowledge has its base in a literal, physical network: the neural network of the nervous system. We must distinguish process and product in this regard. The process of grasping a fact is a *mental* activity; the storage of that grasp is accomplished *physically*, by some alteration of the neural network.

I can say a little, in a general way, about the mechanics of the interaction between the mental process and its physical products. When one brings together two or more items in one frame of awareness and grasps how they relate — such as that they are similar in a certain way or that one causes the other — that grasp, if intense enough, gets "saved to disk" — i.e., is encoded physically by a specific type of change in the brain. The stored and recallable grasp of a factual relationship *is* the stored knowledge, the knowledge qua permanent product. (Note that even when asleep, one still possesses knowledge — which exists as a potential: the ability, when awake, to recall things previously grasped; that potential is due to permanent neural encoding.)

But this ability of the brain to form lasting connections is of little cognitive or practical value if done by random association. When the two items in focal awareness are co-present only by coincidence, what the brain stores (when such storage occurs) is a random association, not a logical connection. The difference is all-important. Only a conscious, rational process can distinguish mere coincidence from a logical relationship. What logic demands is not *random association* but *integration*, and to achieve integration requires working to achieve both clarity and precision. Attaining clarity and precision is a precondition of checking for consistency. One cannot check the unclear or the vague for its coherence with the rest of one's knowledge.

The random associations that occur in the normal course of life pose no problem — provided one recognizes them as being random associations. For instance, it is said that most people remember where they were when they learned of some shocking event, such as the shooting of John F. Kennedy or the attack on the World Trade Center. But everyone is aware that this is random association: it is obvious that there is no logical connection between, say, one's having been on a picnic in Pasadena and Kennedy's having been shot in Dallas. In other areas, however, people can be unaware that they have mistaken correlation for causation, details for essentials, familiarity for universality.

The ability to rise above random associations is what separates man from the animals. Animals function by random association of perceptual concretes. An animal that is burned by a flame will subsequently fear and avoid anything that is perceptually similar. A man can analyze the factors that make the flame more or less dangerous, such as the flame's intensity and proximity; he can learn what is flammable and what is not, and use the latter to shield himself from the flame's heat; he can learn what extinguishes a flame and what fuels it. Thus, he learns how to tame fire and make it serve his needs.

The wider point is that logic directs us to work to reach a clear, precise awareness of the specific nature of the relationships existing among things. Logic directs us not to rest with "fire has to do with stuff that burns," but "fire requires heat, oxygen, and a flammable substance that serves as its fuel."

Prometheus' gift of fire would have had no value to a being restricted to the gross, unanalyzed associations occurring on the perceptual level. A conceptual being is able to break down the perceptually given into its characteristics and components and to identify each conceptually. Man's mastery of nature stems from this ability to rise to the conceptual level, to use concepts to analyze concretes, to logically identify causal factors, and thus turn the nature-given causal powers of entities to the service of his needs.

All items of knowledge are interrelated, and every item of knowledge is acquired, maintained, and used according to its relationship to the rest of one's knowledge.[102] Knowledge is a network of discriminated and interrelated content, not scattered bits acquired in separate "revelations." Expanding one's knowledge is like adding the next pieces to a jigsaw puzzle: each new item must attach to those adjacent to it, if it is to cohere with and add to the whole.[103] Thus, the point that knowledge is contextual goes to the essence of what knowledge is: a growing network of interconnected material.

The *immediate* context of an item is the knowledge directly connecting to it — as the knowledge that Phoenix is in Arizona connects directly to the knowledge that Arizona is a U.S. state. The *wider* context consists of the things directly related to that, and then the things directly related to them, and so on — such that the *full* context is the totality of one's knowledge at a given time.

Since every fact bears some relationship to every other fact, however remote, one must work to *integrate one's knowledge into a non-contradictory whole.* Rand's important summary statement is:

---

102 Even the first item of knowledge one acquires is contextual. Knowledge begins with perception, and perception is not of an isolated datum but of the world, with its panoply of entities. Perception is inherently wholistic and contextual.

103 The jigsaw metaphor was suggested by Jean Moroney.

No concept man forms is valid unless he integrates it without contradiction into the total sum of his knowledge. [AS, 1016.][104]

Doing the work of integration is a multifold process, requiring more than good intentions. One has to understand and follow the rules of the "non-contradictory identification" that constitutes logic. Take: "Tax cuts would stimulate the economy." Is there any contradiction in that idea? That question cannot be answered by simply posing it. There are myriad questions and subquestions one has to consider in order to deal *logically* with that issue. The whole science of economics and of its philosophic base, as well as a knowledge of history and of the nature of man, is involved in reaching a logical conclusion.

In integrating something into the total sum of one's knowledge, there are two stages. First, one checks the coherence and consistency of the new item with its "nearest relatives" forming its immediate context. One needs to ask oneself, "How does this relate to the things in the next wider category (its genus)?" "What are its immediate causes (both of the thing and of one's knowledge of it)?" "What are its direct applications and/or implications?" and, "What are other examples or instances of this?" In each case, one is both looking for positive connections and checking for possible contradictions. (Depending on the results one reaches, this may call for further integration.)

The second stage of integration is wider: one sets a "standing order" in one's mind — a settled intention — to carry forward the process of integration into the future. That is, if one has reached a conclusion (or formed a hypothesis), one commits oneself to being alert to additional information that one can connect to the item.

The injunction to integrate, i.e., to "hold context," pertains to the application of knowledge as well as to its acquisition. In applying one's knowledge, one must give due attention to the specifics of the case at hand. Concepts and generalizations cannot be treated as contextless formulas or rote rules. The mechanical, context-blind application of knowledge constitutes a fallacy, one identified by Aristotle and now known as "The Fallacy of Accident."[105]

---

104 In this passage, Rand uses "concept" to mean any conceptual product, including propositions, theories, etc.

105 A Wikipedia article gives a good example of this fallacy: Cutting people with a knife is a crime. Surgeons cut people with a knife. Therefore, surgeons are criminals.

Rand's term "context-dropping" names the wider error: ignoring available facts that would alter or contradict one's conclusion.

A simple form of context-dropping is that involved in irrational behavior. An action is irrational if it stems from evading the long-range consequences. It is context-dropping to function on the basis of a kind of tunnel-vision that restricts one's range of view to the here and now. Overspending facilitated by a credit card may be satisfying for the range of the moment, but it carries a long-term penalty. Defrauding someone may bring you cash today, but in the full context it exacts an unpayable price: setting yourself up as an enemy of every honest man and instituting a state of war with reality.[106] Any action that sacrifices the long-range to the short-range represents context-dropping.

Peikoff recounts a striking example of what context-dropping means. Here is his analysis of Neville Chamberlain's appeasement of Hitler's demands regarding Czechoslovakia, at the Munich conference in 1938:

> Mr. Chamberlain treated Hitler's demand as an isolated fact to be dealt with by an isolated response; to do this, he had to drop an immense amount of knowledge. He did not relate Hitler's demand to the knowledge already gained about the nature of Nazism; he did not ask for causes. He did not relate the demand to his knowledge of similar demands voiced by aggressor nations and even local bullies throughout history; he did not ask for principles. He did not relate his own policy to mankind's knowledge of the results of appeasement; despite ample indications, he did not ask whether his capitulation, besides satisfying Hitler, would also embolden him, increase his resources, hearten his allies, undermine his opponents, and thus achieve the opposite of its stated purpose. Chamberlain was not concerned with any aspect of a complex situation beyond the single point he chose to consider in isolation: that he would be removing Hitler's immediate frustration.
>
> Deeper issues are involved in this example. Chamberlain was proposing a course of action while ignoring the field that defines the principles of proper action, ethics. He did not ask whether his course comported with the virtues of honor, courage, integrity — and, if not, what consequences this portended.

---

106   On the latter, see OPAR, 267–276.

He dropped the fact that foreign-policy decisions, like all human actions, fall within a wider context defined by moral philosophy (and by several other subjects as well). The prime minister wanted "peace at any price." The price included the evasion of political philosophy, history, psychology, ethics, and more. The result was war. [OPAR, 124–125]

The more one works to integrate, the better one's mental filing system and the easier further integration becomes. A proper filing system deals in *essentials*.[107] As a consequence, the task of integration becomes progressively more efficient. And of course one does not set about integrating at random ("Does my conclusion about tax cuts integrate with the Pythagorean theorem?"). Moreover, if one has formed concepts properly, one's mental file folders will have a certain hierarchically nested structure, and that also aids the integrative process. One asks: "What is taxation?", "What are the consequences of taxation on the individual? On government financing?", "What is the source of economic progress?", etc.

The effects of tax cuts are part of the science of economics, which is part of the social sciences. Knowing the "tree of knowledge" vastly accelerates the needed integration, allowing for things to be integrated wholesale. The Pythagorean theorem, for instance, is part of geometry, which is part of mathematics; the required integration is not that of tax cuts with the theorem but rather the integration of the entire field of mathematics with the entire field of the social sciences. The overall integration of two such sciences is very abstract, but fairly straightforward, and one would have no reason to expect to find an inconsistency between them. (E.g., economics presupposes and uses mathematics, since economics deals with quantitative relations, but mathematics does not presuppose or use principles of economics; mathematics, though devised by man, studies all quantitative relationships, whereas economics studies an aspect of man—his interactions in production and trade; mathematics is a science of method—of calculation and measurement, whereas economics is a theoretical science, etc.[108])

---

107 The Objectivist theory of "essential" will be discussed in the next chapter.

108 In fields other than philosophy and mathematics, integration usually requires acquiring new data by fresh perceptual observations. (For philosophy, the observational base is the common knowledge we have gained as civilized adults; for mathematics, the base is provided by simple observations about quantity and shapes. In neither field does one need to acquire new information about concretes to get new data—although doing so may aid one's thinking.)

Integrating an idea into the full context is a demanding activity — far more demanding than the simple act of combining two premises in a syllogism. Proper integration consists of a conscientious process of checking the idea against (the essentials of) all of one's knowledge, actively looking for possible contradictions or counter-data. It also requires the commitment to doing fresh thinking should any interesting or problematic facts arise in the future (such thinking is normally an enjoyable, rewarding process.)

The fact that knowledge is contextual has crucial implications for the field of epistemology: the standards of judging an idea's validity must take into account the contextual nature of knowledge. No cognitive standard can require one to have more knowledge than is possible at a given stage of cognitive development. One cannot require that, for instance, in order to attain certainty, one must know everything that could bear upon one's conclusion — i.e., be omniscient. One cannot downgrade or invalidate actual cognition because it is contextual. Standards must adjust to reality, not begin with a fantasy (omniscience) and downgrade what is real by reference to what is dreamed up. [BINSWANGER, 1981] Standards must judge by reference to what is possible within the available context of knowledge.

If an idea is supported by observation and integrates with all the knowledge available, that idea is valid. Its validity is not retroactively undone if, as occasionally happens, the idea has to be subsequently qualified, or even rejected, on the basis of new data. Given the context of knowledge that one possessed, the idea was either reached logically or it wasn't — and that fact about the past situation never changes. The issue is not: "What would one conclude if one were omniscient?" but: "what is the proper conclusion to draw given all the facts available now?" *Epistemic standards are prospective, not retrospective.*[109]

Contextuality thus has a dual application: 1) one must be consistent with *all* the knowledge currently available, and 2) a standard cannot require consistency with the as-yet-unknown. "Man *cannot* know more than he has discovered — and he *may not* know less than the evidence indicates, if his concepts and definitions are to be objectively valid." [ITOE, 46] The purpose of standards is to guide one's *present* choices.

---

109 Even retrospectively, the issue is: "What should I have done, given what I knew (or should have known) at the time?"

HIERARCHY

In CHAPTER 4, I discussed the hierarchical nature of concepts, but hierarchy is a much wider phenomenon: every aspect of conceptual knowledge is hierarchical. Hierarchy is essential to logic, and the anti-hierarchical approach is the one factor most responsible for the confused and chaotic state of today's intellectual world.

"Hierarchy" as a general term pertains to a number of ways in which things exist in an order of dependency, but the specific meaning of hierarchy I will focus on is: the hierarchy of learning—i.e., *the necessary order of acquiring knowledge*. This is the kind of dependency that occurs when knowing *A* is a prerequisite of learning *B*, as knowing arithmetic is a prerequisite of learning algebra. In this hierarchical relationship, *A* grounds *B*.

The dependency here is *causal* dependency—but the causality is that operative in cognition, not physical causality. "Hierarchy" refers to how certain *knowledge* makes possible other *knowledge*, not to what causes what in the external world. For instance, consider the order of grandfather and father. Existentially, the grandfather came into being before and caused the existence of the father; but epistemically, the order is exactly the reverse: first one forms the concept "father," and only then can one grasp the idea of a parent's father—i.e., "grandfather."[110]

The hierarchy of knowledge is epistemological; it is not some structure that exists in the external world (see CHAPTER 4). But the hierarchy reflects two metaphysical facts. First, the range of things that the senses can respond to is metaphysically given. We cannot, for example, respond to ultraviolet light, so our knowledge of ultraviolet depends hierarchically upon inference from what we do perceive. Second, some differences are too great to be accommodated by our limited "crow" capacity. For instance, the differences between trees and dogs are more numerous and extensive than the differences between dogs and cats. Accordingly, to integrate "dog" and "tree" into "organism," we need to advance in "crow-friendly" steps. Only after we have formed and become familiar with the concepts "animal" and "plant," are we able to contrast both of them to non-living things, such as rocks and rivers.

---

110 The hierarchy of knowledge pertains to the content of knowledge, not to its external conditions. E.g., to learn algebra, one has to stay alive, but knowing how to obtain food, shelter, etc. is not part of the hierarchical base of algebra. The hierarchy of knowledge concerns *cognitive prerequisites*: the earlier identifications that have to be used in grasping later ones. To grasp "the father of a father," one must use the knowledge of what a father is; to grasp that 2 + 2 = 4 one must use the knowledge of what 2 and 4 are.

The intermediate concepts are condensations that make "room" for grasping how dogs and trees are similar. (By analogy, ladders are necessary to reach things that are too high; and the spacing of rungs is set by the size of man's step, just as man's cognitive tools must be adapted to the size of the "crow.")

A vivid illustration of how the "crow" creates the need for a sequence of condensations, and thus hierarchy, is provided by numbers. To grasp the concept "million," a child first has to have formed the concepts of the numbers one through ten, then "hundred" as ten tens, "thousand" as ten hundreds, before he can finally reach "million" as one thousand thousands.

Hierarchy is an aspect — the structural aspect — of context. Hierarchy is the context insofar as it exhibits epistemic dependencies. For instance, the concept of "dog" and the concept of "cat" are clearly related parts of one *context*, the context of one's knowledge of domesticated animals. But there is no *hierarchy* between "dog" and "cat": one does not need to form "dog" on the basis of already having formed "cat" or vice-versa. In contrast, the concept of "kennel" is not only contextually related to the concept of "dog," it is *hierarchically* dependent on "dog." One could not form the concept "kennel" if one did not already have the concept "dog."

Peikoff summarizes the relation of hierarchy and context:

> A hierarchy is a type of context. The contextual view of know-ledge states that cognition is relational. The hierarchical view identifies a particular kind of cognitive relationship: it states not only that every (non-axiomatic) item has a context, but also that such context itself has an inner structure of logical dependence, rising gradually from a base of first-level items. The principle of context takes an overview; it looks at the sum of knowledge already acquired and says: it *is* a sum. The principle of hier-archy looks at the process by which a given item was learned and says: the simpler steps made the more complex ones possible. [OPAR, 132][111]

The need to obey hierarchy has long been recognized in regard to infer-ence. The well-known fallacy of "begging the question" (*petitio principii*) consists of a hierarchy violation: illicitly using what was to be proved, in the attempt to prove it — i.e., circular reasoning. The textbook example of question-begging is: "There must be a God because the Bible says there is,

---

111 In general, I depend heavily on Peikoff's discussion of hierarchy in OPAR pp. 129–132, and in many of his articles and lectures.

and I know the Bible is true because it is the word of God." That is a hierarchy violation: *A* cannot be established by *B*, if *B* has to be established by *A*.

More widely, the injunction to obey hierarchy means never to treat an idea as if it could be known or used in disregard of the knowledge that is hierarchically prior to it — i.e., on which its grasp and intelligibility depend.

In contemporary philosophy, some minimal attention is given to the issue of an item's immediate context, but there is total, blithe unconcern with hierarchy. To understand the issue of hierarchy, one must be very clear on the difference between uttering a word and grasping its meaning. But, under the influence of nominalism, philosophers have denied there is any difference between "socially approved linguistic behavior" and grasping the meaning of a concept. Thus, the philosophic establishment first opposed, then became blind to the issue of which concepts depend on which prior concepts.

For instance, a leading philosopher of the 20th century, Willard van Orman Quine, proclaimed:

> Any statement can be held true come what may, if we make drastic enough adjustments elsewhere in the system. Even a statement very close to the periphery can be held true in the face of recalcitrant experience by pleading hallucination or by amending certain statements of the kind called logical laws. . . . Revision even of the logical law of the excluded middle has been proposed . . . .
> [QUINE 1953B, 43]

Quine's is not a minority position.[112] But his flippant dismissal of hierarchy flops when examined. E.g., there is no way that "pleading hallucination" could work to hold as true "Sand is food." And what "adjustments elsewhere in the system" could make it possible to reject the laws of logic? Those laws, including Excluded Middle, are the hierarchical base of all conceptual functioning. The very idea of "revision" implies that the revision is what it is, that it is not what it is not, and that it is not a nothing. What "adjustments" could preserve algebra while denying arithmetic? Or could hold onto the concept "orphan" while denying the concept "parent"? Quine is here denying the patent fact that some knowledge uses and builds upon prior knowledge — i.e., he is

---

112 For one of the most stunningly anti-hierarchical passages in the history of thought, see Nelson Goodman's claim that one could form the concepts "green" and "blue" on the basis of (impossibly) first forming his (absurd) concepts "grue" and "bleen." [GOODMAN, 79–80]

denying hierarchy. His motive is to "espouse a more thorough pragmatism." That means: to negate the axioms of existence, identity, and consciousness.

Quine's opposition to hierarchy represents an epistemological egalitarianism: all propositions are held to be equal, so that we can deny any one of them and avoid the consequences by revising, at whim, any of the others. In terms of the construction industry, this would mean: we can remove the ground floor and support the second floor by hanging it from some of the higher floors. But what supports those higher floors? Can we deny the evidence supporting a given conclusion and still "hold onto" that conclusion? Only by *making things up* to support the preferred conclusion. And in some cases, such as denying axioms, even that is not possible. Try denying that existence exists and holding onto, say, "Wines can be red or white" when one has just claimed that wine, along with everything else, does not exist.

Another 20th-century philosopher, Wilfrid Sellars, launched a highly influential attack on the very foundation of hierarchy: the perceptual base of all knowledge, which he describes as "the myth of the given." This is a colossal stolen concept: the concept of "myth" denotes a product of imagination in distinction from that which is based on observation — i.e., on the perceptually given. To say it is a myth that perception is the given is to say that basing ideas on observation flouts the need to base ideas on observation. If the self-evident status of perceived fact were a myth, what, then, would distinguish myth from non-myth? What would it mean to say, "Centaurs are mythical creatures"? Nothing. And it means precisely nothing to say "the given is a myth."

THE SPIRAL PROCESS OF KNOWLEDGE

Although knowledge cannot be acquired out of hierarchical order, the growth of knowledge is not just a unidirectional, linear progression. There is also a process of spiraling back — the use of hierarchically later knowledge to add depth and content to hierarchically prior knowledge. The hierarchical order may be A–B–C, but relating C back to A will nonetheless add to one's understanding of A. Here, I distinguish "understanding" from "grasp." The hierarchical order states the order in which items must be grasped. That means: to grasp C, one must have already grasped B, which in turn required a prior grasp of A. But once a fact has been grasped, one's *understanding* of it can grow in all directions, expanding with each integration one makes to other items of knowledge, even to the hierarchically later knowledge that it grounds.

For instance, grasping the concept of "wine" is hierarchically prior to making distinctions among types of wine — red vs. white, dry vs. sweet, Burgundy vs. Merlot — but coming to know each of these subsequent facts adds to one's understanding of wine, enhancing and enriching it.

Grasp is an all or nothing affair — either one has taken secure cognitive hold of a fact or one has not — but *understanding* admits of degrees. One understands a topic better and better as one learns more and more about it. (But omniscience is not the standard: gaining an expanded understanding of something does not mean that previously one had understood nothing at all about it.) Understanding an item comes from connecting it to other knowledge, and the more connections made, the fuller the understanding. As Rand observes:

> To understand means to focus on the content of a given subject . . . to isolate its essentials, to establish its relationship to the previously known, and to integrate it with the appropriate categories of other subjects. Integration is the essential part of understanding. [RP, 68]

For example, take the simple recognition that the sun moves across the sky from east to west. *Grasping* that fact was hierarchically required in order to reach the knowledge (discovered by Copernicus, et al.) that the Earth rotates on its axis while it orbits the sun. But having reached that later knowledge adds to one's *understanding* of the sun's apparent motion. For instance, in conjunction with the later knowledge of the tilt of the Earth's axis, it explains why the sun's path across the sky changes with the seasons, why the seasons are reversed in the Southern Hemisphere, and it makes intelligible the observed fact that sunspots move across the sun (the sun is rotating on its axis, too).

In the case of concepts, there is another important order besides hierarchical order: the order of generality. The hierarchy of concepts is the order in which concepts must be formed. Starting from the perceptual level, the conceptual hierarchy proceeds in two directions, "up" (wider integrations) and "down" (subdivision) (see CHAPTER 4). In order to learn "collie," one must have grasped the concept "dog"; and in order to go "up" from "dog" to "animal," one must have conceptualized some other animals — e.g., "cat," "horse," and "pig." But once all these concepts have been formed, they are organized in one's mental filing system according to their generality, which gives a different order: collie-dog-animal.

Whatever the order in which concepts are formed, a given concept, once formed, subsumes its subdivisions, and when a file folder is stored inside a larger one, it "inherits" the knowledge that the larger folder contains. Conversely, the larger folder gains in content when subfolders are added inside it. Again, although one cannot grasp what it is for something to be a Burgundy before knowing what it is to be wine, one gains a fuller, richer understanding of wine when one learns that wines can have the color, flavor, and body of a Burgundy in distinction to those of a Merlot.

Spiraling back through the hierarchy also enriches the narrower concepts that were used to form wider ones. Consider how forming "animal" adds to one's understanding of what it is to be a dog. Even if "dog" was one of the concepts that a given child used in forming "animal," his realization that a dog is an animal gives him a wider knowledge of dogs. For instance, it enables him to see how dogs differ from plants and are similar to other animals — including their similarity to the very animals from which dogs were differentiated when he formed the concept "dog."

Going even wider, the realization that dogs are living organisms requires that one see dogs as being similar to trees and grass but different from stones and automobiles. In other words, here too, the later concept illuminates the earlier concept on which it depends.[113]

For a more interesting example of the spiral, take the child's progression in understanding money. "Money" is an integration wider than the concept of some specific form of money — dollars, francs, yen, etc. But consider an American child who has learned "money" from his experience with only American bills and coins. He understands that these bills and coins are things universally accepted as payment (i.e., serve as a medium of exchange) and that they can be saved (i.e., are a store of value). Later, he learns that in other countries, money takes different forms — euros, pounds, pesetas. Still later, he learns that in other times gold, silver, and even salt or sea shells served as money. He did not need this advanced information in order to grasp "money," but learning it enhances his understanding of money.

The general point captured by "the spiral process of knowledge" is that integrating an item into an expanded context of knowledge enhances the understanding of each item in that context — whatever its hierarchical

---

113 I am not sure that it is quite accurate to say that a wider concept depends on any particular one of the narrower concepts used in forming the wider concept, since one could have used some other narrower concept to make the widening. But this subtlety is unimportant to the overall discussion of spiralling.

provenance. But gaining that understanding presupposes that one has grasped the item in the first place, which requires the hierarchical progression.

Logic is not a desiccated concern with the rules of deduction or a game of manipulating symbols. Logic is the means of keeping conceptual cognition connected to reality. Since conceptual cognition is a process of progressive, stepwise integration, the two essentials of logic are context and hierarchy. Logic demands that one ground each conclusion in perceived facts or in knowledge derived from perceived facts, and that one integrate the conclusion into the full context. What this means in actual practice is the subject of the next chapter.

7

LOGIC: PRACTICE

U P TO THIS POINT, THE MATERIAL COVERED HAS BEEN DESCRIPTIVE
rather than normative. I have described how we know — when we do
indeed attain knowledge, i.e., when the process of cognition has succeeded.
But the purpose of describing what successful cognition consists of is to
define the oughts — i.e., the norms and standards to which our thinking
must adhere if we are to acquire actual knowledge of reality. Theory is for
practice, and I turn now to the practical application of all the preceding
theory: the rules of logic. This is not a textbook, however, and completeness is not my aim in the following presentation. I have sought to restrict
the topics I cover to those that are essential to logical thinking, giving
more attention to topics that are likely to be new to the reader — either
because classical, Aristotelian logic has come to be neglected in college
courses on logic, or because the material was originated by Ayn Rand
(or, in one or two minor instances, by me). It is widely assumed today that
logic deals only with inference, but logic exists to provide guidance for all the
conceptual functions that are subject to volitional control. Thus, logic covers:
concept-formation, propositional judgment, and inference. The present chapter
takes up each of these, in turn.

Logic and Concepts

In the preceding chapter, I stressed the need to recognize the hierarchy of concepts — the fact that some concepts (e.g., "sophomore") can be grasped only on the basis of first grasping prior concepts ("student"). This gives rise to a question: since the hierarchy represents a *necessary* order of forming concepts, why does logic need to tell us to obey it? Why isn't the alternative simply: either one goes through the proper, hierarchical progression or one is flatly unable to proceed?

The first answer is that obeying the hierarchy is necessary — to form actual *concepts*. On the higher levels of abstractions, many people form only approximate concepts, words used by imitating the way others use them. Such half-baked, semi-formed concepts cannot be applied accurately to their units. Accordingly, Rand calls them "floating abstractions."

Floating abstractions are cognitive cripplers. They represent, in Rand's words, "condensing fog into fog into thicker fog — until the hierarchical structure of concepts breaks down ... losing all ties to reality." [ITOE, 76]

Consider the vague, woozy manner in which many people hold and use such higher-level concepts as "love," "freedom," and "justice." Such people are clear on the application of these concepts to a few simple concretes; they know, for example, that a slave held in chains is not free. But, not having gone through the hierarchical steps necessary to attain a full, clear grasp of these concepts, people can use them in bizarre and contradictory ways, resulting in romantic, political, and moral chaos, respectively.

There is a second reason why the hierarchical progression, though necessary, can yet be violated. Even if one did go through all the required steps when first forming a given concept, one may not remember that hierarchy years later. Thus one may not notice the fact that a given proposition uses that concept in a way that violates the conceptual hierarchy, resulting in committing the fallacy of the stolen concept.

The main remedy for both floating abstractions and stolen concepts is the process of *definition*. "A definition is a statement that identifies the nature of the units subsumed under a concept." [ITOE, 40]

The Function of Definitions

A definition serves the function of isolating a concept's units, thus providing the concept with a specific identity.

Every word, except proper names, denotes a concept. An average English speaker knows something like 30,000 words. How is he to keep each concept attached to its specific referents in reality, particularly when the same concrete can be classified under many different concepts? I am a referent of "man," "animal," "philosopher," "American," "husband," "stockholder," "taxpayer," "civilian," and dozens of other concepts, so merely bringing an image of me to mind would not enable you to distinguish these concepts from each other. How can one organize 30,000 concepts? What keeps order in one's mind and distinguishes a given concept from every other? The definition.

The definition is analogous to the *label* on a (physical) file folder. The label indicates, as concisely as possible, what the folder contains — i.e., the nature of the information it stores — just as a concept's definition allows one to quickly recognize the meaning of the concept — i.e., the nature of the units it integrates. A proper label also permits organizing the file folders, so that one can place related files together inside larger file folders, put those into file drawers, and organize file drawers into file cabinets and banks of file cabinets. With 30,000 such files, this is not a mere "convenience," but a matter of cognitive necessity.[114]

(Certain concepts can be defined only *ostensively* — by pointing to or otherwise indicating instances and contrasting them with appropriate foils. Rand places in this category axiomatic concepts, such as "existence," "identity," and "consciousness," and concepts of the primary aspects of experience — "sensations" in her terminology. [ITOE, 40–41] Neither what it is to exist nor what it is to feel pain or to taste the sweetness of sugar can be analyzed into anything prior. To isolate or communicate these primaries, one can only give examples and foils.)

The Rules of Proper Definition

A definition's vital function can be performed only if it meets certain requirements. We owe the rules of proper definition to Aristotle. The Aristotelian rules have importance far beyond their role in definition; they illustrate the pattern of conceptual cognition as such: differentiation and integration. Traditionally, however, these rules are stated in negative terms; I have reformulated them as positives. I also have reorganized them slightly and

---

114 Reflecting her stress on the need for definitions, Rand defined over 100 philosophic terms in her nonfiction writings. See *Glossary of Objectivist Definitions*, Kunze & Moroney, 1999.

put them into an Objectivist context, giving them new names, when doing so clarifies their function.

The justification of these rules is that they serve the *purpose* of a definition: they spell out the method of identifying a concept's meaning — a method adapted to the identity of man's consciousness.

1. The rule of genus and differentia

One of Aristotle's great achievements is the idea of defining concepts by means of genus and differentia. The *genus* is the wider class containing both the concept's units and those things from which they are differentiated. E.g., for "triangle," the genus is "polygon," which is the wider class that contains triangles, quadrilaterals, pentagons, etc. The *differentia* is the characteristic(s) that distinguishes the units from the other existents in the genus — here "three-sided." A "triangle" is a three-sided polygon. (In Objectivist terms, the genus is the class of things having the Conceptual Common Denominator, CCD, along which the units are differentiated from foils; the differentia is a range or category of measurements within that CCD.)

The definition must consist of a genus and a differentia.

The genus-differentia structure is the most efficient means of isolating the concept's units from all other existents. Beginning the definitional process by identifying the genus narrows one's focus, so that instead of considering the entire universe, one is focusing on a class that is only one step wider than the "species" — i.e., the class of things one is seeking to define. Identifying the genus gets one into the proverbial "ballpark," making it fairly easy to go on to differentiate the concept's units from their nearest "relatives." Moreover, the most efficient means of organizing concepts is to set up a nested progression: species within genus, within still wider genus, and so on — e.g., "triangle" within "polygon," within "plane figure," within "shape."

The genus-differentia structure of a definition helps one to, in effect, quickly re-form the concept, and thus recapture the concept's meaning. Rand writes:

> The rules of correct definition are derived from the process of concept-formation. The units of a concept were differentiated — by means of a distinguishing characteristic(s) — from other existents possessing a commensurable characteristic,

a "Conceptual Common Denominator." A definition follows the same principle: it specifies the distinguishing characteristic(s) of the units, and indicates the category of existents from which they were differentiated.

The distinguishing characteristic(s) of the units becomes the *differentia* of the concept's definition; the existents possessing a "Conceptual Common Denominator" become the *genus*.

Thus a definition complies with the two essential functions of consciousness: differentiation and integration. The differentia isolates the units of a concept from all other existents; the genus indicates their connection to a wider group of existents. [ITOE, 41]

A proper definition must have both a genus and a differentia. When the genus is omitted, a mistake often made by uncritical thinkers, the result is an unorganizable approximation, as in "An 'automobile' is what you drive." A proper definition of "automobile" must contain its genus: "motor vehicle."

One popular form of omitting the genus is the barbarous use of "is when": "A 'crime' is when someone violates another's rights." A proper definition would be: "A 'crime' is an action violating another's rights."

The other breach of this first rule is the omission of the differentia. "A 'table' is an item of furniture." "'Literature' is an art-form." There is nothing wrong with these statements as statements, but they are not definitions because they do not isolate the concept's referents from non-referents within its genus.

A proper definition must not only contain both a genus and a differentia, it may not add in any extraneous element. A definition consists *only* of the genus and differentia.[115]

"Man is a rational animal." Not: "Man is a rational animal, like my father."

Extraneous information distracts from the essentials and violates the rule of unit-economy (rule 5, below).

Identifying a concept's genus is comparatively easy but immensely valuable. It brings clarity to one's thinking and is indispensable to the integration of one's knowledge.

---

115 In some cases, additional terms are required to meet special cognitive needs. Two such cases are: 1) including the recognizable, sensory qualities of physical objects (as "flat level surface" is included in "table"), and 2) including the process by which a product is made (e.g., for "cake" including that it is baked, and for "knowledge" including that it is based on perception and/or reason).

A personal example will serve to dramatize the crucial role of the genus. While teaching college logic, I had one interchange that helped me appreciate the importance of the genus. Having just covered the topic of definitions and worked through some simple examples, it was time to give the students a harder term to define. Since inflation was a growing concern at that time, that was the term I asked the class to define. I began by asking for the genus of "inflation." The answer I wanted was something like "economic condition."

One student volunteered the answer that the genus of inflation is "money." But "money" is a kind of thing, an entity, whereas inflation is a condition. Hoping to lead him to see that he had the wrong basic category ("entity," instead of "condition"), I asked the student: "What is the genus of "money"? Without hesitation, he answered: "survival." Stunned, but intrigued, I asked him, "And what's the genus of survival?" "Food" he answered. We went on like this through several more concepts, wandering around in his hopelessly disorganized mental filing system, until I gave up.

This student was connecting concepts by random association, failing to notice major differences among types of relationships, e.g., subsumption vs. causation. The organization of his mental files amounted to: inflation relates to money, money relates to survival, survival relates to food — and so on. All those relationships do exist, but each is a different type of relationship, and none identifies the genus of its subject.

The failure to specify and differentiate such relationships sabotages logical thinking. If one has inflation filed under its proper genus — economic condition — thinking about inflation will activate in one's mind the proper, logical context. A logical context will make prominent the data on closely related economic conditions — in this case: deflation. That is the data that is most logically relevant. Without that context, one is prey to all sorts of confusions. For instance, suppose one is considering the popular notion that inflation is due to greed. If one has filed inflation as the contrary of deflation, one is primed to notice a problem with the greed-explanation: if inflation is due to greed, then deflation would be due to lack of greed, too much self-denial. But that clashes with other facts. For instance, in the last huge deflation — the Great Depression — people were not less concerned with ("greedy" for) money.

Identifying the proper genus leads one to ask the right questions — here: "What distinguishes inflation from deflation?" On a common-sense level, inflation is marked by a rise in the general level of prices, deflation by a fall. And that raises a new question: "What is the general price-level?" The genus of "general price-level" is "price." The genus of "price" is: an amount of money (the differentia is: "paid per unit in purchase of a good"). A price is thus a ratio (money spent per good), and the general price-level is the equivalent aggregate ratio: the economy-wide spending divided by the total quantity of goods sold. A rise in the general price-level is an increase in that ratio, a fact drawing our attention to the two things that can make that ratio increase: an expansion of the money supply or a diminished supply of goods. (More investigation would be required to get a proper understanding of inflation, but the foregoing should be sufficient to illustrate the cognitive efficacy afforded by knowing the proper genus of each of one's concepts.)

In order to have an organized, efficiently functioning mind, one must have stored one's concepts in a nested series of genera. This amounts to having automatized such connections as: a dog is an animal, an animal is an organism, an organism is an entity. Or: dollar bills are currency, currency is money, money is a commodity (or claims to a commodity), a commodity is an entity. That is the kind of structure of links that brings order to one's mental files, making them into a system organized around essentials.

A definition is a proposition; propositions establish a specific relationship between a subject and a predicate, allowing the knowledge stored in the predicate to be applied to the subject. The species-to-genus relationship is extremely direct and intimate. It is the relationship of, e.g., tables to furniture, and of triangles to polygons. When one identifies the genus of a species, the link formed between the species and the genus becomes very strong — perhaps the strongest form of cognitive link there is, because one of those concepts (e.g., "furniture") can be formed by abstracting from the other ("table"). Therefore, keeping the genus in mind means that the most directly relevant information is potentiated for entry into conscious awareness.

2. The rule of reference

A definition isolates the units of a concept from all other existents. In order to do that, its formulation must actually direct the mind beyond mere words, to what those words stand for.

The definition must specify a group of referents in reality.

There are at least four ways in which a definition can fail to identify the concept's referents and thus violate this rule.

1. SYNONYMY: One cannot define a term by simply giving synonyms, nor can a definition depend upon the use of a synonym of the term being defined. Relying on synonyms simply transfers the question to the definition of the synonym, rather than pointing out referents in reality. E.g., take: "Fear is an emotion of being afraid." Since "afraid" is a synonym of "fear," this attempted definition does not specify referents in reality but merely switches the burden onto "afraid." (A valid definition of "fear," in general terms, would be: an emotion resulting from the evaluation of something as a threat to oneself or one's values.)

2. CIRCULARITY: A is defined in terms of B, when B has to be defined in terms of A. E.g., "Economics is the science pursued by economists." But "economist" has to be defined in terms of "economics." (The circularity may involve more than just two steps: it is still a circular definition when A is defined in terms of B, which is then defined in terms of C, which is then defined in terms of A.)

3. VAGUENESS: If the terms of the proposed definition are vague or unclear, referents are not specified. E.g., "Faith is the substance of things hoped for, the evidence of things not seen." Or Tolstoy's definition of "art": "Art is a human activity having for its purpose the transmission to others of the highest and best feelings to which men have risen." This definition fails to differentiate art from other human activities — e.g., from oratory and writing love-letters.

4. METAPHOR: Figurative language cannot substitute for literal truth. E.g., "Architecture is frozen music" makes an interesting comparison of music to architecture, but the statement does not serve the function of a definition: one could not use it to demarcate instances of architecture in reality.

3. The rule of scope

If a definition satisfies the rule of reference, so that it does isolate a specific set of existents, the next question that arises is: has it picked out the *right* set — i.e., exactly the things that are the units of the concept being defined? The definition's scope must match that of the concept; the definition must apply to all of the concept's (normal) units and only to them. In the negative formulation: a definition must be neither too broad nor too narrow.

The definition must have the same scope as the concept that it defines.

The issue here is truth. A definition that is too broad is false qua definition: it implies that things are units that are not, or vice-versa. For instance,
"A 'table' is an item of furniture with a flat top surface" implies that beds are
tables. A definition that is too narrow implies that some things that are units
are not units. For instance, "A 'table' is an item of furniture with four legs
and a flat, level surface for supporting smaller objects" implies that six-
legged tables are not tables. A proper differentia must characterize all and
only the units within the genus.

A proposed definition can easily be both too narrow and too broad.
For instance, "Man is a white animal" is both too narrow, excluding non-
Caucasians, and too broad, including polar bears.

Plato, in his dialogue the *Meno*, raised a problem that has bedeviled this
rule of definition: don't we need to know the definition in order to know
what the concept includes? But the rule directs us to judge the definition
by reference to what the concept includes. For instance, how do we know
whether or not a six-legged table is to count as a table, prior to having the
definition of "table"?

The answer to this apparent circularity becomes quite obvious once
one recognizes the basic fact that *concept-formation precedes definition*.
Prior to having a definition of a concept, we know what its units are.
We start from observation of reality, not from definitions. The definition is the final step in the process, not the first. The first step is observation of similarities and differences — the definition merely makes
explicit the similarity involved. We are aware pre-definitionally that
a six-legged table is similar to the other things we are classifying as tables.
The scope of a concept is determined by fundamental similarities and differences, and these are grasped prior to formulating a definition. The file exists
before one writes a label for its folder.

Sometimes one does indeed learn a concept by hearing another
person's definition of it, but this is learning from others, not learning from
direct observation of reality. And however many men learn the concept from
another man's definition, someone must have formed the concept for himself
in order that there be anyone to teach it to others. Furthermore, the student must bring to mind examples of the concept's referents in order to
properly understand the concept. The fundamental order here is: first one
has in mind the units of a concept, then one begins to formulate a definition
of that concept.

Not only is the scope of the concept set before the defining process begins, the definition, once formed, is not a substitute for the concept. The definition is merely the summary of the units' nature — the label on the file folder.

When applying the rule of scope: the "all and only" requirement applies to the *normal* units of the concept. For instance, in defining "man" one is not concerned to draw the line in evolution at which man evolved from the apes. Borderline cases are borderline cases, not tests of the definition. This follows from the fact that a concept pertains to a *range* of measurements. There is an issue of degree here, and one does not need, and cannot demand, infinite precision. A proper definition allows for borderline cases.

Likewise, it is no objection to defining "man" as "the rational animal" that immature, senile, or brain-damaged human beings lack the ability to use reason. These people are still members of the human species, and that is the species whose means of survival is the use of reason — which is what "rational" actually means in the definition. (Moreover, the genus "animal" already includes the fact of immature, defective, or diseased instances.) In general, defining is not a mechanical process; judgment is required.

The primary purpose of a definition is not to provide criteria for deciding whether or not a given item is to be subsumed under a given concept. Though a definition can serve as an aid in classifying an item, a definition is primarily for use in the other cognitive direction: pointing from a concept to its referents. Definitions tie a concept to its units, the units that constitute its meaning.

4. The rule of fundamentality

The next rule becomes necessary when, as often happens, there is more than one characteristic (or set of characteristics) that could serve to isolate the concept's units from the other existents within the genus. For example, all (normal) men and only men have a certain kind of shape, have the ability to make tools, have the ability to reason. Which of these distinguishing characteristics should be used as the differentia in the definition of "man"? The rule of fundamentality tells us:

The definition must state the fundamental distinguishing characteristic(s).

This rule is traditionally phrased in terms of stating the *essential* characteristic of the concept's referents. The essential characteristic is one of the distinguishing characteristics, the one that is *fundamental*. This fundamentality is a *causal* issue: the fundamental characteristic is the one that causes and explains the greatest number of other characteristics. Rand writes:

> When a given group of existents has more than one characteristic distinguishing it from other existents, man must observe the relationships among these various characteristics and discover the one on which all the others (or the greatest number of others) depend, i.e., the fundamental characteristic without which the others would not be possible. This fundamental characteristic is the essential distinguishing characteristic of the existents involved, and the proper *defining* characteristic of the concept.
>
> Metaphysically, a fundamental characteristic is that distinctive characteristic which makes the greatest number of others possible; epistemologically, it is the one that explains the greatest number of others.
>
> For instance, one could observe that man is the only animal who speaks English, wears wristwatches, flies airplanes, manufactures lipstick, studies geometry, reads newspapers, writes poems, darns socks, etc. None of these is an essential characteristic: none of them explains the others; none of them applies to all men; omit any or all of them, assume a man who has never done any of these things, and he will still be a *man*. But observe that all these activities (and innumerable others) require a *conceptual grasp* of reality, that an animal would not be able to understand them, that they are the expressions and consequences of man's rational faculty, that an organism without that faculty would *not* be a man — and you will know why man's rational faculty is his *essential* distinguishing and defining characteristic. [ITOE, 45–46]

Consider, for example, the attempt to define man as "the tool-making animal." This definition fails the test of fundamentality, because man's ability to make tools is a *consequence* of his ability to use reason. The same error is committed, less grossly, by the common definition of man as "the animal that uses language." What explains man's ability to speak a language? His ability to form concepts — i.e., his rational faculty.

Note that both of the inferior definitions create further conceptual muddles. Is a bird's nest or a beaver's dam a "tool"? Is the twitter of birds a "language"?

The "dance" done by bees to indicate the location of a pollen-rich field has been called a "language." But an actual language uses propositions composed of *concepts*, and concepts are formed by a process of reason. Thus, fundamentality dictates that the definition be: "man is the rational animal."

(In general, concepts must be not only defined but also formed in the first place on the basis of fundamental, not superficial, similarities and differences. More on this will follow.)

The rule of fundamentality explains and subsumes the traditional rule against negative definitions ("A definition must not be negative where it can be positive"). Negatives are grasped in relation to the positives from which they differ, so negatives are non-fundamental. For example, take this negative statement: "Man is the animal that is not limited to the perceptual level." The "not limited" is a consequence, not the fundamental: man is not limited to the perceptual level *because* he has a rational faculty.

It must be noted, however, that some concepts *are* inherently negative. For instance, "dry" is the absence of moisture. "Blindness" is the absence of the ability to see. "Freedom" is the absence of coercion. The rule of fundamentality entails that a definition must be negative when the concept being defined is negative — i.e., specifies the absence of something.

Finally, note that to be fundamental a characteristic need not explain *all* the other distinguishing characteristics: the requirement is that it must explain the greatest number of distinguishing characteristics. It is not obvious, for example, that man's possession of an opposable thumb is explained by his possession of a rational faculty. But man's possession of a rational faculty does explain an enormous number of his distinguishing characteristics, incomparably more than does any other candidate.

5. The rule of unit-economy

A definition is not an exhaustive summary of the units' characteristics. Nor is it a substitute for the concept. A definition is a cognitive tool — a means of quickly recalling the nature of the units, as the label on a file folder informs one of the nature of the folder's contents. Accordingly, the definition must be short — the shorter, the more condensed, the better. (Shorter definitions also make the genus prominent, which aids organizing one's concepts into a series of progressively wider genera.)

The definition must be a single, economical sentence.

Consider the following as a definition of "man": "Man is the animal whose faculty of awareness possesses, from the time of late infancy through senility, in normal cases, the capacity for the formation and use of concepts."

Obviously, that won't do. It would not serve as a "label" for one's "file." Aristotle's definition of man is unit-economical: "Man is the rational animal."

Another example of a violation of this rule (and others) is John Dewey's definition of "inquiry": "Inquiry is the controlled or directed transformation of an indeterminate situation into one that is so determinate in its constituent distinctions and relations as to convert the elements of the original situation into a unified whole." [DEWEY, 104] A unit-economical definition of "inquiry" would be: "Inquiry" is a systematic process of gathering information about a delimited subject.

These five rules are not arbitrary *dicta*. They are statements of what is required for the definition to perform its function. That function is: to enable one to know what one is talking about — i.e., which things one is referring to and what their essential nature is. Definitions allow concepts to function as concepts, rather than as inarticulate sounds or floating abstractions. Defining a concept in compliance with these rules, if done rationally and tested against a range of examples, gives one's concepts a firm identity in one's mind and ties them to their referents in reality.[116]

Definitions as Contextual

A definition is a condensation of knowledge, knowledge of a concept's units and of their place in the entire structure of one's knowledge. Knowledge is not frozen in a static sum; it grows in the individual's development, as he advances from childhood to educated adult, and it grows with the progress of science. Definitions, to function as optimal condensers of knowledge, must expand to keep abreast of an expanding context of knowledge.

Definitions, in other words, are contextual. They are established in a given context of knowledge, and they are to be judged by reference to the context of knowledge in which they are used. A broadened or deepened knowledge of the units requires a corresponding change in the concept's definition.

---

116 I have found that the best method of developing a definition on one's own is: 1) select two or three *clear and simple* examples of the units and, as foils, one or two "near relatives"; 2) identify the genus that includes all of the selected examples; 3) ask what fundamentally differentiates the units from their "relatives" in that genus; 4) package the results into a clear, economical sentence. (The rules are one's guide throughout the process and, until they have been automatized, it is a good idea to check one's definition against each.)

Take the concept "gold." In a primitive context of knowledge, the (implicit) definition of "gold" might be "a hard substance of a particular, yellowish color." This definition, I am assuming, is sufficient to distinguish gold from all other materials known at the time. Later, however, other hard, yellow substances, e.g., "fool's gold," are encountered. At that point, the statement "gold is a hard, yellow substance" — though still true as a statement — no longer serves to differentiate gold from other things known. Accordingly, the definition must be expanded (not contradicted, but expanded) by adding new differentiae. Suppose the other yellow substances are not as dense and malleable as gold. Then, at this point, the definition of "gold" would be expanded to become: "dense, malleable yellow substance."

That definition may suffice for quite a while, but eventually, as civilization develops, men will create alloys, e.g., of gold and silver. Since these alloys look and feel too similar to gold to be distinguished perceptually, the expanded definition will include more advanced differentiae, such as "insoluble in such and such acids," and (per Archimedes' discovery), "having such and such a density relative to water."

As science progresses, the genus of the definition must also be expanded. When the concept "metal" is formed (from observation of different metals), the genus of "gold" becomes "metal." Still later, "metal" will be refined to "element." These expansions of the genus are necessary to maintain the definition's role in *organizing* one's concepts.

When the atomic theory of matter is established, a new change will be required: "gold" will be defined in terms of its atomic number, which states the number of protons in the gold atom. The result is our present definition: "gold" is an element having the atomic number of 79. In our current context of knowledge, this definition states the *fundamental*. It is the fact that gold has 79 protons that *causes and explains* its having 79 electrons, which, in turn, causes and explains its possession of its distinctive properties — including its malleability, its density, and its characteristic yellow color.

Throughout the evolution of these definitions, gold remains gold, with all the properties that characterize it. Gold does not change, nor does the *concept* change. And the earlier definitions remain true as statements: gold is still yellow, hard, malleable, etc. But reference to these properties no longer satisfies the cognitive function of a *definition*.

In all such cases of definitional revision, the facts stated by the earlier definitions remain facts, the old definitions remain *true as statements*, but they no longer suffice to define the concept. Thus, the change in definition required by the growth of knowledge represents a process of expanding, not of contradicting, the concept's earlier definition.

The cases calling for definitional expansion are: 1) the discovery of new concretes (e.g., "fool's gold") that need to be distinguished from the concept's units; 2) the gaining of new knowledge about the genus ("element"); and 3) the discovery of a deeper characteristic (atomic number 79) that causes and explains those previously used as differentiae.

As an example of definitional expansion, Rand cites the case of a child's evolving definitions of "man" (definitions that are, of course, only implicit for the child). The child's first implicit definition of "man" might be, she suggests, "a thing that moves and makes sounds." At a later stage, after the child learns more, his (implicit) definition might become: "a living thing that walks on two legs and has no fur," and, still later: "a living being that speaks and does things no other living beings can do." As an adult, he reaches a still deeper, and now explicit, definition: "a rational animal."[117] Man's possession of a rational faculty is the fundamental characteristic causing and explaining the vast complexity of "does things no other living beings can do."

If one recognizes that definitions are cognitive tools, not a substitute for the full concept, there is no problem in embracing the contextuality of definitions.

Valid vs. Invalid Concepts

The rules of definition presuppose that one has formed a valid concept.[118] Though we live in a "non-judgmental" age, the fact is that the concepts one forms are either *right* or *wrong*: a given conceptualization is either pro-cognition or anti-cognition. Rand writes:

> There are such things as invalid concepts, i.e., words that represent attempts to integrate errors, contradictions or false propositions, such as concepts originating in mysticism — or words without specific definitions, without referents, which can mean anything to anyone. . . . Invalid concepts appear occasionally in men's

---

117 Rand also endorsed the idea that a biologist's definition of "man," as opposed to a general philosophic definition, would include sophisticated terms like "primate." [ITOE, 235]

118 Aristotle noted that a concept of imagination, like "unicorn," does not have a definition, but only a "formula" — i.e., a sentence explaining how the word is used in fantasy.

languages, but are usually — though not necessarily — short-lived, since they lead to cognitive dead-ends. An invalid concept invalidates every proposition or process of thought in which it is used as a cognitive assertion. [ITOE, 49]

The two basic mistakes that produce an invalid concept are: 1) making a concept for non-existent units, or 2) making a concept that uses an invalid standard, resulting in misclassifying units.

1. Concepts that Lack Units

Concepts lacking units are those that attempt to refer to the contradictory or to the arbitrary. The test for the validity of a concept here is whether or not it can be reduced to perceptual reality. (For an example of this process, see Peikoff's reduction of "friend" through such intermediate concepts as "man," "knowledge," "affection," and "esteem." [OPAR, 134–135]) If a concept cannot be reduced to any perceptual base, it is an error, distortion, or fantasy.

A made-up example of a concept that does not reflect facts would be "biangle": a two-sided polygon — which is impossible.

Actual examples of invalid concepts are, of course, more controversial, since to be common enough to figure as "real-life" examples, many people must take them as valid. But it is worthwhile to discuss some concepts that I, at least, regard as invalid, because doing so will illustrate how the rules of epistemology have important application to real-world issues.

The first case is that of invalid concepts "originating in mysticism," in Rand's phrase above. These would include "god," "fairy," "angel," "devil," "afterlife," etc. These concepts are nothing but arbitrary inventions, rather than being based in any way on logical processing of perceived facts. The fact that their origin lies in make-believe becomes clear when one contrasts them with valid, scientific concepts that designate non-perceivable existents. "Electron" and "ultraviolet" are concepts reached by logical inference from what is perceived — whereas "god" and the like are based on nothing but primitive men's awe before such phenomena of nature as lightning, floods, and earthquakes. (Concepts of imagination, like "angel" and "hobbit," can have a valid role in imaginative literature, but they are invalid if used "as a cognitive assertion," in Rand's careful phrasing.)

The injunction to reduce a concept to the perceptual level is *not* the demand: "Show me referents I can see, touch, or otherwise perceive by my

senses." Rather, it is the demand: "Show me how, by logical steps, starting from perception, one can reach this concept — and why one needs it."
Our senses cannot perceive cosmic rays or genes or a budget-deficit, but each
of these concepts is definitely reducible, through a long chain of intermediate
concepts and knowledge, to perceptual data.

It is not just religion that is guilty of using mystical or groundless
concepts. The history of philosophy offers an embarrassingly large array of
non-reducible, arbitrarily constructed concepts. Some examples, of many, are:
Plato's "Forms," Spinoza's "intuition," Leibniz's "monads," Kant's "noumena,"
Hegel's "dialectic," Marx's "forces of production." All of these terms, and
many more, are introduced without any logical derivation from perceptual
reality. They are all invalid concepts, of interest only to the historian.

There are also scientific concepts, such as "epicycle" and "phlogiston,"
now known to contradict observed data (even if they were legitimate
as hypothetical concepts in an earlier context of knowledge). But even
contemporary science (or pseudo-science) exhibits invalid concepts, such as the
concepts deployed by "parapsychology" (itself an invalid concept): "telepathy,"
"telekinesis," etc.

In contemporary physics, the accusation raised against "string theory"
is that it is an arbitrary construct, based on playing with mathematics,
rather than supported by observational data. I am not a physicist, but if this
accusation is correct, its concepts, notably including "eleven-dimensional
space," are invalid.

The examination of concepts for validity is much needed in regard to
concepts used in the social sciences. Freud's concepts of "Id" and "death-
instinct," the concept of "socialization" in sociology, and the concepts of
"perfect competition" and "externalities" in economics are all arguably invalid,
most of them on grounds of being arbitrary constructs, lacking units in
reality. But "socialization" and "externalities" are terms commiting a much
subtler type of error: the misclassification of units.

2. Concepts that Misclassify Units

Concepts in this category deal with actually existing phenomena, but
mis-organize them, classifying things in a way that is confusing, misleading, or otherwise anti-cognitive. How can a concept be anti-cognitive?
Isn't any "conceptual scheme" just as good or bad as any other, provided
that its units exist? No — no more than any filing system is as good or bad

as any other. Here is an extended example that demonstrates the folly of this non-judgmental, relativist attitude.

Suppose a biologist were to set up a classification system for living organisms (a "taxonomy") based on superficials instead of fundamentals. In making the highest-level distinction, covering all organisms, he rejects the traditional division between the plant kingdom and the animal kingdom, distinguishing instead between "stripes" and "solids" — according to whether or not the surface of the organism shows stripes. This would mean the "stripes" kingdom would contain, for instance, zebras and tigers, along with certain snakes, bees, and plants; these would be divided from the "solids" kingdom, which would contain horses and lions, along with other snakes, bees, and plants — plus all single-celled organisms.

Now imagine making further subdivisions along equally superficial lines, such as whether an organism's stripes are monochromatic or colored, and then whether its shape is elongated or not. This conceptual scheme, though absurd, could be entirely consistent: all and only the "stripes" would have stripes, all and only the "longs" would have relatively elongated shapes. So, for instance, both what we now call "whales" and what we now call "oaks" would be "elongated, monochromatic solids." Both what we now call "tigers" and what we now call "honeybees" would be "polychromatic stripes," while lions and other bees would be "monochromatic, non-long solids," and so on.

The problem with this taxonomy does not concern any lack of referents or any contradiction to observed facts. Instead, the problem concerns how the referents are being grouped. The classifications are made on the basis of non-essentials — i.e., superficial similarities and differences rather than fundamental ones. Classifying by superficials puts fundamentally different things together and separates things that are fundamentally the same.

The result is the kind of groupings that frustrate the needs of cognition, turning biological classification into an unintegrable jumble. Rather than providing cognitive leverage, rather than aiding cognitive specialization (as between botany and zoology), the stripes-solid taxonomy based on superficials would make that specialization pointless. What is to be gained by specializing in zebras and honeybees while leaving horses and wasps to those who study "solids"? This taxonomy would result in the utter stultification of biological science — if any biologist could actually stick to it, rather than covertly reverting to the traditional system of classification.

This example makes it dramatically clear that, contrary to the claims of conceptual relativism, there is an *objective* right and wrong in how we classify.

The basis of that right and wrong lies in the need to obey the identity of man's conceptual equipment. Specifically, it is "the crow epistemology" that gives rise to the need for economizing on units, and thus for judging classifications from the standpoint of their unit-economy.

Carving nature at the joints — i.e. on the basis of fundamentals — provides the most unit-economical system of classification. What makes a characteristic fundamental is that it causes and explains the greatest number of other characteristics. Thus, in a classification by fundamentals, the greatest number of characteristics can be condensed into one unit and treated wholesale. E.g., horses and zebras have many characteristics in common, allowing for a condensation of units in dealing with them together, whereas far fewer characteristics are common to zebras and honeybees, and their differences overload the "crow." A concept formed on the basis of superficial similarities, ignoring fundamental differences, is *invalid*.

To validate a concept and establish its proper definition, one should ask oneself: *What facts of reality give rise to the need for such a concept?*

If no such facts are ascertainable, the concept cannot be considered valid, and one should not attempt to use it cognitively. But most of the concepts that we form remain in the language because they do reflect fundamental similarities. In those cases, identifying the need for the concept brings those fundamentals to light, helping one to form a proper definition.

Rand provides an intriguing example of this process in regard to the concept "justice":

> For instance: what fact of reality gave rise to the concept "justice"? The fact that man must draw conclusions about the things, people and events around him, i.e., must judge and evaluate them. Is his judgment automatically right? No. What causes his judgment to be wrong? The lack of sufficient evidence, or his evasion of the evidence, or his inclusion of considerations other than the facts of the case. How, then, is he to arrive at the right judgment? By basing it exclusively on the factual evidence and by considering all the relevant evidence available. But isn't this a description of "objectivity"? Yes, "objective judgment" is one of the wider categories to which the concept "justice" belongs. What distinguishes "justice" from other instances of objective judgment? When one evaluates the nature or actions of inanimate objects, the criterion of judgment is determined by the

particular purpose for which one evaluates them. But how does one determine a criterion for evaluating the character and actions of men, in view of the fact that men possess the faculty of volition? What science can provide an objective criterion of evaluation in regard to volitional matters? Ethics. Now, do I need a concept to designate the act of judging a man's character and/or actions exclusively on the basis of all the factual evidence available, and of evaluating it by means of an objective moral criterion? Yes. That concept is "justice." [ITOE, 51]

Rand's Razor

In the preceding passage, note her final question: "Now, do I need [such] a concept?" An answer of "Yes" is not to be simply assumed (particularly not in the case of neologisms). As we saw in the example of "stripes" vs. "solids," not every recurring fact warrants the formation of a new concept; the vast majority of such facts are, properly, identified in descriptive propositions, such as "Tigers have stripes." In contrast, the fact that there is a fly on the ceiling theoretically could be, but wouldn't be, elevated into a permanent, open-ended concept — say, "ceiling-flies." But properly, one handles that fact descriptively by combining into a proposition the existing concepts "fly," "on," and "ceiling."

Forming a concept is not a free lunch; there are "overhead" costs involved in storing it, carrying it forward, updating it, etc. One should form a new concept only when the cognitive gains of doing so exceed the cost. If the concept would not be thus cognitively profitable, forming and using it constitutes a waste of mental resources, complicating one's mental filing system. Needless multiplication of concepts results in decreased cognitive efficacy.

In recognition of this fact, Ayn Rand formulated an epistemological version of Occam's Razor, which has come to be called "Rand's Razor":

> ... concepts are not to be multiplied beyond necessity — the corollary of which is: nor are they to be integrated in disregard of necessity. [ITOE, 72]

What is meant by "necessity" here? What factors would make a new concept necessary? Rand names three such factors:

"The descriptive complexity of a given group of existents, the frequency of their use, and the requirements of cognition (of further study) are the main reasons for the formation of new concepts. Of these reasons, the requirements of cognition are the paramount one." [ITOE, 70]

Rand discusses the kinds of concepts whose formation is necessary, according to these criteria:

There is a great deal of latitude, on the periphery of man's conceptual vocabulary, a broad area where the choice is optional, but in regard to certain central categories of existents the formation of concepts is mandatory. This includes such categories as: (a) the perceptual concretes with which men deal daily . . . (b) new discoveries of science; (c) new man-made objects which differ in their essential characteristics from the previously known objects (e.g., "television"); (d) complex human relationships involving combinations of physical and psychological behavior (e.g., "marriage," "law," "justice"). [ITOE, 70]

Failing to conceptualize "television" or "marriage" would mean depriving oneself of a file folder one needs.

In contrast, consider the case of flatly unnecessary concepts. The worst of these are not concepts that merely duplicate existing ones, but rather concepts formed on the basis of non-essentials, such as "ceiling-flies." It is clarifying to consider here the analogy with physical (or digital) files, say for correspondence. To make files for "letters received when the moon was full," "letters opened while I was standing up," and so on, would defeat the *purpose* of a filing system. A policy of making files like these whenever one was struck by any random similarity would produce chaos — just as forming concepts to capture random similarities would produce chaos in one's inner, mental office.

The chaos is compounded by the fact that concepts become *automatized*:

A concept substitutes one symbol (one word) for the enormity of the perceptual aggregate of the concretes it subsumes. In order to perform its unit-reducing function, the symbol has to become automatized in a man's consciousness, i.e., the enormous sum of its referents must be instantly (implicitly) available to his conscious mind whenever he uses that concept, without the need of perceptual visualization or mental summarizing — in the same manner as the concept "5" does not require that he visualize five sticks every time he uses it. [ITOE, 64]

Automatizing needless concepts intensifies their destructiveness. Automatized concepts spring to mind when triggered, leaving less mental space available for retrieving and using proper concepts (per "the crow epistemology").

Concepts permit a cognitive division of labor, with all the benefits flowing from specialization. But specialization is beneficial only under certain conditions — only when it is a specialization in things sharing a fundamental unity. Imagine a business formed to specialize in products that begin with the letter "N" — nails, nasal sprays, nasturtiums, etc. That kind of "specialization" would bring not profits but bankruptcy. In the same way, cognition is not aided but obstructed by forming a concept on the wrong basis, i.e., according to superficials at the expense of fundamentals.

In considering the cognitive cost of forming a concept, one must keep in mind the fact that a concept is something that is to be carried forward, used, and updated. Concept-formation is only the beginning of an ongoing process, not something that is over and done with after performing the initial mental integration, nor even after defining the concept. Concepts are open-ended because they are tools of cognition, tools that are formed in order to be used. The *raison d'être* and purpose of conceptualization is application — application in forming propositional judgments, in the acquisition of knowledge, and in planning, deciding, and acting to achieve existential goals. *Concepts are a human being's basic equipment for successfully coping with the problem of survival.*

It is against this background that the choice to add or not to add an additional concept must be evaluated. The question is: would forming this additional concept aid cognition, clarify thinking, add to my life-guiding equipment — or would it merely add clutter, distract me from fundamentals, and lead to dead ends in thought and action?

To better understand violations of Rand's Razor, recall the mechanics of concept-formation (CHAPTER 3). A concept is formed by grasping similarity (measurement-proximity) against difference. In what way can this process go wrong? Not in regard to grasping similarity: there is no problem in correctly comparing the measurements involved. In contrasting a circle, an ellipse, and a triangle no one makes a mistake about which figures are close in shape-measurement; it is perceptually evident that the circle and the ellipse have similar shapes when contrasted with the triangle. Nor, on a much higher level of abstraction, does anyone take an inflation rate of 8% to be more like a *de*flation rate of 10% than an inflation rate of 10%. In terms of measurement-relationships, no one mistakes proximity for remoteness.

It is not errors about what is nearer in measurement that create invalid concepts. Instead, it is the set-up itself that is at fault: one chooses the wrong items to compare, thereby establishing the wrong CCD. Comparing a zebra and a striped snake to a lion brings to the foreground the issue of stripes vs. lack of stripes, which is an extremely superficial characteristic in the context of an overall biological taxonomy. The primary cause of misorganizing the referents — i.e., of violating Rand's Razor — is *using the wrong CCD*.

False division

Concepts that violate Rand's Razor are categorizable as either "false division" or "false integration."

Concepts that I am terming "false divisions" are those that make subdivisions based on non-essential differences. These concepts focus attention on superficial or cognitively insignificant differences at the expense of fundamental similarities.

Rand provides a made-up example: "Beautiful blondes with blue eyes, 5'5" tall and 24 years old." [ITOE, 71]

Suppose we were to make a concept for this group of women — call them "blins." There would be no cognitive gains to be achieved by cognitive specialization in blins. Virtually all the facts that one could learn about blins would be equally true of beautiful blondes with blue eyes who are 26 years old or 5'2" tall — despite the fact that the concept "blin" calls for us to canonize, in a concept, the distinction among them.

Further, if "blin" is to be formed, by what *principle* would one refuse to form concepts for every other combination and concatenation of characteristics? Either one adheres to the principle of unit-economy, or one does not — in which case one's mental filing system becomes progressively more clogged and progressively less functional.

"Blin" is a deliberately absurd concept. But consider a real-life, political example of false division. Since the 1930s, the political spectrum has been conventionally divided between two poles: fascism as the extreme "right" and communism as the extreme "left." This is a lethal false division. There are no *fundamental* differences between fascism and communism. Both are forms of *dictatorship*. Both are based on the theory and practice of collectivism. They differ in their outward forms — fascism demands the submission of the individual to a national and/or racial collective, communism demands the submission of the individual to an economic collective — but, both deny completely the rights of the individual, requiring him to live for the state. This is not to claim that the two systems are identical; a few minor, quite secondary, distinctions can indeed be made between fascist dictatorship and communist dictatorship. Rather, the point is that it is disastrously wrong to set up as the poles of the whole political spectrum two varieties of dictatorship. (Note the absurd implication that a free society occupies a "middle" between two forms of dictatorship, as if it combined elements of each.)

False integration

Concepts that I am terming "false integrations" are widenings based on non-essential similarities, at the expense of essential differences. For instance, suppose I were to make up the concept "cutter" to denote anyone who cuts human flesh with a sharp instrument. "Cutter" would include both surgeons and Jack the Ripper. Clearly, automatizing and working with "cutter" would produce cognitive chaos and lead in practice to gross injustice. It is not that one couldn't tell who was and wasn't a "cutter," but that the CCD here — flesh-cutting — is grossly superficial.

"Cutter" is a made-up example. In actual practice, false integration frequently occurs when an existing and perfectly valid concept is given a "definition by non-essentials," in violation of rule 4. Defining an otherwise valid concept by non-essentials converts it into something that "integrates in disregard of necessity," making the concept into what Ayn Rand terms an "intellectual package-deal."

For instance, Bertrand Russell defines "freedom" as: "the absence of obstacles to the realization of one's desires." Consider some of the known facts — the wider context — that this definition ignores. To a 17th-century man in Northern Italy seeking to travel into Switzerland, the Alps are an obstacle to the realization of his desires. Do the Alps deprive him of his freedom? To a man who wishes to have sex with a given woman, her unwillingness is an obstacle to the realization of his desires. Does her refusal deprive him of his freedom? What about *her* freedom, which would be violated by his act? And what about historical conditions? In contemporary America, with its unprecedented standard of living, there are — in one sense — far fewer unrealized desires than there were in 1800. Does that mean that individuals in contemporary America have more freedom than Americans living in 1800?

Russell's definition is centered on a man's *desires*, using their frustration or fulfillment as the CCD. But a desire results from evaluations that may be rational or irrational, correct or incorrect. Desires may even come from evaluations that flout metaphysically given facts: recall Dostoyevsky's "underground man" who did not like the fact that two plus two equals four ("The Formula 'two and two make five' is not without its attractions.") But Russell's definition treats desires as irreducible givens, when in fact they are effects, not primaries. His definition converts "freedom," a crucial term of political philosophy, into a "package-deal."

A definition of freedom grounded in all the facts I have mentioned would result in a concept quite different from Russell's; it would be a concept defined in terms of the absence of physical coercion by others. But Russell's concept treats human acts of coercion as if they were essentially the same as inanimate obstacles, the laws of nature, and even the laws of logic (which present the "obstacle" that you can't have your cake and eat it, too). Russell's definition converts "freedom" into a massive package-deal, obscuring the life-and-death need to be free from coercion by human beings, who act by deliberation and choice, not necessity (see CHAPTER 10).

Several neologisms that have been injected into contemporary political discussion exhibit the same kind of anti-cognitive focus on superficials at the expense of fundamentals. The arch-example, as Rand explains, is "extremism."

> . . . "extremism" is a term which, standing by itself, has no meaning. The concept of "extreme" denotes a relation, a measurement, a degree. The dictionary gives the following definitions: "Extreme, adj. — 1. of a character or kind farthest removed from the ordinary or average. 2. utmost or exceedingly great in degree."
>
> It is obvious that the first question one has to ask, before using that term, is: a *degree* — of what?
>
> To answer: "Of anything!" and to proclaim that any extreme is evil because it is an extreme — to hold the degree of a characteristic, regardless of its nature, as evil — is an absurdity (any garbled Aristotelianism to the contrary notwithstanding). Measurements,

as such, have no value-significance — and acquire it only from the *nature* of that which is being measured. [CUI, 177–178]

In politics, the issue that is *fundamental* is: freedom vs. state coercion.[119] But the term "extremism" puts together, as if it were one basic phenomenon, positions that are "extremely" pro-freedom and "extremely" anti-freedom. It packages into one "file" and treats as equivalent George Washington and Adolf Hitler. Washington was "extremely," i.e., radically and consistently, dedicated to establishing a nation based on the free exercise of the inalienable rights of the individual. Hitler was "extremely" dedicated to eradicating individual freedom and establishing a totalitarian state based on racial collectivism. Packaging them together under one concept is a crime against logic (and morality). "Extremist" whitewashes Hitler and Nazism by associating them with Washington, and it blackens Washington and liberty by associating them with Hitler.

It is a fact that both Washington and Hitler held extreme views. And it is a fact that both zebras and certain plants have stripes. But in neither case is there justification for selecting these facts, rather than fundamentals, as the basis for forming a new concept (or mis-defining an existing one).

The formation of a concept has to be justified. Concepts, though not pre-set by nature, are to be judged by *objective* standards. Justifying a concept requires showing that it refers to existents, rather than fantasy or error, and that it is pro-cognition, i.e., that it satisfies "Rand's Razor," rather than christening an unnecessary division or obscuring fundamental differences. The rules of proper definition, especially the rule of fundamentality, serve as checks to ensure that one has not violated Rand's Razor by sacrificing fundamentals to superficials.

For completeness, I will discuss briefly the "optional" cases — concepts whose formation is neither mandatory nor prohibited. Such concepts represent "borderline cases," in the sense that they fall between mandatory concepts and invalid ones.

"Optional" concepts, Rand writes, are mainly "subdivisions that denote subtle shades of meaning, such as adjectives which are almost, but not fully, synonymous." [ITOE, 72] Consider "slender" as a subcategory of

---

119 What makes this the fundamental are two facts: that reason is man's basic means of survival and that only coercion — i.e., physical force — can prevent a man from exercising his reason in the service of his life. Thus, the alternative of freedom vs. force reflects the alternative of life vs. death. See Rand, "Man's Rights" and "The Nature of Government" [VOS, CH. 12 AND CH. 14] and Peikoff [OPAR, 310–324 AND 350–369].

"thin." Although "slender" marks a shade of difference from other cases of "thin" (such as "skinny"), one could not say that one would be bereft of any important distinction if one lacked the concept "slender" and instead used descriptive phrases, such as "attractively thin." In contrast, consider the cognitive overload that would result if one eliminated the concept "justice" and tried to rely instead on descriptive phrases, such as "evaluating people and their actions by taking into consideration all the evidence and only the evidence."

The optionality of certain concepts is reflected in the fact that some languages make distinctions that others do not. English, for instance, has the two terms "forest" and "woods," but German describes both as "Wald." (Of course, in German one can use descriptive phrases to make the distinction, which pertains to the size of the wooded area; the issue is whether a single concept is used.)

Optional cases pose a "problem" only for the Realist theory of concepts, according to which concepts are based on a "universal" that must be either present or absent in the concretes. "Where do we draw the line between green and yellow?" the Nominalists ask in attacking Realism — as if some precise line were necessary. On the Objectivist theory of concepts, which accommodates continuous measurement-variation, no such sharp division is necessary. Borderline cases are handled perfectly well by a descriptive phrase (e.g., "greenish yellow"); no special concept is required.

The very purpose of forming concepts is to use them to identify facts. This is the function of judgments, and judgments are made in the form of *propositions*, to which I now turn.

LOGIC AND PROPOSITIONS

As defined in CHAPTER 5, a "proposition" is "a grammatically structured combination of concepts to identify a subject by a process of measurement-inclusion." It is possible for propositions to err, to assert that a thing has characteristics that it actually does not have. In other words, with the making of propositional judgments comes the issue of truth or falsehood. (Concepts, being tools, are not properly described as true or false, but as valid or invalid.)

The factor making invalid *concepts* possible is choice — specifically, the choice of what to contrast with what. The possibility of false *propositions* arises because of choice and because of an additional factor: *time.*[120]

Propositions as trans-temporal

Perception is time-bound: it is awareness of the present state of things. Concepts are open-ended in regard to time. The very purpose of forming concepts is to have a means of carrying knowledge forward, of applying to future units what one has learned from studying past units; propositions are the means of doing that.

To say of a given thing, "This S is P" is not merely to say, "This S appears to be P from here right now" but to assert what S is in reality — that is, across all conditions of perception — past, present, and future. For instance, to (mistakenly) describe the distant hills as "blue," in effect, predicts that from closer up they will still look similar in color to blueberries and the sky. But that implicit prediction turns out to be contradicted by later perception, and thus is false. Similarly, in the case of a stick half-submerged in water, to call it "bent," predicts, in effect, that when it is pulled out of the water, its perceived shape will still be like that of other bent sticks — in contradiction to what one actually will perceive.

Propositions, of course, do not deny the fact that things can change. "That is an ice cube" is not shown to have been false if the ice cube later melts. But a stick does not change its shape by being lifted out of the water, so "The stick is bent" was false all along.

The use of propositions to make judgments is fallible because to judge is to apply a predicate, which is a concept, and concepts are open-ended with regard to time. Concepts are trans-temporal: they integrate, summarize, and imply how a kind of thing *is, was, and will be* — across all conditions.

Because concepts are trans-temporal, in using them to make a conceptual identification one needs to integrate what he perceives at one time with what he perceives at any other time. A judgment that contains or implies a contradiction is false. In fact, the false is precisely the contradictory.

---

120 Concepts themselves involve time, since they are open-ended in time, applying to all existents of a certain type — past, present, or future. But the alternative of a concept's validity or invalidity is only indirectly related to this fact. The invalidity of the concept "extremism," for example, is due to its being based on a superficial characteristic at the expense of fundamental differences, rather than that "extremism" will run up against a contradiction in future observation.

There are no contradictions in reality. One never perceives a contradiction, an *A* that isn't *A*. When we talk about contradictions in one's thinking, what we actually mean is inconsistency: at a given time, one thinks, "This is *A*," but at another time, in regard to the same, unchanged thing, one thinks, "This isn't *A*." The inconsistency means that one of the two thoughts is in error.

On the perceptual level, there is no such phenomenon as "inconsistency." Inconsistency, and thus error, is a phenomenon of the conceptual level: the open-ended, trans-temporal nature of concepts is what makes inconsistency possible. To subsume something under a concept implies that it is relevantly the same as the other units of that concept; if it is, in fact, relevantly different from them, the subsumption is in error.

(In CHAPTER 2, I rebutted the Argument from Illusion, which attacks perception by appeal to cases like that of the stick half-submerged in water. I said that the error lies in the judgment made, not in the perception itself. The trans-temporal nature of conceptual identification provides the deeper explanation of this point: the conceptual identification uses open-ended concepts and thus extends into the future. That is why a conceptual identification can contradict what is later perceived.)

Thus, consistency — non-contradictoriness — is the standard of truth for propositions. To paraphrase Rand's statement quoted in CHAPTER 6: No proposition man forms is true if it cannot be integrated without contradiction into the total sum of his knowledge.[121]

Defective propositions

The truth or falsehood of a proposition is distinguishable from the validity or invalidity of its formation. Truth and validity are highly interrelated: the truth of a proposition depends upon its having been validly formed, and that validity usually depends upon the truth of prior propositions. Truth and validity are given separate discussion in what follows, but one must bear in mind that they are interconnected.

A precondition of considering the truth or falsehood of a proposition is that the proposition be meaningful; that, in turn, depends upon how the proposition was formed. A proposition is formed by combining concepts; a validly formed proposition consists of valid concepts, validly combined. If the parts are invalid or if they are combined illogically, the resulting proposition is defective. If the defect is severe enough, what

---

121 Rand's original statement was: "No concept man forms is valid unless he integrates it without contradiction into the total sum of his knowledge." [AS, 1016]

one is dealing with is not a proposition at all but a pseudo-proposition, a string of words that fails to make an intelligible statement.

To have a definite meaning, a proposition must ascribe a properly conceptualized predicate to a clearly designated and properly conceptualized subject.[122] Further, to be cognitively meaningful, the proposition must be based not on fantasy but on some evidence. Sentences uttered on the premise "I just feel it" or "Why not believe it?" or "It came to me in a dream," are pseudo-propositions, not cognitive assertions. Such utterances are outside the domain of cognition. They are neither true nor false, but *arbitrary*. (The topic of arbitrary assertions will be discussed at length in the next chapter.)

Let's look closer at the two cases: propositions that are defective due to using invalid concepts and propositions defective on account of invalidly combining legitimate concepts.

1. Propositions using invalid concepts

Every concept used in a proposition must be valid; an invalid concept renders defective any proposition that uses it. Take the earlier example of "biangle," which supposedly stands for two-sided polygons. Since "biangle" is an invalid concept, the sentence "Biangles can be large or small" is not a proposition at all. The issue of whether it is true or false does not even arise, because "biangle" involves a contradiction.

The same is true when a proposition uses a less obviously invalid concept. The false integration "extremism" renders defective any proposition like: "George Washington was an extremist." As a matter of logic, one must reject the proposition, rather than attempt to decide whether Washington was or was not an extremist.

There are concepts that would be valid if given a proper definition but are invalid as defined, implicitly or explicitly, by the person using them. Propositions using such invalidly defined concepts are defective as used by that person. There are two cases here: concepts that are misdefined and concepts that are undefined. "Freedom" can be given a logically valid definition, but since Bertrand Russell defined it as "the absence of obstacles to the realization of desires" that invalidated any use *he* made of the term. If Russell ever said, "Freedom is a good thing," that was a defective proposition for *him*, because of how *he* defined "freedom."

---

122 If the subject term is a proper name, it must clearly specify a particular thing.

The same applies in the case of someone who uses terms while lacking an adequate understanding of them, rather than operating with an explicit but illogical definition, as Russell does. Suppose that, for instance, someone says: "Love is the solution to all problems." There is no point in trying to assess the truth or falsehood of this statement, because it clearly reflects the speaker's unclarity about what "love" means. "Love" in his mind is a floating abstraction, or it is a "package-deal" that combines actual love (an emotional response to values) with something fundamentally different: a temporary relief from guilt, resulting from being granted an unearned forgiveness.

Having clear, unambiguous, properly defined concepts is a precondition of making cognitive assertions by combining those concepts. If the components are defective, so is the proposition combining them.

2. Invalid combination of concepts

Even when each of the concepts used in a proposition is valid, a defective proposition will result if these concepts are improperly combined. To be valid, a proposition must meet three criteria: it must be a) grammatical, b) consistent, and c) referential.

a) The grammaticality requirement

The first requirement of valid proposition is that it be formulated in a grammatical sentence. The following is not a proposition: "Is of in in." But less radically ungrammatical propositions are still malformed. For example: "Tom told his uncle that he was working too hard" — was it Tom or his uncle who was said to be working too hard? Or, "Nearing home, the familiar driveway was seen." (A dangling participle: the driveway was not nearing home.)

Of course, such minor issues are often merely linguistic sloppiness and can be fixed by editing (though re-writing frequently requires doing real work to clarify one's thought). But grammatical issues extend to the philosophical level as well. Consider the following argument for the existence of God: "Every event is caused by something, and the something that causes every event is what we call God." The grammar here equivocates on "caused by something." The conclusion states that the same one thing (God) causes each different event that occurs. But that is not the meaning of the premise (or else the premise begs the question). The conclusion that follows from the assumed meaning of the premise would be: each event has its own particular cause — a statement carrying no theistic implications.[123]

A more interesting class of cases concerns what I call "philosophical grammar." While ordinary grammar concerns the right use of the parts of speech, philosophical grammar concerns the right use of the metaphysical categories — entity, attribute, action, relationship, etc. To take a pedantic example, there is nothing *linguistically* ungrammatical in the statement, "Saturday is in bed." But "Saturday" is not an entity and so cannot be in or out of bed.

Amateur writing often exhibits philosophically ungrammatical constructions. Consider this statement from a Wikipedia entry on the philosophy of education:

> Instead of being taught in philosophy departments, philosophy of education is usually housed in departments or colleges of education, similar to how philosophy of law is generally taught in law schools.

The writing in this passage is philosophically ungrammatical: it switches confusingly between metaphysical categories. *Where* (in what department) philosophy of education is taught cannot be compared to "*how*" (in what manner) philosophy of law is taught. It is beside the point that one can still reconstruct the idea the author had in mind: "how" is a word from the wrong category of existents, so using it requires the reader to do the mental work of figuring out the correct comparison, which takes mental resources away from grasping and integrating the point the author wishes to make.

The writing in this example can be easily salvaged by doing a little editing; the important cases are those in which it is the thought behind the words that is invalid, especially when violations of philosophical grammar occur in philosophic writing. It would be ungenerous to cite vaguely poetic statements, like "God is love," so take the following passage penned by the early 20th century philosopher Henri Bergson.

> . . . philosophers agree in making a deep distinction between two ways of knowing a thing. The first implies going all around it, the second entering into it. [BERGSON 1946]

---

123 The equivocation is the same as the one in the old joke: "Every man loves some woman — who is she?"

Knowing a thing is a mental activity; it is not a matter of movement in space. Nor can all the objects of knowledge be treated as if they were physical entities to be moved around or entered into (whatever that would mean). Take the knowledge that $2 + 2 = 4$. How does one move around it or enter into it? Perhaps the words are to be taken metaphorically. But if so, it is wholly improper to introduce an allegedly basic philosophical distinction by means of a metaphor — especially not such an opaque one. Nor does he follow up with any literal statement of what this "deep distinction" actually consists of. (Lest you think I'm quoting Bergson out of context, this passage comes from the very first sentence of the chapter titled "An Introduction to Metaphysics.")

A more famous sin against philosophical grammar is displayed in Martin Heidegger's pronouncement, "The Nothing nothings." ("Das Nichts nichtet.") [HEIDEGGER, 1929] Likewise, his question: "Why is there something rather than nothing?" misuses the term "why," ignoring the fact that it is a request for the identification of a cause. The expanded meaning of his pseudo-question would be: "What is the something that causes there to be something rather than nothing?" — which is unintelligible. The same statement also reifies "nothing," treating it as a thing rather than as the absence of a delimited positive (as in "There is nothing in my pocket" — i.e., none of the palpable physical objects that might have been there.)

Unintelligible language is not the only result of philosophically ungrammatical writing; such misuse of categories can also produce monumental and tragic errors. A notorious example is the following passage by John Stuart Mill, in his alleged proof that morality requires the sacrifice of the individual to the collective (under his ethics of utilitarianism):

> The only proof . . . that an object is visible is that people actually see it. The only proof that a sound is audible is that people hear it; and so of the other sources of our experience. In like manner, I apprehend, the sole evidence it is possible to produce that anything is desirable is that people do actually desire it. [MILL 1957, 44]

Mill here uses "desirable" in a philosophically wrong way. "Desirable" does not mean "capable of being desired"; if it did, it would include immoral desires, such as the desire to murder. Rather than denoting a capacity, "desirable" pertains to an entirely different category — the category of normative concepts. "Desirable" denotes what *ought* to be pursued or obtained, in marked distinction from whatever people just happen to desire.

Compounding the felony, Mill goes on, two sentences later, to this philo-sophically ungrammatical horror:

> . . . each person's happiness is a good to that person, and the general happiness, therefore, [is] a good to the aggregate of all persons. [MILL 1957, 45]

What is "the aggregate of all persons?" Mill's statement implies that this aggregate is some collective entity floating above and beyond the individuals residing in a given region. The "aggregate of all persons" is treated as if it were a sentient organism that had its own pursuits, goals, and emotions. It is not merely the linguistic formulation but the thought behind it that does vio-lence to philosophical grammar. Yet such pseudo-thought has characterized most ethical-political theorizing over the last two centuries; the same philosophical muddling occurs in the near-universal notion that "society" is an entity capable of providing benefits to its members, and that "the com-mon good" or "the public interest" is something requiring laws that sacrifice the interests of individuals (who are thus excluded from "the public").[124]

All such collectivist utterances, from Mill's on down to those of today's can-didates for office, are defective propositions, pseudo-propositions actually; they cannot be treated as expressing something definite that could be true or false. Sometimes the person putting forward a defective proposition has an actual thought in mind that he can put into a new (and different) statement that is logical. But more often such statements either are irreme-diably confused (as Mill's are), or, when made intelligible, stand revealed as patently false.

b) The consistency requirement

The second requirement of valid combination is: consistency. First, the proposition must be internally consistent, as opposed to such illogical combinations of concepts as "That circle is square." But the more interesting, and oft-flouted, requirement is that a proposition must be consistent with its own *hierarchy*: it must not use concepts in a way that contradicts the

---

124 We know where this collectivist road leads: "We recognize only two Gods: A God in Heaven and a God on earth and that is our Fatherland," Adolf Hitler, *Volkische Beobachter*, Sept. 23, 1928 [COHEN, 411] and: "[T]he dictatorship of the proletariat is the rule — unre-stricted by law and based on force — of the proletariat over the bourgeoisie," Josef Stalin, *The Foundations of Leninism* [COHEN, 173].

knowledge required to form them. That kind of contradiction is involved in utterances that commit the fallacy of the stolen concept. I have noted this fallacy several times earlier in the book; now I can treat it in full detail.

The stolen concept fallacy is a form of hierarchy inversion: it consists of the attempt to use a derivative concept in a way that contradicts its own presuppositions — i.e., that negates or ignores a prior concept that is required in order to grasp and use the concept in question. Suppose someone were to announce, "I know there are desserts, but there is no such thing as a meal." Here the stolen concept is "dessert"; a dessert is a dish that follows a meal. The concept that is said to be "stolen" is the one that is used without a *logical* right to that use, in analogy with using someone else's property without a *legal* right to do so. In this case, "dessert" is the stolen concept.

When a concept is "stolen," it is being used in a way that severs its connection to perceptual reality and thus deprives the concept, as used, of meaning. "Dessert" could not have its present meaning if meals did not exist. The same type of contradiction is contained in each of the following examples.

- *I reject the existence of consciousness.*
  "Rejection" is an action of consciousness.
- *Logic is a Western prejudice.*
  A "prejudice" is that which is pre-judged, in advance
  of *logical* evidence.
- *Life is all a dream.*
  A "dream" is meaningful only in distinction to wakeful perception.
- *Property is theft.*
  "Theft" is forcibly taking property from its rightful owner.
- *The laws of logic are arbitrary.*
  The "arbitrary" is distinguished from the logical.
- *You can't prove reason is valid.*
  "Proof" can be grasped only as a certain process of reason.
- *Physics is defined as: what physicists do.*
  "Physicist" can be grasped only in relation to "physics."
- *The universe is moving.*
  "Motion" is change of place; "place" is the surrounding entities;
  the universe is *everything;* nothing surrounds it, and it has no place.

In the above, the stolen concepts — the concepts rendered meaningless — are, in order, "reject," "prejudice," "dream," "theft," "arbitrary," "prove," "physicist," and "moving."

The last three examples involve not denying but *ignoring* the stolen concept's roots: ignoring the dependency of "proof" on "reason," of "physicist" on "physics," and of "motion" on "place" and "entity" (or "existent").

All of these statements deprive the concept that is stolen of its hierarchical base, rendering the concept as meaningless as the nonsense sound "slatch." Sentences containing a stolen concept express no thought, make no judgment, and are therefore only pseudo-propositions.

Concept-stealing is arguably the most frequent and most destructive fallacy in the history of philosophy. The mother of all stolen concepts, one rampant in post-Cartesian philosophy, is the primacy of consciousness: the attempt to use concepts of consciousness while denying or ignoring that consciousness is consciousness *of something*, something that exists (see CHAPTER 1).

c) The referentiality requirement

The third requirement of making a valid combination of concepts is that it be referential. The proposition must succeed in designating a subject. The trivial case of a failure in this regard is a proposition based on a false presupposition, such as the proposition Russell devised: "The present king of France is bald." There is no present king of France, so the combination of concepts in the sentence's subject fails to refer, and the sentence is thus not a proposition and is neither true nor false. (The non-referential term could be in the predicate, as in: "That man is the king of France's nephew.")

A more interesting way of violating the requirement of referentiality is by making statements which commit what I call "the fallacy of pure self-reference." The simplest example of the fallacy is:

THIS STATEMENT IS FALSE.

On inspection, it seems that if this statement is true, then it is false. If it is false, then it is true.

That statement is representative of a whole family of self-referential paradoxes. These would remain parlor-tricks were it not for the fact they have spawned disastrous conclusions in the fields of mathematics and logic. Morris Kline's definitive book on the history of mathematics includes a history of the effect of these paradoxes, and the book is appropriately titled: *Mathematics: The Loss of Certainty.* Kline reports that the discovery of these paradoxes, "and the realization that similar paradoxes might be present, though as yet undetected, in the existing classical mathematics, caused mathematicians to take seriously the problem of consistency." [KLINE, 216] These paradoxes gave skepticism and subjectivism a boost. "The pride of human reason was on the rack." [KLINE, 257]

Take a closer look at "This statement is false."

The solution to the paradox is to realize that the sentence is neither true nor false; it makes no judgment; it is not a proposition at all, but a pseudo-proposition, because it fails to refer to anything. To see this, take the easier case — the same sentence minus its unnecessary twist:

THIS STATEMENT IS TRUE.

What does that assert? That it is true? But that *what* is true? The sentence has no content. To be true or false, a statement must *first* refer to something. Only then can we evaluate its content as either corresponding to or con-tradicting the facts. In both "This statement is true" and "This statement is false," there is no statement, and therefore nothing to be either true or false. Neither sentence *says* anything. A proposition declares what its subject is or does. But the subject of these sentences is "This statement" — meaning its content, not its words as shapes on the page. Since there is no content, no statement is made. Thus, both sentences are pseudo-propositions.

Such sentences attempt the impossible: to refer *only* to their own act of referring. Their own referring — to what? To their own referring to their own referring to . . . ? We are caught in an infinite regress. There is nothing capable of being either true or false until after the sentence has content — a stage we can never reach in cases of pure self-reference.

The fallacy of pure self-reference is an instance of the fallacy contained in any version of the primacy of consciousness: "A consciousness conscious of nothing but itself [an act of pure self-reference] is a contradiction in terms: before it could identify itself as consciousness, it had to be conscious of something." [AS, 1015]

"Pure self-consciousness" is a contradiction in terms. One can certainly be self-conscious, but self-consciousness can occur only after and on the basis of first being conscious — i.e., being aware of something that exists.

Extrospection must precede introspection. Before extrospection, there is no consciousness to introspect. First there is awareness of something, say of a tomato; only then can one be aware of being aware of the tomato. As I put it in the first chapter: consciousness precedes self-consciousness.

This necessary order applies to statements as well. A statement *can* refer to and include itself, but only *after* and on the basis of having first referred to something. For instance, "All propositions refer to something" is a valid and true proposition, and it includes itself: it has a subject to which it refers (namely, "propositions"). But it includes itself only because and on the basis of *first* referring to propositions other than itself — such propositions as "Dogs are animals."

Consider a contrasting case: "This sentence is grammatically correct." That sentence is grammatically correct — and true. It contains no pure self-reference: the sentence refers to its own grammatical structure, but that is a linguistic matter. Its grammatical structure is independent of its conceptual content — i.e., of the particular state of affairs it refers to. It remains grammatically correct if we reverse its assertion: "This sentence is *not* grammatically correct." That is also a grammatically correct sentence; it asserts something, but what it asserts contradicts the facts, so it is false.

The principle that reference must precede self-reference also resolves more convoluted cases, such as that of the Russell paradox. That paradox is based on "the set of all sets that are not members of themselves." Is *that* set a member of itself or not? The answer is: no, it is not self-including. But that does not imply that the set fits its own definition and thus *is* self-including. In fact, the set's definition cannot be applied to itself. A simplified version of the paradox will make this point easier to grasp.

Let's call a man "well-named" if his name correctly describes him. Thus, Mr. Black is "well-named" if he is black, but "ill-named" if he is white. Likewise for Mr. Rich and his financial status. But what about Mr. Ill-Named?

The answer is that Mr. Ill-Named is neither well-named nor ill-named. He is in the same boat with Mr. Jones. "Jones" does not ascribe any feature to its bearer, and neither does "Ill-Named." Pure self-reference is impossible. A name cannot refer only to the inaptness of its own reference — to what?

Mr. Ill-Named is not well-named. Period. Mr. Well-Named is not well-named. Period. And the set of all non-self-including sets is not self-including. Period. One cannot go on to assert that this implies it *is* self-including: self-inclusion presupposes that the predicate has meaningful content, which is not the case when self-application involves an infinite regress.[125]

---

125 The hardest case is perhaps: "This sentence is meaningless." But the principle is the same: that sentence is meaningless, and one cannot object: "But that's just what it says it is!" It does not "say" anything. All paradoxes of pure self-reference dissolve when one realizes that they either attempt to refer to only their own referring, and thus fail to refer, or attempt to evaluate only their own evaluation (of what?) and thus fail to say anything.

Finally, consider Gödel's theorem in mathematics; it is believed to show that there is a certain "incompleteness" in logical-mathematical systems. Carl Boyer says of Gödel's theorem, "it appears to foredoom hope of mathematical certitude." [BOYER, 656] To the extent that, beneath the mathematical formalism, this theorem trades upon "This statement is unprovable,"[126] the same fallacy is involved: there is no proposition there to be proved and thus no "incompleteness" in logic or mathematics for being unable to prove a non-statement.

The emptiness of "This statement is unprovable" shows nothing about proof or completeness; the same circularity is exhibited by "This statement is magnificent." No statement can refer to or evaluate *only* itself.

The Russellian paradoxes arise because philosophers have attempted to treat truth as if it were a matter of the correspondence between *words* and *facts*, and to turn proof into a mechanical procedure in a purely formal system. The validity or defectiveness of a proposition is reduced to an issue of typography — of accepted symbols and physically defined criteria for "well-formed formulas" — in the belief that one can thereby avoid such "mentalistic" ideas as "concept," "meaning," and conscious reference to reality.

In fact, these paradoxes constitute a refutation of the formalist approach to logic. Purely physical criteria provide no means of distinguishing vacuous, self-referential sentences from those with cognitive content. To distinguish propositions from pseudo-propositions, one must recognize the fact that concepts are words given a cognitive content by a mind seeking awareness of the facts of reality.

A validly formed proposition has a clear, unambiguous meaning. It asserts that its subject possesses the characteristic(s) conceptualized by its predicate. This presupposes that the subject and predicate terms are valid concepts, validly defined, and that they are organized in a way that makes the whole they constitute both intelligible and graspable.

Truth

Having outlined the requirements for the logical validity of a proposition, we are now in a position to discuss the nature of truth, and what makes a proposition true.

---

126 Gödel himself denied he was trading upon this circularly self-referential statement. [GÖDEL, 41 N13] This remains a disputed issue.

Truth, as Rand characterizes it, is "the recognition of reality." [AS, 1017] Although a true proposition is often described as one that "corresponds to" the facts, truth actually pertains not to some match-up but to an *awareness*, a mental grasp, of the facts.

Awareness is not a series of isolated responses to isolated stimuli; awareness is a global activity of differentiating and integrating. Products of that activity, such as concepts and propositions, are organic outgrowths of the activity, not self-standing items; concepts and propositions are better analogized to the branches of a tree than to automobiles coming out of a factory. Propositions grow out of a context, and their meaning depends upon that context. No proposition exists or has meaning out of context. The statement's background context is infused into that statement and shapes its meaning.

Part of that context is the hierarchically prior items grounding the proposition. A proposition is formed out of concepts, and the vast majority of propositions depend hierarchically upon prior conclusions. If these hierarchically prior items were different, the proposition, though expressed in the same words, would have a different meaning—i.e., it would be a different proposition.

As an illustration, take the proposition, "Lying is wrong."[127] Its meaning depends on the content of the ethics and metaphysics that informs that statement. For a religionist, "wrong" means "against God's commandments," for Rand, "wrong" means "destructive of man's life on this earth." And for the religionist, the basis of the moral judgment is the unaccountable will of a supernatural being; for Rand, the basis is the natural causal order. [PWNI, CH. 10] A Humean, Kantian, or Existentialist philosophy would fuse still other ideas into "Lying is wrong," so that the same words would actually express very different propositions.

To judge a proposition as true or false, one must know its meaning, and its meaning exists as part of the total cognitive context of which the assertion is an outgrowth.[128] In considering a proposition's truth one cannot detach the proposition from the fabric of one's knowledge. Truth is the relationship that

---

127 I am indebted to Peter Schwartz for making this point, using a similar example, in his lecture "Contextual Knowledge" (https://estore.aynrand.org).

128 This does not mean that truth itself is "contextual"—i.e., the advance of knowledge does not change a true proposition into a false one or vice-versa. Sometimes future knowledge shows that what one believed to be true had never been true, but if a proposition is true, it is timelessly true. (Even a truth about what was the case at a certain time, such as that the Civil War ended in 1865, will remain true forever.)

a part of a cognitive whole bears to the facts of reality, when that proposition expresses in conceptual terms a recognition of those facts.

A false proposition is one that contradicts something. The contradiction may be internal, as in "This circle is square," or the contradiction may be to other knowledge, as in "Pears grow on vines." A proposition is false if it contradicts *any* fact.

An infrequently noticed form of contradiction occurs in philosophical statements that commit what Rand calls "the fallacy of self-exclusion." This fallacy is committed when the *act of asserting* a proposition contradicts its own content (thus the speaker is illicitly excluding his own utterance from what he is claiming). For example, "There are no absolutes" — asserted as an absolute. (Even if one says, "Probably, there are no absolutes," *that* is being asserted as an absolute.) Or, "Man can know nothing for certain" is asserted as something known for certain.

The fallacy is also committed in fields outside of philosophy. Freudian psychologists like to assert: "All thinking is just the rationalization of unconscious impulses" — but then is that statement itself just a rationalization of unconscious impulses? Marxist economists claim: "All thinking is determined not by objective considerations of logic but by the material factors of production" — but then is that statement itself determined by the material factors of production, not logic? Neuroscientists exclude their own statements if they claim that the genetic structure of the brain dictates all human activities — what, then, about the activity of pursuing truth in neuroscience?

Such statements are guilty of self-exclusion no matter who makes them or how, and their content is thus shown to be false. These are the most important instances of the fallacy, but in other cases whether or not the fallacy is committed depends on who makes the statement and how. "I do not exist" exhibits the fallacy of self-exclusion no matter who says it, but "Harry Binswanger does not exist" is a self-exclusion only if I say it. "There is no such thing as the English language," commits the fallacy because it is itself stated in English; but "There is no such thing as the French language," though obviously false, does not commit this particular fallacy.

The manner of making an assertion can contradict the assertion's content. If someone says in an angry, denunciatory tone: "That's a value-judgment!" he is making a value-judgment himself. (In contrast, the mere observation "That's a value-judgment," without an implied moral condemnation, commits no fallacy; it might even be said as a compliment.) A statement is false when it contradicts any fact, including facts about its own utterance.

The next question is: when do we achieve truth? Is being logical in every respect enough? Normally, it is. Normally, if a proposition is fully logical — valid in form and reached by an unbroken chain of logical processing grounded in perception and integrating with everything one knows — it will be true. But logical validity alone does not *guarantee* a proposition's truth. There are unusual cases in which a proposition that one is fully justified in taking to be true, based on all the available evidence, nevertheless turns out to contradict facts not available to one at the time, and thus is false. (Such cases will be discussed in the next chapter.) Thus, "logical" and "true" are not fully coextensive. Moreover, there is a distinction in perspective between "logical" and "true." The focus of "logical" is on the process, of "true" on the product — specifically, on the product's relationship to reality.

A true proposition is one that is both logically valid and expresses an awareness of fact. To achieve that awareness, a proposition must be based on prior observations, conceptualizations, and, in many cases, inferences. I have already discussed perception (CHAPTER 2), concept-formation (Chapters 3 and 4), and the general nature of propositions (CHAPTER 5). The remaining level to be discussed is that of inference.

LOGIC AND INFERENCE

Inference is the mental process of deriving a proposition from observation and/or other propositions. Inferences are either deductive or inductive. Deduction is the simpler process, so I will take that up first.

Deduction

Deduction is the application of the general to the particular (or to the less general). The most elementary act of deduction is the syllogism, which is the "atom" of deduction. In the standard "Socrates" syllogism, the premise "All men are mortal" is the generalization that is applied to the particular fact, "Socrates is a man," to produce the conclusion that he is mortal. The syllogism, with its two premises and three terms, is the smallest unit of deduction; all the more complex and extended processes of deductive reasoning can be reduced to chains of syllogisms.

Almost all of everyday reasoning is deductive. Deduction is the process used when one goes from "It is raining" to "I should take an umbrella" (using the suppressed premise: "When it rains, I should take an umbrella"). Deduction is the form of inference that a jury uses to reach its verdict. (One such deduction might be: "The murderer had type B blood" combined with: "Of the people then in the vicinity, only the defendant had type B blood.") Even the act of making a simple statement, like "That is a dog," is deductive, at least in pattern, because it applies a general term (dog) to its subject.[129]

Because a deduction represents the application of general knowledge that one already possesses, the conclusion was *implicitly* contained beforehand in the generalization used. But the deduction is hardly in vain: the purpose of the deduction is to make that implicit connection *explicit* — i.e., to bring it into conscious awareness. Deduction draws to mind the implications of what one knows. Deduction makes the implicit explicit.

Deduction has been well understood ever since Aristotle identified the syllogism and analyzed which forms are valid and which invalid. There are 256 theoretically possible variants of the syllogism, according to different combinations of the factors known as Quantity, Quality, and Figure. Only 17 of the 256 are formally valid (i.e., have a structure that actually succeeds in applying the general to the particular). But of the 17, only two or three valid forms are used in real-life thought. As to the invalid forms, in my experience only two are apt to occur in ordinary reasoning: equivocation and undistributed middle. Consequently, little needs to be said to improve people's use of syllogisms, and that little can be quickly gleaned by consulting any traditional textbook.[130] (There is much merit, however in familiarizing oneself with the so-called "informal fallacies," such as Ad Hominem, Appeal to Authority, Begging the Question, and a dozen or so others; these are "informal" not in being casual but in pertaining to content not form, and to the validity or relevance of the premises used. It was Aristotle who identified almost all of the informal fallacies.)

Induction

The other type of inference is induction: the process of generalizing from particulars (or from the less general). Where deduction applies the more general to the less general, induction moves from the less general to the more general.

---

129 See CHAPTER 5 and ITOE, 28.

130 I recommend older textbooks, such as *Logic: An Introduction*, by Lionel Ruby (re-issued by Paper Tiger).

Induction has been under attack for centuries, and is now regarded as something uncertain or subjective. But the validity of induction cannot in fact be denied or even questioned: induction is the fundamental means of acquiring conceptual knowledge. Without induction, there would be no general premise for a deduction to apply. *Deduction presupposes induction.*

Since all inferences either are inductions or require inductively reached premises, the attack on induction is an attack on all inference — which is self-refuting, since the attacks themselves require making and applying generalizations reached by induction. In other words, the statement "Induction is invalid" commits the fallacy of self-exclusion. The same is true of milder attacks, such as "Induction cannot give certainty" which is itself a claim to certainty about a generalization.

Though there is no "problem of induction," there are legitimate questions regarding *how* induction works and what is required for an inductive generalization to be valid. (In the same way, there never was any "problem of deduction," but Aristotle's discovery of the principles of deduction marked an historic advance.)

A revolutionary understanding of induction has recently been provided by Leonard Peikoff. Rejecting the conventional statistical approach, Peikoff's treatment of induction focuses on the crucial role of *concepts*:

> One must grasp how the constituent concepts of a generalization are related to reality before one can grasp how the generalization itself is related to reality. The theory developed here is based on Rand's theory of concepts. . . . [V]alid concepts, in her definition of "concepts," not only make possible but also guide our search for true generalizations.[131]

The two essentials of Peikoff's theory reflect two points of Objectivist epistemology emphasized in this book: 1) the hierarchical nature of knowledge, and 2) the open-endedness of concepts.

1. Hierarchy applies to generalizations just as it does to concepts. Accordingly, when seeking to understand induction, we cannot plunge in at any random stage of the hierarchy. We could not understand concept-formation if, in ignorance of hierarchy, we began with and focused only on

---

131 Leonard Peikoff, Introduction to *The Logical Leap*, by David Harriman. [HARRIMAN 2010, xi] This book, prepared under Peikoff's guidance, presents in written form the theory that Peikoff gave as lectures; Harriman illustrates the theory by discussing, philosophically, a series of the key discoveries in the history of physics.

higher-level concepts, such as "inflation," and attempted to discover how these concepts could be formed directly from perception. Likewise, we cannot understand induction by taking higher-level generalizations, such as "Water boils at 212 degrees Fahrenheit," as our paradigm case, since this is a higher-level generalization and is not formed directly from perception.

A sensitivity to the hierarchical nature of induction enables us to recognize that advanced generalizations depend on less advanced ones, so that the right cases to examine first are those at the hierarchy's base. The base is *first-level generalizations*, generalizations that do not presuppose any prior generalizations. Peikoff's examples include: "Fire burns paper," "Drinking water quenches thirst," "Pushing a ball makes it roll."

The facts that first-level generalizations formulate are self-evident — i.e., available to direct perception. Moreover, the concepts used to formulate those facts are concepts validated by direct perception, and not subject to error. E.g., the similarity in the *rolling* of a baseball, a golf ball, and an egg is perceptually given, so the concept "roll" needs no justification or reduction. (The same is true of concepts of perceptually given attributes, relations, etc. One cannot make an error or violate Rand's Razor in forming such concepts as: "blue," "soft," or "on."[132])

All these cases of first-level generalizations — "Water quenches thirst," "Fire burns paper," and "Pushing a ball makes it roll" — are identifications of causal connections. This is true of inductions in general, on any level.[133]

Some cause-and-effect relationships are complex and can be identified only on the basis of abstract concepts, but the causation operative in these simple cases is *available on the perceptual level.*[134] A toddler can see and feel

---

132 *The Logical Leap* refers to concepts like "roll" and "thirst" as "first-level," which has generated some confusion. One must distinguish between two somewhat different ways of assigning a concept's "level": the level pertaining to learning-order, and the level pertaining to justification. (On this issue, see CHAPTER 4, p. 153, footnote 74.) A child directly perceives the difference between the motions of things that roll and the motions of things that slide or tumble, and thus he cannot get "roll" wrong (as he can get wrong "vector" or "freedom").

    It is self-evidency (not place in the order of learning) that is required of the concepts used in one's first inductions. A generalization, to be first-level, must contain only concepts that are perceptually self-evident, not subject to error, and need no justification. That is indeed the case for all the concepts in "Pushing a ball makes it roll" and the other examples of first-level generalizations.

133 A possible exception is the case of generalizations about part-whole relationships, e.g., "All matter is composed of atoms," and, "All living organisms are composed of cells." But even these could be construed as identifying what Aristotle called "the material cause."

134 Peikoff credits this point to Gregory Salmieri.

the effects of giving the ball a push; he can see the fire burning the paper, he can feel the water quenching his thirst. The causality here is nothing like that involved in such abstract generalizations as: "An increase in supply causes a fall in price" or, "Stars generate their light and their heat by nuclear fusion." These two statements do identify causal connections, but not ones that are perceptually given, as is the causal connection identified in the statement "Pushing a ball makes it roll."

To make a valid inductive generalization, one must know the operative causality (either perceive it directly or reach it conceptually). To generalize from "This particular S is P" to "All S is P," one must know that this S is P *because* it is S, not because of some other fact about it. One needs to know that to be S is to be P.

For example, Archimedes discovered that an object immersed in water is buoyed up by the weight of the water it displaces. This is a fact about physical objects as such, not about, say, the material of which they are made. To be an object is to have weight — thus, to displace water (which is incompressible). It is not qua stone or wood or metal that a thing is buoyant. An immersed object qua object displaces its weight in water.

"S qua S is P" implies "To be an S is to be P." That fact is the basis and the meaning of the generalization "All S is P."

Concepts of characteristics, like "weight," enable one to isolate and identify causal factors and thus to know qua what a given entity acted as it did. That knowledge is necessary for one to reach a higher-level generalization.[135]

2. The second part of Peikoff's theory is its explanation of the mechanism of generalizing — e.g., of the mind's movement from "This (paper) did that (burned)" to "Fire burns paper." The factor permitting such generalizing is the *open-ended* nature of the concepts the child applies. In conceptually identifying the fire as fire, the burning as burning, and the paper as paper, the generalization follows perforce. The open-endedness of concepts is what permits the application of concepts to new concretes, and the potential for making that application is the essence of what it is to generalize.

We must bear in mind that first-level generalizations, like all propositions, are *contextual*. A child observing a newspaper burning in a fireplace can form the open-ended proposition "Fire burns paper" without having the responsibility of testing the scope and conditions of this generalization:

---

135 This analysis in terms of S qua S, and the formulation "To be an S is to be P" are not taken
from Peikoff or Harriman, and the responsibility for any errors in this way of conceiving
higher-level generalization is my own.

the context of his knowledge does not permit doing so, and no valid standard requires the impossible. Here, as in ethics, "ought" implies "can."

Consider the case at hand: going from seeing a newspaper burn up in a fireplace to "Fire burns paper." Our beginning inducer is perhaps two or three years old. At his rudimentary stage of knowledge, the child, as Peikoff points out, could not and does not need to ask himself such questions as, "Is it only the first edition of *The New York Times* that acts this way?" "Is it only in wood fires that a sufficient temperature is reached?" He knows of no such issues. When he learns them, years later, he may add any needed contextual provisos to his induction. The key point (to be pursued in the next chapter) is that his later knowledge does not overturn his earlier knowledge. On the contrary, the later discoveries *depend on and expand* his original discovery that fire burns paper.

Take an extreme case: the fact that paper can be treated with flame-retardant, in which case it will not burn. This fact, which is way beyond the young child's ken, in no way contradicts or invalidates his generalization; in fact, the invention of flame-retardants was made possible by the prior knowledge that fire burns paper.

The point is that the later statement, "Fire burns paper, unless counter-acted by flame-retardant," constitutes *more* knowledge than "Fire burns paper." Learning about flame-retardants moves the child from having one item of knowledge on the topic to having two, rather than from one item of (apparent) knowledge back to zero.

There is more work that needs to be done regarding induction, especially with regard to the precise *standards* for inducing and validating higher-level generalizations in science. [SEE HARRIMAN, 2010] But from what has already been sketched in here, it should be clear that Peikoff's theory answers the basic questions, and that the key to understanding induction is the application of logic — i.e., of context and hierarchy — to the topic, on the base provided by Ayn Rand's theory of concepts. (Of special importance is Rand's point: "No concept man forms is valid unless he integrates it without contradiction into the total sum of his knowledge." [AS, 1016])

LOGIC IN A NUTSHELL

Logic is the reality-based method of conceptual functioning. To be logical, a process must be grounded in and derive its content from observation of reality. Logic is based on the basic fact of reality: the Law of Identity, with its two corollary Laws: Non-Contradiction and Excluded Middle. Logic consists of integrating and differentiating on the basis of the identity that things are observed to have — i.e., according to their observed character-istics and the measurement-relationships obtaining among them.

Logic also requires obeying the identity of man's means of cognition. This means recognizing that knowledge is gained in a context and is built up in a hierarchical progression from perceptually given data. And it means accepting the principle of unit-economy, in recognition of the limit on the number of distinct units a consciousness can hold in focal awareness and deal with at one time.

To summarize: logic is observation-based, non-contradictory, and unit-economical.

8

PROOF AND CERTAINTY

THE PRECEDING CHAPTERS HAVE FOCUSED ON THE ACQUISITION of knowledge. Now I turn to the issue of validation — the process of ensuring that an idea is correct, does constitute knowledge. Some ideas can be validated by direct perception, but other ideas require a multi-step process of validation: *proof*.

The need for proof arises not only in regard to ideas one hears asserted by others but also in regard to any of one's own past conclusions whose logical basis one no longer clearly recalls. The question then is: is the idea true or false? Is it derivable by logical means or not? What is its epistemic status: is it certain, likely, possible — or is it invalid?

The epistemic status of an idea depends upon the evidence supporting it and on the logical validity of the reasoning premised on that evidence. If someone is asserting an idea, and its basis in reality is not obvious, the first thing one should do is to ask him directly: "Why do you say that; what's your evidence?" — a question asked too rarely. In validating a belief of one's own, a logical first step is to ask oneself: "How did I arrive at this belief, by what steps?" — not as autobiography, but as a lead to identifying the steps by which one could validly reach this conclusion. Thus, one attempts to "reverse engineer" the idea, seeking to determine if it can be reached logically from prior knowledge.

To prove an idea, one needs to link it back to perceived fact. The Objectivist term for this process of going back "down" the hierarchy to prove an idea is: *reduction.*

> The responsibility imposed by the fact that knowledge is hierarchical is: the need of *reduction.* . . . Reduction is the means of connecting an advanced knowledge to reality by traveling backward through the hierarchical structure involved, i.e., in the reverse order of that required to reach the knowledge. "Reduction" is the process of identifying in logical sequence the intermediate steps that relate a cognitive item to perceptual data. Since there are options in the details of a learning process, one need not always retrace the steps one initially happened to take. What one must retrace is the essential logical structure. [OPAR, 132–133]

Heraclitus said that the way up and the way down are one and the same — referring to a staircase. The same can be said of the staircase of knowledge. Contrary to contemporary notions, there is only *one* logic, not both a "logic of discovery" and a "logic of proof." Instead, there are two different *directions* of motion along the same logical, hierarchical structure: *derivation* moves "up" from the perceptually given, while *proof* moves back "down" to the perceptually given. (There may be intermediate upward steps.)

A derivation moves in thought from what is closer to perception to what is farther from perception. Reduction is the same process in reverse, moving back down the same hierarchical structure, with the hierarchy terminating in the self-evident data of perception. Derivation is from perception; proof is back to perception.

The two directions — derivation and proof — apply to both deduction and induction. In deduction, we take knowledge gained from past observation and apply it to a new instance. For example:

Lassie is a dog.
Dogs are animals.

Lassie is an animal.

The conclusion is more abstract — farther from perception — than the first premise. One gains a wider knowledge of Lassie by means of applying to Lassie the prior generalization that dogs are animals. (For this to be new knowledge about Lassie, the prior generalization would have to have been formed from observation of dogs other than Lassie.)

Now consider a somewhat different case of deductive derivation:

> There is smoke coming from that hill.
> Where there's smoke there is fire.
> _____
> There's fire on that hill.

Here, the conclusion is no more abstract *in itself* than the first premise, but it is a conclusion not perceptually available *now,* from *here*; it is further removed from currently available perception than is the starting premise, "There is smoke coming from that hill."

In any deductive derivation, we use a general premise ("Where there's smoke there's fire") as a bridge to make a new application. We reach thereby not new *general* knowledge, but new knowledge about the concrete (viz., that particular hill).

In contrast to derivation, proof goes in the other direction, to check the validity of the conclusion (or to prove a hypothesis). The thought process would be something like the following.

"Is Lassie an animal? What is an animal? It's a living being with consciousness and locomotion, like pigs, snakes, and dogs, as opposed to plants. Since Lassie is a dog, and, like all dogs, she is conscious and moves herself around, Lassie is an animal. Q.E.D."

(One is not by this process checking the validity of the syllogism used in the deduction; in simple cases, that does not need to be checked; instead, the process is one of reducing "animal" back to perception, to see whether there can be an application made. Of course, the example is artificial, chosen to illustrate the pattern of a reduction rather than for realism.)

For a case of inductive derivation, consider the following schematized (not complete) example. It starts from Peikoff's example "Fire burns paper," and goes one level more abstract:

> Fire burns paper.
> Focusing sunlight on paper with a magnifying glass burns it.

Putting paper in a very hot oven burns it.
The common causal factor in these cases is high heat.
Therefore, high heat burns paper.

(Let's put aside any doubts as to whether this derivation is iron-clad: my point here is the hierarchical progression — the logical structure — not the certainty of the result.)

The corresponding reductive proof goes in the other direction:

"Does high heat burn paper? Yes, because fire burns paper, highly focused sunlight burns paper, and a very hot oven burns it, but applying less heat in each case does not, so the common factor is high heat."

This artificial example is too simple to be a process one would actually need to step through, but it shows the pattern that would be involved in more complex reductions. Take, for instance, the reduction of the Law of Demand in economics: "The quantity of a good that will be demanded varies inversely with its price." This can be reduced by first getting clear on what is meant by "good," "demand," and "price." (Roughly: a "good" is an item with exchange value — i.e., which is bought and sold; "demand" is money spent on the purchase of a good; price is the amount of money paid per unit of the good when it is bought.) Next, one identifies the intermediate generalizations on which the Law of Demand is based, such as the fact that more people can afford to buy a good if its price goes down, fewer if it goes up. Continuing the reduction "downwards" to concretes: when Ford's Model T lowered the price of an automobile, a vastly greater number of people could afford to buy one, and did. Likewise, falling prices for big-screen televisions have greatly expanded their sales. To have a logically complete reduction, more would be needed — for instance, reducing "afford" to its base (a step unnecessary in most real-life cases) — but the example should make clear the pattern of reduction.

The complete validation of an idea — the justification for accepting it as a grasp of fact — requires both that it be proved by reduction to perceptual reality and that it be integrated into the sum of one's knowledge. A conclusion has been fully proved only when it has been related, step by step, back to perceptual data (the task of reduction) *and* has been checked for consistency with the rest of one's knowledge (the task of integration). Between these two processes, man achieves a "double check," as Peikoff terms it, on the validity of his conclusions. [OPAR, 138]

The integration required is a positive act, not merely the failure to find a contradiction, such as the failure to find any contradiction between the observed price of tomatoes and the inferred size of the planet Jupiter. Instead, a true idea will positively "fit into place" with the rest of one's knowledge, unifying it into a coherent whole. For instance, the inference to Jupiter's size coheres with: its brightness in the night sky, the orbits of its moons, its gravitational effects on the other planets and the sun, and even the comparative rarity of asteroids hitting the Earth (Jupiter's huge gravitational field, on one theory, acts to sweep asteroids away from the inner planets).[136]

Since reality is an interconnected whole, an adequate grasp of reality will capture the connections found in reality. In fact, we grasp reality *by means of* becoming aware of relationships. Consciousness *is* an awareness of differences and similarities.

For instance, consider the knowledge that the Earth rotates on its axis. This knowledge is reducible through a series of steps back to what one sees in the nighttime sky. But this knowledge also *explains* facts that are not among those used to reach it. As noted earlier, it explains why weather in the Northern Hemisphere moves predominantly from west to east. Also, the Earth's rotation on its axis *coheres* with the facts, observable by the naked eye, that sunspots move in only one direction across the sun (because the sun, too, rotates), and with the fact that ordinary objects, such as a thrown rock, virtually never move without rotation.

New conceptual knowledge is derived and validated by making logical connections to antecedent knowledge. Implied thereby is an important principle: *no new knowledge contradicts old knowledge.*

New knowledge can contradict old mistaken beliefs, but not old *knowledge.* Knowledge is a mental grasp of the facts of reality. Contradictions do not exist in reality; newly grasped facts cannot contradict previously grasped facts. Yes, the facts under consideration can change, as when a rock that had been cool is warmed by sunlight; but a change in the object of know-

---

136 One can even, through sufficient intermediate steps, find significant relationships between the price of tomatoes and the size of Jupiter. E.g., the price of tomatoes is studied by economics, the size of Jupiter by astronomy, so one belongs to the social sciences, the other to the natural sciences; one fact is "man-made" in contrast to the other's status as "metaphysically given" (see CHAPTER 2); both the price and the size are measurements and thus involve a standard of measurement (the dollar and the meter); both standards of measurement have to be based on a unit adapted to the human scale of perception [ITOE, 8], etc.

ledge is not what the principle refers to. Now, in the noonday sun, the rock has become warm, but it remains eternally true that the rock was cool at dawn. One's knowledge of its state at dawn is not contradicted by learning the changed state of affairs. (In addition, the change is lawful and proceeds in accordance with the nature of the rock and of the incident sunlight; if tomorrow, under the same conditions, the rock did not warm, *that* would be a contradiction.)

The principle that new knowledge does not contradict old knowledge rules out notions such as, "For the medievals, the world was flat; for us it is round." Such attacks on knowledge and certainty depend upon treating as equivalent fact and error, truth and falsehood, science and fantasy — as if the Earth had actually been flat until Columbus' voyage somehow curved it. But it is the error of the primacy of consciousness to imagine that the nature of existence depends upon men's beliefs, wishes, or social practices.

A slightly different line of attack on certainty is found in the popular notion that the discovery of new conditions demolishes conclusions that did not countenance them, as in the idea that "Swans are white" was demolished by the discovery of black swans in Australia, or that Newton's law of gravity was refuted by Einstein's theory of general relativity. But neither discovery destroyed any previous knowledge; in fact, both discoveries expanded the previously existing body of knowledge.

The generalization "Swans are white" could not *logically* have warranted making the assertion: "There are no black swans anywhere in the world." That is *not* what was known at the earlier stage. The new knowledge is: "Swans are white, except in Australia where some are black." Thus, the end result is more knowledge, not less. Similarly, Newton's law of gravity was supplemented, not refuted, by Einstein, because that law never extended to the kind of conditions (super-huge masses and/or submicroscopic distances of separation) that Einstein's theory embraces.[137]

Knowledge is not an assemblage of out-of-context absolutes, as the skeptics assume in their attacks on knowledge. Any conclusion exists in and depends upon a context, the context of the antecedent knowledge used to establish it. Peikoff writes:

---

137 Einstein's theory applies generally, even to the range of masses and distances that Newton did refer to; but within this range, the deviation from Newton's inverse-square law is too small for Newton to have observed. This too is accommodated by a proper statement of his law, which incorporates the proviso, "to the limits of accuracy in measurement presently attainable."

If a fact is inherent in human consciousness, then that fact is not an obstacle to cognition, but a precondition of it. . . . In this approach to philosophy, there is no "problem" of the senses, of concepts, of emotions — or of man's non-omniscience.

Man is a being of limited knowledge — *and he must, therefore, identify the cognitive context of his conclusions.* In any situation where there is reason to suspect that a variety of factors is relevant to the truth, only some of which are presently known, he is obliged to acknowledge this fact. The implicit or explicit preamble to his conclusion must be: "On the basis of the available evidence, i.e., within the context of the factors so far discovered, the following is the proper conclusion to draw." Thereafter, the individual must continue to observe and identify; should new information warrant it, he must qualify his conclusion accordingly.

If a man follows this policy, he will find that his knowledge at one stage *is not contradicted* by later discoveries. He will find that the discoveries expand his understanding; that he learns more about the conditions on which his conclusions depend; that he moves from relatively generalized, primitive observations to increasingly detailed, sophisticated formulations. He will also find that the process is free of epistemological trauma. The advanced conclusions augment and enhance his earlier knowledge; they do not clash with or annul it. [OPAR, 172–173]

Knowledge is a mental product. If one forms that product by employing the right method (logic) on the right material (prior knowledge), one is fully entitled to claim the result as knowledge. Yes, there are occasional cases in which one will be entitled to claim as knowledge a conclusion that later turns out to have been a mistake, but that is not grist for the skeptics' mill. Man is neither infallible nor omniscient, and epistemic standards must embrace this fact. The purpose of any standard is to guide men in how to proceed *within what is possible.* There is no justification for erecting a fantasy standard of judgment. [See BINSWANGER, 1981]

Using rational epistemic standards permits us firmly to distinguish between an actual error ("Swans are pink" or "Gravity depends upon the cube of the distance") and a truth that has come to need qualification ("Swans are white, except in Australia" or "Gravity depends upon the square of the distance, and on relativistic factors"). In making this distinction, it is helpful to consider the causes of error.

Cognitive errors result from a defect in the thought process or in its input material. More concretely, cognitive errors result from one of three causes: 1) illogic, 2) false premises, or 3) incomplete information.

1. *Illogic.* When one departs from logic, the conclusion one reaches does not follow from the evidence and premises used. A simple example is that of making an error in adding up a long column of figures. If one follows the rules of arithmetic, one will not err, but we sometimes slip up, depart from the rules, and thus get the wrong sum.

In very simple, one-step reasoning, error is not possible. No one can make a mistake in adding 2 + 1, or in combining "That's ice," and "Ice is cold." But logical missteps are not uncommon in complex calculations and in the complex, multi-step reasoning used in everyday decision-making.[138] The possibility of error looms much larger in inductive inference, which requires integration on a much wider scale. (See HARRIMAN, 30–35.) A person's departure from logic may come from wanton irrationality, sloppiness, slight negligence, ignorance, or just an innocent slip-up; but whatever the illogic's cause, its product is not knowledge.

2. *False premises.* Falsehood used as "input" to the process of inference cannot result in a grasp of fact. Truth cannot be built upon error. One cannot become aware of reality by weaving in elements of the unreal. (Even if a given conclusion could have been reached from true premises, it does not represent knowledge — i.e., a grasp of fact — when it is reached from false premises.[139])

The truth or falsehood of a premise is not a primary: any idea now being used as a premise was itself reached as the outcome of an earlier conceptual process. And the concepts composing the premise were formed in earlier processes of concept-formation. The ultimate starting point of the conceptual is perception, and perception cannot be in error (see CHAPTER 2). Thus, the truth or falsehood of a conclusion depends upon the nature of the conceptual processes one has used to reach it — not just the current processes but also the earlier processes, which led to the premises and to the concepts used.

---

138 Slip-ups become possible when the task exceeds the limits of the "crow," and material has to be shifted in and out of short-term memory.

139 Thus, the contemporary logical doctrine that "false implies true" is a serious error. Although one can draw (narrowly) logical inferences about the consequences of believing falsehoods, a conclusion based on a falsehood does not itself represent truth. A conclusion based on a falsehood is not a recognition of reality. (However, the hypothetical form of the proposition may be true: "If this were true, then such and such would follow.")

So, errors resulting from false premises usually reduce to the first cause of error: illogical processing (remembering that the standards for determining what is logical must be based on what is possible, not on an impossible omniscience). These two causes of error reduce to: current illogic and past illogic resulting in false ideas now being used as premises. (For completeness: there is also the rare case of false premises resulting from the next factor.)

3. *Incomplete information.* Although this occurs very infrequently, there are cases in which, despite being flawlessly logical, one reaches a false conclusion because the data were both insufficient and apt to mislead, because of their similarity to other things known. The simplest kind of case is erring in identifying perceptual concretes — e.g., thinking the distant hills are blue, that the straight stick semi-submerged in water is bent, or taking a man's twin to be him. Though these conclusions resulted from (we may assume) logical conclusions concerning what was seen, ignorance of certain facts result in one drawing conclusions that are errors nonetheless. The judgments "Those hills are blue," "That stick is bent," "There's Joe," are simply false, as further observation reveals.

As noted in the previous chapter, being logical does not *guarantee* the truth of one's conclusions. Nevertheless, standards of cognition must be restricted to what is possible within the context of the information available to the individual. The standards cannot require omniscience, which is an impossibility. Thus, conclusions resulting from *logical* processing (of material that is itself actual knowledge) are entitled to be claimed as knowledge. That remains true even in the rare cases when later information shows that the conclusion was an error. If it was fully rational to judge as sufficient the information available when the conclusion was drawn, the conclusion, though erroneous, was logical, *and it would have been illogical and irrational to draw any other*. (This raises the topic of certainty, which will be discussed shortly.)

A method of cognition is *right* if it is adapted to the requirements of success; the fact that it does not make failure impossible does not weigh against the basic method, only against the specific procedure that led to the failure. (More on this topic will follow.)

The discovery of an actual error — even of a huge, fundamental error — always represents cognitive *progress*. One knows more after discovering the error than one did previously. And, determining the cause of the error, and resolving to be on the lookout for its recurrence, makes one less likely to err in the future, thus strengthening one's cognitive position. Some discoveries of error are painful, as when one discovers that what one took to be a wart is in fact a cancerous growth. But the horrible shock is due to the nature of the facts discovered, not to having been in error — as shown by considering the reverse case: when what one took to be a cancer turns out to be merely a wart, no one's reaction in this case is: "Damn! I was in error!" Leaving aside the content of what was discovered, the discovery of error is always a gain in knowledge and, in that respect, is to be welcomed.

As one learns more about reality, one's context of knowledge grows. Contrary to the skeptics, it is not an error but an *expansion* of knowledge when one discovers the existence of a new factor to be taken into account. It is expansion, not refutation, when one learns in economics that prices can rise due to inflation rather than to real changes in supply and demand (as opposed to nominal changes), or when one learns that blood types thought to be compatible with each other (type A with type A) are incompatible if the newly discovered Rh factors do not match. [OPAR, 173–174] Likewise, it is not an error but an expansion when greater precision or a wider scope of measurement results in a more complete formulation of a mathematical relationship. (E.g., Tycho Brahe's careful measurements of the orbits of Mars enabled Kepler to identify that the planetary orbits Copernicus thought to be circular were actually slightly elliptical.[140])

Localized errors may arise on occasion, but if one adheres to logic, knowledge taken globally is a growing sum. Even when limited information results in a (justified) error, the processes of reduction and integration mean that errors are limited and are correctable in the light of new data. Also, identifying the cause of any error allows one to guard against it in the future. One learns that the color of hills is *not* to be judged as blue on the basis of how they look from a distance, that a stick half-submerged in water is *not* bent, or, to take a recent scientific correction, that some radiation *does* escape a "black hole."

(There are also lessons one can draw from cases of illogic; these involve a refinement of one's methodological tools — e.g., by becoming aware of and guarding against logical fallacies, such as that of the stolen concept.)

Rather than being traumatized by the fact that logic does not immunize one against all error, one must recognize that the identification of error as being error is itself an illustration of the fact that we do know what we know. For it is only on the basis of subsequent *knowledge* that an earlier conclusion can be identified as erroneous.

---

140   Usually, it is not only greater precision in measurement but also a re-conceptualization that is involved.

Instead of bewailing the fact that automatic omniscience is unavailable, we must establish and adhere to cognitive standards that distinguish between the *right* and the *wrong* ways of using one's mind volitionally. Cognitive standards cannot require the impossible; only what is under one's volitional control can be judged.

CERTAINTY

Not all claims to knowledge are elaborate or in need of proof. In the case of "There goes a fire truck," one makes the observation, applies the relevant concepts, and that's that. Similarly, for knowledge reached by a chain of rote steps, as in arithmetical calculations, one need only check that the steps were followed. But there are other cases, cases in which an item of knowledge is acquired and validated by the accumulation of evidence over time. For instance, at a jury trial, the presentation of the evidence may take months, with an objective verdict becoming possible only at the end. In geology, the theory of plate tectonics was first proposed in 1912, but it took half a century of investigation before the theory qualified as having been proved.

Such cases, in which the evidence for a conclusion grows over time, give rise to the idea of an *evidentiary continuum* and to the concepts that mark off ranges along that continuum — notably: "possible," "likely," and "certain" (and informal subdivisions, e.g., "barely possible" and "quite likely").

In measuring evidence, the standard is set by the goal: proof. A given position on the scale can be measured by what (approximate) portion of the journey to proof has been completed. Thus, the unit of evidence is fractional: the ratio of the evidence at hand to the total set of evidence required for proof.

An idea is "certain" when the evidence for it is conclusive: one has acquired and integrated all the evidence needed for proof, and contrary ideas have no supporting evidence. An idea is "possible" when the evidence in its favor is small in comparison to what would constitute proof, and there is some evidence for contrary ideas. "Likely" is the middle case: one has a lot of supporting evidence, but at least one contrary idea still qualifies as possible.

The relationship between certainty and knowledge needs clarification. "Certainty" and "knowledge" are closely related but distinguishable concepts. Knowledge is primarily differentiated from ignorance; certainty is primarily differentiated from states that are less than certain: the possible and the likely. "Certainty" refers to the *cognitive status* of an idea, which means it is a purely epistemological concept; "knowledge," in contrast, has both a metaphysical and an epistemological component: to know something, the thing known must exist (must be a fact) and one must have a mental grasp of it. "Fact," in contrast, is a purely metaphysical term: facts are facts whether or not anyone knows them or has any evidence of their existence.

But do we actually need the concept "certain"? After all, "proved" already names the status of being established by conclusive evidence. If "certain" merely duplicates "proved," then we should eliminate it, in accordance with Rand's Razor. But "certain" does add something to "proved": the implications for *action*. Proof establishes truth; certainty denotes the confidence that one can have in acting, existentially and cognitively, on the idea. To identify an idea as "certain" is to recognize that one can act on it without hesitation, without doubt, without needing further deliberation or investigation.[141]

An important implication of this understanding of certainty is: *one can be certain but mistaken*. A man can be objectively certain of a conclusion that is, unbeknownst to him, false (although this occurs but rarely). There is no contradiction in saying, "I was certain but wrong." The meaning is: "Given the state of the information I had at the time, I was fully justified in believing it — the evidence required me to — but in the light of what I now know, my conclusion was mistaken; the facts were not as I thought they were, what I took to be knowledge turned out to be a mistaken belief."

Thus, *certainty is contextual.* "Conclusive evidence" means "evidence that is sufficient within a given context of knowledge," not with an impossible omniscience as its standard. But certainty's contextuality does not make it subjective: the standard of "sufficient" is not defined in terms of personal feelings or social conventions, but in terms of logic. In a given context of knowledge, the evidence for a conclusion is conclusive, rendering the conclusion *certain*, when the totality of the evidence logically requires it. That is, within a properly delimited field of alternative hypotheses, only one conclusion explains and is consistent with all the data, all the other hypotheses being excluded as contradicting some or all of that data.[142] In such a case, the evidence, taken as an integrated sum, *supports and is consistent with one and only one conclusion.* That conclusion is then contextually certain.

---

141 Any further information that comes along will be useful cognitively, will add to the fabric of one's knowledge. But, with regard to action, there comes a point at which gaining more information cannot be expected to change one's action-decision.

142 What I mean here by a "properly delimited field of alternative hypotheses" will be explained shortly.

Note that the evidence must logically *imply* the conclusion, not the other way around. Certainty is not achieved merely on the grounds that a given hypothesis, *if* true, *would* explain the observed facts. What one needs for certainty is that *only* a given hypothesis can explain all the observed facts. And that "only," in turn, assumes that one knows enough about this kind of phenomenon to be certain that one of a relatively few hypotheses has to be the correct one.

For example, suppose one observes tracks in the soil that have been made by some passing animal. Suppose that the tracks are not too clear but have a general shape consistent with the animal having been a fox. One cannot reason: "Foxes produce tracks shaped like these, so it is certain that a fox walked by," because tracks with roughly similar shapes can also be produced by dogs, wolves, and coyotes. The track shapes, given the appropriate context of knowledge, do establish that it is *possible* that a fox walked by, but to claim certainty would be to commit the fallacy of Affirming the Consequent: "If a fox walked by, then tracks with these shapes would be present; tracks with these shapes are present, therefore a fox walked by." Again, what is needed is: "*Only* if a fox walked by would this kind of track be present." That statement is equivalent to: "If this kind of track is present, then a fox has walked by" — which allows for the valid form of the hypothetical syllogism known as "Affirming the Antecedent."[143]

Now let's add to the example other facts about the observed tracks beyond their shape: their distance apart, their depth in the soil, the implied nature of the gait, etc. If one has a knowledge of animal-tracking and knows what animals inhabit the locale, and if only foxes produce tracks with all those characteristics, then the evidence is conclusive that a fox made the tracks. There is then no *logical* alternative hypothesis. The conclusion is certain.

The mere fact that one is ignorant of any alternative possibility is not sufficient grounds for claiming certainty; certainty does not flow from ignorance. Nor can one base certainty on the psychological issue of what alternative explanations one can or cannot think up. A presupposition of attaining certainty on a given topic is that one knows enough to make a rational delimitation of the hypotheses, so that one knows that the true hypothesis is within that delimited set.

---

143 Affirming the Antecedent: If A, then B; A; therefore B — valid. Affirming the Consequent: If *A*, then *B*; *B*; therefore *A* — invalid. E.g., "If there is traffic, he will be late; there is traffic; so he will be late" — valid. "If there is traffic, he will be late; he will be late, so there is traffic — invalid: he could be late for other reasons.

These issues arose in the Workshops on Objectivist Epistemology, when Rand was asked a question about the so-called "hypothetico-deductive" method in science. Here is the exchange, as reprinted in the Appendix to ITOE:

> Prof. M: Would you consider the following method of confirming a scientific principle to be valid? One formulates the principle being guided by one's knowledge of fact. Using the principle, one next deduces how entities under certain conditions should act. Then, if one observes such action, and within the context of one's knowledge can account for it only by the principle which predicted it, it follows that the principle has been confirmed. In summary, one induces the principle, deduces its consequences, and if only that principle is known to give rise to those consequences, which in turn exist, then the principle is confirmed as a contextual absolute.
>
> AR: This is outside the province of my book; this is the theory of induction. But within this context, I would say, no, this would not be the right procedure, and there is a danger of a very, very grave error here. Because if you follow the procedure you outline here, and you make certain predictions on the basis of a hypothesis, and the entities do act accordingly, you conclude that you can hold as a contextual absolute that it was your hypothesis that was operating and that it is therefore true. You are assuming an omniscience that contextual knowledge cannot permit. Because since you are not omniscient, within the context of your knowledge you cannot say that your particular hypothesis was the *only* possible cause of the entities acting the way you predicted. You would have to say this offers great confirmation of your hypothesis, but it still remains a hypothesis and cannot be taken as knowledge. Why? Because so many other possibilities are involved. And I don't mean unknown or unknowable factors — I mean that it would be impossible, for any complex principle of science that you are trying to establish, to eliminate, even within your own context of knowledge, all the other possibilities.
>
> What I would question is this part of the procedure: "if only that principle is known to give rise to those consequences" — that's the mistake of arrested knowledge, right there.

Prof. M: Even though it is relative to what you know at that time?

AR: Even though it's at that time and it's your full context of knowledge. Because you cannot conclude that *something which is not fully known to you* can be produced only by one hypothesized factor. On the basis of that same context of knowledge, any number of hypotheses could be constructed. Which is why we need hypotheses. If it were otherwise, then your hypothesis to begin with would almost have to be a certainty. [ITOE, 301–303][144]

In a scientific induction, or in an extended investigation to determine a concrete fact (e.g., crime detection), one uses background knowledge to establish a kind of "genus" that delimits the field to cases that warrant investigation. This narrowing of the field to a genus of possibilities must be based on knowledge; one must be certain that the truth lies in one of the possibilities in that genus. Only that delimitation enables one to conclude objectively that certainty is reached when only one hypothesis supports and is consistent with the totality of the evidence.

Normally, the available evidence is consistent with only a small genus of possibilities and rules out the rest of the universe, as it were. If only three people had access to the crime-victim during the time when the crime was committed, then these three are ruled in and the rest of the world's population is ruled out. These three become "suspects," in view of the fact that the available information is consistent with any of them being guilty and inconsistent with anyone else being guilty.

The assessment of an idea as "possible" or "likely" is not a guess or speculation but a cognitive assertion — a claim to have some actual *knowledge*, for instance, knowing that foxes leave tracks of a certain shape. To evaluate an idea as being either possible or likely, one must *know* the evidence for it and *know* that it *is* evidence — i.e., that it advances cognition, moving it forward in the direction of the conclusion. But when alternative hypotheses are still possible, i.e., still have some evidence supporting them, the idea remains a hypothesis, not a certainty.

Evidence is data that advances us toward knowledge. This means that evidence must distinguish among alternative hypotheses, favoring one over others. In crime detection, for instance, suppose we ask: when the perpetrator's blood is found at the scene of a homicide, does its blood type constitute

---

144   See also the discussion of inertia and gravity on p. 370.

evidence? That depends on whether it discriminates among the suspects. Suppose we know with certainty that the killer is one of three people, but they all have the type B blood that was found at the crime scene. In that case the blood type is not evidence as to which man is the murderer. But if one suspect has type O blood, then the blood analysis is evidence because it weighs against the hypothesis that he is the murderer.

Now take a case of induction from the history of science: Galileo's investigation of the nature of motion. In his era, the dominant view was that objects move in a circular path unless something forces them to move in a straight one. The evidence for this idea is the motion of the heavenly bodies, plus the fact that an object thrown follows a curved path. Galileo considered the alternative hypothesis: objects move in a straight line unless some force constrains them to a curved motion. The evidence for this contrary hypothesis is that a dropped object moves straight downwards and that a curving motion involves a continuous change in direction, and changes must have a cause. But what is ruled out? The idea that objects "naturally" (without constraints) move in a zigzag, back-and-forth motion. There is no evidence for this dreamed-up notion. Or, the idea that objects' unconstrained motion depends upon their color or the day of the week or someone's prayers.

In his study of motion, Galileo constructed experiments demonstrating the independence of the horizontal and vertical components of motion. The experiments expanded the context of knowledge, enabling Galileo to conclude that it is motion in a straight line, not circular motion, that is "natural." (Later knowledge, particularly of gravity as a force exerted by all matter on other matter, confirmed Galileo's hypothesis by explaining the circular motion of heavenly bodies.) In induction, as in crime-detection, observational evidence is the only coin of the realm.[145]

On the basis of this understanding of the role of evidence in assessing the cognitive status of an idea, we are prepared to rescue certainty from a long-standing attack.

For a conclusion to be certain, there must be no other rational hypothesis that qualifies as possible. But the concept of "possible" has long been subjected to a disastrous "package-deal" — a false integration that packages epistemic possibility with metaphysical possibility. The two are entirely different. Metaphysical possibility denotes an ability, potentiality, or capacity. Epistemic possibility denotes the status of the evidence.

---

145 On standards of certainty in scientific induction, see *The Logical Leap* [HARRIMAN, 2010], especially pp. 184–187 and 238–239.

In English, metaphysical possibility is expressed by "can" and epistemic possibility by "might."[146] I *can* shoplift, I am able to do it, but that does not imply I *might*. Metaphysical possibility, by itself, does not warrant the assertion of epistemic possibility. *Can* be does not imply *might* be.[147]

To say that something might be the case is to treat it as a hypothesis. Forming something as a hypothesis is a positive mental act that has to be justified. The required justification is evidence. *Hypotheses require evidence.*

For something's metaphysical possibility to serve as evidence warranting making it into a hypothesis, one must have grounds for thinking that the metaphysical possibility has been actualized.

I can whistle "Yankee Doodle": I know how to whistle and I know the tune. But my having that ability does not, per se, provide any evidence that I am whistling it now, as you read this. For you to be justified in thinking that I *might be* now whistling "Yankee Doodle," you would need some evidence for that idea, some reason to think that I am actualizing my potential to whistle it. If I am scheduled to perform at a public whistling event at about the present time, and if "Yankee Doodle" is on the program, then knowing all that would justify thinking that I might be whistling it right now. But the mere fact that I *can* whistle it — that it is metaphysically possible for me to whistle it — does not count as evidence that I am doing so now. And in the absence of evidence, the idea is not to be accepted or entertained, but dismissed.

Dismissing "X might be the case" does not mean holding X to be impossible; the term "impossible" has only a metaphysical use. To know that something is impossible is to know that it contradicts the facts. It is impossible for man to fly by flapping his arms — that would contradict the nature of man, the nature of gravity, and the nature of flight. In dismissing possibilities asserted only because they are metaphysically possible, one is not saying that the thing dismissed is impossible. One is simply refusing to entertain it as a hypothesis — because there is no reason to do so. It is not impossible for me to whistle "Yankee Doodle" — unless I am asleep, I am gagged, etc. But "not impossible" does not translate into positive evidence, and it would be irrational to entertain the possibility that I might now be whistling "Yankee Doodle" —

---

146 "Might" and "may" differ in degree of likelihood. "I may attend" indicates a stronger likelihood than "I might attend." Thus, everything I say about "might" applies with even more force to "may."

147 Equivalently, "possible for" is metaphysical and "possible that" is epistemic. The fact that it is possible *for* me to shoplift does not imply it is possible *that* I will shoplift.

or shoplifiting, dancing a polka, reading Gray's Anatomy, or doing any of an unlimited number of things, merely because my doing them is not impossible.

The "crow epistemology" comes into play here. Treating something as a hypothesis has cognitive costs: one has to form a mental file for the issue and carry the issue forward for further pursuit, consideration, and integration. Having too many hypotheses at once overloads the "crow," frustrating attempts at cognition.

When there are too many alternatives for the mind to work with on an ongoing basis, these alternatives do not qualify as epistemic possibilities. In the terminology of law-enforcement, one cannot have one thousand "suspects." That would be a misuse of the concept "suspect." And in general, to grant something the epistemic status of "possible," one must have evidence — evidence that is specific to the case at hand and that a mind limited by the "crow" can work with on a continuing basis.

Thus, when an idea is supported by contextually conclusive evidence, one's certainty in that idea is not threatened by the mere metaphysical possibility of an alternative.

THE LAW OF RATIONALITY VS. THE ARBITRARY

One's proper attitude to evidence is summarized in what some logicians have called "The Law of Rationality." In my formulation, this law states:

In reaching conclusions, consider all the evidence and only the evidence.

Because evidence is the only means of gaining inferential knowledge, the rational mind accepts all that which the evidence shows, only that which the evidence shows, and only to the extent that it shows it. Only evidence — not someone's assertion, not feelings, not authority, not faith — can provide the basis for proceeding cognitively.

The question then arises: what does one do when there is zero evidence in favor of a claim?

Let me make up a scenario in which there is zero evidence in support of an idea. Suppose the idea pops into your mind that you will inherit a fortune from some distant relative whom you have never heard about. I assume that the idea has no evidence to support it. That means *it has no cognitive content.* The notion does not fall on the evidentiary continuum. It is neither possible, nor likely, nor certain. It has no cognitive status. If such an idea is nonetheless asserted as being cognitive, it has an anti-cognitive status: *arbitrary*.

The term "arbitrary" does not refer merely to a state of ignorance but to ignorance taken as an epistemological license, as if the ability to *imagine* something made it cognitive. "Arbitrary" means: put forward on the premise that evidence is unnecessary, that one can assert anything one has dreamed up, and that this assertion stands until and unless it is refuted. An arbitrary assertion is one made in defiance of the need for such a thing as evidence. As such, it represents an assault on logic and cannot be countenanced.

The cognitive status of an idea is an outgrowth of the process by which it was reached. To be cognitive, that process must be one of observing facts and drawing logical inferences therefrom. Absent that, the idea is non-cognitive. To accept it anyway — even to entertain it as a possibility — is cognitively toxic. Yet, indulging in arbitrary assertions, possibilities, and "constructs" is standard operating procedure today in philosophy, in the culture, and in political debate; it has even infected the field of law (see the upcoming example of arbitrary "what ifs" raised by the defense in the O. J. Simpson trial).

Knowledge is a mental grasp of fact. When there are no rational grounds for an idea, there is no *means* of achieving that grasp. Nor does an arbitrary claim constitute even a step on the path to gaining knowledge: it does not represent an awareness of anything and thus does not represent a cognitive advance. It leaves one in the same cognitive state one was in prior to its assertion. In my example, the idea that you will inherit a fortune does not move you closer to grasping any fact on any subject.

To be engaged in cognition, one must accept and implement the means of acquiring knowledge. The means of acquiring knowledge is awareness of evidence — facts, implications, relationships, causal connections, etc. — information that moves one toward one's cognitive goal. An arbitrary idea, by definition, has no such means. As such it is a cognitive nullity, and the Law of Rationality requires that one refuse to consider it; the claim must be summarily dismissed. (Again, this is not to hold that what is claimed to be the case is impossible.)

The analogy here is to an action at law. The mere lodging of a complaint is not sufficient grounds for holding a trial. The plaintiff must provide sufficient evidence to show that a trial, a costly and onerous affair, is warranted. Absent such a showing, the complaint is dismissed. This dismissal is not a determination that no legal wrong occurred, only that there is no basis for holding a trial; analogously, in epistemology, the dismissal of an arbitrary assertion is not a determination that the assertion is false, only that there is no rational basis for entertaining the notion — not even for undertaking to refute it. In the cognitive sense, there is no "it" to deal with.

In merely entertaining the arbitrary, one has suspended logic, since logic deals with evidence. Accordingly, logic cannot be used to guide what one does with the arbitrary. The anti-logical premise that admitted the baseless idea into consideration prevents one from knowing what to do with it, how to integrate it, and what it means or implies. Either one accepts the requirements of cognition, or one does not. If one does not, there is no answer to: what is the *logical* next step to take in working with this idea?

Although logic is not a game, like a game it has rules. Consider, then, the analogy to changing the rules of a card game at whim. Suppose that during a game your opponent announces "My three of clubs is now a king of clubs." If you accept that, how do you know how to proceed in the game? Can you now play your three of hearts and have it accepted as a king of hearts? What happens when the actual king of clubs appears? Does it become a three of clubs? Or, if it stays a king of clubs, what is its relation to the other "king of clubs": higher? lower? equal? When will the next arbitrary rule-change be announced, and what will it mean for your play? There is no way to answer these questions once one accepts the premise that the rules may be changed at whim. And there is no way to answer questions about the meaning and implications of an idea once one accepts arbitrary assertions as being cognitive.

Arbitrary ideas are products of imagination. Imagination is entirely proper — in fact, indispensable — across a broad range of rational activities, but *imagination is not cognition.* Imagination is not limited by logic or evidence; it is the rearrangement of stored images, ideas, or words, according to internal considerations, such as wishes or fears, which may or may not be realistic. One can take the idea of gold and the idea of mountain and combine them in imagination to project a golden mountain. This may be entirely appropriate as part of a fairy tale. But to treat such fantasies as acts of cognition is an act of high treason against logic.

To have cognitive content, a claim must first have content — it must formulate a definite, intelligible idea. The assertion, "Something bad is going to happen" lacks such content, as does "My computer's problems are due to gremlins." Arbitrary ideas ultimately lack content *because they are made up.* The content of an arbitrary idea consists of whatever the person dreaming it up says it consists of — until he announces that it has changed ("The gremlin teleported himself to another planet as soon as you started looking for him inside the computer").

A content of imagination has only as much identity as its imaginer has conferred on it so far, with the duration of his whim replacing the stability of existents. As an experiment, picture a toothbrush in your imagination. How many bristles does it have? There is no answer to that question; you might provide a number, by making a decision as to what the number shall be, but there is no objective quantity of bristles waiting to be counted. Now, imagine brushing your teeth with it. Did it lose any bristles in the process? There are no facts to find out here, only a *decision* to be made as to what you wish the answer to be. The imagined has no independent identity. The arbitrary, because it lacks an independent identity and has no connection to the rest of one's knowledge, cannot be dealt with cognitively. The arbitrary is a cognitive dead end. It stops the mind.[148]

In saying that the mind is stopped by the arbitrary, I mean the rational, cognizing mind. Imagination can, of course, proceed. The crucial point is not to confuse imagination with cognition, not to pretend that one is pursuing cognitive contact with reality when the means of doing so — evidence — is absent.

The arbitrary is *not* involved when someone supports a claim by what he believes to be evidence but turns out not to be. In these cases, there *is* a rational way to proceed: one can expose the errors in the assertor's reasoning, showing how the "evidence" he offers is not actual evidence for his conclusion. Here, in order to dismiss the claim, one is logically obligated to deal with any proffered evidence (unless it is transparently absurd); one has to show that the evidence has been misinterpreted, or that it is not factual, or that it doesn't support the conclusion. One cannot arbitrarily assert that a claim is arbitrary.

When the alleged basis for a claim has been invalidated, the claim returns to a non-cognitive status, as though it had never been brought up in the first place. But if the assertor does not accept this dismissal, if he continues to assert the idea in defiance of its demonstrated baselessness, there is no way to deal with him or his claim. Lacking *cognitive* content, the idea must be dismissed without consideration. Otherwise one is surrendering logic, abandoning one's cognitive guide.

---

148 This is a point made in several lectures by Leonard Peikoff; see the general discussion in OPAR, 163–171.

The consequences of granting even a "maybe" to arbitrary assertions are deadly. Consciousness is a biological faculty. Its survival role is to guide an organism's actions toward that which serves its life and away from that which threatens it. Man's control over his conceptual faculty gives him the ability to create in imagination new combinations of his mind's stored contents; but if he confuses the content coming from reality (evidence) with whatever he chooses to rearrange in his mind, if he confuses combinations dictated by logic with those generated by his imagination, his mind's output is simply junk, not a means to guiding his actions and succeeding in his life.

Again, one needs imagination in regard to planning, self-motivation, literature, amusement, and other purposes; but in these cases, one is not holding that the imagined content is *true*.

Once granted *cognitive* standing, the arbitrary cannot be rationally confined, because reason has been dispensed with. Any "limits" set would themselves be arbitrary — which means they could be adjusted, extended, or revoked arbitrarily. Since reason *never* endorses the arbitrary, since the acceptance of the arbitrary is always counter to reason, a compromise with the arbitrary surrenders the supremacy of reason. Henceforth, feelings dictate where reason is to operate and where it is not. Reason and logic then function only by permission of feelings.

One must have a *principle of methodology*: either one recognizes that imagination is imagination, or one does not. If one compromises the principle here, the result is that reason is no longer supreme in one's mind.

The gates to the realm of the arbitrary bear the inscription: "Abandon all hope of cognition, ye who enter here."

One cannot object: "But sometimes the arbitrary idea will turn out to have been true." There is no such thing. Whatever transpires, it cannot represent an arbitrary claim "turning out to have been true." Non-awareness cannot "turn out to have been" awareness. Yes, the *words* used to make an arbitrary utterance may be the same as the words used later, in a cognitive context, to express a true proposition; but that does not mean the arbitrary utterance was an act of awareness or that one judged correctly. When an idea is put forward without any grounds, it is not expressing a *judgment* at all, merely engaging in imaginative projection.

Since the arbitrary is actually fantasy, it is instructive to compare it with dreams. Suppose a man asleep dreams that he meets a beautiful red-headed woman, and suppose that the next day he does. It is not the case that his dream "turned out to be true." The woman he meets is not "the woman from his dream." His dream had no actual referent in reality. A reference to reality requires an awake mind with mental content that has some cognitive connection to reality, i.e., some awareness on which it is based. Where that awareness is absent, there is no reference at all. Dream images are merely a succession of internal experiences; the images may resemble things encountered in the external world, but they are not *about* the world; they make no cognitive reference to reality. To paraphrase the old legal preface to fiction stories: any resemblance between the dream's content and actual persons or events is purely coincidental.

To see the vacuousness of an arbitrary assertion, take the following case. Suppose a parrot squawks, "It is raining now." Sometimes when it squawks that, it *is* raining, sometimes it is not. But the parrot does not go from uttering truth to uttering falsehood with the changes in the weather. The parrot squawks are, for it, just squawks. Words do not have an *intrinsic* connection to reality: that reference depends on the mental actions of the speaker or listener. (In terms of just the sounds, "It is raining now" is identical to "It is reigning now" and "It is reining now," so clearly any reference of parrot-sounds to the weather depends on the meaning supplied by the human being listening to them.)

Accordingly, an arbitrary claim is not to be taken as true, nor as even possibly true. But neither is it false. To be false, a statement must first say something: it must attribute some definite characteristics to a clearly designated subject.[149] An idea's falsehood is established by reference to a body of knowledge — knowledge contradicting the idea. [OPAR, 166] When you know that something *isn't so*, you know it by reference to your awareness of what *is*. But arbitrary assertions, lacking evidence, provide no such awareness, so they do not reach even the level of being false.

As explained in CHAPTER 5, negative terms like "not" mean "different from." Take a reasonable but false statement, such as: "There is a soup bowl on Joe's dining room table." (Assume that it is now dinner time and that one knows that Joe often has soup at dinner, making this a reasonable statement.) To learn that this claim is false, one could look at Joe's tabletop and see what *is* — i.e., the wooden expanse and whatever other objects are on it; what one sees has a different identity from that of a soup bowl. The evidentially supported (but false) statement "There is a soup bowl on Joe's dining room table," is definite and intelligible. Contrast it with: "There is an invisible aura surrounding Joe's dining room table." That has neither intelligible content nor

---

149 See CHAPTER 5 on the meaning of a proposition.

cognitive standing. We don't know what it even means; we don't know what would serve as evidence for it or against it.

The Law of Rationality, again, states: *In reaching conclusions, consider all the evidence and only the evidence.* The Law does not merely demand that you justify your *conclusions*, it also demands that you justify your cognitive *actions* — justify even spending time considering a claim. It is irrational to consider that for which there is no evidence.

Thus, arbitrary ideas are not even to be entertained as hypotheses, as "maybes." Things that are on the way to being established as true or false (hypotheses grounded in evidence) are different from notions that are just dreamed up. Arbitrary assertions are not propositions at all, but pseudo-propositions: words with the linguistic form of a proposition, but without cognitive meaning.

There are an unlimited number of imaginary notions that one can construct, once evidence is regarded as unnecessary. For any given arbitrary idea, one could construct 10,000 alternative ideas on the same non-basis. Take the earlier example of the arbitrary assertion that you will inherit a fortune from an unknown relative. If that is to be granted cognitive respect, why not: "You will inherit a crushing debt"? Or, "You will inherit a dog," "You will inherit a cat," "You will inherit a baseball autographed by Mickey Mantle," "You will inherit a lamp with magic powers," and so on ad infinitum? There is no logical way to prefer any one of these notions to any other. And one cannot deal with a deluge of alternative hypotheses.

Newton famously wrote *"hypotheses non fingo"* (I feign no hypotheses). In light of the Law of Rationality, one could formulate "Newton's Razor": hypotheses are not to be multiplied beyond the evidence, nor are they to be dismissed in disregard of the evidence.

The rational response to an arbitrary assertion is to *dismiss* it — i.e., not to assume its truth, not to assume its falsity, not to take it as a hypothesis, not to try to refute it, but to recognize it as fantasy and turn one's attention to reality.

It is important to realize that for an idea to be disproved, for it to qualify as *false*, the principle of dismissing the arbitrary must already be accepted and adhered to. Otherwise, there can be no disproof and nothing can be established as false (or as true). The refutation of any claim presupposes that the arbitrary is *not logically entitled to* a refutation, that it has no cognitive standing. Otherwise, there is always the comeback, "Maybe you erred," or "Maybe you're dreaming all this."

Thus, the idea that dismissing the arbitrary is only tentative, compared to having a disproof, is contradictory: dismissing the arbitrary is a precondition of disproof.

The Ad Ignorantiam Fallacy

Consider what qualifies as evidence and what does not.

The mere fact that someone has asserted something is not evidence for its truth. (Testimony from a credible source about what he observed is fundamentally different from raw assertion.[150])

The fact that no counter-evidence has been offered is not evidence. The absence of evidence *against* is not evidence *for*. By the same token, the absence of evidence *for* is not evidence *against*. Yes, there are cases in which one has looked for positive evidence, where such should have been available, and found only facts different from those asserted (as with seeing only Joe's tabletop where one would have seen a soup bowl if it had been there). But this is awareness of facts, facts from which an implication can be drawn contrary to a rational hypothesis. The logical point is: sheer unawareness of evidence is not itself a form of awareness, is not evidence. To assume otherwise is to commit the logical fallacy known as *Ad Ignorantiam* — the appeal to ignorance. *Nothing follows from ignorance.*

I must register another caveat regarding what counts as evidence. The epistemological issue of the amount of evidence is not to be confused with mathematical probability. A judgment of an event's probability uses known facts plus a rational theoretical framework to predict a relative frequency, as in calculating how many times out of 100 a fair coin can be expected to land heads up when tossed. The epistemic question is different: how well established is a given idea?

For instance, there is a mathematical probability assignable to winning a lottery. But your holding one ticket out of a million sold does not count as any evidence that you will win. Your winning is not impossible, but neither is it a "maybe." It is valid to say "The odds of my winning are one in a million," but "I *might* win" is not a valid hypothesis for you to form.

---

150 In the case of another's testimony, the evidence one needs is not of the content of his report (beyond its being consistent with what you know) but of its credibility as a report — i.e., knowledge of the honesty, reliability, and accuracy of the reporter. The reporter, if thus qualified, is serving as your eyes and ears. This is why courts do not allow as testimony *conclusions* that a witness drew, but only the facts that he observed.

If you were to regard winning as a hypothesis, you would, by the same principle, have to form hypotheses for all other "not impossible" events, such as contracting a rare tropical disease, getting hit by falling space-debris, happening upon the U.S. Ambassador to Guatemala around the next corner — and so on, without limit. But one cannot hold an unlimited number of hypotheses. Attempting to do so would merely make the word "hypothesis" into an empty sound, and a new word would have to be used to refer to ideas having some actual evidence, not just a mathematical probability.

The lottery example spotlights the absolute difference between refusing to consider something, even as a hypothesis, and claiming to know that its opposite is true. To dismiss the idea of winning the lottery is *not* to say, "I know for a fact that I won't win." You do not know that. To *dismiss* is to *refrain* from doing something — i.e., it is nonaction. Dismissing the arbitrary is refusing to squander limited cognitive resources on pursuing notions merely on the grounds that they cannot be ruled out as impossible. Dismissing X is very different from claiming not-X. They share the complete rejection of X, in the one case by rejecting it as arbitrary and in the other by rejecting it as contradicting known facts. The difference is the same as that between not investing in a given stock and selling the stock short.

However, to know that something is false is not a "stronger" rejection than dismissing it as arbitrary. The person who rejects the idea of God as arbitrary, as imagination, does not have a "weaker" rejection of that idea than the person who rejects the idea of square circles. Whether an assertion is groundless or contradicts known facts makes no difference to one's epistemic attitude toward *it*. In both cases, one totally refuses to accept it. There's no "strength" added to one's rejection of an idea that comes with seeing that it is impossible, as if one could say: "Previously, I merely rejected the idea, now I really reject it." That's nonsense.

THE BURDEN OF PROOF PRINCIPLE

One doesn't need a reason *not* to consider something a fact. One doesn't need a reason *not* to entertain something as a hypothesis. The reverse is true: *The burden of proof is on him who claims knowledge.*

Knowledge is an effect of the operation of certain causes. For the effect to be present, the causes must have been present. Ignorance, not knowledge, is the default condition. Thus, a claim to have achieved knowledge (even knowledge of possibility) must be supported by showing that the cause was present and operative. The cause is awareness — direct perception of the thing or awareness of evidence logically supporting it. In the absence of such awareness, the claim to know is arbitrary and thus is to be dismissed.

Some formulations of the Burden of Proof Principle make reference to asserting a "positive." But "positive" is an ambiguous term that raises a tangle of unnecessary questions here. In one sense, any claim is a "positive": it is a claim to having achieved knowledge. Even the claim that something is possible is a claim to knowledge — the knowledge of certain facts and the knowledge of how far they support the conclusion. In another sense, only claims that assert the existence of an entity are taken as "positive." In a third sense, claims that assert that an entity possesses a given characteristic or is acting in a certain way are taken as "positive."[151]

But these are needless issues. "Concepts are not to be multiplied beyond necessity." That canon ("Rand's Razor") applies to forming concepts of "positive" and "negative" statements: there is no need for those concepts. Instead, the required distinction is between the cognitive and the arbitrary. The Burden of Proof Principle does not concern the kind of *content* a claim has but that it is a claim to be aware of something, to know something. What has the burden of proof is any claim to have achieved knowledge (even of possibility).[152]

To know something, one must have used the means of gaining knowledge: evidence. That is *all* that the Burden of Proof Principle states. When there is no evidence for "S is P," there is no awareness of S being P, nor of anything indicating that S is P. That means there are no grounds for hypothesizing that S is P.

The Burden of Proof Principle also applies to negative statements: "S is not P" or even "S does not exist." Take the statement, "There is no life elsewhere in the universe." Given the state of our ignorance (or, if you prefer, the

---

151 Here is a real-life example. I just flipped a coin, and it landed on my desk. It came up either heads or tails. If you, who don't know which side came up, assert "It was heads" is that "the positive"? The proper assessment is: you know, from your knowledge of coins, that it is possible that it was heads and it is possible that it was tails. To claim that it was one over the other is arbitrary. Both "It was heads" and "It was tails" are claims to knowledge and thus both face a burden of proof — which in this case you cannot meet. (P.S., it came up tails.)

152 The negative propositions discussed in CHAPTER 5 (e.g., "Lassie is not a beagle") are negative in structure, not in content. Such propositions do make claims and thus require justification. What does not require justification is non-consideration; that is the default state. One needs a reason to consider, not a reason not to consider.

ignorance of 100 years ago), there is no evidence for this "negative" claim — as there is none for the corresponding positive: "There is life elsewhere in the universe" (probabilistic appeals to the huge number of stars in the universe notwithstanding). Where there is no evidence on a subject, the Law of Rationality directs us not to pretend there is — i.e., not to consider it, one way or another. Thus, there is a burden of proof for claiming to know that something does *not* exist, because that means claiming to know facts that exclude it. Both "I will get leukemia in the next month" and "I will *not* get leukemia in the next month" have a burden of proof. In the absence of evidence, neither idea is to be entertained.

By the same token, the familiar idea that it is impossible to prove a "negative" actually means: it is impossible to disprove an arbitrary assertion; it is impossible to proceed under the assumption that any assertion stands until refuted, or that only a disproof of an assertion would justify not accepting it as a "maybe."

One does not need evidence *against* an idea in order to dismiss it — i.e., *not* to entertain it. For dismissal, the most that one needs is to show that one is informed of the state of the evidence and has found that there is none supporting the idea. (This is not a claim to be aware of non-existence: it means that one has looked where that evidence should have been but has found only data *different from* evidence for the assertion.) And, if there has been anything put forward mistakenly as evidence, in order to dismiss the claim one must identify why the purported evidence is not, in fact, evidence.

The Burden of Proof Principle is a corollary of the Law of Rationality; the principle implies that when a claim to knowledge is unsupported by evidence, we must not even consider it. *Ad Ignorantiam* adds the fact that ignorance is not a source of evidence.

There are no degrees of meeting the burden of proof: it is either met or not, period. "Proof" requires conclusive evidence, evidence beyond a reasonable doubt. (Unreasonable doubts are arbitrary.) When an idea has fully met that burden, it is *certain*. Even though a lesser degree of evidence qualifies an idea as *likely* or *possible*, the burden exists for proving conclusively, with certainty, that it *is* likely or possible. Possibilities have to be proved. To prove possibility is to prove that the idea is evidence-driven, that one knows a subset of the facts required to attain certainty on the issue.

Take the earlier example of seeing certain tracks in the soil. Assume that one is warranted in saying, "I know that a small animal walked by here; the tracks are unclear, but it is possible that they were made by a fox, since the tracks are consistent with fox pawprints and foxes do inhabit this region." By pointing out that evidence, one has fully met the burden of proof for concluding: "It is *possible* that a fox recently walked by here." But now take a case when that burden of proof is not met. Suppose there are no tracks, and the only "evidence" is that one dreamed last night that a fox walked by. In that case, the idea has no cognitive content, and The Law of Rationality demands dismissing it as arbitrary.

Or, take the issue of the existence of God. The burden of proof is on him who claims to know that God exists, or even that "maybe" God exists. One doesn't need a reason *not* to believe in God. Rather, one needs a reason *to believe*. In the absence of such reason, one is logically required not to believe. This is not agnosticism, but atheism. Agnosticism is the claim that God is a valid hypothesis — "maybe God exists, maybe not, we can't know." This kind of fence-sitting is precisely what the Burden of Proof Principle rules out. Given that there is no rational evidence in support of a God, either one entertains the idea anyway or one does not. There is no "third" or "middle" position.[153]

When the burden of proof is not met, the claim must be rejected, no disproof being required. The process of disproof presupposes that one accepts logic as an absolute, that one is not granting cognitive significance to arbitrary assertions. But on the premise that the arbitrary is *entitled* to a refutation, that it is good until and unless disproved, nothing can be proved or disproved. As to disproof, the assertor can always dream up new arbitrary content to back up his prior claim. The ultimate such arbitrary backup is: "I say there is a mistake in your refutation; now you have to prove there isn't." Whatever one says in response to that, the assertor of the arbitrary need only repeat his claim, asserting that you are mistaken about *that*. You have agreed to play a game that you cannot win.

On any given issue, there is only one truth but an unlimited number of non-truths. To spend one's time eliminating non-truths (if one could even do that) would mean getting nowhere cognitively. One would be preventing oneself from spending that time learning about reality.

---

153 Given a semi–intelligible definition of God — e.g., an omnipotent, omniscient, immaterial consciousness — one can show the contradictions in such a notion; but doing that is not required in order to reject God's existence, even as a possibility. And note that such disproofs do not faze committed theists, who immediately take refuge in arbitrary rejoinders such as, "Such contradictions are resolved from God's perspective," or "You can't know someone won't come up with a definition of God not subject to your criticism."

The application of the Burden of Proof Principle to the possibility of errors due to incomplete information deserves more discussion.

Suppose you have a longstanding friendship with a man. By everything you know, he is an honest, industrious person. But later you discover that for the past year he has been embezzling from his firm. Let's assume that during this year you were objectively certain that he was honest, having years of evidence of his honesty and absolutely no evidence of his current misdeeds. Nonetheless, you were mistaken; you lacked the crucial information: that he had stooped to embezzlement (and of his inner state that made this crime possible to him). The painful discovery of this man's dishonesty is, however, no grounds for doubting the honesty of your remaining friends. The fact that a good person *can* go bad, even coupled with your experience with the embezzling friend, provides no grounds for doubt of anyone else. It would be grossly unjust to start entertaining the possibility that another friend is secretly dishonest. Since man has free will, the choices made by one individual provide no grounds for judging what another individual will choose. (On free will, see CHAPTER 10.)

Despite the fact that being logical does not guarantee immunity from error, one has to go by the available evidence, without engaging in groundless doubts. First, there are conclusions about which no contrary data could arise — e.g., that two and two is four, that dogs are animals, or that the Earth rotates on its axis. But even for conclusions that are, in principle, subject to correction by new data, such as your judgment of a man's moral character, the mere fact that, on rare occasions, new data will reverse a prior certainty provides no grounds for doubt in any new and different case. What is supported by conclusive evidence is *certain*, and this certainty is unaffected by the fact that it is *not impossible* for a certainty to be overthrown by new information.

The arbitrary assertion of possibilities is widespread today. The equivocation between metaphysical and epistemic possibility — between *can* and *might be* — is the stock in trade of skeptics in their attacks on certainty. The skeptics' argument here is from the fact of fallibility. Because you *can* make a mistake, they argue, you always *might be* mistaken about anything. But *can* does not imply *might be*. The capacity to make a mistake provides no evidence that a given conclusion *is* mistaken, and thus gives no grounds for doubting one's conclusions — just as my capacity to whistle "Yankee Doodle" gives no grounds for thinking I am whistling it now.

"Maybe" is not an epistemological free lunch. One has to have grounds for entertaining a possibility, even the possibility that a given conclusion is illogical (when one has conclusive evidence that it *is* logical) or that it will be refuted by facts that will be discovered in the future.

Along with crediting the arbitrary claim, "Maybe you've made a mistake," most people assume that an idea begins with the status "possibly true," as its default state. They believe that an idea has cognitive standing until and unless someone refutes it. For example, in the 1994 O. J. Simpson murder trial, the defense made many arbitrary claims—about an alleged police conspiracy, cuts on Simpson's hands being due to "golf injuries," and so on. The premise was that unless the prosecution could somehow refute these baseless claims, "reasonable doubt" existed as to Simpson's guilt. But in fact, such doubts were flagrantly *unreasonable*.

There is no difference in principle between those unreasonable doubts and more bizarre assertions of the arbitrary, such as those of astrology or the Book of Revelation.

Throughout the history of thought, it has been common for philosophers to take arbitrary claims as their starting points. For instance, Spinoza begins his entire system with this as his axiom (Proposition I): "By cause of itself I understand that whose essence involves existence, or that whose nature cannot be conceived unless existing." [SPINOZA, 41]

This pseudo-axiom treats as irreducible primaries such notions as "cause," "essence," and "conceiving." These are proper concepts—if understood in terms of *prior* concepts (particularly, "existence," "identity," "action," and "consciousness"). But just plopping them into a "Proposition I" deprives them of any base in reality, rendering them arbitrary.

Kant launches his *Critique of Pure Reason* with the entirely arbitrary distinction between "analytic" and "synthetic" judgments, and between "a priori" and "a posteriori" knowledge—distinctions without rational basis.[154] The second paragraph of his "Introduction" arbitrarily announces:

> But though all our knowledge begins with experience, it does not follow that it all arises out of experience. For it may well be [!] that even our empirical knowledge is made up of what we receive through impressions and of what our own faculty of knowledge (sensible impressions serving merely as the occasion) supplies from itself.

---

154 See CHAPTER 5.

"May well be" — based on what evidence? (In fact, the idea of knowledge whose source is purely internal denies the very need of evidence.)

To parody the grounding of philosophic systems in arbitrary claims, Rand projected a philosopher announcing: since man has only two eyes, he can see only two things. (This then, in her parody, gives rise to two subsequent schools: one maintains that only two things actually exist, the other acknowledges that many things exist but asserts that man actually has more than two eyes.) [PEIKOFF 2013, 73]

The first step in judging the validity of an idea is to identify its source: is it based on fact or fantasy? If the idea is evidence-based, one can check the interpretation placed on that evidence; but that which is asserted arbitrarily — proceeding from "what if?" or "why not?" or "it may well be" — offers no evidence to be interpreted. Such ideas are not in the realm of logic but of make-believe.

WHAT IS OBJECTIVITY?

When a mental product results from the deliberate application of logic to evidence, it has a unique status: it is *objective*. Ayn Rand provides a new understanding of what objectivity is and requires.

In its metaphysical usage, "objective" simply means: existing independently of consciousness. But now we are concerned with "objective" in its epistemological meaning — i.e., the objectivity of a mental process or product. What is it for a mental process or product to be "objective"? To properly understand the concept of "objectivity," we must pose Rand's key question: what facts of reality give rise to the need for such a concept?

Among many such facts, three stand out: 1) the primacy of existence: existence exists independently of consciousness, and consciousness is awareness of that which exists; 2) the law of identity: contradictions do not exist in reality, so, "non-contradictory identification" (logic) is the method of acquiring knowledge of reality; 3) volition: man can choose to regulate his own cognitive activities, applying his knowledge of logic to guide them and to check his conclusions.

Do we need a concept that distinguishes between those cognitive activities that are *deliberately* guided by logic and those that are not? That is, do we need the concept of *objectivity*? Yes, because processes guided by logic are fundamentally different from those that are not. Only if one knows and consciously applies logic can one warrantedly claim to have knowledge as opposed to mere belief. Only by reference to logic can one have a standard of certainty.

One can, of course, *be* logical before one knows that that is what one is doing. A child does not need to study logic in order to go from "Lassie is a dog" and "Dogs chew bones" to "Lassie chews bones." Adapting a statement from John Locke, men didn't have to wait for Aristotle to become logical. Although that is true, men did in fact have to wait for Aristotle in order to know, beyond the most rudimentary level, what logic consists of and to therefore be able to make their thinking *objective*. Before having a decent understanding of how to validate an idea, men could say no more than, "My idea just seems right to me."

Even when one can give reasons to support his beliefs, objectivity about one's conclusions requires something more: knowing how to distinguish valid from fallacious reasoning, what constitutes evidence, what kind or quantity of reasons constitutes proof.

To be objective involves standing back from one's mental processes, viewing them as if they were external, making the form and method of one's thinking into the *object* of awareness (thus the term "objective"[155]). An objective thought-process is one that is observed, inspected, judged — just as are the objects of perceptual awareness. On the perceptual level, one makes, say, a flower into an object of perception by turning one's gaze to it; on the conceptual level, one makes a thought-process into an object of judgment by turning one's attention to it. By adopting this self-conscious standpoint, one can subject his thought to critical examination, judging its validity by the canons of logic. Some of this can be done in "real time," while the thought is occurring, but often it requires retrospection.

Unless one uses logic to critically evaluate one's own thinking, one is absorbed by and caught up in the content of the thought, in which case it is precisely objectivity that one has not yet achieved. Prior to making the thought into the *object*, one is thinking "through" the thought; in a sense, one *is* the thinking process. By reflecting on the thought, one becomes its judge, not its advocate. One establishes a certain separation between self and the thinking, making it easier to avoid distorting factors, such as a too narrow viewpoint, or psychological defense-mechanisms, such as rationalization.

---

155 "Objective" also connotes: object-based — i.e., based on evidence not on the wishes of the subject, the person holding the idea.

Consider what so often happens when one argues over abstract issues, such as politics. After one has presented an extended argument that one takes to be conclusive, the other party is neither persuaded nor silenced. Rather, the other party replies with a stream of objections and counter-arguments. After several such back-and-forths, no resolution is in sight. In order to know who made a logical case, one needs to know what making a logical case consists of. In order to get beyond the mere *feeling,* "I made a good case, he did not," one needs to know how to analyze, criticize, and check an argument — one's own even more than that of a disagreeing party. In order to have an *objective* assessment of the reasoning offered in support of an idea, one must know logic explicitly. The explicit knowledge of logic is what Aristotle supplied.

Just as being "scientific" in one's thinking requires having some explicit knowledge of the scientific method, so being "objective" in one's thinking requires having some explicit knowledge of logic. In contrast, to be "rational" simply means to exercise the faculty of reason, something that all men, even savages and young children, can do when they form concepts, use them to make identifications, and draw logical inferences. But to achieve objectivity is to go beyond that; objectivity enters when one consciously applies the rules of logic to guide and check one's cognitive processes. That is a higher-order phenomenon, and to reach that level requires an explicit knowledge of logic.

For reasoning of any complexity, to determine what one knows, as opposed to what one merely believes or assumes, one must check the reasoning against the standards and methods of logic.

(This does not mean, absurdly, that to be objective a person has to be continually saying to himself any such things as: "I am now using a syllogism of type AAA-1," or "I am now testing my definition against rule 2." For one thing, the proper methodology becomes second-nature — or would, granted a proper education. But to be objective, one must be able, if the need arises, to state at least roughly the reasons for his conclusion, the meaning of his terms, and what makes his reasoning valid and complete.)

Since logic, for Objectivism, is based on the identity of both the object and man's cognitive equipment, Peikoff defines "objective" as follows:

> To be "objective" in one's conceptual activities is volitionally to adhere to reality by following certain rules of method, a method based on facts and appropriate to man's form of cognition.
> [OPAR, 117]

His shorter formulation describes objectivity as: "Volitional adherence to reality by the method of logic." [OPAR, 116]

This theory is a deepening of the colloquial meaning of "objective." Colloquially, to be objective is to be unbiased, to go by the facts, to place no consideration above determining the truth. The opposite is being *subjective*, in which case one's conclusions are produced by internal factors — wishes, hopes, fears, and whatever happens to pass through one's mind. The means of ensuring that one is proceeding in a reality-based manner is logic. And, to apply the Objectivist understanding of logic, this includes (once learned) rules derived from the nature of man's conceptual faculty (see CHAPTER 7).

In our formation and use of concepts, nothing forces us to proceed logically — i.e., to hold the full context and retain the links back to reality by following a hierarchical progression. The rules of logic are not pre-programmed into the brain; they must be discovered. Even once learned, the rules of logic do not apply themselves: one needs to institute them by an active process that is not automatic but volitional. In every moment and issue, one faces the alternative of putting forth the effort to engage in logical processing of observed facts, integrating one's ideas into the full context and checking for contradictions — or passively riding with anything less than that, as in going by authority, urges, guesses, pretenses, or faith.

An objective process has truth as its goal and its normal result, but being objective does not *guarantee* that one's conclusion will be true. Truth, like knowledge, has both a metaphysical and epistemological component: a true conclusion must both state a fact and reflect awareness of that fact.

"Truth" and "knowledge" are "win-words" — i.e., terms that apply to cases of cognitive success. In contrast, "objective" denotes the nature of the *process* (and the status of its products), whether or not the process succeeds in reaching awareness of fact. And objectivity, like certainty, is compatible with being in error; but objectivity is one's best protection against such error.

Objectivity is a deliberate, honest, truth-seeking, methodical process — as opposed to surrendering control of one's mind to emotional urges and random associations (or of actively evading facts available to one). Derivatively, a mental *product*, such as a conclusion or theory, has the status of "objective" when it has been reached by and checked by an objective process, a process of deliberately subjecting one's thought to the rules of logic.

A Trichotomy in the History of Thought

The concept of "objective" opens the way to a new and deeper understanding of the history of thought, including the history of theories of how we know.

Traditionally, theories of knowledge have oscillated between two poles of a false alternative: either man's knowledge is gained passively and automatically, or his knowledge is due to his own "interpretation" and is not a valid grasp of fact. Rand terms these false alternatives *intrinsicism* and *subjectivism*. As against both, she offers a third possibility: *objectivity*.

Thus, there is not just a dichotomy but a trichotomy in regard to theories of mental processes and their products. The revolutionary nature of Rand's philosophy is to define, in area after area, a position that is neither dogmatic nor skeptic, neither Platonist nor Humean, neither intrinsic nor subjective, but objective. That is why she named her philosophy "Objectivism."

The intrinsic-subjective-objective trichotomy offers a new and fundamental way to classify theories in philosophy. Moreover, all of the humanities and social sciences manifest intrinsic, subjective and objective schools of thought. For an application of this trichotomy to issues throughout philosophy, see *Objectivism: The Philosophy of Ayn Rand*. Here, I will illustrate it only in regard to theories of concepts, the basic issue of epistemology.

The Objective Status of Concepts

The recognition that concepts, if properly formed, are *objective* contrasts with the two false theories that have dominated the history of epistemology. Looking again at the schools discussed in CHAPTER 3, the Realist school holds that a concept refers to something non-specific that exists *intrinsically* in the external world, whether as a separate Platonic "Form," an Aristotelian "essence" inside concretes, or a Lockean non-specific attribute (e.g., "whiteness"). The Realist theory represents *intrinsicism* because it holds that a concept is the mental representation of this intrinsically existing "universal." Concept-formation is treated as something akin to a revelation: the passive absorption of the pre-existing, pre-packaged universal that exists "out there," waiting to be taken in by the mind. Thus, the intrinsic theory assimilates the conceptual to the perceptual. We just "see" abstract truth with "the eye of the intellect."

Describing the intrinsicism of Platonic Realism, Peikoff writes: "In the end, [Plato] thinks, the mind need merely remain motionless, passive, receptive, and the light of truth will automatically stream in, taking the form of a synoptic and ineffable intuition." [OPAR, 142]

Later intrinsicist theories of concepts are less overtly mystical, but retain the idea that concepts are a percept-like vision of an intrinsic universal that lies within concretes. For Aristotle and Locke, the process of abstraction is one of subtracting away from a given concrete all that is specific, after which the intrinsic "universal" is there to be "seen" in that single concrete.

The intrinsicist theory of concepts results from the failure to recognize the role of the identity of conceptual consciousness, including its volitional nature. The premise of intrinsicism is that for concepts to be valid, the mind must passively mirror something in the external world.

In reaction to the intrinsicism of the Realists, the Nominalists advance the equally false idea that concepts are *subjective*. The Nominalist theory recognizes that, apart from man's mind, everything that exists is specific through and through; no non-specific characteristic or "universal" exists. There is thus nothing in reality for the mind to passively mirror. But from that the Nominalists conclude that concepts are subjective inventions of man's consciousness. Concepts are regarded as invalid, as nothing more than arbitrary social conventions. Since "nature doesn't tell us" what concepts to form — i.e., since concepts are not intrinsic — they are subjective, according to the Nominalists.

Rand sums up and provides the overlooked alternative:

> The extreme realist (Platonist) and the moderate realist (Aristotelian) schools of thought regard the referents of concepts as *intrinsic*, i.e., as "universals" inherent in things (either as archetypes or as metaphysical essences), as special existents unrelated to man's consciousness — to be perceived by man directly, like any other kind of concrete existents, but perceived by some non-sensory or extra-sensory means.
>
> The nominalist and the conceptualist schools regard concepts as *subjective*, i.e., as products of man's consciousness, unrelated to the facts of reality, as mere "names" or notions arbitrarily assigned to arbitrary groupings of concretes on the ground of vague, inexplicable resemblances. . . .
>
> None of these schools regards concepts as *objective*, i.e., as neither revealed nor invented, but as produced by man's consciousness in accordance with the facts of reality, as mental integrations

of factual data computed by man — as the products of a cognitive method of classification whose processes must be performed by man, but whose content is dictated by reality. [ITOE, 53–54]

Objective knowledge is a mental product that one knows one made in the right way. Objectivity, i.e., being self-consciously logical, comes down to *integration:* integrating "downward" to perception (i.e., reduction) and integrating generally, in all other "directions."

Thus, to state the point negatively, objectivity means: *shun the unintegrable.* Do not pretend that what cannot be integrated into the full context of one's knowledge is nevertheless cognitive.

An idea may be unintegrable for either of two reasons: 1) it involves a contradiction, or 2) it is arbitrary — i.e., there is no means to integrate it. Being nonobjective means either holding contradictions or entertaining the arbitrary.

The first step toward objectivity is the rejection of the arbitrary — i.e., the recognition that claims to knowledge have to be justified, that the mere presence of an idea in one's mind is no basis for assenting to it or treating it as cognition rather than fantasy. The need for objective validation applies not just to propositions and theories but also to their root: concepts.

> Objectivity begins with the realization that man (including his every attribute and faculty, including his consciousness) is an entity of a specific nature who must act accordingly; that there is no escape from the law of identity, neither in the universe with which he deals nor in the working of his own consciousness, and if he is to acquire knowledge of the first, he must discover the proper method of using the second; that there is no room for the *arbitrary* in any activity of man, least of all in his method of cognition — and just as he has learned to be guided by objective criteria in making his physical tools, so he must be guided by objective criteria in forming his tools of cognition: his concepts.
>
> Just as man's physical existence was liberated when he grasped the principle that "nature, to be commanded, must be obeyed," so his consciousness will be liberated when he grasps that *nature, to be apprehended, must be obeyed* — that the rules of cognition must be derived from the nature of existence and the nature, the *identity,* of his cognitive faculty. [ITOE, 82]

9

PRINCIPLES

A THEME RUNNING THROUGHOUT THIS BOOK IS THAT KNOWLEDGE is not an end in itself, but a means of acting successfully in the world.

At the same time, however, I have warned against Pragmatism, a philosophy holding that practical success requires rejecting absolutes, certainty, and, above all, *principles*.

Today, to describe someone as a "pragmatist" is considered to be paying him a compliment. Anyone who adheres to principles is attacked as being an "ideologue." But, in fact, principles offer the only guide to practical success. Consider one striking data-point: the fate of Richard Nixon. Nixon was, by general acclaim, a virtuoso of pragmatism. The lesson of his downfall is clear: nothing is as impractical as the attempt to function without principles.[156]

A principle is a fundamental generalization. To understand principles, and their practical potency, one must understand the nature of fundamentality.

---

156 *The Washington Post*, in a 25-year retrospective on Watergate, discusses the transcripts of secret tapes President Nixon made of his meetings, which reveal his unconcern with moral principles: "The transcript reveals that Mr. Nixon, on his own initiative, discussed accommodating blackmail demands on at least a half-dozen occasions during the meeting without once suggesting that paying the men for their silence would be wrong." (www.washingtonpost.com/wp-srv/national/longterm/watergate/articles/050174–2.htm)

FUNDAMENTALITY

Fundamentality pertains to a certain kind of hierarchical order. In addition to the hierarchy of knowledge, there are other kinds of hierarchical order — for instance, there is the hierarchy of composition (part-whole): subatomic particles, atoms, molecules, macroscopic entities, astronomic entities (such as galaxies).

Fundamentality refers to causal sequences. For example, the military chain of command refers to who gives orders to whom, and the Commander in Chief is the fundamental of the military hierarchy.

In contrast, though the ground floor of a building causally supports all the higher floors, the causal sequence is too simple for the ground floor to be called the building's fundamental. Fundamentality concerns causal sequences that have a branching, tree-like structure of causation, from trunk, to major divides, to large limbs, to smaller limbs, to twigs.

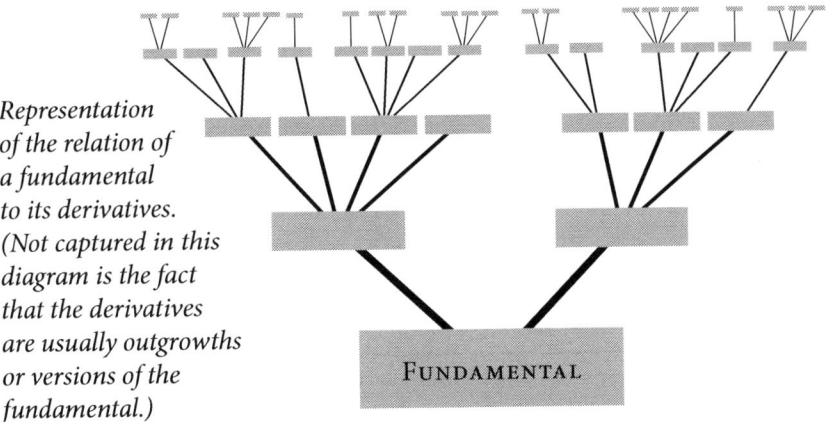

Representation of the relation of a fundamental to its derivatives. (Not captured in this diagram is the fact that the derivatives are usually outgrowths or versions of the fundamental.)

FUNDAMENTAL

The existence of this kind of ramified set of relationships, stemming from one root cause, is the fact that gives rise to the need for the concept of a "fundamental." As a preliminary definition, a "fundamental" is a causal factor on which a multi-level, branching series of effects depends. The dependency here is causal: the fundamental is a necessary condition — a *sine qua non* — of the derivatives' occurrence.

(Sometimes the same overall type of result can be produced by a number of different causes. For instance, when a rock is dropped into a pond, it causes a series of ripples to spread across the pond, lapping upon the distant shores, making a faint sound. Similar results would have been produced by dropping a bottle into the pond. But the series of consequences that did in fact occur depended upon the dropped rock; that was the root cause of *those* consequences. It is irrelevant that a different cause would have produced a different "tree" of consequences.[157])

A "family tree" nicely illustrates the kind of causal relationship a fundamental bears to its derivatives. The founding patriarch and matriarch are the fundamentals of the line of descent in that their union was a necessary condition of that whole line. Although the founders brought into existence only their own children, not their grandchildren or any later generations, the founders are the fundamentals: but for their union, there would be no ancestral line at all.

Similarly, the division of labor is a fundamental of all economic-financial phenomena; without the division of labor, there can be no supply and demand, no credit, banking, stock exchanges, arbitraging, etc. It is only by reference to the division of labor that we can understand all these diverse activities, by integrating them as forms that the division of labor takes.

The existence of a domain of causally interrelated phenomena, existing on different levels, is one fact that gives rise to the need for the concept of "fundamental." Thus, a fuller definition would be: a "fundamental" is a factor necessary to the existence, nature, and explanation of a ramified set of items in a given domain.

In the biological realm, the fundamental factor is natural selection. Natural selection causes and explains the whole "tree of life." It also causes and explains the adaptedness of the structure of organisms on every level of taxonomy: the structure of any particular species of flowering plant, of flowering plants in general, and of the entire plant kingdom. Whether one is seeking to explain the specific shape of the pistil in the rose, the fact that flowers have bright colors, or the presence of chlorophyll in plants, one will find that the contribution made to the plant's survival is the causal factor that forms the deepest part of that explanation. Note that natural selection is a *necessary* factor: without it, evolution would not have occurred.

---

157 If one is considering a category of causal trees, not just the particular one caused by the rock, one must state the fundamental in correspondingly general terms (e.g., "the impact of a solid body"). The issue is: from what are the effects being differentiated?

Note, however, that for the field of biology as a whole, natural selection is a *derivative*, because it depends on the fact that life is conditional on successful action and on the nature of reproduction. Something is fundamental only in relation to a specific domain, not per se. Natural selection is a fundamental in relation to the evolution of organisms, but it is a derivative in relation to the nature of life as such. *Because* organisms are metabolizing systems, capable of reproduction in kind but with variation, there is a natural selection of variations favorable to descendants.

(The only things that are fundamental *simpliciter* are the philosophic axioms — primarily, the axioms of existence, identity, and consciousness — and the basic essentials of epistemology. These state the necessary conditions of all knowledge, including the knowledge of any domain of related items. All other fundamentals qualify as such in relation to a delimited domain.)

A fundamental is a factor causing and explaining the items in a given domain. More informally, a fundamental is both wide and deep — "wide" in terms of explaining the ramified set of things in the domain, and "deep" in identifying their root cause. One arrives at a fundamental when many concrete phenomena can be traced back to the same overall cause.

For example, in a business: why is the boy in the mailroom doing what he is doing? Because his boss assigned that kind of task to him. Why did his boss assign that kind of task? Because of the direction supplied by his boss. Following the chain back will lead one to the overarching direction supplied by the CEO. The CEO has the same ultimate authority over the activities of the salesmen, the legal staff, the accounting staff, and every employee of the firm, including its executives. The CEO is the firm's *fundamental* employee.

Or, the U.S. President, as Commander-in-Chief, has the fundamental role in directing America's military; his decisions underlie and explain the orders given by the generals, which underlie and explain the orders given by the colonels, and so on, down to the enlisted men.

In a given domain, a fundamental is the factor that integrates and explains the existence and interrelations of all items within that domain. All the items in that domain, on whatever level, are subordinate to the fundamental; they are its consequences, implications, and/or variants.[158]

---

158 I say "consequences, implications, and/or variants" to cover different types of dependency. Although all fundamentals identify first causes, in some cases the causality pertains to the external world and in others to man's cognition.

What Identifying Fundamentals Accomplishes

Knowing fundamentals is a source of immense cognitive power. That power results from the *unit-economy* provided by a knowledge of fundamentals. Since a fundamental causes and is expressed in everything in the domain, it is the one factor to be held in mind when dealing with anything in that domain. For instance, in the military, every soldier's actions are devoted to carrying out the fundamental order given by the Commander-in-Chief (an order that may reduce to a directive as simple as: "Defeat the enemy"). Every military decision must be judged solely by its potential contribution to that fundamental goal. (The addition of qualifications, such as "with minimum casualties to our soldiers" does not alter the fundamentality of the goal.) Or, in a business, the fundamental goal is making a profit by following the firm's business model, and that fundamental sets the standard used to judge every decision on every scale of operations. Losing sight of that fundamental leads to decisions that may look good out of context, but are harmful in the long run.

The cognitive power of fundamentals is dramatically illustrated in the history of astronomy by the shift from the geocentric to the heliocentric conception of the solar system. Since motion is relative, the geocentric model is just as factually correct as the heliocentric model. If we take the Earth as our frame of reference, the celestial bodies do move as described in the geocentric system. However, the sun's gravity is the fundamental cause of all the relative motions, and this makes the heliocentric model objectively superior. The baroque complexity of the Ptolemaic model, with its epicycles and deferents, results from taking a non-fundamental (Earth) as the frame of reference; the simplicity (unit-economy) of the heliocentric model stems from taking the *fundamental* as its frame of reference.[159]

Organizing one's knowledge on the basis of fundamentals permits a "crow-friendly" condensation of the whole "tree" of phenomena. This not only adds clarity, it also allows for automatizing what is most cognitively fertile.

---

159 The inclusion of relativistic effects, such as the precession of the perihelion of Mercury, does not change the point: a stubborn geocentrist could handle the precession by simply adding further *ad hoc* devices, similar to "epicycles" and "deferents." In reality, the motion of A around B is the very same phenomenon as the motion of B around A — i.e., the fact is that A and B are moving *relative* to each other.

Automatization is essential to building new knowledge on old, because of, once again, "the crow epistemology." Rand explains the process.

> . . . all learning involves a process of automatizing, i.e., of first acquiring knowledge by fully conscious, focused attention and observation, then of establishing mental connections which make that knowledge automatic (instantly available as a context), thus freeing man's mind to pursue further, more complex knowledge. [ITOE, 65]

By repeatedly tracing the connections of the different branches down to the trunk (and, conversely, seeing how the trunk ramifies into branches) one can automatize the whole tree-structure — not as a random pattern but as theme and variations. For example, the fundamental in chess is the goal of killing the opponent's king. Without having that goal as the automatized, taken-for-granted context, the moves and arrangements of pieces make no sense. A chess expert, who has automatized many derivatives in relation to that supreme goal, can look at the board of someone else's game midway through it and see at a glance what is going on. Or, in music, automatizing the relation of each note of the scale to the scale's keynote (the "tonic") is what allows the music to be intelligible. Music is key-relative and the keynote is the fundamental of the notes in that key.[160]

The power of simple, automatizable fundamentals is what accounts for the decimal system having replaced Roman numerals. The decimal system allows for automatizing one fundamental: the "place" of the digit; that governs what power of 10 the digit represents — ones, tens, hundreds, etc. Having long ago automatized this fundamental, you now have no difficulty understanding the number 644,012 even though it is very unlikely that you have ever encountered it before. But in grasping Roman numerals, we must alternate among three different procedures. First, we increment by conjoining another of the same symbol: I to II to III; then, to denote the next number, we switch to subtracting one from the symbol to the right: IV; then, to continue incrementing, we drop the subtraction and use just the new symbol: V; after that, we revert to the first method: VI. And all three procedures are often combined: XCVII (97), making for a far more cumbersome system, than the decimal one.

---

160 In the C major scale, the tonic is C, and one automatically perceives all notes in relation to C. For instance, the notes E and G will be heard in their specific harmonic relations to C: as the pleasingly consonant 3rd and 5th scale degrees. But C# will have a radically different, very discordant, musical (and emotional) meaning.

PRINCIPLES AS FUNDAMENTAL GENERALIZATIONS

Fundamentality can concern a particular cause in relation to a particular tree of effects, as with our sun and the particular planets of our solar system. But the real cognitive value to be reaped comes from the generalization to a type of cause and a type of tree of effects, as with: "Any star is the basic causal factor controlling the orbits of its planets." When such generalizations reach a certain level of scope, they qualify as *principles*.

A "principle" is a fundamental generalization that serves as a standard of judgment in a given domain.

We need standards to guide our thinking, including the thinking devoted to deciding what to do existentially. E.g., the law of universal gravitation is a principle guiding the thinking of the physicist, and the principle of honesty guides (or ought to guide) each man's thinking about his own conduct.

Principles are differentiated from other action-guiding generalizations, such as rules of thumb or statements of "good policy." A principle, by identifying a fundamental cause, informs us of requirements that are absolute: one cannot have effects without their causes. In contrast, a rule of thumb has no such absolutism. "Don't buy stocks upon the release of good news" (because the news is probably already reflected in the stock's price) may be sound advice in the main, but sometimes stocks do go up on good news. "Never draw to an inside straight" is a correct statement of the odds in poker, but the less usual does occasionally happen. Unlike probabilistic generalizations, a principle can never be flouted with impunity. In this regard, "Honesty is a virtue" states a principle, whereas "Honesty is the best policy" merely makes a probabilistic recommendation.

Principles are also distinguished from those generalizations that, even though absolute, are not wide and deep enough to qualify as principles. "Don't shoplift" is absolute, not probabilistic, but does not rise to the level of a principle — the principle here being: "Respect the rights of others."

The same depth-requirement applies to principles that guide cognition rather than conduct. In mathematics, the commutative law ($a + b = b + a$) is a principle, but "The sum of two even numbers is even," though exceptionlessly true, does not have the requisite scope. Or, in the field of grammar, "Subject and verb must agree in number" is a principle, whereas "The word 'none' takes a singular verb" is too narrow to qualify for that appellation.

One must keep in mind that the issue of fundamentality pertains to a specified domain (and a given context of knowledge). Honesty, for instance, is the fundamental issue at stake in a wide range of situations, but honesty itself depends upon deeper philosophical generalizations, such as the law of causality; causality is a fundamental relative to a much wider domain. The same is true of a (literal) tree: a major branch is the fundamental of all the sub-branches, twigs, and leaves, but that branch is itself one of several outgrowths of the trunk of the tree.

THE NEED FOR PRINCIPLES

The need for principles is psycho-epistemological: principles provide a unit-economical, long-range view of consequences. Because principles deal in fundamentals, principles integrate and condense all the derivatives — i.e., all the consequences, implications, and variants.

Life is complex; principles allow us to simplify it. This is a view of principles very different from the traditional one. Principles have been looked upon as externally imposed rules aimed at keeping us from doing what we actually want to do.

The popular, but mistaken, view of moral principles is the paradigm case in this respect. Moral principles are widely regarded as being a series of Thou Shalt Nots, commanded from on high. The same shadow of grim duty darkens other fields — e.g., the principles of grammar are typically viewed as arbitrary prohibitions, rather than as enablers of clear, precise expression. Even the principles of logic have been viewed by some as galling limitations on their "freedom."[161] But in a proper understanding, principles are a *means of cognition* — which is why they serve as standards of judgment to guide cognitive or existential action.

By spotlighting root causes, principles make one aware of a long train of consequences — not just the immediate effects, but the sum across a lifetime. Principles are thus indispensable for acting long-range. In this regard, Peikoff makes an apt contrast of man with animals:

> An animal cannot grasp or deal with the total of its lifespan and does not need to do so. . . . Man can and must know not merely tomorrow's requirements or this season's, but every identifi-

---

161 Dostoyevsky's "underground man" famously vents his rage at "two plus two makes four" and "a wall is a wall."

able factor that affects his survival. He can assess not merely the proximate, but also the remote consequences of his choices. It is not enough for him to consider the chance of a toothache next week; he also needs to know whether he is courting bankruptcy next month, an anxiety attack next year, an invasion of human predators in the next decade, or a nuclear holocaust in the next generation. [OPAR, 216–217]

Thus, one needs principles because they provide the overview, the road-map outlining the kind of consequences that follow from choosing one way or another. Principles identify cause-and-effect relationships. Acting in defiance of a valid principle means pretending that there can be causes without effects or effects without their causes. Both attempts are inherently self-defeating.

Principles as Cognitive Bridges

Since principles are generalizations, they are reached by a process of induction. And since principles are high-level generalizations, they are formed from generalizations that are one level less abstract, rather than from cognitive ground-zero.

For example, in physics, the principle that all matter attracts other matter is a very wide generalization integrating narrower ones, such as generalizations pertaining to the rate at which falling bodies accelerate, Kepler's laws of planetary motion, and the periodicity of the tides. (Finally, one "spirals back": the seemingly unrelated phenomena that one integrated to grasp the principle come to be seen as manifestations of that principle.)

To reach a principle, as we have seen, is to grasp a general type of root cause, a factor explaining a whole "tree" of derivatives — as the principle of identity (A is A) underlies and explains the rules of valid deduction, valid induction, proper definition. Likewise, the principle of individual rights identifies a fundamental requirement of moral dealings with others, whether on a personal, social, or political level.

One grasps a principle by a process of abstraction, just as one does in concept-formation. And abstraction, we have seen, is not subtraction but *interrelation*. Neither concepts nor principles are formed by "intuition," "insight," or any process other than observing the similarities and differences among concretes.

Principles offer a conceptual approach to cognition and conduct. Like concepts, principles are integrations; by integrating narrower generalizations, principles provide unit-economy. The condensed grasp of facts achieved by a principle gives us a mountain-top view of the particulars with which we must deal, cognitively and existentially. Principles enable us to apply what we have learned about observed cases to those as yet unobserved.

For example, to oversimplify somewhat, the principle "One must be honest" codifies, in abstract terms, the lessons learned from observing and reflecting on the nature of particular cases of honesty vs. dishonesty. The oversimplification is contained in the phrase "the nature of particular cases." To grasp the principle of honesty, one must not only see that the particular acts of dishonesty led to bad consequences in those circumstances, one must also grasp what in the nature of those acts caused the results to be bad and why some form of negative outcome is inevitable. In other words, the principle must be a valid induction — i.e., one that identifies a causal connection, not just a statistical correlation.[162]

Generalizations serve as cognitive bridges leading from cases that have been studied to those that have not been. As with a literal bridge, the value of a principle is that it allows one to cross over — i.e., to take knowledge gained by investigating the concretes from which one generalized and apply it to concretes not yet investigated.

The diagram below illustrates the process of moving in cognition from observed concretes A, B, and C to identify a principle, then moving back "down" to apply the principle to a new concrete, S.

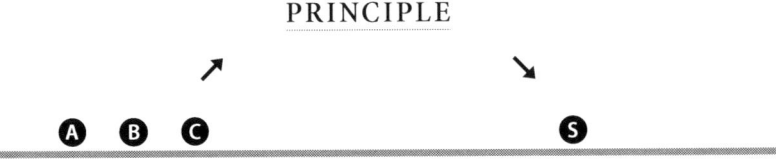

PRINCIPLE

CONCRETES

<hr />

162 Dishonesty is destructive because it is the attempt to fake what cannot be faked: the actual facts. Moreover, reality is an interconnected whole, not a mosaic of isolated compartments, so the faking cannot be limited to one domain but, to be maintained in the face of the growing disparity with reality, must grow ever wider — until the whole system of lies collapses. This is the lesson of the Bernie Madoff fraud.

Knowledge is not an end in itself. The value of all knowledge, whether concrete, mid-level, or fundamental, lies in its *application* — which, ultimately, means its use in guiding action. Whether one induces "Arsenic is poisonous" or "All bodies attract other bodies in inverse proportion to the square of the distance between them," the value of knowing the generalization lies in its application — e.g., to avoid dying from arsenic-poisoning or to put satellites into orbit. The use of principles consists in deductive applications of the induced generalizations.[163]

Principles, since they identify fundamentals, are more cognitively powerful than lesser generalizations: they have a wider scope and isolate a more potent, longer-range causal factor. For instance, the law of gravity is more powerful, in this double sense, than "Objects fall downwards."

Contra Plato, only concretes are real; abstractions, including principles, are merely man's method of understanding and dealing with concretes. A principle, if valid, is an invaluable tool for learning about the concretes and their long-range consequences; but the principle is only a tool, not a substitute for study of the concretes with all their particular characteristics. Principles tell us where to look — what considerations to hold in mind — when dealing with concretes, but we still have to look.

Even thinkers who reject Platonism may inadvertently adopt a Platonic approach by converting principles into formulas, which are then imposed mechanically upon unexamined concretes.[164] The proper application of principles uses them as an abstract frame of reference to guide a diagnosis of concretes, based upon sensitive attention to their particular characteristics. A physician observing that a patient is coughing would not reason: "Tuberculosis causes coughing, so this patient has tuberculosis," but would look at all the patient's symptoms, his medical history, the prevalence of tuberculosis in the environment, and many other factors, including test results. In the same way, the proper application of principles requires careful attention to all the facts about the concretes, some of which may modify the way the principle applies or, in unusual cases, even indicate that the concrete has special features that place it outside the principle's domain.

---

163 *Analogies* function as temporary bridges, based on grasping a relevant, but isolated, similarity between some concretes that are well understood and others that are made more intelligible by reference to that similarity. Analogizing principles to a bridge is itself such a case. The "bridge" is temporary in that the isolated similarity does not warrant forming a concept to permanently integrate the analogized items, because they are too different, overall.

164 In Objectivist terminology, this represents "psycho-epistemological Rationalism."

This procedure also provides a check that one has induced a valid principle, and has defined its proper sphere of application.

An extreme example of the Platonic, Rationalistic misuse of principles is Kant's notorious position that the principle of honesty requires telling the truth to an armed homicidal maniac demanding to know where one's children are — an absurd and outrageous example of context-dropping.[165]

Principles as Simplifiers

Since one learns principles by observing concretes (*a*, *b*, and *c* in the preceding diagram), the question arises: why are principles necessary? Couldn't we just observe the new concrete(s) as we observed the original ones? Part of the answer is that having a principle eliminates the need to continually re-investigate the same issue; the principle is an invaluable shortcut. But there is a deeper answer. Concretes differ in their complexity. *Principles enable the clear, simple cases to shed light on the obscure, difficult ones.*

This is the answer to those philosophers who scorn principles as being "tautologies" or "truisms." These philosophers say, for instance, that the Law of Non-Contradiction is "empty," citing the fact that we gain no new information from being told "It cannot be raining and not raining at the same place." But, in fact, holding in mind the principle of non-contradiction reminds one to check for *non-obvious* inconsistencies; it directs one to work to integrate every conclusion into the full context.

It is from simple cases like raining vs. non-raining that we draw the lesson: check for non-obvious contradictions. E.g., there is a non-obvious contradiction in an economy having both full employment and a minimum-wage law.[166] Or, take the idea that man, as a "sinful" being, cannot avoid immorality; what is unavoidable is not subject to moral judgment: morality exists to judge *choices.* Thus, the idea of unavoidable sin implies a contradiction.

A recent study on the sociology of scientific research found that from half to two-thirds of experiments on the frontiers of knowledge do not produce the expected results. The study also found that there is a tendency, especially among junior researchers, simply to ignore the anomalous results. As one distinguished biologist reported, graduate students and post-doctoral researchers frequently dismiss anomalous results as being due to "phases of

---

165 "On a Supposed Right to Lie from Altruistic Motives." [KANT 1949, 427]

166 Minimum wage laws mean that a man whose services are worth less to an employer than the mandated minimum wage cannot be employed.

the moon."[167] In fact, there is much to be learned from anomalous results, whether about how to avoid errors in procedure or about the existence of previously unknown factors. Bringing to mind the principle "Every effect has a cause" is an important reminder of the need for investigating the cause of all results — expected or unexpected. Likewise, the principle that knowledge is an integrated whole, not isolated bits, reminds the researcher to bring to bear on the problem everything relevant, not just the details of one particular run of one particular experiment.

Principles as Contextual

Like all conceptual knowledge, principles are contextual. The context of a principle is the knowledge from which it derives and the conditions under which it applies. For instance, the context of moral principles is the actions of a volitional being. The fact that there are no moral principles for ants is not any defect in ethics or moral principles.

Other issues of context are not as obvious (a point that itself illustrates the fact that principles clarify non-obvious cases by connecting them to more obvious ones). For instance, in ethics there is the oft-heard challenge, "What would ethics prescribe for two men in a lifeboat that can hold only one?" This sort of pretend-philosophizing drops the context of ethics, which is: normal conditions of existence, in which a long-range course of action is possible, and in which the survival of one does not threaten that of another.[168]

Even arithmetic has been attacked by using the same context-dropping approach. In objection to the principle that $1 + 1 = 2$, it is said that one lion plus one lamb equals one well-fed lion, and that one drop of water plus one drop of water equals one (coalesced) drop of water. But the context of $1 + 1 = 2$ is not physical combination but mental comparison. The physical results of an interaction are outside the context of arithmetic.

Often an invalid, concrete-bound formulation of a principle is exploited to attack it. For instance, one philosopher claimed that the existence of airplanes proves that gravity is not a principle. But the actual principle here is not "Heavy things fall"; it is "All bodies are attracted by other bodies." And an airplane is, of course, subject to that force of attraction — which is why the plane needs the power of its engines in order to fly.

---

167 Judith Berliner, UCLA, personal communication.

168 On such "lifeboat cases," see Rand, "The Ethics of Emergencies," VOS, CH. 2.

The fact that principles apply only within a delimited context does not make them dispensable or second-rate — except by a Platonic standard of evaluation, proceeding from the arbitrary idea that knowledge concerns relations between Forms existing in another dimension. A principle is an abstraction derived from observing and integrating facts, and its sphere of proper application is therefore determined by reference to the context of knowledge on which it is based.

Principles as Absolutes

Within their proper context, principles are absolutes. This follows from the nature of a principle: the law of causality has no exceptions. Thus, a valid principle can never be violated with impunity.

A principle allows for the operation of countervailing factors (as the force of gravity can be balanced by the force of an airplane's lift), but there is no such thing as a cancellation of the law of causality. Within their context, principles hold exceptionlessly.

Why, then, do people so often violate their own principles? In some cases, the explanation is that the principle is false. In that case, the principle tells one to follow a course of action that is demonstrably self-destructive. In other cases, the problem is one's failure to grasp and hold a principle in an authentic, first-hand manner. If a man's "principles" are merely his internalization of the blindly accepted assertions of his parents, his teachers, and his neighbors, then he holds arbitrary, undigested rules, not actual principles — i.e., not road-maps to the achievement of his own values.

Finally, man is not automatically rational: one does not automatically activate his abstract, conceptual knowledge. It takes no effort to be aware of short-range consequences; they are glaringly evident, here and now. But principles are highly abstract; it takes some conceptual effort even to realize that a principle is at stake, and more effort is required to apply the principle to a new, concrete case — and to hold onto the resulting knowledge under fire. So, in some cases, simple mental lethargy explains why people act against the better knowledge their principles make available to them.

A frequent rationalization used to justify violating a principle is that it will be violated "just this once." But the absolutism of principles cannot be escaped. First, if the principle is true, then it is true. That means one cannot succeed — whether one is attempting to acquire knowledge without obeying the principles required to do so, or trying to reach an existential goal without obeying the causal principles that identify the necessary means. Principles provide the map that identifies the location of a goal that one cannot directly see. If the map shows that the goal lies to the north, whatever the temporary attraction of heading south, doing so takes one farther from one's goal. Even if one seeks a "compromise" by heading northwest, one will miss the goal.

Violating a principle does not work; sooner or later, it results in failure. Failure exacts existential and psychological costs: wasted time and resources, and weakened self-confidence and self-respect.

Consider a second, and deeper, penalty for violating a principle. There is a logic to principles, and a logic to what happens when one acts against them. In acting against a principle, one faces consequences not just in regard to the case at hand, one is also implicitly endorsing an opposite principle and beginning to establish it in one's soul. For instance, if one tells a "white lie" to spare a friend's feelings, one is endorsing the (false) principle, "Avoiding negative feelings is more important than facing reality." One is also endorsing certain principles about the nature of friendship, such as that it is based not on mutual esteem but on pity and shared weaknesses.

To the extent that one is rational, one's principles define what one judges to be rationally necessary. Thus, flouting a principle jettisons both reason and causal necessity. This amounts to endorsing two wrong wider principles: metaphysically, the notion that reality is a fluid, non-absolute realm; epistemologically, that reason is not an absolute and that one's rational judgment is dispensable.

The latter, epistemological point is not just a theoretical implication. The unadmitted meaning of violating a principle is the dethroning of reason. One's operating premise is: "I'll go by reason — unless I don't feel like it." The meaning of this is a new (and false) principle: feelings trump reason. It doesn't matter what one advances as the factor before which reason must retreat — a hunch, social mores, short-range advantage, God's will — that factor cannot be something endorsed by reason. The idea of a rational limitation on reason is a contradiction in terms: if reason endorses the use of some consideration, then it is not beyond reason but part of reason; if reason does not endorse it (which is always the actual case), then it is against reason. And as explained in the preceding chapter, accepting the arbitrary is as irrational as accepting the contradictory. What is not rational to believe is irrational to believe.

The issue is: on what grounds does one mark off an area with the sign, "Here reason does not enter"? It cannot be on rational grounds: the attempt to use reason to exclude reason from a given domain is a contradiction: it means holding, "By the nature of the things in this domain, reason cannot know them." Yet, supposedly, it is precisely the nature of those things that reason cannot know. Let us even assume that the things in the domain are not held to be contrary to reason, only inaccessible to reason. But how does one know that? Not by reason, because reason has been excluded. It must be that the "limits" set for reason are imposed by faith, or by whatever non-rational, non-validatable means of knowledge one claims to possess.

Thus, the claim reduces to: "I have no reason to think that there are things inaccessible to reason; I accept that on faith." Which is to say that it is an arbitrary assertion and therefore against reason.

Whenever someone asserts: "There are areas that the human mind cannot penetrate," he has either just penetrated it (in contradiction to his claim), or else he has made an arbitrary assertion. (There is a third possibility: he could claim to be superhuman.)[169]

Since the only demonstrable human faculty that can stand opposed to reason is emotions, the violation of a rational principle necessarily inculcates the principle that emotions are superior to reason. Since reason is the faculty required to identify the facts of reality, taking emotions to be superior to reason means taking them to be superior to reality — which is the primacy of consciousness. Beneath all the sophistries and rationalizations, the man who violates a rational principle is saying: "This will work, because I *want* it to work."

"Just One Contradiction"

A principle identifies an action that is required by the facts at hand. To violate a principle is to act as if what is required were not required — a contradiction. The oft-heard excuse "Just this once" means: "It's safe to accept just this one contradiction." But accepting a contradiction undercuts the whole structure of one's knowledge. It forces a puzzle-piece into a space it does not fit, spoiling the overall picture (and leaving no place to put the right piece).

---

169 This fallacy is committed in a secular form by the Positivists (e.g., Ernest Nagel) who assert that the laws of logic are not truths about reality, but merely ways that the human mind is compelled to think. This entails the self-contradictory claim: "Contradictions may exist, but we cannot conceive that they exist" — a claim that begins by *conceiving* that contradictions do exist. [NAGEL, 1949]

Clinging to the contradiction undercuts method as well as content: one becomes unable to check ideas for consistency with *all* that one knows. Without that consistency-checking, one cannot distinguish knowledge from mere belief or feeling. The contradiction leads one into a swamp of subjectivism, bereft of epistemic guidance. The only way out is to renounce the attempt to "get away with" a contradiction, repair the damage done, and resume the task of non-contradictory integration, as a matter of *principle*.

To see the cognitive consequences of accepting a contradiction, consider the simplest possible case: accepting a contradiction in arithmetic. Let's take a hard case: a "small" contradiction not at the base of arithmetic, but further down the line. Suppose one accepts the contradictory idea that 14 = 15. Can't one still have arithmetic?

No, because arithmetic is an integrated whole. Consider: if 14 = 15, then what is the result of 15 − 14? Is it 1? Is it 0? There's no way to know. What is 14 + 14? It could be 28, 29, or 30.

Such undecidable questions cannot be quarantined. What is the result of 2 x 14? Is it the same as 2 x 15? Is 14 even or odd? Since 14 is supposed to be the same quantity as 15, we can't answer. What happens to the Pythagorean Theorem if we have a right triangle with one side 14 inches long and one side 15?

A contradiction, if maintained, *paralyzes* thought. One can proceed only by abandoning logic and just making up an answer as an arbitrary dictum. Ultimately, the alternative is: adherence to logic or cognitive paralysis.

AN EXAMPLE: INDIVIDUAL RIGHTS

A vivid concretization of the contextual absolutism of principles is provided by the principle of individual rights. On an objective theory of rights, rights are moral *principles*. Rights are the application of the principles of morality to man's dealings with others; they demarcate the individual's proper sphere of independent action. To say that a man has the right to do X is to say that he should be the one to choose whether or not he does X; no other person or group may force their choices upon him. Rights prescribe freedom by proscribing coercion.[170]

---

170 "A 'right' is a moral principle defining and sanctioning a man's freedom of action in a social context." [RAND, "MAN'S RIGHTS," VOS, 110] See this essay for a new theory of what individual rights are and how they are validated.

Principles are contextual. Rights are contextual in that they arise only in civil society; they provide guidance in organizing a proper social-political system under government. Locke's "state of nature" is outside the context to which rights apply. There are no rights on a desert island, or between two 17th-century fur trappers who cross paths in a deserted wilderness. Likewise, rights do not apply to the survivors of a shipwreck clinging to a life raft on the high seas.[171] But in civil society, in non-emergency conditions, rights define *objectively* the proper sphere of an individual's freedom of action.

Within their proper context, principles are absolute. The principle of individual rights starkly illustrates the absolutism of principles: rights exist to define what takes precedence over what in cases of conflict, social or individual. In such cases, rights define the supreme moral consideration—that over which nothing can take precedence. The right to free speech, for example, cannot be superseded by any other ethical or political consideration. If one holds that free speech may be abridged for the sake of "promoting virtue," preventing "blasphemy," or for achieving any other "social good," one has thereby implied that free speech is *not* a right, but a permission.

In any decision-making process, two competing considerations cannot both be supreme. It's either/or—either rights are inalienable, unconditional, absolute—or they are not and can be overridden by something else. If the latter, then they are not rights. Just as reason cannot "leave room" for faith, so rights are precisely that which cannot be compromised.

The popular idea of "conflicting rights," which must be "balanced" against each other, is a contradiction in terms (e.g., the conflict between a homeowner's property rights and the public's alleged right to eminent domain). There are certainly cases in which it has not yet been determined which party has the right and which party must yield. But the idea of a conflict among the very principles used to resolve conflicts is incoherent. A political right functions like a right-of-way in driving or boating: both are designed to settle the issue of who may proceed and who must yield. If someone were to claim that two cars approaching an intersection each have the right of way, it would be clear that he fails to understand what a right of way is (or else that the rules of the road have been improperly defined). The same is true for anyone claiming that political rights can be in conflict. Rights are the

---

171 In the fur-trapper example, the individuals remain obligated, by individual morality, to treat each other justly and peacefully (unless threatened); but if one constructs a lifeboat example in which it is impossible for all to survive, one has placed it outside the context in which the virtue of justice applies.

principles defining who may act independently, without interference, and who must refrain from interfering. Just as two competing principles cannot each be supreme, so two disputants in a conflict cannot each have the right to have his own way.

Rights are thus absolute — within their proper context.

PHILOSOPHY AND PRINCIPLES

Philosophic principles, like those of any other science, are reached by induction from experience. Philosophic principles are the fundamentals of the widest domains: existence and consciousness. Rand defines "philosophy" as the science that studies "the *fundamental* nature of existence, of man, and of man's relationship to existence." [PWNI, 2]

Philosophic principles have real-world application, as do principles in any other field. People understand that the principles of, say, physics have immense practical value, but they fail to see that philosophy has even more. Indeed, philosophy, in identifying the nature of existence and the rules of cognition, is the base of physics. The formation of any lesser generalization and the recognition of its value *depend upon* the implicit acceptance of its philosophic base. For instance, the generalization "All matter attracts other matter" could not have been discovered by consulting sacred texts or waiting for revelation; nor could it be reached on the premise that the world is governed not by natural law but by the decree of an omnipotent super-spirit; nor could it have any value to those who hold that this life is God's punishment for sin — all of which is why this generalization was not reached in the one-thousand years ruled by religious mysticism.[172]

Every adult, whether he has formally studied philosophy or not, has, in fact, stored a whole host of conclusions that reach a philosophic level. It is philosophical ideas that are being expressed in colloquial formulations such as: "Facts are facts" or "What's true for one person isn't necessarily true for another"; "There's an explanation for everything" or "Lots of things must remain as impenetrable mysteries"; "I can understand things" or "I can't ever be certain on my own — it's safer to follow others"; "I'm in charge of my

---

172 "For in much wisdom is much vexation, and he who increases knowledge increases sorrow." (Eccles. 1:17–18) And: ". . . there is scarcely anything so lowly or so simple to understand that man can thoroughly grasp or fully understand. . . . [W]e should live in the constant presence of death." [INNOCENT III, 12, 24]

own life" or "People are as society makes them"; "My life is my own to live" or "My duty in life is to serve the needs of others."

> You have no choice about the necessity to integrate your obser-
> vations, your experiences, your knowledge into abstract ideas,
> i.e., into principles. Your only choice is whether these principles
> are true or false, whether they represent your conscious,
> rational convictions — or a grab-bag of notions snatched at
> random, whose sources, validity, context and consequences you
> do not know, notions which, more often than not, you would drop
> like a hot potato if you knew. [PWNI, 5]

Philosophic principles, like those of physics, have real-world application — deductive application. One's actions are shaped by one's philosophic
conclusions — implicit or explicit, rational or irrational, correct or mistaken.
The influence of one's worldview on concrete issues and decisions is unavoidable, because the worldview is automatized. (Indeed, it forms an integral part
of who one is.) Just as the investor who has automatized the importance of
diversification looks at his investments from that perspective, so one who has
automatized the idea that what's true for you is not necessarily true for me
will view disputes between men from that perspective.

Since philosophy consists of the highest-level principles, since it is
supported, rationally or irrationally, by the widest range of particulars, since
adults have automatized it and built their lives upon it, philosophy's effect on
men's lives — and on history — is fundamental.

Ironically, it is the principles of philosophy men have accepted or
absorbed that explain the current widespread contempt for principles and
for philosophy.

In American culture today, anyone who operates short range, reversing
himself moment to moment, is admired as being "pragmatic" and not "rigid."
Our leaders continually tell us to adapt to "new circumstances," and claim
that "the tired, old solutions of the past" will no longer work (ignoring the
fact that *that* idea is one of the tiredest, oldest "solutions" of the past).

This cultural contempt for principles is relatively new. America's Founding Fathers were men of principle. (Note that they rose in rebellion against
very light taxes on stamps and tea.) Opposition to principles originated with
philosophers, especially the Pragmatists William James and John Dewey.
They influenced the educators (Dewey launched "progressive education")
and other opinion-leaders, who then spread the anti-principle attitude across

the culture. The average man is not a philosophic innovator; he gets his philosophic framework from the intellectual leadership, as it filters down to the educators, editorial-writers, artists, journalists, etc.

For over a century, philosophers and the intellectuals they have influenced have opposed principles. Their scorn for principles is a consequence of their underlying opposition to concepts. Due to the lack of a proper theory of how concepts are formed and how objectivity is attained, there was no proper defense of principles. The only (seemingly) pro-principle voices have come from the religionists (who defend not actual principles but frozen dogmas). The resurgence of religious fundamentalism, unleashed by the intellectuals' evisceration of reason, is only the other side of the false alternative: commandments vs. whims. The actual alternative to both commandments and whims is: rational principles, principles reached by a hierarchically ordered series of abstractions based upon perceptual observation, principles held as *contextual absolutes*.

To understand and defend principles, one must recognize that the law of identity applies to consciousness fully as much as to the external world. The knower, not just the known, has a specific, delimited nature. Three facts about the identity of man's consciousness are fundamental to epistemology: 1) man's senses provide an awareness of the world, in a form determined by his sensory physiology, 2) man's consciousness can hold only a limited number of units in a single frame of awareness ("the crow epistemology"), and 3) the conceptual level is volitional (the subject of the next chapter).

Together, these facts explain the cognitive function of concepts — and thus of principles. Concepts and principles are consciousness-expanders: starting from the data of perception, they expand the range of one's awareness, overcoming the "crow-limitation" by means of condensing an open-ended multiplicity into a unity. Concepts integrate a limitless number of perceptual concretes into a single unit, retained by one word; principles integrate a limitless number of derivative truths into one fundamental relationship, retained by one proposition. Concepts carve steps into the cliff face; principles describe the essentials of the scene spread out before one, after one has mounted those steps to reach the summit. The summit's view is not available to those who reject principles.

Both Pragmatists and religionists hold that "real life" cannot be governed by reason, that concepts do not integrate percepts, that theory is opposed to practice, and soul is opposed to body. In all these false dichotomies, the religionists side with the soul, the Pragmatists with the body. The motto of Pragmatism is: "It may be good in theory, but it doesn't work in practice."

The religionists (or Platonists) tell us, "It's good in theory, forget practicality; that's materialistic." The objective (and Objectivist) answer to both is: "What makes a theory good is that it names the fundamental requirements of successful practice; there can be no mind-body dichotomy." If a theory does not work in practice, that means the theory is wrong or misapplied. If the practice is to succeed in promoting life on this earth, it must obey the requirements identified by a valid theory.

Concepts and principles are neither social conventions nor ends in themselves. Concepts are the means of grasping knowledge beyond the animal level of "here now this." Principles are neither commandments — "Thou Shalt Nots" set against the needs of living on earth — nor ad hoc rules of thumb. Rather, they are cognitive maps of the world. Using the map analogy, Rand summarizes the anti-principle attitude:

> The present state of our culture may be gauged by the extent to which principles have vanished from public discussion, reducing our cultural atmosphere to [one] . . . that haggles over trivial concretes, while betraying all its major values, selling out its future for some spurious advantage of the moment . . . and by panicky appeals to "practicality."
>
> But there is nothing as impractical as a so-called "practical" man. His view of practicality can best be illustrated as follows: if you want to drive from New York to Los Angeles, it is "impractical" and "idealistic" to consult a map and to select the best way to get there; you will get there much faster if you just start out driving at random, turning (or cutting) any corner, taking any road in any direction, following nothing but the mood and the weather of the moment. [CUI, 144–145]

Principles are a biological imperative for Homo sapiens. To say to a human being, "Don't be theoretical" is like saying to a bird, "Don't fly."

Principles are the fullest realization of *how we know*. That is why they are how we survive and prosper.

10

FREE WILL

I HAVE EMPHASIZED THE FUNDAMENTAL DIFFERENCE BETWEEN THE perceptual level and the conceptual level. Perception is automatic, unchosen; conceptual activities are volitional — they are subject to *choice*. But what does choice mean and imply? Choice operating where? Caused by what? Affecting what? Now is the time to meet those questions head on — i.e., to take up the topic of free will.

Free will has traditionally been thought of as the ability to choose among alternative physical actions, e.g., choosing between going to work and going to the corner saloon. This view is not false, but it is quite superficial. Physical actions are not primaries; one's body does not unaccountably lurch off in one direction or another. The actions of one's body are controlled by the actions of one's mind: one *decides* what to do.

A decision, however, is also not a primary: it is the outcome of a decision-making process, and the input to that process is constituted by one's beliefs and values, specific and general.

One's beliefs and values are, in turn, the products of earlier processes. The process fashions the product. All conceptual products — all ideas, values, theories, and convictions — are caused and shaped by the processing that one employs in reaching them.

That processing can be performed rationally or irrationally. One can reach conclusions by a conscientious, fact-centered process of thought, or by any irrational substitute, such as emotion-driven leaps in the dark or unthinking absorption of the beliefs and values of others.

Here we have reached the actual primary: the rationality or irrationality of one's mental processes. It is this that is under one's direct, volitional control.

This is the understanding of free will originated by Ayn Rand,[173] and hers is the first philosophy to recognize that free will is fundamentally an epistemological issue, that it pertains to conceptual cognition as such.

> ... *man is a being of volitional consciousness.* Reason does not work automatically; thinking is not a mechanical process; the connections of logic are not made by instinct. The function of your stomach, lungs or heart is automatic; the function of your mind is not. In any hour and issue of your life, you are free to think or to evade that effort. But you are not free to escape from your nature, from the fact that reason is your means of survival — so that for *you*, who are a human being, the question "to be or not to be" is the question "to think or not to think." [AS, 1012]

Man's free will consists in his sovereign control over how he uses his own mind. How a man uses his mind determines the rest: the conclusions he reaches, the goals he sets, the action-decisions he makes. But nothing, in turn, controls how he uses his mind; that is his "sovereignty": the causal chain begins within one's own mind. Having the power to initiate a rational process makes man an autonomous, self-regulating being, not a robot programmed by outside forces.

Sovereign control is not omnipotence; one cannot take actions that would violate the identity of one's conceptual faculty. One cannot, for example, will to be infallible or omniscient. Nor is one immune from the effects on cognition of drugs or a blow to the head. But given a normal, healthy brain, one's sovereign control means that such factors as genes, upbringing, subculture, and desires do not control whether or not one engages in rational thought.

---

173 William James, in *The Principles of Psychology*, recognizes that free will is psychological, and his discussion there of will as control of attention is quite similar, though not identical, to Rand's idea of "mental focus." [JAMES, 1890] Also, an Aristotelian of the 2nd century A.D., Alexander of Aphrodisias, proposes essentially the same idea [*Quaestiones* III.13].

The doctrine that denies this sovereign control is known as "determinism." Determinism is the theory holding that antecedent factors beyond man's control necessitate everything he is and does, including the nature of every mental process he performs. Determinists claim that one's sense of control over one's own mind is illusory. According to determinism, every event in one's consciousness is only a reaction, necessitated by prior events, which were in turn necessitated by still earlier events, and so on, reaching back in time to before one's birth, before human beings evolved, before the Earth was formed. According to the theory of determinism, whatever happens in consciousness, as in the material world, had to happen, with no alternative, no actual control, no freedom, no genuine choice.

But if a man's mind were in thrall to some factor that forced ideas upon him, he could not validate his conclusions objectively, and thus he could not distinguish knowledge from mistaken belief. Objectivity requires guiding one's thinking by logic (see CHAPTER 6); the operations of a deterministic mind would be ruled not by logic but by some necessitating factor — genes, social "conditioning," brain structures, "confirmation bias," etc. A deterministic mind would only emit outputs, like a computer; it could not make objective judgments, distinguish the logical from the illogical, or separate truth from falsehood. As I show later in this chapter, if conceptual processes were deterministic, they would be like perceptual processes: metaphysically given and incapable of error. But denying the existence of error lands one in a contradiction: "The belief that error exists is an error."

If men could not think or act otherwise than they do, neither ethics nor epistemology would make sense: one cannot evaluate the impossible. To say that one ought to take some action presupposes that one can choose to take it.

For instance, logic instructs one to hold the full context in mind in making judgments — which presupposes that one can do so, that nothing blocks one from consulting all the relevant information available, that no mental content or thought is barred from awareness, that one is free to consider all sides, pro and con.

The same sovereign control is presupposed by all the principles of logic. "Dismiss the arbitrary" presupposes that one can dismiss it, and "reject the Appeal to Authority" presupposes that one can reject it, that one is capable of independent thought, rather than being deterministically "conditioned" by parents, teachers, and social practices.

In short, logic, as a normative field, presupposes that nothing "runs" one's mind, that one has sovereign control over its operation.

Such control is precisely what Ayn Rand identified as the locus of man's free will. Man's ability to take charge of his mind gives him control over all the other aspects of his life: how he uses his mind shapes his conclusions, goals, actions, and character.

> That which you call your soul or spirit is your consciousness, and that which you call "free will" is your mind's freedom to think or not, the only will you have, your only freedom, the choice that controls all the choices you make and determines your life and your character. [AS, 1017]

Focus

One's power to take hold of the mental reins is always present — but it is present as a choice. One does not have to take charge of one's mind; one is always free to drop effort, control, concern with reality, and just "space out." In Rand's terms, one has the choice between *focusing* one's mind or not:

> Thinking requires a state of full, focused awareness. The act of focusing one's consciousness is volitional. Man can focus his mind to a full, active, purposefully directed awareness of reality — or he can unfocus it and let himself drift in a semiconscious daze, merely reacting to any chance stimulus of the immediate moment, at the mercy of his undirected sensory-perceptual mechanism and of any random, associational connections it might happen to make. [VOS, 22]

Mental focus is wider and deeper than thinking; it is the precondition of thinking. Focus is the purposeful mental "set" that underlies and drives the process of thought. (Thought is focus sustained on a specific topic, to answer a definite question.)

Optical focus is a state of clarity and sharpness. Focusing one's mind, as with focusing the image from a movie projector, aims at making things clear — clear conceptually, in the case of mental focus. As Peikoff aptly describes it, " 'Focus' (in the conceptual realm) names a quality of purposeful alertness in a man's mental state. 'Focus' is the state of a goal-directed mind committed to attaining full awareness of reality." [OPAR, 56]

The essence of focus is *purposefulness*. To focus is to set and enforce a goal — the goal of gaining a clear, integrated understanding of the world, and of oneself.

Purposefulness is not a static state but a process of steering one's mind, adjusting its activities to the requirements of attaining full, clear knowledge of reality. To be in focus means to *manage* the operations of one's own mind in pursuit of a cognitive goal.

But one also can choose to mis-manage one's mind: to deliberately slam one's mind shut in the attempt to deny the reality of something that one knows, clearly or dimly, *is* real. This is *evasion*, which Rand describes as:

> . . . the act of blanking out, the willful suspension of one's consciousness, the refusal to think — not blindness, but the refusal to see; not ignorance, but the refusal to know. It is the act of unfocusing your mind and inducing an inner fog to escape the responsibility of judgment . . . [AS, 1017]

Evasion has a purpose, but that purpose is non-awareness. To avoid acknowledging some unpleasant or frightening fact, one steers one's mind away from it, working to get it out of awareness.

To focus is to set the goal of awareness, as distinguished from two other states: evasion and "drift." To drift is to fail to set the goal of awareness; to evade is to set the goal of non-awareness.

Either one sets one's mind to the task of knowing reality, or one does not. Every use of one's conceptual faculty — whether to choose a course of behavior, or choose a value, or make a judgment, or form a concept — can be done in focus or out of focus. In focus: as a purposeful, self-monitored, reality-oriented process. Out of focus: either as aimless, unsupervised drift or as emotion-driven evasion.

Being in focus is like steering a car. Steering has two aspects: observing the road ahead and turning the steering wheel. Likewise, steering one's mind involves both monitoring and directing. Monitoring consists of observing what is going on in one's mind; directing is issuing to oneself the words, or wordless equivalents, that will cause the next step.[174]

---

174 The words act upon one's subconscious, which is embodied in neural mechanisms. The study of how the conscious mind interacts with the subconscious is the province of "psycho-epistemology" [see RM, 18].

For instance, suppose one monitors a sense of confusion in response to reading a statement about financial planning. In that case, directing one's mind to deal with it might take the simple form of asking oneself: "What's confusing me?" Or just: "Huh?" In other cases, some groping might be involved, as in this sample mental monologue:

> "I'm uncomfortable. What's wrong? I'm confused. What's confusing here? Oh, the phrase 'yield to maturity.' What's confusing about it? I don't know what 'to maturity' adds. What can I recall about 'to maturity'?"

(Here, I have put the mental process into full sentences, to express it for the reader. Often one will use a mental shorthand, so that the whole sequence might occur in a foreshortened form, like: "What? 'To maturity'?")

The process of seeking clarity is not automatic. First, nothing makes one monitor at all: a person can feel confusion but fail to attend to it, fail to identify that confusion is what he is experiencing. Or, he can be aware that he is confused but not ask himself: confused about what? Or, he might ask himself that, and even get the answer "I'm confused about the meaning of 'yield to maturity,'" yet shrug it off with: "Who knows?" All of these are states of less than full focus.

(In the last case, an in-focus decision might well be, to again put it in a full sentence: "I don't understand 'yield to maturity,' but, all things considered, it's not worth my time to figure it out, so I will note that I don't understand it and table this issue for now." The issue of focus concerns taking active control, being "hands on," not the particular judgment one makes.)

To be in focus means to make full, unconditional awareness an absolute of one's mental functioning: "It means one's total commitment to a state of full, conscious awareness, to the maintenance of a full mental focus in all issues, in all choices, in all of one's waking hours." (VOS, 28)

Rationality

Epistemologically, focus means rationality. Rationality is the exercise of reason; reason is the conceptual faculty. "Focus" names the introspectible sense or "feel" of the psychological state; "rationality" names the kind of activities that one performs in that state. The choice to function rationally is the choice to utilize one's conceptual faculty, activating one's full cognitive resources. This choice consists in exerting the effort to take charge of one's mind, to set it to the task of understanding what one is dealing with, to monitor one's own mental operations and direct them toward what one judges to be their most effective, rational deployment — as opposed to anything less than that.

In contrast, sensory perception is automatic, physiologically determined, and not subject to introspective monitoring. In looking at a table, one is not aware of the neurophysiological processes that make possible the perception of the table. In fact, we learn of the existence of the neurophysiological processes only extrospectively, by scientific investigation.

But on the conceptual level of awareness, the process of cognition is conscious, deliberate, and introspectible. The elementary act of grasping a new concept requires doing conscious mental work. Even the child learning the term "table" from a parent has to put forth the effort to attend to similarities and differences among the objects he perceives, make conscious comparisons to recollected objects, and grasp that the word "table" stands for all similar concretes, irrespective of when he considers them. (Forming such simple concepts is so easy for a human being that even an out-of-focus child will eventually pick it up, though without the in-focus child's sense of achievement.) More mental work is required for an adult learning advanced abstractions, such as "yield to maturity." Some people put forth the effort required, some do not. The choice is up to each individual.[175]

No effort is required to see the words on this page, but to understand what is written, to integrate it, grasp its implications, judge its validity — that requires the choice to do mental work. You don't have to will your eyes to see, but you do have to will your brain to think. Perceptual processes are automatically in contact with the world; conceptual processes are not. Conceptual processes performed out of focus result in mental content that is invalid, subjective, out of touch with reality.

To engage in a process of rational thought, one has to take charge of one's mind and set it to the task of identification and integration — that is, one has to focus one's mind. The alternative is not simply that of full, consistent rationality or a complete retreat to near the perceptual level; there are various levels of conceptual awareness in between, and (unfortunately) most

---

175 Choosing not to form a technical concept is not objectionable and doesn't imply being out of focus; but using a term without concern for whether one understands it or not *is* and *does*.

people drift somewhat passively among them. Full focus is not a momentary foray into the cognitive realm but an ongoing commitment to full awareness.

The basic volitional choice, to focus one's mind and proceed rationally, does not concern differences in intelligence, interest, or prior knowledge, but solely the difference in the degree of purposeful effort put forth to understand reality. E.g., at a university lecture even the slowest, most uninterested and unprepared student has the power to concentrate on the lecture and seek to understand, integrate, and judge it. Conversely, even the most brilliant and well-informed "A" student can simply let his mind go, tuning out the lecture.

The Reality-Orientation

Metaphysically, rationality consists of instituting the "reality-orientation," in Peikoff's phrase. [OPAR, 66] Rand writes that rationality, "is the recognition of the fact that existence exists, that nothing can alter the truth and nothing can take precedence over that act of perceiving it, which is thinking . . . ." [AS, 1018]

Thus, being rational means recognizing that existence has primacy over consciousness, recognizing that the mere presence of an idea in one's mind, no matter how correct it might *feel*, offers no assurance that it corresponds to the facts of an independently existing reality. An irrationalist functions on the opposite implicit premise, the premise of the primacy of consciousness, according to which facts snap into line with whatever passes through one's mind or whatever one wishes the facts to be.

Does one go by evidence or by whims and authorities? Does one latch onto whatever idea first strikes him as plausible, or does he work to integrate it into the sum of his knowledge, checking for contradictions? The basic alternative here is one's orientation: does one accept reality and seek to know it, come what may? Or, does one consider reality expendable when it clashes with one's desires, one's self-image, or the beliefs of others?

The basic choice is a single primary but, as we have seen, it has several aspects and thus is describable as focus, rationality, purposefulness, self-monitoring, managing, adopting the reality-orientation, and in still other ways.[176] Rand writes:

> Psychologically, the choice "to think or not" is the choice "to focus or not." Existentially, the choice "to focus or not" is the choice "to

---

176   For more discussion, see OPAR, ch. 2, and Binswanger, 1991.

be conscious or not." Metaphysically, the choice "to be conscious or not" is the choice of life or death. [VOS, 22]

MOTIVES AND FOCUS

The basic choice to focus and take charge of one's mind is independent of any *specific* motive.[177] If being in focus were conditional upon some specific motive, we would remain in a daze until something grabbed our attention, and upon losing interest, we would go out of focus. And if some topic was unpleasant or frightening, we would automatically evade it. In other words, if the choice to focus had to wait on and remain subject to some lure from without or within, then we would be hopelessly passive, irrational — and mankind could not have survived.

Rather than requiring a specific motive, the choice to focus is *unconditional*. You can will yourself to manage your mental operations and adopt the reality-orientation without needing a concrete incentive to do so. Even when you feel that you really don't want to focus, you can still will it. Not only do you need no specific motive to focus, you can focus in the teeth of a desire to evade that responsibility.

If man were unable to focus unless he felt like it, he would not be the rational animal; he would be precisely the irrational animal that scores of philosophers have claimed him to be.

People can be irrational. They can, by their own choice, make the exercise of reason wait upon the permission of their feelings. Their operating premise is: "I look at reality — when my feelings permit it." But rationality is precisely the unconditional commitment to perceiving reality, the commitment to grasping and accepting any relevant fact, whether pleasant or not.

Peikoff makes the point that motives cannot compel consciousness, because motives presuppose consciousness.

> The choice to activate the conceptual level of awareness must precede any ideas; until a person is conscious in the human sense, his mind cannot reach new conclusions or even apply previous ones to a current situation. There can be no intellectual factor

---

177 Focusing is not an end in itself. It has what can be called a "metaphysical" motive: the desire to live, which means the commitment to acting in and achieving values in reality. This fundamental motive is, however, universally applicable, in contrast to any narrower motive (which presupposes the desire to live and function).

which makes a man decide to become aware or which even partly explains such a decision: to grasp such a factor, he must already *be* aware.

For the same reason, there can be no motive or value-judgment that precedes consciousness and which induces a man to become conscious. Instituting the reality-orientation must precede value-judgments. Otherwise, values have no source in one's cognition of reality and thus become delusions. Values do not lead to consciousness; consciousness is what leads to values. [OPAR, 59–60]

This point above applies not only to the alternative of consciousness versus unconsciousness but also to intermediate, semi-conscious states. Semi-conscious content need not be accepted as real and binding; it can be treated just as stray thoughts or imagination.[178] In a state of less than full focus, by definition, one is not committed to the reality of reality; one is acting as a passenger in one's own mind, merely spectating upon snatches of out-of-context ideas. An idea or goal that floats through a semi-focused mind has only such causal power as one gives it: one is free to choose whether to stop, consider it, take it seriously (i.e., to deal with it in full focus) or to let it pass away, as if it were unreal (i.e., to remain in semi-focus or actively evade).

While in a semi-focused state, a man may happen to feel a desire to focus and think (or at least to know more about something that has arisen). But while in that state, the desire is not an absolute commitment; it can be a faint desire, a wistful longing, a vague sense of guilt — all in contrast to the active resolve to know the full context and the full truth. Moreover, while not in full focus, the prospect of "really looking" may sometimes seem unpleasant or even frightening. The primary choice is whether or not to "really look" despite any such feelings.

The possibility of semi-focus or half-hearted efforts to know reality does not get around the point that it is either/or: *either* the actions of one's consciousness are surrendered to transient feelings, including feelings about focusing itself, *or* one is committed to full awareness of reality.

---

178 I owe this point to Peter Schwartz (personal conversation).

THE CHOICE OF ACTION

As I have stressed throughout this book, consciousness is a biological faculty whose function is to guide action. How, then, does the choice to focus relate to one's bodily actions?

First, I must clarify what I mean by "action." I do not include those local muscular contractions that occur without conscious initiation and control, such as the "knee-jerk" reflex. Some borderline cases are sneezing, coughing, vomiting. These may well have an origin in consciousness, but they "come over us," rather than being voluntary actions. A greater involvement of consciousness occurs in brief, trivial acts, of which one is only peripherally aware, such as absent-mindedly scratching one's scalp.

Philosophy is concerned with "human action" in the full sense of the term: purposeful action, action consciously initiated and sustained in pursuit of a pre-envisioned end. Although even very minor decisions are subject to volition and can be made rationally or irrationally, the most fruitful kinds of examples to keep in mind in thinking about the choice of action are the more dramatic cases, such as deciding which candidate to vote for in an election, choosing between buying a new house and remaining in one's present home, choosing a career.

In these kinds of practical, existential choices, and in all lesser variants, what is the role of the basic choice? Perhaps surprisingly, the answer is: the same as its role in cognition. In deciding how to act, as in deciding how to think, the state of focus remains the fundamental, controlling factor. The conscious ego is capable of controlling both the operations of thought and the muscles of one's body; both mind and body can be guided rationally, in focus, or not, according to one's choice. The essential causality is the same for directing one's mind to take up a particular topic and directing one's body to go to a particular location. Both are subchoices, implementing the primary choice to focus (to the extent one is out of focus, they are not decisions at all but capitulations to internal emotional pressures).

In discussing the relation of volition to action, it is crucial to avoid Platonism, with its view that the intellect is sundered from action in the world. Although I have generally presented the primary choice in intellectual terms — e.g., as the will to know — the premise has been that one is seeking that knowledge in order to guide one's course of behavior, directly or indirectly, concretely or abstractly. I have been speaking from a biological, not a Platonic, orientation.

Consciousness is biological equipment. Awareness evolved for its survival function — to guide the actions of conscious organisms. Directly or indirectly, the motive for knowing anything is to use it in action. To capture the life-centered view of cognition, free of any trace of other-worldliness, Rand crafted a statement that makes a dramatic reversal of Hume's "is"–"ought" dichotomy: "Knowledge, for any conscious organism, is the means of survival; to a living consciousness, every 'is' implies an 'ought.'" [VOS, 24]

Fundamentally, consciousness is navigational: it is identification used to guide action. A prime example is the process of deliberating upon alternative courses of action. Deliberation seeks to identify the consequences of alternative actions, judging which one is best; if successful, its conclusion is a decision to act. Deliberation is at once a quest to find truth and to direct action; it is at once intellectual and practical.

The deliberative process need not be performed at all — one can simply act on emotional urges. Even when one does do the work of deliberating, the process can be performed rationally or irrationally — i.e., in focus or out of focus. This is a matter of directly volitional choice.

The relation of the basic choice to a course of behavior is then clear: one has the choice to deliberate and decide through a rational, in-focus process — or not. For both cognitive and existential action, the volitional element — the act of direct will — pertains only to the rationality of the mental processes that lead to the action.

Some minor decisions, such as to pick up and read the newspaper, require nothing more than an instant's thought. Even more momentous decisions can sometimes be made quickly and easily, because all the evidence points in one direction and one is free of doubt and conflict — as when one gladly accepts an unanticipated promotion at work. But what about cases that are not open and shut, cases in which one has doubts or is in conflict?

For instance, suppose that you have the thought of reading the newspaper, but it is accompanied by a vague, as yet unidentified, sense of guilt. Suppose that this feeling's actual source, also not yet identified by you, is that you had resolved to start preparing your income tax return. You are experiencing the result of two contradictory ideas: 1) It would be good to read the newspaper now, 2) It would be wrong to do that now. Here, you face the three volitional alternatives: focus, drift, or evasion. The act of pushing the guilty feeling out of your mind, in order to avoid awareness of what you have only vaguely glimpsed, would be evasion. Drift would be relinquishing cognitive effort, allowing your behavior to be determined by whichever feeling — desire or guilt — eventually predominates.

The in-focus process consists of seeking to understand — to understand both the world and yourself. In this example, that means: asking extrospective and introspective questions — such as (extrospectively) "What is actually best for me now, in the full context? What's my schedule?" and (introspectively) "What is the bad feeling that I'm having now?" (answer: guilt) "Why am I having it? Guilt over what?" (answer: not doing my taxes now).

These are only some possible questions and answers; I cannot, of course, predict what the actual questions and answers would be. The point is that a *rational* process is available to you to resolve such conflicts, or to at least make progress toward resolving them. And that rational process is devoted to discovering the full truth. Drift, in contrast, is goal-less, and evasion is devoted to avoiding knowledge.

Deliberation, decision-making, selection among alternatives — all these acts can be done in-focus, conscientiously, or out-of-focus, i.e., negligently or by a deliberate act of evasion that attempts to wish away unpleasant facts.[179]

Whether a decision concerns what to do next with one's mind or what to do next in existential action, the decision-making process is simultaneously cognitive and action-oriented. Cognition is not severed from the action. One finds out (cognition) what to do (action). And, looking in the other direction, purposeful human action is the physical expression of having reached a conclusion about what to do.

Man has the ability to reflect upon and evaluate his own decision-making processes, and thus to control the processes that control his actions. One can step back and rationally make a wide variety of judgments, such as:

- The considerations are too complex and/or too confusing to decide at this time.
- I need to get further information before deciding.
- I am too tired to make a good decision now; I will revisit the question later, when I am rested.
- I need to check that there is not an option that I have overlooked.
- I have to decide right now, even though I am uncertain, so I must pick the option that looks best now.

---

179   In the Objectivist ethics, evasion is the fundamental act of immorality.

In cases of confusion or conflict, one can reach full certainty regarding such "meta-cognitive" judgments.

To reach rational certainty on any topic requires applying a standard of certainty.[180] To be certain one must have conclusive evidence, and that requires knowing, explicitly or implicitly, what counts as "conclusive evidence." Rough, generalized standards are available to anyone who can distinguish between evidence and assertion, logic and illogic, reason and feelings, fact and fantasy. (The objective standard, as explained in CHAPTER 8, is that the integrated sum of the evidence supports and is consistent with one and only one hypothesis, within a rationally delimited set of hypotheses.)

Just as thought in general ranges from the easy to the difficult, so do the development and application of standards. It is trivially easy to judge an object's length by reference to the standard of the inch as marked off on a ruler. It is quite difficult to devise and apply an appropriate standard for judging a nation's aggregate economic production. But whether a given standard allows for precise measurement or only a rough approximation, the use of a standard of judgment takes decision-making out of the realm of emotion, of what just "feels right," and into the realm of objectivity.

Cases of grappling with uncertainty spotlight the need to manage one's mind; only a self-conscious, fully focused state allows for stepping back to judge how best to deal with the uncertainty.

An Extended Concretization

Here is an extended example of managing one's mind vs. not doing so — resulting in different actions taken. I project the thought process going on in two students' minds, on the night before their final exam in a course on Ancient Greek philosophy. Each student is deciding whether or not to study for the exam.

First student's thoughts:

> Am I going to study tonight, or watch TV? I guess I ought to study — but that course — ugh! Professor Winston is so boring. I don't see why I should have to force myself to study something if the teacher can't make it interesting. He wants us to do all the work while all he does is read his lectures from a script. He must have written that lecture decades ago; there are jokes from the '80s

---

180 I owe this point to Shrikant Rangnekar (personal conversation).

in them. I bet he hasn't done any new work in years. Just takes it easy. He's probably watching TV right now. What's on TV tonight? Oh, that great old Bogart film. That's the one I saw last year with Maureen. I remember how she cried at the end of the film. That was really nice. Maureen is nice. I don't know why I didn't pursue a relationship with her. Hey, I could ask her over right now to watch that movie on TV. Repeating our old date — that would come across as real romantic.

Oh, but what about the final? Aw, I guess I'm prepared enough, and everyone knows you can bluff your way through philosophy tests. [He reaches for the phone.]

Second student's thoughts:

Am I going to study tonight or watch TV? What's at stake? My grade-point average. If I don't do well on the final tomorrow, I'm going to get a C in the course, and that's not going to look too good when I apply to graduate school. But is studying tonight really going to make a difference to my grade? Well, how well do I already understand the material this exam will cover? Well, what will it cover? Oh yeah, Professor Winston said it will be mainly on Aristotle's ethics. What are the topics of Aristotle's ethics that we are going to be responsible for? [Looks at his notes.] Happiness as an end in itself, the golden mean, pride as the crown of the virtues.

Now how well prepared am I on those topics? Well, I wrote my term paper on the golden mean — I know I've got that down pat; no problem with the virtue of pride — that's simple. But happiness — didn't that have some technical stuff in it — what was it? Something about the soul? Yeah, that was confusing. Professor Winston sure wasn't clear about that. But then what is he ever clear on? He expects the class to figure out what he's saying, rather than taking the trouble to explain anything. He just reads his old lectures, and never — wait, that's beside the point; let me get back on track.

Okay, if I'm hazy on happiness, I'm not going to do too well. Winston's hinted more than once that Aristotle's view of happiness is important. I could re-read my notes on happiness and check a secondary source.

But then that's going to take time, and that great Bogart film is on TV tonight. I'd hate to miss it. And after all, I'm entitled to some pleasure in life. No, that's just an excuse. Could I even enjoy the movie, with tomorrow's exam looming over me? No, I really, really want to get into a good grad school; my whole future depends on that.

But I want to see that movie! Do I have to miss it? Is there some other way? Wait — it must be out as a video. Yeah, I'll rent the video tomorrow night after the exam as a reward for nailing down Aristotle's view of happiness tonight. [He reaches for his study materials.]

The second student's focused, rational process of thought, which I tried to make prosaic rather than extraordinary, led him to the clear, unconflicted recognition that studying was the thing to do — the thing he actually *wanted* to do. The alternative, as he came to see it, was the investment of one evening's work or jeopardizing a long-range value of great personal importance to him. Plus, his thinking in the last two paragraphs completely reversed his initial evaluation of seeing the movie that night; it no longer seemed tempting. But his seeing the issue this way was the consequence of his maintaining full focus.[181]

In contrast, the first student's out-of-focus ramblings led him to the opposite decision (or pseudo-decision). The choice as he saw it, given his contracted range of awareness, was between an enjoyable date watching a good movie while impressing a girl — or a painful and boring evening carrying out an unjustly imposed duty. His decision in favor of watching the movie followed from his out-of-focus mental set.

The example concretizes how the alternative of focus vs. non-focus underlies all the lesser alternatives one confronts. In the face of the same alternative studying or not, one student chose rationally, the other irrationally. That difference reflected their opposite mental "sets": one student was committed to full awareness, the other was not. To be rational, a decision must be made in focus. If a decision (or a lurch into action) is made while out of focus, it is not rational. Rational action means action proceeding from the full

---

181 Notice that he does not deny his emotions ("But I want to see that movie!"). He acknowledges his desire, but he keeps thinking, and thus is able to find an overlooked way to get the enjoyment without sacrificing his higher value.

and honest use of reason. And that, in turn, means that one must generate the effort to keep the full context clear, real, active — as the second student did — instead of passively letting short-range emotional pushes and pulls substitute for rational self-direction.

Whether one is functioning in focus or out of focus, the actions one takes depend on the mental content that enters one's mind. A series of ideas, images, value-judgments, and emotions serve as input to the choice of what to do. But the nature of that input depends on one's level of awareness: the actively managed awareness of a man in focus brings to his mind and makes real to him considerations that would not occur to a man operating on a lower level of awareness. While out of focus, one is intensely aware of the immediate, perceptually present factors and only weakly aware of more abstract, long-range considerations — as the first student is strongly aware of the pleasure of watching the Bogart movie with his former girlfriend, but only weakly aware, if at all, of the effects on his future of doing poorly on the exam.

Understanding men's actions in this way enables us to give a good explanation of the phenomenon that so puzzled the Ancient Greek philosophers: how people can act against their own knowledge. People sometimes take an action while saying, "I know I shouldn't be doing this." The explanation is: they *don't* actually know at that moment that they shouldn't be doing it. They are not choosing to make that knowledge real and active in their minds.

Thus, the alleged clash of reason and emotion can be reduced to the issue of context-holding vs. context-dropping. The clash is not between two independent "parts of the soul," but between a wider and a narrower context of knowledge, between the way things appear (and how one feels about them) when considered rationally, in the full context — vs. how they appear when one relinquishes effort and allows the unsupervised, automatic response of one's subconscious to set the terms.

One's emotions are produced by the brain's automatic application of one's stored beliefs and values to the perceived facts. But one's level of focus affects which set of material, out of all that one has stored, is activated and therefore operative at any given moment. Different beliefs and values may be activated — and different emotions result — according to whether one works to bring the full context to mind or myopically stumbles along on the basis of whatever out-of-context beliefs and values get triggered by what one perceives. In my example, the in-focus student no longer feels the desire to watch the film on TV once he considers the full context, which includes the fact that he can later watch the video.[182]

In summary, one's fundamental choice is between purposeful, rational management of one's own mind and purposeless drift or deliberate evasion.

VOLITION AND CHARACTER

By adulthood, one has formed a certain character, which includes dispositions to behave in certain ways and not in others. The question thus arises: what is the relation of free will to character? Does a man choose his own character? Does his character, once formed, control his choices?

What is "character"? The term refers to a person's moral makeup, as manifested in his *characteristic* way of behaving. Some people are characteristically hard-working, some are slackers, some are mixed. Peikoff's definition names the fundamental: "'Character' means a man's nature or identity insofar as this is shaped by the moral values he accepts and automatizes." [PEIKOFF, 1976, LECTURE 2]

The kind of moral values one accepts depends upon one's rationality or irrationality in thinking about issues of morality; one's automatization of moral values comes from action — from repeatedly acting honestly, justly, industriously, etc. or failing to do so — which, in each instance, depends upon one's state of focus. Thus, the moral values that one ingrains in one's soul, resulting in a good character or a bad one, proceed from one's direct area of free will: one's choice to be rational or irrational, to maintain full focus or to drift or evade.

A man's character is the net product of all his choices, over his life up to the present. Man does not choose his character directly, but the nature of the choices he makes adds up to a characteristic way of acting.[183]

Consider how one's repeated choices in regard to the basic issue of focus affect the development of one's character. Focus concerns the level of awareness at which one functions mentally. At a low level of awareness, only the

---

182 This is not to say that all conflicting evaluations can be resolved so easily. But the point remains that one can go by either a rational, in-context evaluation or the snap judgment produced by the unsupervised actions of one's subconscious.

183 Of course, one can consciously dedicate oneself to instilling a good character in oneself; the point is that that choice can be implemented only in each of the concrete choices one confronts in the course of daily living, and that one's character is formed or changed not over hours or days but over years.

Self-made
soul

perceptually evident concretes and the emotions they automatically generate shape one's behavior. To the extent that one refuses to focus, surrendering instead to short-range urges, one is establishing a weak-willed character. In making the effort to function on a higher level of awareness, one is establishing a self-disciplined character.

It is in this sense that we *indirectly* choose our characters — we forge our characters, step by step, according to the nature of the specific choices we make, for good or ill. Man, Rand writes, "is a being of self-made soul." [AS, 1020] The self-making occurs gradually, in an ongoing process.[184]

The sum of past choices does not eliminate choice in the present. The choice to focus cannot be <u>automatized</u>, because it is precisely the choice to take charge of one's mind rather than letting the automatized take over.

Character does not eliminate choice. One can act "out of character." But one's character limits how far one can go — at the moment.

A man who is characteristically rational and self-disciplined might in a given instance wrongly permit himself an out-of-character rationalization — say, to indulge in a diet-breaking snack. That sort of out-of-focus action remains possible to him. On the other hand, there are things that would *not* be possible for such an individual to do. He could not take it into his mind to beat up his wife. He could not arbitrarily decide to inject himself with heroin. He could not suddenly start acting in obvious contradiction to his basic convictions. While other individuals, with a record of evasion (and the psychological disintegration it wreaks) can do such things, the rational man's character neither permits that scale of self-betrayal nor gives him any motive to act that irrationally.

Evasion normally sets off an internal "alarm" — a sense or signal from one's subconscious that something is wrong. After all, by evading, one is engaging in a pretense, in a form of self-deceptive double-think: "I mustn't look at that; it's not there." But if it actually were not there, why the order not to look at it? The implicit contradictions involved in acts of evasion produce a range of emotional signals, from the simple sense of confusion and bafflement on up to acute feelings of anxiety and guilt.

The individual with a rational character, with a long history of conscientiously facing all the facts, pleasant or painful, is unaccustomed to hearing such alarms. If he evades, the alarm is a striking exception to his normal sense of clarity and calm. Thus, to continue the evasion would require more

---

184 By saying "gradually," I do not mean to imply that all choices are tiny; there can also be momentous choices that have huge consequences upon one's character.

Long range values
short range emotions

of him than it would for a less rational person: it would require that he evade the alarm as well as the original evasion that set it off. In contrast, the individual who evades frequently is used to these alarms; to him they are the normal background. One more alarm almost gets lost in the general din. Thus, for him, one more evasion may not require any special effort.[185]

In addition, in order to act out of character, one must have a motive. To be in focus is to place long-range values over short-range emotions. But a lifetime of doing just that means that one is precluded from even being tempted to take certain actions. Taking heroin is not emotionally attractive to a man with an unbroken history of relying on and valuing his mind. Even when momentarily out of focus, taking heroin is not on the table; both his reason *and* his emotions scream against it. Or, he may on an occasion get quite furious with his wife, but nothing within him would urge him in the direction of striking her.

The reverse situation holds as well: it would be impossible for a man with a long history of evasions to suddenly start acting just as a rational man would. (Reforming his character and methodology is possible, but only through a long, gradual process.)

Hume
actions
≠
character

Hume had it exactly wrong when he claimed that an action has no effect if it is "out of character":

> Actions are, by their very nature, temporary and perishing; and where they proceed not from some cause in the characters and dispositions of the person who performed them, they infix not themselves upon him. . . . [the act] leaves nothing of that nature behind it. [HUME, II, III, 2]

But the causal nature of man's consciousness means that *every choice leaves its trace.* Choosing a certain way once makes it a little easier and more natural to choose that way the next time. Giving in to a temptation increases its motivational pull; dispelling the power of a temptation, by making oneself aware of the long-range consequences, decreases any subsequent motivational pull. The volitional aspects remain volitional, but the subconscious is geared toward automatization; like an obedient servant, it gets the message, the modus operandi, being established by the choices one makes. Moreover, each choice has existential consequences, which themselves are either identified, ignored, or actively evaded. As Aristotle said,

---

185 The soul of an evader is dramatized and dissected by Ayn Rand in the character of James Taggart in *Atlas Shrugged*.

it is by *acting* virtuously or viciously that we come to have (and maintain) a virtuous or vicious character.[186]

Though one's character limits the range of actions possible to him, that range is not fixed. It can be gradually shifted, in a better or worse direction, by the choices one makes in the present. The character-degrading effect of bad choices is well illustrated in literature, from Aesop's fables on. These stories show how giving in to temptation strengthens the temptation and makes possible actions that are progressively more irrational, and how, on the other hand, making the right choice serves to reduce the temptation to take wrong actions, strengthening one's "character-muscles," as it were.[187]

It is not only one's motivation but also one's "psycho-epistemology" that is affected by how one chooses to use his mind. To the extent that one focuses, one's mental files are kept in good order. One not only obtains more information to put in those files, one also becomes more easily aware of their logical relationships, which acts to establish and maintain order among the files. A simple example is that of identifying the genus of something; that identification, especially if one treats it as important, acts to place its file folder within the wider folder that represents its genus.

Establishing a track-record of full focus thus tends to make one, perhaps wealthy, but certainly healthy and wise — healthy motivationally and emotionally, wise in the sense of having well-organized, essentialized, smoothly functioning files (i.e., concepts) to store one's knowledge. Conversely, a history of drift and evasion produces emotional conflict, psychological problems — and inner chaos, psycho-epistemologically.

The process of character development begins in early childhood, before one has philosophic knowledge and full self-control. How, then, can one be morally responsible for a character that begins forming when one is at such a primitive stage?

First, the young child's character remains in a very fluid state for many years, perhaps through late adolescence, the time when he does begin to deal

---

186 "... men make themselves responsible for being unjust or self-indulgent ... for it is activities exercised on particular objects that make the corresponding character." *Nichomachean Ethics*, III, 5, 1114a5–7. Aristotle, in this same section, seems to advance, by implication, a theory of free will similar to Rand's: "each man is somehow responsible for the state of his mind" (a point he makes in answer to the claim that how men evaluate things is not under their control). See 1114a31–b25.

187 The latter is the theme of the movie "Back to the Future" (Part I), which is both highly entertaining and deeply philosophical.

consciously with more abstract issues. Empirically, we do observe that children can change character markedly between, say, age four and twenty-four. Some children remain on the same path, but some do not.

Second, the basic issue of focus or non-focus confronts the child from the beginning of his entrance to the conceptual level, as he experiences the fact that he needs to *do* something, to put forth effort, if he is to understand the things with which he deals. From late infancy on, there is all the difference in the world between the mentally active, focused child and the mentally passive, unfocused one. That difference is one of direct, volitional choice.

It is not necessary for a child to have philosophic instruction or highly abstract concepts in order to know in some form that it is good to know things, and that learning things requires that he *do* something, that he *try*, that he put forth *effort.*

In what specific form does the choice to focus arise in early childhood? Picture a boy at age three or four, sitting on the floor playing with some blocks. He is trying to stack them as high as he can. He has piled them about a foot high, but when he places the next block on top, they all come crashing down. This may be a frustrating, upsetting experience for him. Suppose he feels a wave of negative emotions sweep over him. That emotional response is automatic, but the volitional issue is: what does he then *do*? Does he dissolve in tears, kick his blocks away, and run to Mother for solace, shunning blocks from then on? Or does he, perhaps after a moment, take himself in hand, look back at the blocks, and try again, thinking about what went wrong and how to correct it?

Here, on a kindergarten level, the child confronts the issue of reason vs. emotion, a directly volitional issue. According to how he chooses to use his mind, according to whether he places his feelings above facts or facts above feelings, he is making deeper a groove in his brain; he is forming his character.

Now picture the boy at age seven at the dinner table. A thought has occurred to him and he raises it: "Daddy, if God created the world, who created God?" (Children do ask that.) Let's suppose his father is the worst kind of lout: he flies into a rage at the "blasphemous" question, and shouts "You damn smart aleck! You'll go to Hell if you ask that kind of thing!" and he reaches across the table and slaps the boy.

The boy is hurt and confused. He bursts into tears. But the issue here is: what goes on in his mind, after the heat of the moment is over? Does he think about what happened, or just wallow in hurt, resentment, and self-doubt? He is not a philosopher, he is only seven, but what can he already conclude, if he chooses to think? He can conclude: "I only asked a question. A question that made sense to me. Daddy didn't answer my question, he only got mad and hit me, for no good reason. I still want to know the answer to my question."

And most importantly, he can judge his father: "Daddy was bad to me; he shouldn't have yelled and hit me. He stops *me* when I hit my brother. It can't be wrong to ask questions." As a practical matter, he can resolve to keep quiet about this and other topics that might anger his father. He can resolve not to say such things aloud, but to keep thinking them in his own mind. The wonderful thing about thinking is that it is private. Parents cannot hear what their child is thinking. They cannot control whether he thinks or not. And, as a general rule, parents do not even seem to know whether their child thinks or not.

According to whether the boy maintains the will to understand or drops it, he is forming his character — not just in regard to each concrete, but in relation to values as such. He builds the premise that the world is a welcoming place, where good things await him, that life is an active, joyful adventure — or the opposite premise, that the world is fraught with unpredictable dangers, that values are always threatened, and that life is miserable.

One might think that from his father's brutality the child in my example would necessarily form a bad premise about people — that they are unpredictable, dangerous. But this is not so, because the boy always has at least one counter-instance refuting any such over-generalization. The counter-instance is *himself*. If he judges his father's action as wrong, he can, at the same time think: "*I* would never do that." And it is not only possible for him to judge his parents, it is his moral responsibility to do so.

The difference between being mentally active and mentally passive makes a huge difference in the developing psychology of the child. The active, focused child builds *self-esteem*. He learns that he can figure things out, and that gives him a sense of pride and confidence. He learns he can trust his mind. He develops the sense that he is good — because he knows, wordlessly, that he achieved his understanding volitionally, by trying hard, by doing work with his mind.

By this gradual process, concrete by concrete, choice by choice, a child forms over the days of his life conclusions about himself. He comes to regard himself as competent or incompetent, good or bad. Which way he goes depends on how he chooses, how he exercises his free will.[188]

---

188 For an extended discussion of the role of choice in a child's cognitive and characterological development, see Rand, "The Comprachicos." [RP, 51–95]

kids

Starting in earliest childhood and continuing throughout life, one does indeed forge one's own character, as one continuously chooses, in issues large and small, to function rationally or irrationally.

VALIDATION OF THE THEORY

What is the basis for holding that focus is volitional? Introspection — the only direct source of information about the nature and actions of consciousness. My modus operandi in this chapter is to call to the reader's attention and name facts that he can directly introspect. The reader, presumably, recognizes introspectively his own ability to monitor and direct his mind's operations, to seek full awareness, adopt the reality-orientation — in other words, to focus his mind. Thus, my presentation of what focus is, has simultaneously been a presentation of the evidence that focusing is directly volitional.

Comparing the in-focus state to the out-of-focus state presents a certain difficulty: to the extent that one is out of focus, one is not introspecting. But upon coming into focus, it is easy enough to recall the preceding moment. That is what one does when one catches oneself daydreaming. The difference between a recalled state of non-focus and a present state of focus is striking and undeniable: being alert, purposeful, actively in charge vs. being passive, aimless, not in charge (or actively evading).

But there is no introspectible process of deliberation that occurs before focusing. In fact, one has to already be in focus to be thinking about anything, including about whether or not to focus. Focusing is therefore unlike other choices, such as that between items on a restaurant menu. One simply either puts one's mind in gear or one does not.

What, then, can be said about the form in which one experiences the specifically *volitional* nature of focus? Granted that there is a clear difference between being in focus and out of focus, how can one introspect one's volitional control over which state one functions in?

Volition is experienced directly in one's sense of *agency* and *effort*. One cannot avoid being aware of oneself as the active agent in the cognitive process. Initiating and sustaining focus is something that one *does*, not something that just happens to one. Part of this sense of agency is the experience of *effort*. It takes an effort to think; it even takes an effort to engage in purposeful sensory observation. ("Effort" does not mean strain or suffering; there is effort required to walk, talk, and eat, but these physical activities, like the mental activity of seeking to know, are normally pleasant.)

Taking charge of one's mind, setting the goal of full awareness, directing one's attention, asking oneself questions, making judgments — these are things that one *does*, as opposed to things that happen to one, as when an idea "pops into your mind" or a feeling "comes over you." The effort to understand a confusing issue stands in stark contrast to, for instance, a tune that one cannot get out of one's head. Supplying the effort required to understand an issue is up to you to do, which is to say: it is volitional.

Consider the contrast with emotions. Emotions are an *automatic* response. Feeling anger is something that happens to you, not something you do. One says: "I am getting angry," not: "I am doing angering." Emotions are effortless responses, based upon stored value-judgments which are triggered super-rapidly by what one perceives. In contrast, naming one's emotional responses, identifying their causes, judging their actual appropriateness to the facts of the situation — these cognitive acts do require effort. Such reflective analysis does not occur automatically; one must choose to do mental work.

To further distinguish the automatic from the effortful, consider the case of memory. For instance, what happens when you read the following: "Two plus two is . . ."? The word "four" is triggered automatically and effortlessly. But now try to remember what clothes you wore a week ago today. You probably have to do work to retrieve the answer, if you even can retrieve it. And you can stop trying at any time. But you cannot normally stop yourself from hearing "four" in your mind when I triggered your memory of that sum. Some recall is automatic, some takes effort, and we are very aware of the difference.

These examples should make clear the manifest difference between the automatic and the volitional, between that which enters your mind without effort and that which you *do* in an act of *effortful* self-direction.[189]

DETERMINISM: THE DENIAL OF FREE WILL

To say that man has free will is to say that man is capable of making genuine choices, that the cognitive and existential actions he performs are up to him, rather than being made necessary by antecedent factors. The opposite theory, determinism, holds that choice is an illusion, that what we think of

---

189 Effort is a sign of volition, but not every expenditure of effort indicates a *proper* use of volition; evasion, the antithesis of focus, also requires effort — the effort *not* to know.

as being up to us is actually necessitated by the factors, internal and/or external, operating at the time of the alleged choice.

Man's actions, determinists readily concede, have much more complex causes than those governing the movement of inanimate objects, such as a rock tumbling down a hillside. But, determinists hold, a man's actions are just as necessitated as the rock's. After all, they observe, a computer is also very complex, but no one is tempted to posit free will in the physical processes that go on inside the computer and produce its output. Human action, mental and physical, is held to be similar: just "output" that is pre-determined by the person's makeup plus the conditions obtaining.

Determinism implies that if we knew all the facts, we could predict everything about your future — what you will think, what you will feel, what you will do. Determinism, however, is basically a metaphysical position, not one concerning what we can or cannot predict. It is defined as the doctrine that all man's actions are necessitated by factors beyond his control.

Numerous attempts have been made throughout the history of philosophy to reconcile free will and determinism, but no such reconciliation is possible. There is no middle ground between: 1) the act of focusing one's mind is necessitated by antecedent factors, and 2) the act of focusing one's mind is *not* necessitated by antecedent factors.

Determinism and free will are contradictories; determinism is precisely the denial of free will.[190]

Determinists claim that the introspective experience of free will is illusory. "You feel that you choose freely," they say, "but only because you are unaware of the motives and reasons controlling your decision-making." This idea has an element of truth — when directed against theories that locate free will in existential choices, such as whether to study or go to a movie. Such choices are indeed not causal primaries. But the choice to focus or not is.

The evidence of free will is not that we deliberate but that to deliberate rationally one must *do* things that take *effort*. Determinists cannot deny that we experience agency and effort. Instead, they must argue that a deterministic being could also experience effort and agency, a hard sell.

Rather than rebutting what the determinists might say on this topic, I turn now to exposing the error in the main positive argument for determinism: the false belief that free will would contradict the law of causality.

---

190 "Compatibilist" theories inevitably side with determinism, and re-define volition out of existence, as in the claim that "free" means "uncoerced." The absence of coercion is an issue of social-political freedom, not of metaphysical freedom.

Causality and Volition

The popular belief that there is a conflict between free will and causality stems from a mistaken conception of the law of causality. The proper view of causality, originated by Plato and Aristotle, recognizes that causality is a relation between the nature of an entity and its actions. An entity of a given kind has the properties it has, which gives it certain potentialities and no others. The actions possible to an entity are determined by its identity, by what it is.

There is nothing in this proper understanding of causality to clash with free will. Man, by virtue of his nature, has the potentiality of initiating a process of rational thought, but he does not have to actualize that potentiality.

However, as far back as the 17th century, the proper, Platonic-Aristotelian understanding of causality lost favor, and came to be supplanted by an arbitrary construct: the notion that causality concerns "events," not entities and their actions, and that every event is a necessitated reaction to previous events. Unfortunately, it was Galileo who popularized the new event-to-event view, as historian Wilhelm Windelband notes:

> ... the idea of cause had acquired a completely new significance through Galileo. According to the [preceding] scholastic conception ... causes were substances or things, while effects, on the other hand, were either their activities or were other substances and things which were held to come about only by such activities: this was the Platonic-Aristotelian conception of the aitia [causes]. Galileo, on the contrary, went back to the idea of the older Greek thinkers who applied the causal relation only to the states — that meant now to the motions of substances — not to the Being [identity] of the substances themselves. Causes are motions, and effects are motions. [WINDELBAND, II, 410; emphasis deleted]

This notion of causality does lead to determinism. But the event-to-event view is wrong. We do not encounter any such thing as free-floating "events"; actions are actions of entities. The event-to-event model of causality cannot be applied even to its proponent's favorite case: billiard balls. When one billiard ball collides with another and sets it in motion, the interaction is causally determined by the nature of the entities involved, including their state of motion. To see this, one need only consider the consequences if either ball had a different identity. What if one or both balls had a different shape, say a cylindrical one, or were made of gelatin, or were only a thin, brittle shell, hollow inside? The actions resulting from collisions would be different if the entities' natures were different. Causality relates entity, identity, and action — not event to event.

The identity of a material object consists not only of its state of motion but also of the kind of material of which it is made, and the structure in which that material is arranged — both the macro-structure, overall shape, and micro-structure, down to the scale of molecules, atoms, and subatomic particles. What a material object does in interaction with other material entities depends on all these factors, on its (and their) total identity, not just their state of motion.

Accordingly, the proper understanding of the law of causality is that the actions of an entity are an expression of its identity; the interaction of entities is an expression of the identity of each. What an entity can *do* is determined by what it *is*. "The law of causality is the law of identity applied to action."[191]

This understanding of causality represents an integration of three concepts that are irreducible primaries: "entity," "identity," and "action." We perceive entities acting. We form concepts for their actions by observing them act. We form "walking," for instance, by observing men and animals walking. The concept of "walking" includes the fact that legs are involved in the action. Thus, we know that a billiard ball cannot walk — the action would be a violation of its identity, since it has no legs (and lacks many other requirements). Or, "burning" is a concept we form from observing the burning of wood, paper, and other combustible materials. This implies that the miracle of "the burning bush that was not consumed" is incoherent: for a thing to burn *is* for it to burn up — i.e., to be consumed.

At any given time, we may not know what features of an entity are necessary for it to perform a given action. Pre-scientifically, for instance, men did not know that combustion is the combination of an oxidant with the material composing the burning substance. But from their first grasp of causality as such, men know that the actions possible to an entity are caused by facts — whether known or yet to be discovered — about the makeup, the *identity*, of the entities involved.

---

191 [AS, 1037] Here I might be in disagreement with Rand's view of causality, since I see it as involving what an entity *can* do, and some of her statements are phrased in terms of what an entity *will* do.

Next, by observation and induction, we discover that the material world is governed by mechanical causation. Matter as such is inert; it cannot set itself in motion. As scientific knowledge progresses, we learn that even the self-generated actions of living organisms, in their *physical* (non-conscious) aspects, are essentially like those of inanimate objects — i.e., are deterministic. The difference is that living organisms possess an internal store of physical energy, and their structure enables them to route that energy to power different types of action.[192]

The motions of material objects, and of the material aspects of living organisms, are subject to strict necessity: whatever they do, they had to do. The same matter in the same circumstances will act the same way. But the form of causation applicable to man's consciousness is different — because man's consciousness is a different kind of phenomenon. The nature of man causes him to have the power of choice — fundamentally, the choice to focus his mind or not. By virtue of his makeup, including the makeup of his nervous system, man has sovereign control over the operation of his conceptual faculty. When a man chooses to use that faculty to pursue conceptual understanding, the action is not causeless — *his choice* is the cause. The same applies when he lets himself drift passively or chooses actively to evade.

Free will is a specific form of causation, not a cancellation of causality, a form of causation that arises from and depends upon the functioning of one's nervous system and body, as one interacts with the world.[193]

Can the choice to focus itself be explained causally? The answer depends on what one means by "explaining the choice." The very existence of a choice between focus and non-focus can be explained causally: man, by virtue of his makeup, has such a choice; lower animals, which lack the conceptual faculty, do not have this choice. But the specific *outcome* of the choice — the fact that a given man chose to focus rather than not — can be explained only in the sense that one focuses for a reason: in order to be fully aware. But this reason is not a necessitating factor. It is only a potential reason; the actualization of that potential takes an act of will. At root, the actuali-

---

192 See my discussion of "self-generated action" in Binswanger 1990, 40–54, where I conclude that "an action is self-generated when it results from the utilization of an internal energy source integral to the agent according to a directive mechanism."

193 The relationship of mental activity to brain function is a difficult and largely scientific issue. Philosophy can establish only two general points here: consciousness has causal efficacy in relation to man's body, and the choice to focus is volitional. But clearly the mind depends causally upon the healthy functioning of the brain, and the entire discussion of free will presupposes that we are considering normal, healthy brain states.

zation of that potential — i.e., setting the goal of full awareness — is what the exercise of free will consists of.

What one cannot do is "explain" the choice to focus (or not to) in the sense of specifying some antecedent factor that *made* one choose the way one did. This fact constitutes a philosophical problem only for those who equate causality with necessitation. And there is no way to justify that equation. Taking causality to mean necessitation is an over-generalization from the kind of causation applicable to matter. But consciousness is not matter; it is not inert, but active.[194] To insist that consciousness must be governed by the specific form of causation exhibited by matter is to approach man with an arbitrary, a priori commitment to materialism.

In an extemporaneous discussion of this issue, Rand said:

> The appearance of a conflict between causality and free will is due to taking causality to be only that which governs the material world. Consciousness is an existent having a nature different from that of matter. The law of causality implies, accordingly, that the type of action consciousness can take will be different.[195]

Free will means choice, and *choice is a phenomenon of consciousness*. The nature of consciousness is different from the nature of matter, and the law of causality says that different natures entail different forms of action.

Consciousness, on the conceptual level, is self-initiated. The nature of conceptual consciousness is to be volitional, not deterministic — i.e., to be able to activate its full resources, to set awareness as its goal. This is not an exception to, but an instance of, the law of causality. The law of causality does not prohibit the existence of choice, of self-initiated action, of starting a causal chain. In the case of volition, one starts a causal chain by willing the state of full awareness, as a "first cause" within consciousness.

---

194 Why is free will possible to consciousness but not to matter? I suspect that the difference is due to the fact that consciousness is an organic whole, without parts but with a rich "internal" identity. Material objects are ultimately collections of "atoms" — using this term broadly for whatever are the ultimate constituents of material things. These ultimate "atoms" of matter, having no parts, can have no internal structure. If so, then they can have no unactualized potentialities and can only go on doing that which they have always done. Material objects, being nothing but arrangements of these "atoms," could not, then, act differently in the same circumstances. But consciousness is not a compound of parts; it is an organic whole having a complex identity, with many unactualized potentialities.

195 From my notes of a personal conversation with Ayn Rand, circa 1980. (I can vouch for the exact wording of only the first sentence.)

(Furthermore, the law of causality entails that causes, once instituted, have necessary effects. This applies to volitional acts as well: initiating rational, focused cognition necessarily produces different effects, existentially and psychologically, from those produced by drift or evasion.)

The exercise of reason is a *causal primary*.[196] A "causal primary" is a factor that 1) determines a series of effects, and 2) is not, in turn, determined by any prior factor. The exercise of reason exhibits both of these relationships: 1) the rationality (or irrationality) of a man's mental processes determines the nature of his conclusions, his decisions, his actions, his character, and his psychology; 2) no prior factor determines whether or when he will function rationally or irrationally — that is a matter of his direct volition.

Another question arises in regard to integrating volition with causality. In the case of material objects, the same thing put in the same circumstances will act the same way. Does this apply to man? Can we say that a given man placed again in the same circumstances must use his mind in the same way he did before — assuming, for the sake of argument, that both the external and the internal, psychological, circumstances could be absolutely identical?

In one sense, the man must act the same way: he must choose. He cannot shed his volitional nature; as a human being, he cannot avoid the ongoing choice of how to use his mind: rationally or irrationally. But, contrary to what I formerly believed [BINSWANGER 1999], this does not erase the fact that, from a more concrete perspective, what he chooses can differ. Analogously, if one man votes Republican and another votes Democratic, they are, on an abstract level, "doing the same thing": voting. But, more concretely, they are doing different things: voting Republican and voting Democratic.

Secondly, we must not reify the "choosing" that is involved in the choice to focus. The choice to focus is not like the choice of what shirt to wear: there is no process of deliberation (which itself would have to be done in focus or out of focus). In the case of focusing, the "choosing" is not a separate process: one simply either focuses *by choice* or one does not, again *by choice*. The phrase "by choice" expresses the volitional nature of either action; it does not mean that the two actions are "really" the same.[197]

Again, the applicable type of causality depends on the entity's nature: "same conditions, same outcome" applies to inanimate matter but not to man.

---

196 I owe this way of putting it to Allan Gotthelf (personal conversation). Some other causal
      primaries are: existence, identity, and the nature of the ultimate constituents of matter.

197 I am indebted to Lee Pierson for pressing me on this issue.

Focus and "The Problem of Agency"

One recurrent objection to free will is known as "the problem of agency." According to this objection, a being with free will would, paradoxically, not be a rational agent, would not be the author of his own acts. As one determinist put it: "Either our wills are determined by prior causes ... or they are the product of chance and we are not responsible for them." [HARRIS, A15] A rational agent's existential actions are caused by the content of his mind, by what he thinks. But, the objection holds, free will would be something that breaks the connection between thought and action, thereby preventing one from acting as a rational agent. Personal responsibility, this objection concludes, requires determinism: acts for which one is responsible are those caused by one's deliberative reasoning, not by a blind act of "willing."

This objection, however, is not applicable to Ayn Rand's theory of free will: the objection evaporates once one recognizes that "will" consists in choosing to engage in and implement a rational process. The will is not some blind force coming in from the dark, disrupting the connection between one's thinking and one's action. Rather, one wills to institute rationality — or one does not. The "will" *is* one's capacity to generate and sustain rational thought. One is responsible for one's actions, cognitive and existential, precisely because one is responsible for the state of mind — in-focus or out-of-focus — that caused those actions. (And if we could not control the state of our minds, if what our minds churned out were necessitated by some antecedent factor, we would not be self-responsible beings.)

It was this wrong view of the will that led A. J. Ayer to proclaim that: "if it is a matter of pure chance that a man should act in one way rather than another, he may be free but can hardly be responsible." [AYER, 278] But it is *choice*, not "chance," that governs man's actions — the choice to generate a state of full focus or to default on that responsibility.

In notes Ayn Rand made in her personal journal, at age 29, she wrote:

> The will does not have to be *without reason*, or motivation, in order to be free. One's act may be motivated by an outside reason, but the *choice* of that reason is our *free will*. ... Doesn't the "free will" question come under the general question of human reason — and *its* freedom? ... Does a *free* action necessarily mean an *unreasonable* one? [JAR, 68–69]

When one chooses to take a certain action, one has a reason for what one chooses. The choice is not blind or causeless. But that reason does not force itself upon one; its presence in one's mind and its motivational power result from how one is using one's mind — i.e., from one's level of awareness. By choosing the level of awareness on which one functions, *one chooses what kinds of reasons will become operative.*

The example of the two students dramatized this. Each student had a reason, in the sense of mental content, that explained why he acted as he did. The first student's reason for not studying was to see an enjoyable movie and avoid what he felt, while out of focus, would be a painful evening of studying. The second student's reason for studying was to get a better grade in the course and thus improve his chances of getting into a good graduate school. Different reasons governed their decisions because they exercised their free will differently: the first student engaged in out-of-focus, associational wandering, which kept the long-range consequences out of his mind; the second student took charge of his mind, directing it to the task of finding out the full truth, which included the long-range consequences.

Each student's choice was free, not determined, because it was shaped by his *chosen* way of using (or misusing) his mind. The decision each made did not "just happen." It was not a "chance" outcome. The decision of each was based on what was in his mind, which in turn resulted from his level of awareness. Having free will did not mean that either student acted without a reason, but rather that each chose whether or not to have a *rational* reason.

Does the determinist have a comeback? Can he say about focus itself: either you focus for a reason, in which case focus is determined by that reason, or you focus for no reason, in which case, it is arbitrary and irrational?

No. There is always a reason to focus, because focus means the acceptance of reality. Reality is always there and always needs to be focused on. But reality does not have the power to make one focus on it. The point can be stated this way: there is always a *potential* reason to be in focus — namely: to know reality and guide one's actions by reference to one's grasp of the facts. But that potential reason is not actualized automatically; one has to *make* that reason be operative, by a self-initiated choice.

Moreover, there can be "reasons" (i.e., motives) for *not* focusing. You can *feel* at a given moment that full awareness would be a bad thing, requiring you to face something you don't want to face. But you cannot make a rational assessment of the consequences of facing something until you face it — i.e., until you choose to focus.

When you are out of focus, focusing can feel like a very bad idea. But your choice is whether to accept that feeling or to go by reason — i.e., to focus or not. The fact that something — even focus itself — prompts a *feeling* of aversion cannot dictate whether or not you go by feelings. And that is what the choice to focus is: the choice to go by facts, not by feelings.

So it is absurd to say, as some determinists would, that one's feelings determine whether or not one goes by feelings. Just as it is absurd to say, as other determinists would, that the facts determine whether one goes by facts. If that were true, no one would ever be irrational.

Focus is precisely the choice of which will govern how one proceeds: facts or feelings. The inescapable issue is: which do you put in charge — your best perception of the facts or your feelings? Neither facts nor feelings are *automatically* in charge. The question is which side has authority, and you have to decide that; it is up to you.

Neither reality nor your feelings is the equivalent of the Supreme Court here. Neither reality nor your feelings can seize control of your mind. *You* are the Supreme Court determining which factor, reason or feelings, governs how you proceed.

Thus, the determinist cannot re-apply his argument about "the problem of agency" to the issue of focus itself. He cannot claim that focusing would be irrational unless the (potential) reasons to be in focus *made* one focus. The choice to exercise reason is not irrational. The choice to accept reality is not arbitrary. "Arbitrary" means: not based on the facts of reality. If the very acceptance of reality is called "arbitrary," then the concept of "arbitrary" loses all meaning, becoming a stolen concept.

The acceptance of reality is not necessitated by anything prior; we are neither forced to function rationally nor forced not to.

The determinist objection that free will would be a blind lurch is directed against a straw man. The actual target of that objection is not free will but the doctrine known as "indeterminism." Indeterminism holds that human action is not necessitated because some actions allegedly have no causes at all. According to this notion, in certain cases it is a sheer, causeless accident — Ayer's "chance" — which of two actions a man performs. But choice is not chance or an Epicurean Swerve — i.e., free will is not indeterminism.

Nor would indeterminism do man any good. Whether a man's life were ruled by iron necessity, or by a necessity interrupted by freak accidents, man would not be in control of himself. Free will is not non-causation but a form of causation: self-determination.

Volition as Axiomatic

Volition is not only self-evident — directly introspectible — it is fundamental to conceptual cognition. One's volition controls the extent to which conceptual cognition exists, and the alternative of whether conceptual functioning exists or does not exist is a fundamental alternative.

(A mind completely out of focus is still operating "conceptually" in the sense that words go through such a mind, and some minimal conceptual content will necessarily be involved, due to the triggering of automatized connections. But out-of-focus, associational wandering, though beyond the capabilities of an animal, is not *cognition*. Cognition is the pursuit of knowledge of reality; striving to know, adopting the reality-orientation, setting the goal of full awareness — these are precisely the things that require volitional activation.)

As both self-evident and fundamental to the conceptual level, volition is an axiom of the conceptual level. Axioms cannot be proved to be true, since they are the very basis of proof, but granted their truth, one can demonstrate that they are axioms rather than derivative truths. As discussed in CHAPTER 1, the demonstration that a truth has the status of an axiom consists in showing that it is *inescapable* — that it is, in Rand's words, "a statement necessarily contained in all others, whether any particular speaker chooses to identify it or not." [AS, 1040] This means applying the test of "re-affirmation through denial," as I did in CHAPTER 1, for the axioms of "existence" and "consciousness." I will now show how this test applies in the case of volition: how even those attempting to deny free will have to covertly assume it.

Determinism as Self-Refuting

One's volitional control over one's conceptual faculty indeed passes the test of re-affirmation through denial. Suppose someone states, "I do not have volitional control over my mind." If so, then he cannot claim that *that* statement is true or represents knowledge, only that whatever runs his mind forces him to believe it. He has to assume he is free to consider the facts on the subject of free will vs. determinism, in the very process of denying he is free to do so.

Freud, an arch-determinist, quoted approvingly the statement of Georg Groddeck: "We are 'lived' by unknown and uncontrollable forces." [FREUD, 13] That statement, if true, would itself be the product of unknown and uncontrollable forces — and thus not entitled to rational consideration.

As with any assertion of determinism, the claim commits the fallacy of self-exclusion. To include itself would mean asserting: "I am 'lived' by unknown and uncontrollable forces." Anyone saying that, not as a joke but as a serious report of his condition, would be recognized as psychotic (and possibly dangerous). All forms and varieties of determinism negate themselves, because the very essence of determinism is to assert that one has no control over the operations of his own mind.

A determinist cannot escape this self-invalidation by maintaining that what runs *his* mind are facts and logic. How, on the determinist premise, could he know that this was the case? After all, other men reach different conclusions, opposite to his, on many subjects. He is claiming to be, in effect, programmed to think in a certain way. How can he assess the validity of his programming (vs. the invalidity of others' programs)? Any attempt at validating his "programming" is doomed to failure. If he asserts that his programming is validated by a given test, that will merely raise the question: how do you know *that*? A deterministic mind could be programmed to announce that it passed a test when it actually failed, or to accept an invalid test as valid. And any further sentences he utters to defend against this objection would simply raise the same question over again: what makes you say that *that* is logical, if whatever you say is merely a reaction to the forces impinging on you at the moment?

The determinist is asserting that he cannot be objective — that his mind is in the grip of something that runs it. If so, then he also cannot be objective about his meta-level beliefs — i.e., beliefs about what determines him and what its nature is. By his own theory, he cannot judge either facts or his own judgments. Instead of judgment, there is only stimulus and response.

A *volitional*, self-regulating mind can directly will itself to focus on reality, to work honestly to integrate its conclusions into the full context of its knowledge, without any factor censoring it. If a man knows the basic rules of logic, he can choose directly to employ them and thus be objective. No feelings or external factors can keep him from engaging in rational thought and checking, without prejudice, the validity of his thinking.[198]

A volitional mind is never forced to be irrational, forced to deviate from observations, forced into fantasy. It always retains the power to exclude such invalidating conditions by a direct act of will. A deterministic mind, in contrast, could not exclude invalidating conditions.

---

198 It is irrelevant that in extreme circumstances emotions can make rational thinking temporarily impossible. It is easy for one to recognize that one is in that kind of state (e.g., a panic) and to wait for a calmer moment in which one can resume rational thought.

Consider a determinist who says that what runs his mind is logic. Logic is not an entity that can exert forces on a brain. In contrast, when one sees an apple, light reflected from the apple physically stimulates the receptors in one's retina. But no such object-generated causation is available on the conceptual level. There is no such thing as Logic Itself, Truth Itself, or Reason Itself to act upon one.

Nor is logic some set of concrete operations that could be wired into the brain. Logic is a process that adheres to reality by considering all and only the evidence. But a deterministic mind would "output" whatever was necessitated by the *biased* set of material, real or imaginary, that the determining factor permitted entry into its consciousness. A deterministic mind would be operating under constant censorship.

Thus a deterministic mind would be in the situation of a man forced at gunpoint to read aloud what is written on a piece of paper shoved in front of him. His utterances, in that case, would be cognitively valueless. Suppose a bystander asks the victim, "How do you know that what you are forced to say represents a valid, logical identification?" The gunman writes something on a piece of paper, shoves it over to his victim and orders him to read, "I know it because . . ." It doesn't matter what the next words he reads are: it is still without cognitive content for the victim. That is the dilemma that man would always be trapped in, under the assumption of determinism.

The concept of "logic" cannot be applied to a deterministic consciousness. Logic requires *independent judgment* — independent of any prejudicial, potentially censoring factor. The volitional ability to function rationally is required to attain that independence. Free will means having the power to choose to consider whatever is relevant, and hence to attain objectivity.

Determinism is actually a secularized version of Descartes' "evil demon":

> I will now suppose . . . an evil spirit, as powerful as he is cunning and deceitful, who has employed all his powers to deceive me; I will suppose that the sky, the air, the earth, colors, shapes, sounds, and all the other external things that we perceive, are only illusions which he uses to snare my credulity. [DESCARTES, 62–63]

Once this fantasy is (arbitrarily) adopted, there is no way out. It is no answer to say, "God would not allow such a being to radically deceive me" (Descartes) or "The demon forces me to believe only those ideas that are in fact true," or "The demon forces me to be rational and logical." In each case, there is no answer to the reply: "*That* is just another false idea fed to you by the demon." Or, putting it another way, all such assertions are arbitrary.

Once one has asserted, "The things I think and say are fed to me without my being able to reject them or independently test them," there is no refuge.

At the deepest level, determinism implies not just that there is no such thing as knowledge, but that there is no such thing as belief, assertion, judgment — no such thing as even *claiming truth* for an idea. To believe, assert, or judge that something is the case involves committing one's consciousness to the reality of that thing, and that commitment takes an act of will. A computer-like consciousness would output whatever it had to output, but it would be incapable of making a commitment, across time, to anything being true: what it will output tomorrow will be necessitated by the state tomorrow of the factors that run it. A free, self-controlled mind, in contrast, can resolve to hold to a conclusion over a lifetime (provided that the evidence continues to support it).

On every front and from every perspective, determinism is inconsistent with its own assertion. The attempt to deny volitional control over one's mind has to covertly assume it. Thus, volition passes the test of reaffirmation through denial and is indeed an axiom: a primary, self-evident fact, standing at the base of knowledge.[199] "Choice" is an axiomatic concept.

The debate between the advocates of free will and the advocates of determinism comes down to the issue: which mental functions are automatic? In that regard, the optical metaphor behind "focus" can be misleading: optical focus is a physical state, specifiable in terms of the geometry of the setup. Optical focus can be achieved automatically, as indeed it is for self-focusing cameras. But mental focus is not some concretely specifiable state. To be mentally in focus is to be committed to full awareness, and that means being committed to performing whatever sequence of specific processes one knows of and judges to be logically required. In one situation the process required might be further perceptual observation, in another situation it might be disengaging to do some creative mulling, in another seeking to find an analogy, in another looking for a counter-example, or subsuming something under a known rule, or trying new combinations, making new generalizations, seeking examples — and so on, for all the various cognitive strategies one knows.

---

199 Volition is an axiom of *conceptual* knowledge; perceptual knowledge, such as animals possess, is automatic, not volitional.

Thus, a mind's being "in focus" is like a violinist playing "with virtuosity" — neither state consists of some concretely specifiable sequence of movements. There is no mechanical formula or algorithm whose execution constitutes rationality. Thus, one cannot ask, "Why couldn't the brain be wired so as to be in focus?" The brain could (in principle) be wired to proceed quickly, or with a lot of circuits activated, but there's no such thing as a wiring for "proceeding rationally." There are no physically specifiable neural conditions for using one's best judgment, for finding and adhering to the evidence, nor for intellectual honesty and integrity. There is and can be no neural switch automatically thrown to institute rationality.

The foregoing contradiction in the advocacy of determinism does not constitute a proof of volition. (The existence of such a thing as proof presupposes that one's mind is free to form independent judgments.) Rather, it demonstrates that volition, whose existence we already know from introspection, is cognitively inescapable, and hence has the status of an axiom of the conceptual level.

Free Will and Social Environment

Locating free will in the choice to be rational enables us to answer the following common objection to free-will theories. If free will exists, the objection goes, why do we observe a statistical correlation between people's ideas and their social environment? For instance, the vast majority of Catholics are children of Catholics; most people come to hold the same political views as their parents and/or social subculture; voting patterns tend to occur in blocs. If choice reigns, why these correlations of beliefs with social environment?

Such correlations, however, are not evidence of social determinism but of *conformity*. When one fails to think for oneself, one still has to know what ideas to accept, what values to pursue, and how to act. The easiest and most common "solution" is to conform to the beliefs and values of those around one. Following the beliefs, values, customs, and taboos of others appears, to many, to be an easy substitute for thinking things through on their own. Thus, *conformity is a result of non-thinking*.

Further, note that the percentage of the population that seeks refuge in conformity tends to vary directly with the difficulty of the thinking that would be required in order to function independently: more people are willing to think for themselves about which brand of car to buy than which religion or philosophy to accept.

Rand observes:

> ... a social environment can neither force a man to think nor prevent him from thinking. But a social environment can offer incentives or impediments; it can make the exercise of one's rational faculty either easier or harder; it can encourage thinking and penalize evasion or vice versa. [VOR, 102]

Educational innovator Maria Montessori, who worked extensively with children, reaches the same conclusion:

> Environment is undoubtedly a secondary factor in the phenomena of life; it can modify in that it can help or hinder, but it can never create. [MONTESSORI 1912, 105, emphasis deleted]

FREE WILL AND THE EGO

Across a lifetime, from early childhood on, the proper use of free will consists of the active approach eloquently concretized by Rand in this passage:

> The process of concept-formation does not consist merely of grasping a few simple abstractions, such as "chair," "table," "hot," "cold," and of learning to speak. It consists of a method of using one's consciousness, best designated by the term "conceptualizing." It is not a passive state of registering random impressions. It is an actively sustained process of identifying one's impressions in conceptual terms, of integrating every event and every observation into a conceptual context, of grasping relationships, differences, similarities in one's perceptual material and of abstracting them into new concepts, of drawing inferences, of making deductions, of reaching conclusions, of asking new questions and discovering new answers and expanding one's knowledge into an ever-growing sum. [VOS, 21–22]

Actualizing the full potential of the conceptual faculty in that way is what a life lived in full focus consists of, mentally.

The commitment to full awareness is the opposite of a duty imposed on you: it is thoroughly self-interested. Exercising the will to know reality is a corollary and expression of a metaphysical motive, a motive that transcends immediate circumstances and the vicissitudes of concrete events: the desire to live. From the first volitional act in early childhood until the end of your life, the need and value of awareness are applicable and obvious. You turn on your mind with exactly the same motive that impels you to open your eyes: to be aware, so that you can live.

This means that, from another perspective, the choice to focus is directly the choice to live. Here I am not referring to the fact that in order to maintain and further your life, you have to choose to use your mind, because otherwise you simply won't know how to act. I am now making a deeper point: the choice to focus is the choice to be *fully alive in that moment*. The choice to use your mind *is* the choice to value yourself and fully to live.

In notes she made for *Atlas Shrugged*, Ayn Rand expresses this point:

> Your *self* is your *mind*, and its constant choice is the act of self-affirmation or self-denial, of perceiving or refusing to perceive, the act of *being* or *non-being* by which your mind, like a pilot-light within you, goes on or off. [JAR, 660]

It is by choosing to be fully aware that one chooses to be fully alive, alive in the human sense.

Socrates said: "The unexamined life is not worth living." I am adding: *The unfocused life is not truly lived.*

11
OVERVIEW

THIS BOOK UPHOLDS AN ARISTOTELIAN, NOT A PLATONIC, APPROACH to knowledge, and to consciousness in general. The Aristotelian approach recognizes that consciousness is action and is for action: consciousness consists of mental processes, and its function is to guide existential action.

Consciousness is the faculty of awareness — of seeing, hearing, knowing, remembering, etc. There is nothing supernatural or other-worldly about a hawk's ability to see its prey or a dog's ability to follow a scent. The same is true of man's ability to form and use concepts. The Platonic/religious view makes man's conceptual faculty into a metaphysical outcast, alien to the natural world, and seeking absorption in another. But neither animal nor human consciousness is an emigrant from a World of Forms or a Heaven. *Homo sapiens* evolved from certain primates, and his consciousness is an enhancement of, not a departure from, animal consciousness.

The human brain is a mammalian brain, but with a greatly expanded capacity and with certain crucial add-ons, relating to language-usage and manual dexterity. Man is the rational animal, the animal who *conceptualizes* perceptual material. It is concepts that have enabled man to split the atom and walk on the moon. And radically opposed theories about the nature of concepts have created the battleground for the millennia-long clash between Platonism and Aristotelianism, between mysticism and science, religion and secularism. Behind these polarities lie two opposed ideas about *concepts* — about what concepts are and what they refer to.

For Plato, there is a metaphysical gap, a "divided line," separating the conceptual level from the perceptual level, human consciousness from animal consciousness. Conceptual knowledge, Plato held, is directed to a separate and higher reality, not the concretes of this world.

For Aristotle, the divide is epistemological not metaphysical: there is only one reality, not two, and concepts refer to the things in this world, the world given in sensory perception.

Aristotle got it right. Human consciousness is an enhancement of, not an alternative to, animal consciousness. Animal consciousness is perceptual: it provides an awareness of entities in the world. The world impinges on an animal's senses, and this sensory input is processed by its nervous system, resulting in the animal's perception of the array of entities in its environment. And the animal is capable of *learning*: it forms associational expectations, based on pleasurable and painful experiences. These expectations motivate and guide the animal's behavior in the world.

The sequence is a continuing cycle: the animal moves through the world, acts on the world, perceives the effects of that action, and adjusts its next actions on that basis. Schematically, the causal sequence for animals is:

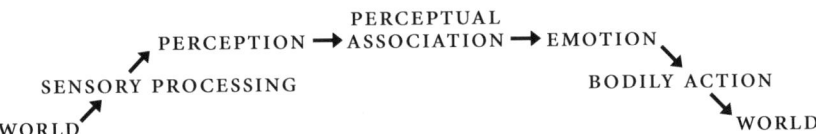

Human consciousness is the same, but with a crucial addition: concepts:

("Perceptual association" here is meant to include any non-conceptual processing of perceptual material. "Emotion" is a stand-in for any affective or motivational element. "Conceptual integration" includes every conceptual process: concept-formation, propositional judgment, and inference, since each involves integration: grasping relationships and making connections.)

CONCEPTS CONDENSE PERCEPTS

The conceptual faculty cannot originate its own content. There is no such thing as "intellectual vision" or "intuition": ultimately, the only source of information about the world is sensory perception. A concept represents a condensation of perceptual data. When higher-level concepts are formed, they, in turn, condense a number of earlier concepts — i.e., they condense condensations of perceptual data.

"Conceptualization," Rand observes, "is a method of expanding man's consciousness by reducing the number of its content's units . . . concepts represent condensations of knowledge." [ITOE, 64–65; emphasis deleted]

Concepts are formed not by "insight" but by interrelating — which means: by perceiving similarities and differences. All the knowledge stored in any concept was obtained, directly or indirectly, from perceptual observation.

In the case of higher-level concepts, the units are not perceptual concretes but prior concepts; nonetheless, higher-level concepts must be reducible, by a chain of intermediate concepts, to perceptual concretes. (If it cannot be reduced to perception, it is invalid.)

Although concepts are integrations of percepts, concepts are not merely words standing for a series of perceptual images, as the Nominalist theory holds. "Table" is not something whose content is exhausted by the image of a table or by several such images. A concept is integrative, not associational. It integrates all the concretes of a given kind into a single mental unit.

The basis of concept-formation is the awareness of similarities — i.e., of measurement-proximities. Tables, for instance, have shape-measurements that are relatively close to each other when contrasted to the shapes of chairs, sofas, and beds. In the case of first-level concepts, the measurement-proximities are perceived directly, in the form of similarity against difference.

Similarities that are abstract, and thus not perceptually available, are used in forming higher-level concepts. But these concepts still depend on perception: they are graspable only on the basis of having first formed the required lower-level concepts. The entire hierarchy is based on and reducible to similarities that are given perceptually.

The cognitive value of concepts lies in the fact that, as condensations, they provide *unit-economy*. Contra Plato, concepts do not have a different *object* from that of percepts; rather, concepts are a way of dealing with perceptual concretes wholesale. A shirt wholesaler still deals in shirts, but not one at a time. Likewise, the concept "table" still deals with tables — not one at a time, but wholesale.

The shirt wholesaler, however, deals merely with groups of shirts bundled together, say ten in a bundle. The bundle has the summed bulk and weight of the ten shirts in it. The shirt-bundling achieves some condensation, but very little compared to the astronomical condensation afforded by a concept, which condenses an unlimited amount of information into a single word. The concept "man," for instance, integrates all the men who have ever existed or will ever exist and stores all the knowledge applicable to them.

Concepts are tools for organizing and condensing perceptual data — for the purpose of dealing more effectively with perceptual reality.

This perception-based, action-oriented understanding of cognition is the polar opposite of the Platonic approach, which declares that concepts are not based on percepts and are not directed toward the world that we perceive. Instead, Platonists treat concepts as static revelations of another, "higher" realm of pure abstractions, whose contemplation is an end in itself, a view that underlies the theory-practice dichotomy, the elevation of "pure" science above applied science, and the widespread contempt for philosophy as "ivory-tower speculation."

Two Primacies

The root of the clash between Aristotle and Plato lies in their opposed views on a fundamental: the relation of concepts to percepts.

Aristotelians uphold the primacy of perception over conception: perceptual awareness precedes, and supplies the base for, conceptual awareness; concepts are abstractions from perceptual material. (In this context, the raw data of introspection, prior to any conceptual interpretation of it, counts as perceptual material.)

Platonists assert the opposite position — i.e., the primacy of concepts over perception. Platonists claim that some or all concepts are grasped by some unspecifiable, ineffable form of awareness of "universals" dwelling in another, "higher" reality. (Aristotelians recognize that there is only one reality, the one that we perceive by our senses.)

In CHAPTER 1, I explained the primacy of existence vs. the primacy of consciousness. A philosopher's stand on the relation of concepts to percepts grows out of his wider view of consciousness and its relation to existence. To help make these two primacies clear and lay out all the different positions, I offer the following two tables.

	The Primacy of Existence	The Primacy of Consciousness
Metaphysics	Existence is independent of consciousness. Consciousness is dependent on existence.	Consciousness is independent of existence. Existence is dependent on consciousness.
Epistemology	Existence must be known before consciousness is known. Knowledge of existence is gained by extrospection.	Consciousness can be known before existence is known. Knowledge of existence is gained by introspection.

The second primacy has a similar structure:

	The Primacy of Perception	The Primacy of Concepts
Metaphysics	Perception is independent of concepts. Concepts are dependent on perception.	Concepts are independent of perception. Perception is dependent on concepts.
Epistemology	Perception is the given. Perception is the standard for judging the conceptual.	Concepts are the given. Concepts are the standard for judging the perceptual.

Two points of clarification are needed in regard to the second table. First, the primacy of concepts metaphysics is described as holding "Perception is dependent on concepts." Only extreme Platonists hold that the *existence* of percepts depends on concepts; but it is commonly held that the *identity* of percepts depends on concepts. E.g., Kant claims that perception is shaped by "categories of the intuition," and in contemporary jargon, perception is "theory-laden." The result in either case is viewing perception as distorted, biased, "merely relative to us," or not of "things as they are in themselves."

It is true that *after* concepts have been formed and automatized, they get automatically integrated with one's perceptions, as Rand notes:

> . . . you cannot perceive a table as an infant perceives it — as a mysterious object with four legs. You perceive it as a table, i.e., a man-made piece of furniture, serving a certain purpose belonging

to a human habitation, etc.; you cannot separate these attributes from your sight of the table, you experience it as a single, indivisible percept — yet all you see is a four-legged object; the rest is an automatized integration of a vast amount of conceptual knowledge which, at one time, you had to learn bit by bit. [RP, 55–56]

This overlay of conceptual content *supplements* perception rather than distorting it — or even changing it, qua perception. Having the concept "table" does not change any table's seen color, shape, or number of legs. The theories a scientist holds do not alter what dial-reading he sees on his instrument. Thus, it remains true that perception is the base of and standard for judging all further cognition.

In the lower table, under "Epistemology," I contrast "Perception is the given" with "Concepts are the given." The "given" refers to mental content that is not shaped by our choices, so the question here is: which mental activities involve choice and which do not? The primacy of perception view holds that only conceptual functioning is volitional. In opposition, the primacy of concepts view, denies the mind's volitional nature and holds that some factor (God, innate ideas, genes, "conditioning") implants ideas into a passive mind. This view leads one to treat conclusions that were in fact reached by fallible, volitional processes as if they were unquestionable givens.

(The primacy of concepts view also carries the implication that perception is volitional. This bizarre notion finds expression in the widespread belief that the senses are capable of "deceiving" us, as if one's sensory physiology could, like a journalist, choose what to present. Those who attack perception often refer to the senses as "giving testimony" and being "lying witnesses" — terms that imply volition.)

Finally, let me compare the two correct positions. The primacy of existence primarily concerns metaphysics; the primacy of perception primarily concerns epistemology. The primacy of existence is a metaphysical principle, with epistemological implications; the primacy of perception is an epistemological principle, with metaphysical underpinnings.

The primacy of existence is essentially the fact that existence exists independently of consciousness, with consciousness being dependent on existence. The primacy of perception is essentially the fact that perception exists independently of concepts, with concepts being dependent on percepts.

The primacy of perception is, in effect, an elaboration of a point included in the primacy of existence: knowledge of existence is gained by extrospection. Extrospection means sensory perception — followed by the conceptual integration of perceptual material. Existence can be known only through physical contact with it, the contact that sense organs provide. Perceptual material is what results when physical existents interact with a consciousness' physical means: the sense organs. Perception is thus automatically tied to existence; but conceptual processes, being volitional, are fundamentally different: they can depart from or contradict existence—and will do so unless one guides them in the required way.

The Platonic approach, in contrast, models concepts on percepts, claiming that we "just see" abstract truth with "the mind's eye." People holding ideas different from one's own are regarded as intellectually blind.

(Here, Plato effectively demotes those who disagree with him to the level of subhumans. Plato holds that those who persist in disagreeing with the ideas of the "philosopher-king" are "incurably corrupt in mind" and *should be put to death* [REPUBLIC, II, IX, 5]. The same attitude is shown by religious fundamentalists who punish "blasphemy" and even murder "infidels.")

The primacy of perception does not in any way deny the importance of concepts—i.e., it is not the same as the "empiricism" of Hobbes, Hume, or the Pragmatists. In fact, the opposite is the case: recognizing the primacy of perception is what enables us to vindicate the conceptual level, to show how it is based on facts and how it serves man's life, as I have done in the preceding chapters, based on Ayn Rand's theory of concepts.

CONCEPT-FORMATION IN SCIENCE

The primacy of perception leads to the recognition that concepts are "where the action is" in the advance of man's knowledge. The history of science is replete with cases of crucial breakthroughs coming from the integration of observed data into new concepts. Such concepts as velocity (vs. speed), inertia, gravity, energy, element, valence, supply, demand, evolution, natural selection, variable, derivative, integral, germ, and synapse, have opened the door to previously unattainable discoveries. Taking three of these concept-forming breakthroughs will illustrate the pivotal value of forming the right concepts.[200]

---

200   *The Logical Leap* [HARRIMAN, 2010] treats many more, and in considerable detail. A brief summary on p. 179 of that work lists seven of the concepts behind the atomic theory.

1. "Inertia"

Prior to Galileo's work, the dominant conception (or misconception) was that of "natural motion" toward a "natural place." Bodies made of "earthy" stuff, in this view, naturally fall toward the center of the Earth, their natural place. Falling, it seemed, is just a given, nothing needing an explanation.

Galileo provided a total reconceptualization: place is relative to bodies (an Aristotelian idea), motion is change in place, speed is the rate of that change, velocity is speed in a given *direction*, acceleration is a change in *velocity*.

This new conceptual framework allowed Galileo to reach the concept of "inertia," expressed fully in Newton's first law of motion: a change in a body's velocity requires the exertion of a force upon it. Because bodies have inertia, their accelerating fall to Earth evidences the operation of a force: gravity. Since the planets' speed and direction change continuously, despite inertia, the question arose as to whether gravity operates on them as well. Thus, forming the concept of "inertia" opens the door to discovering universal gravitation.

2. "Natural selection"

Darwin's concept of "natural selection" allowed biologists to achieve an immensely clarifying new perspective on living organisms, and it led to a new level of integration across the entire science of biology. As the great biologist Theodosius Dobzhansky wrote, "... in biology nothing makes sense except in the light of evolution." [DOBZHANSKY 1970, 5–6] Natural selection — the differential survival rates of alternative genotypes — is what makes sense of evolution and of the adaptedness of organisms' structures and actions to their survival.

3. "Germ"

The concept of "germ" as the agent in infectious diseases (later supplemented by the concepts "virus" and "prion") revolutionized the science of medicine. No longer was "bad air" taken as a causative factor. The germ theory of disease was spurred by the observations of John Snow on the cause of the 1854 cholera outbreak in London. Using statistical analysis, Snow traced the source of the outbreak to water obtained from the Broad Street pump, refuting, in the process, the prevalent "miasma" theory.

Louis Pasteur's experiments proving the role of microorganisms in the fermentation process added evidence for the germ theory. Finally, Robert

Koch proved that a bacterium, *Bacillus anthracis*, was the cause of anthrax. These discoveries, to which many of us owe our lives, allowed Joseph Lister to prove that wound infections were caused not by the "bad air" of a "miasma," but by germs. That led to Lister's introduction of sterile procedures, which have saved millions of human lives — a dramatic illustration of the power of forming the right concept.

Proper conceptualization is essential to the advance of knowledge. Thus, epistemology must focus on concepts — how they are formed, what their cognitive function is, and what makes a concept valid or invalid.

Bottom-up vs. Top-down Theories

The primacy of perception leads to a wider point: knowledge is essentially "bottom-up," not "top-down." Conceptual knowledge is acquired by building up from perceptual data.

Man is born *tabula rasa*: his consciousness is only a potential — until it is actualized by input to his sensory organs. The fetus in the womb does not have theories, thoughts, concepts, or even percepts. An infant born without any senses would never be conscious. A boy may dream that he is driving a car; a fetus cannot. Even to have a dream about cars, one must have perceived them (or have been told about them by someone who has perceived them). Directly or indirectly, perception of cars is necessary to remember cars, imagine cars, form the concept "car," make propositions about cars, draw conclusions about cars, or develop the field of automotive engineering.

Who could deny this? Explicitly, Plato. Implicitly, every Rationalist philosopher, every theologian, every believer in God, Allah, or Vishnu, every advocate of some realm that is neither perceivable nor logically derivable from perception. In other words, the bottom-up nature of knowledge has been rejected, in theory and in practice, by 99 percent of mankind, including the majority of the leading figures in the history of philosophy.

In contrast, I have stressed throughout this book that knowledge begins with perception and builds up hierarchically from perception. The first "upward" step is concept-formation, a process that starts with the perceived similarity of two or more perceived objects. The next step upward comes with the formation of higher-level concepts, in the required hierarchical order. One cannot have a higher-level concept without the lower-level ones on which it rests, and the first-level concepts are formed from perception.

(The meaningless statements that result from concept-stealing show the consequences of severing the chain back to perception.)

When we subsume something under a concept, that is a "downward" step, one that cashes in on the power of previous upward steps. To say "Socrates is a man" is to apply the concept "man" to him—which presupposes one has formed the concept "man." The very purpose of ascending the hierarchy of knowledge is to *use* the knowledge, to apply it, which means applying it back to perceptual reality. In cognition, too, what goes up must come down. The purpose of concepts is conceptual identification. The purpose of theory is practice. The purpose of consciousness is successful action in the world.

The same progression from the perceptual to the more abstract applies to the hierarchy of propositions and to the hierarchy of inferences. The progression is always: from perception to the more abstract (for the sake of subsequent downward application to concretes). The entire hierarchical structure of knowledge rests on perception as its base. New abstract knowledge can, in some cases, be reached by deduction from still more abstract ideas, but those more abstract ideas themselves have to be inductively based.

Induction from perceptual observation is the essential means of gaining new knowledge. Though deductive steps often appear as intermediaries in the process, the overall progression is inductive—bottom-up. To repeat the suspension-bridge analogy to the hierarchy: whenever an item of knowledge, like a part of such a bridge, is suspended from one above it, that higher part must still be supported by the ground; gravity is the ruling principle. Deduction presupposes induction—the induction that supplied the universal premise(s) required to make the deduction valid (no valid deduction can be made without using at least one universal premise).

Even mathematics, the arch-example of supposedly deduction-supplied knowledge, is inductive—bottom-up—at its root. The basic concepts of mathematics—"unit," "number," "equal," "more than," and the like—are graspable only from perceptual experience. Infants do not have these concepts; they must be learned by a process of generalizing from perceptual observation. (Modern "symbolic logic" and meta-mathematics attempt to get around this fact by arbitrarily introducing "undefined primitives" in an "axiomatic system"; but these primitives are just meaningless shapes or sounds unless based on conceptualizing perceived fact.[201])

---

201 Gödel's theorem is the reductio ad absurdum of the entire formalistic (Kantian) approach to logic and mathematics—see CHAPTER 7.

The top-down approach rejects this whole perspective and scorns practical, "materialistic" concerns. Communing with non-material, non-perceivable Platonic Forms or "pure" theory is held to be an end in itself. Reason is thus stripped of its biological function. But life is lived in the concrete, physical, perceptual world; to reject perceptual reality is to reject life itself.

A revealing example of the top-down, Platonic, approach is contained, unfortunately, in Euclid's *Elements*. Euclid begins that great work by giving basic definitions, starting with "point" and "line":

> 1. A point is that which has no part.
> 2. A line is breadthless length.

The second definition contains the most apparent problem spot: what does "breadthless length" mean? There is a Platonic interpretation and an Aristotelian one. The Platonic interpretation has dominated historically, whether or not it is how Euclid himself understood "breadthless length."

In the Platonic interpretation, a line is an abstract entity, like a Platonic Form, and that entity has a width of zero. Perceptual reality contains no abstract entities, only concrete ones — rocks and trees, people and buildings. Concrete entities have both length and width (and thickness). Even the thinnest line drawn on paper has some width. So much the worse for perceptual reality, say the Platonists: "breadthless length" is an "idealization," they claim, a term that reflects the Platonic elevation of "ideal" abstractions over perceptual concretes. Lines are held to inhabit a mathematical world of pure intellection. We deduce geometrical principles by "pure logic," then apply them, as best we can, to the messy, approximate, ignoble perceptual concretes.

Applying the Aristotelian, bottom-up approach enables us to recognize that the concept "line" is formed by a process of *abstraction*. We mentally isolate one characteristic from the others that are co-present, without implying that the characteristic can *exist* apart from those others. We can attend to an entity's length while ignoring its width; we cannot picture or entertain any such thing as length-without-width. Lines do not inhabit some "ideal" mathematical realm; they are aspects of concretes in this world. Specifically, a line is the shape of an edge of a surface. (In ordinary usage, an ink trail on paper counts as a "line." But in geometry "line" does not refer to any such *entity*, but to an attribute: edge-shape.)

Thus, it is wrong to say that lines have small, infinitesimal, or zero width. The geometer's line has neither breadth nor breadthlessness: width is not a property that a geometrical line can have or be bereft of. (See CHAPTER 6, under "Negative Propositions.") It is as wrong to say that lines lack width as it is to say that they lack homes. Lines are neither breadthless nor homeless.

Consciousness is epistemologically active. A concept is the product of an integrative process; it is not an internal reproduction of an external "universal." Having a valid concept of X does not imply that X exists as such in external reality. Just as no intrinsic "universal" is implied in conceptualizing entities, so no *separated* characteristic, such as length, is implied in conceptualizing characteristics. In forming concepts of characteristics, we simply abstract from the co-present characteristics, such as the width of a surface. (This abstraction amounts to the omission of whole categories of measurement.) Neither "line" nor any other concept asserts the absence of the characteristics that are not included in that concept. Concepts do not pretend that what is isolated by a process of abstraction exists separately in the world.

A long tradition of Platonism in mathematics treats not only lines but also shapes, numbers, and mathematical functions as referring to "idealized" mathematical objects—which severs mathematics from the real world. Thus, Kline reports: "To thoughtful scientists it has been a constant source of wonder that nature shows such a large measure of correlation with their mathematical formulas." He quotes Einstein asking: "How is it possible that mathematics, a product of human thought that is independent of experience[!], fits so excellently the objects of physical reality?" [KLINE 1985, 227 & 216]

Robert Knapp identifies the root error that generates this bewilderment:

> The common fallacy that mathematics pertains specifically to a mathematical universe; that mathematics *applies* to the world, but is not *about* the world begins with the first page of Euclid's monumental work. . . . [In fact] mathematics applies to the world *because* it is about the world. [KNAPP, 1]

The "top-down" view also creates the problem Plato raises in the *Meno*:

> . . . how will you look for something when you don't in the least know what it is? How on earth are you going to set up something you don't know as the object of your search? . . . even if you come right up against it, how will you know that what you have found is the thing you didn't know? [MENO 80D]

But one doesn't start a quest for "something I don't know." One looks for more knowledge about something one *does* know. One may know the general nature of something and perform further observation to get the information required to identify it more specifically — e.g., "I see some animal moving through the brush in the distance; I'll get closer to see what kind of animal it is." Or, one may already have the prerequisites of reaching a more abstract identification, and perform the required integrative process — e.g., "These animals look similar when contrasted to those; I will try to isolate the characteristics that make them look similar, in order to use them as a basis of conceptualization."

As discussed in CHAPTER 7, "the problem of the Meno" is often used by skeptics to attack the rules of definition. The Rule of Scope says that a definition must have the same scope as the concept that it defines; it cannot be either too broad or too narrow. But to test a proposed definition against that rule, we must already know what things are units of the concept and what things are not. Yet, the skeptics say, the definition is what tells us which things are to count as units of the concept. For instance, a definition of "man" as "a two-legged animal" is too broad, because that definition would include birds. But how do we know, prior to defining "man," that birds aren't men?

The answer is that cognition is a bottom-up process. We do not begin with a definition. We do not begin with a concept. We begin with perception, including perceived similarities and differences (for first-level concepts). In the case of forming the concept "man," a child begins by *perceiving* the differences of these things (men) from other things with which they share a Conceptual Common Denominator (a characteristic possessed by other animals, including birds). The child attends to the characteristics (such as shape) in which the similarity and difference appear. Next, he isolates the human shape-range from that of other animals. Then he omits the measurements within the human shape-range, integrates the men by using a word, open-ends the "file" thus formed, and *finally* uses all this perception-based knowledge to formulate a definition. The *explicit* formulation of a definition comes only after — years after, in this case — all the hierarchically prior steps of the process have been taken. One already knows what things are and aren't men when one comes to the task of formulating a definition of "man."

"The problem of the *Meno*" serves only as a refutation of the top-down, Platonic-Rationalistic approach to knowledge.[202]

---

202 The Humean-empiricist approach could be styled "bottom-bottom." In denying the validity of abstraction and concepts, it implies that human cognition should not attempt to advance beyond the animal level.

The Prose Principle

To fully defend the bottom-up nature of knowledge, we need to recognize what I call "the prose principle." I take the name from a statement by a character in a Molière play. Upon being told the difference between poetry and prose, the character exclaimed: "By Jupiter! I've been speaking prose for forty years without even knowing it."[203]

The prose principle, then, is: *one can apprehend and use information prior to conceptualizing it.*[204]

Knowledge is often implicit before it is made explicit. Molière's character knew how to speak in prose before he knew that what he was doing could be described in that way.

The prose principle is inherent in the bottom-up approach to knowledge. The fact that perception precedes conception means that pre-conceptual awareness of information precedes the conceptualization of it. The implicit precedes the explicit. To make something "explicit" means: to grasp it conceptually, in words; prior to that act, one is aware of the thing, but pre-conceptually. This process of *explication* is essential to the growth of knowledge.

For example, long before one is able to form concepts of attributes, one is aware of attributes perceptually and *uses* that awareness to form concepts of entities. The child sees the shapes of tables, chairs, and beds, and uses that awareness to form the concept "table," but he will not for a long time be able to form the concept "shape."

Consider some cases in which it is quite difficult to name explicitly the unconceptualized information that one plainly is aware of and uses. For instance, it is fairly easy to recognize a Botticelli painting by its style. But how many people have been able to identify what aspects of the paintings they are using to do that — i.e., what Botticelli's style consists of? A similar difficulty is apparent in trying to identify what makes jazz recognizable as jazz, or a person's face recognizable as *that* person's face. It is difficult, but possible, to make explicit the means by which we recognize such things.

---

203 The character is M. Jourdain in *The Bourgeois Gentleman*.

204 This is my formulation, as a principle, of an observation that Ayn Rand makes in the Workshops on Objectivist Epistemology; she agrees with the suggestion that the first time a child abstracts, he does it without knowing that that is what he is doing: "That's right. He was talking prose and he didn't know it. That joke [from Molière] really is very important. In a certain sense, it names a great many psychological processes." [ITOE, 151]

The prose principle also applies to knowledge of method: we can apprehend and use the right method of cognition before having conceptualized and understood what we are doing. An infant is able to form concepts, even though it has no theory of how concept-formation works. Men were able to reason syllogistically long before Aristotle identified the syllogism and its rules. Early scientists were able to induce long before any principles of scientific induction had been conceptualized.

What then does the explication add? Conscious control. That control has several payoffs: the ability to avoid sources of error, the ability to devise new methods by extrapolating from old ones, and *objectivity*: the ability to distinguish between that which is valid, established, proven — vs. that which merely "feels right."

Principles drawn from attending to the clear, simple cases serve to guide us in dealing with cases that are obscure and complex. As Rand wrote in another connection, "That which is merely implicit is not in men's conscious control; they can lose it by means of other implications, without knowing what it is that they are losing or when or why." [FNI, 53]

The prose principle sweeps aside many paradoxes and claims to innate ideas. Take Noam Chomsky's arguments for regarding the principles of grammar as being innate. Children learning language, at age two or three, appear to be using rules that are much too complex for them to be able to understand or apply. This is shown, Chomsky claims, by the mistakes they make — e.g., using "mouses" as the plural of "mouse," and "gooder" instead of "better." Aren't they following such rules as: pluralize a noun by appending an "s," and: intensify an adjective by appending an "er"? The children are not old enough to understand even the words used in these rules. Thus, Chomsky claims, knowledge of the rules of grammar must be innate.

But by applying the prose principle we can unmask an equivocation here — an equivocation on the phrase "following rules." The children certainly have *implicit* rules, but not *explicit* ones. From their experience with spoken English, they have formed associations and expectations, without having any explicit identification of the rules of grammar. They do learn grammar, but by a wordless, implicit, unconceptualized process.

A child learning to ride a bicycle is, in one sense, "applying the laws of physics." But he has no explicit knowledge of those laws, so his "application of the laws of physics" means only that he is aware perceptually of the concrete pushes and pulls of the forces acting, and uses this perceptual experience in learning to ride. Since a circus bear can be trained to ride a bike, it is abundantly clear that no conceptual knowledge is required. What *is* required is perceptual awareness and perceptual-level association.

The prose principle saves us from being driven into the primitive swamp of "innate ideas"—a supposed knowledge of reality prior to cognitive contact with reality.

According to the bottom-up understanding of knowledge, the essential step in the acquisition of new knowledge is inductive, not deductive. By moving up from perception, one, in effect, reaches a height from which one looks down on the same perceptual reality, but with a wider field of view.

The top-down view of the Rationalists holds that deduction is the basic source of knowledge. But, overall, knowledge cannot be derived top down, by deduction from something still higher—with everything hanging, in effect, from a skyhook.

In regard to generalizations formed by induction, Rationalists hold that only the subsumption of a generalization under a still wider one provides proof and certainty. For them, the starting point of the induction itself is merely a guess or "a free invention of the intellect" (as in the notoriously unsuccessful "model-building" approach of many economists).

This much is true: a generalization, even when proved with certainty by a reduction to perception, does gain something from being subsumed under a wider generalization. The gain, however, is not in certainty (unless the earlier evidence was inconclusive), but in *understanding*.

For instance, it is a cognitive advance to subsume "Shoplifting is wrong" under "Violating others' rights is wrong," or to subsume Kepler's laws under Newton's. Such subsumptions add to our knowledge, but they are not the primary means of acquiring and validating knowledge.

The cognitive value of subsuming a generalization under a wider one does not represent shoring up an induction by a deduction. The subsumption's cognitive value comes from the fact that it integrates an induction with other *inductions*. Such integration strengthens and clarifies a group of independent inductions, but only because the entire structure rests on perception.

By analogy, in building a cabin, the walls support the roof, rather than vice-versa; but the roof adds stability and strength to the whole structure, including each wall—by more fully connecting the walls to each other.

Induction is the primary means of acquiring new conceptual knowledge. To doubt or question the validity of induction itself is to doubt or question conceptual knowledge itself—which is self-refuting (see CHAPTER 7). Thus, it is a mistake to attempt to "rescue" induction by attempting to reduce it to a disguised deduction or to shore it up by deduction.

Peikoff's theory of induction shows *how* induction works; it is not the misbegotten attempt to "prove induction is valid." And the prose principle makes a valuable additional point: we do not need a theory of how induction works in order to induce. Just as, in the physical realm, man did not have to understand the process of combustion in order to tame fire, or utilize a theory of concept-formation in order to form concepts, so one does not need a theory of induction in order to induce. In each case, discovering how the process works is of great value; it brings the process under better control and extends its possibilities, but one can use a physical or cognitive method before one knows how it works, or even has conceptualized the process involved.

Induction is a means of learning from experience by forming the relevant concepts, so that we can then apply them to observed facts; induction is not a disguised deduction.

Induction proceeds by identifying causal connections, and the causal connections grounding first-level generalizations are available *perceptually*. When a toddler pushes a spoon, a pencil, or a ball, he sees and feels the causation. He feels his arm and hand's effort, he sees his hand moving forward and moving the object forward in front of it. He feels the object's resistance to his push and his overcoming of that resistance. He feels the greater effort required to move larger objects, and feels the wall resist and thwart his push. Such perceptual data are what the child uses for his first generalizations.

Just as a child learning to ride a bicycle does not make any explicit "appeal to the laws of physics," so an infant learning that pushing objects makes them move does not make any explicit "appeal to the law of causality." He is aware of causal connections long before he can identify them as "causal connections." He is speaking prose, but he doesn't know it.

Objections to induction stem from the hidden assumption that all learning is deductive, as if an infant needed syllogisms in order to learn or "prove" that pushing things makes them move, that ice is cold, that cookies crumble. That assumption reveals how the top-down, Rationalist approach completely inverts the hierarchy of knowledge.

Beyond the perceptual level, all cognitive processes are hierarchical. By the nature of a hierarchy, its base is a special case, something quite different from the elements that depend on that base. Everyone in the military has to take orders from those of higher rank, but the Commander-in-Chief does not; every organism is composed of cells, but one-celled organisms (from which the others evolved) are not; every concept rests on preceding concepts — except the base: first-level concepts, formed from perception. Treating a hierarchy's base as if it were equivalent to derivative elements is a prevalent form of hierarchy-inversion.[205] In the attacks on induction, that fallacy is committed by treating first-level generalizations as subject to the same requirements as higher-level generalizations — specifically, in requiring justification, proof, or validation in the case of first-level generalizations. One must recognize the context: the facts giving rise to the need for justification. Justification is needed for inductions that are fallible, but first-level generalizations are no more subject to error than are a child's first conceptualizations. Just as there is no such thing as a toddler getting the concept "cookie" wrong, so there is no such thing as him getting "Cookies crumble" wrong. "Wrong" has no meaning in either case. (Nor does "right.") In forming his first concepts, the child sees the similarities he sees, and in forming first-level generalization, the child sees the causality he sees. (Moreover, there is no meaning to "right vs. wrong" or "valid vs. invalid" before concepts of consciousness have been formed.)

For these basic conceptual acts, there is no such alternative as "justified vs. unjustified," "proven or unproven," "hypothetical or certain." Those issues involve reducing the higher levels back to their base, but here it is the base that we are considering.

By analogy, a lawyer might get into the habit of asking about every law, "Is it constitutional?" But if he holds the context and remembers that the base of a hierarchy is not just another element in it, he would not dream of asking: "Is the Constitution constitutional?" But it is no better to ask: "Is the child *justified* in concluding that pushing a ball moves it or that cookies crumble?"[206]

Validation is reduction to perception. The first inductions need no reduction because they don't climb a ladder of abstractions away from perception. The prose principle's negative corollary is: one does not have to know that a process is logical in order for it to be logical. Understanding what justifies a cognitive procedure requires the development of epistemology, and that comes only long after people have been unselfconsciously using that procedure to acquire knowledge.

---

205 Two other forms are: question-begging (*petitio principii*), which attempts to use a derivative to establish its own base, and what could be termed "base-negation," the attempt to use a derivative to negate its own base. Hierarchy-inversion itself is a species within the wider category of hierarchy-violation: any attempt to use an item apart from the prior items that give it meaning and/or validity — e.g., floating abstractions and arbitrary assertions.

206 The wider point is: reduction to a base is a procedure that cannot be demanded of the base itself. (In mathematical recursion, the process of deriving all subsequent elements from the base cannot be required of that base. E.g., a "number" is 1 or any successor of a number — which rules out asking: "Of what number is 1 the successor?")

(Even after one has learned the need to check one's conclusions to determine whether they represent knowledge or mistaken belief, one does not have to know how to justify an idea before being justified in using it. For instance, centuries before Pythagoras came up with his proof of the theorem that bears his name, Egyptian builders knew and applied the geometrical facts that he later proved.)

One does not have to know that one knows before one can know. One can apprehend and use information prior to the conceptual identification of that information. That's the prose principle.

SOME HISTORY

In the broad history of thought, the major proponents of the bottom-up approach are Aristotle and those who accept this aspect of his epistemology (notably, Aquinas, Bacon, and Locke). The major proponents of the top-down approach are Plato and the Rationalists (notably, Descartes and Kant). The clash between Aristotle and Plato reverberates throughout the realm of ideas, both in individuals and in cultures. [See OPAR, 451–460.]

The battle between the two theories takes place on a highly abstract level, but it is impossible to overstate the practical, real-world importance of their impact upon a culture. Science and the Industrial Revolution arose from and depended upon the Aristotelian recognition of the primacy of existence and the primacy of perception. And it was the Platonic primacy of consciousness and primacy of concepts philosophy that led to contempt for this perceptually given world and the abandonment of the achievements of Greco-Roman civilization, plunging mankind into the long, stagnant night of the Dark Ages. In denigrating reality and perception, the Platonists reject life on this earth.

Do I exaggerate? Plato calls the body "a prison" and "the tomb of the soul," [CRATYLUS, 400C]. He says that "true philosophers make dying their profession," [PHAEDO, 67E] and proclaims that a man should have "trained himself throughout his life to live in a state as close as possible to death." [PHAEDO, 67E]

In holding that conceptual knowledge is gained by turning inward to align the soul with a "higher" realm, Plato treats perception as illusion, and holds that sensory observation is a *distraction* from "true knowledge," which is of a non-perceivable "higher dimension":

> ... if we are ever to have pure knowledge of anything, we must get rid of the body and contemplate things by themselves with the soul by itself. ... No pure knowledge is possible in the company of the body. ... So long as we are alive, we shall continue closest to knowledge if we avoid as much as we can all contact and association with the body ... and instead of allowing ourselves to become infected with its nature, purify ourselves from it until God himself gives us deliverance [i.e., death]. [PHAEDO, 66E-67A]

For Plato, learning and discovery never actually occur: all knowledge is innately present in the soul at birth, having been acquired before birth when the soul dwelt in the world of Forms; what we take to be the discovery of new knowledge, he says, is really the recollection of this innate knowledge — a doctrine that is utterly incompatible with science, and with the technological-industrial progress science makes possible.

Descartes' form of the primacy of concepts, while discarding Plato's open mysticism, nonetheless severs knowledge from sensory perception:

> ... no science is acquired except by mental intuition or deduction. ... The first principles themselves are given by intuition alone. ... By *intuition* I understand, not the fluctuating testimony of the senses ... but the conception which an unclouded and attentive mind gives us ... [DESCARTES, RULES III & IV]

Descartes' "intuition" is, of course, hopelessly subjective. To establish an idea's truth, we are to turn inward to inspect the qualities of the ideas as such (their clarity and distinctness), not their relation to perceptual reality. Cartesian "intuition" is the kind of thing that has given self-evidence a bad name. But, in fact, the *perceptually* self-evident has nothing in common with the anti-perceptual "intuition" Descartes is positing.

Kant synthesizes Plato with Descartes, adding a skeptical twist from Hume. Following Plato, Kant holds that the world we perceive through our senses is shadowy, not fully real; the "higher" realm is now called the "noumenal" world, the innate ideas are now called "categories." Following Descartes, Kant's philosophy starts from within consciousness and regards awareness of the external world as problematic; Descartes' "intuition" now becomes the voice of "noumenal" reality heard through (of all things) our alleged sense of "moral duty." Following Hume, Kant regards the external world as utterly unknowable (except for this alleged sense of "duty"); Hume's "habits of asso-ciation" become Kant's innate "synthesizing categories."

Beneath Kant's notoriously convoluted terminology is an all-out separa-tion of the mind from reality. Both perception and conception are cut off from "things as they are in themselves," which remain forever unknowable. Science deals only with "appearances" ("phenomena"), and is, in effect, held to be a shared delusion.

The contemporary attack on science by Popper, Kuhn, and Feyerabend is grounded in Kantianism. In their post-modern version of Kant, science deals not in truth but in public relations, and is the embodiment not of reason but of faith.[207] Thomas Kuhn writes that the scientist must "have faith that the new paradigm will succeed with the many large problems that confront it, knowing only that the older paradigm has failed with a few. A decision of that kind can only be made on faith." [KUHN 1970, 158]

Among more recent philosophers, there are many who regard percep-tion as uncertain, impoverished, concept-laden, non-cognitive. In one form or another, their position is that perception cannot serve as the base of the conceptual level. If so, there are only two ways one can defend concepts: by claiming that concepts are based on and justified by something non-per-ceptual (e.g., innate ideas or mystical revelations) — or by claiming that con-cepts do not need any base — the position known as "anti-foundationalism."

The founder of anti-foundationalism was Richard Rorty. In 1986, Rorty wrote: "Nothing grounds our [cognitive] practices, nothing legitimizes them, nothing shows them to be in touch with the way things really are." [RORTY, 753]

This is utter bankruptcy. The very existence of epistemology depends upon the recognition that beliefs need justification. Such justification must consist in identifying the foundation — the earlier knowledge — on which a con-clusion rests. The alternative to reducing an idea to its base in perception is Platonism unhinged, Platonism gone native, Platonism without a World of Forms, without *any* metaphysical base, championing instead "networks" of interrelated beliefs supported by nothing. Is it supported by "coherence" (consistency)? No, because coherence itself has no support, according to anti-foundationalism. And, remember, even a paranoid schizophrenic's beliefs have that same apparent consistency.

---

207 See Kuhn, 158 and Lakatos & Musgrave, 228–229. On the Kantian roots of this phenom-enon, see Lennox, 1981.

The actual "legitimizer" of beliefs, according to anti-foundationalism, is *the beliefs of other people.* In a confession of profound psychological dependence, of the inability to conceive of objective fact or independent judgment, the anti-foundationalists blithely assert that conformity to others' opinions is the only conceivable justification for an idea. Undeterred by the 20th century's spectacle of millions surrendering their minds and their lives to vicious notions promulgated by Stalin, Hitler, and fatwa-issuing ayatollahs, these pseudo-philosophers nonetheless expect to find safety in justification by "consensus" or "social practices" or ... whatever their latest jargon is for: *what other people say.*

Consider Rorty's response to John McDowell, when McDowell raised objections to Rorty's social view of justification. McDowell used the example of the bogus claims that two chemists made to having achieved "cold fusion." McDowell points out that

> ... whether or not cold fusion has occurred is not the same as whether or not saying it has occurred will pass muster in the current practice [i.e., is in line with the beliefs of one's peers]. ... Without this difference, there would be no ground for conceiving one's activity as making claims about, say, whether or not cold fusion has occurred, as opposed to achieving unison with one's fellows in some perhaps purely decorative activity on a level with a kind of dancing. [BRANDOM, 125]

Here is Rorty's response:

> What, I still want to ask, is so "mere" about getting together with your fellow inquirers and agreeing on what to say and believe? ... How do I tell a world constituted by linguistic practices from a world constituted by facts ... ? *I have no idea.*[208] [BRANDOM, 125–126, emphasis added]

---

208 Rorty "has no idea" what a fact is because, following Wilfrid Sellars, he rejects perception as the base of knowledge. The anti-foundationalist motto is: "Only a belief can justify another belief." The source of this perverse position is the failure to understand how concepts can be objectively formed from perceptual data. The solution is the Objectivist understanding of concept-formation (plus the recognition that perception is a form of *awareness*). [SEE BAYER, 2011]

In all this, Rorty admits that he is taking Kant straight, without a "sugar coating" and as "replacing objectivity with solidarity." [209] [IBID.] In that regard, Rorty is correct: the destruction of objectivity is the ultimate result and goal of Kant's entire system. "I have therefore found it necessary," Kant wrote, "to deny *knowledge* in order to make room for *faith*." [KANT 1958, B XXXI]

To understand contemporary philosophy, one must understand what Kant did to "deny knowledge."

The Kantian Reversal

Kant reversed a crucial distinction, the distinction between the *what* and the *how*—between what one knows and how one knows it. Kant turns the *means* of awareness into the only *object* of awareness. We cannot know extra-mental reality, Kant says, because our means of awareness stand in the way; we are incapable of knowing "things as they are in themselves"; we can know only the *appearances* of things:

> . . . we can therefore have no knowledge of any object as a thing in itself, but only in so far as it is . . . an appearance. [KANT 1958, B XVI]

But, contrary to Kant, an "appearance" is *how* we perceive and know the object. Objects are grasped in a certain *form*, and *what* is thereby known is the *object*, the thing in reality.

By illicitly making the appearance into the *object* of awareness, Kant is able to claim that what we are aware of is the wrong thing—not tables and rivers but only the appearances of tables and rivers. Because we see a table by a certain means and in a certain form, we cannot see the table; we see instead our sight of the table.[210] Likewise, because we conceive tables by a certain means and in a certain form, what we are conceiving is our concept, not tables. The cognitive *how* turns into a *what* that blocks our way to knowing reality, locking us up inside our own minds. The existence of a means of cognition is held to make cognition impossible. Thus, Rand's immortal demolition of Kant:

---

209 "Solidarity" is a euphemism for cognitive surrender to the smiles and frowns of others.

210 As H. J. Paton, a premier Kant scholar, puts it: ". . . the world we know is a world of appearance." [PATON, 62] But "the world we know" means the object of awareness. E.g., when we look at or touch an apple, what we see and feel, Kant claims, is not the apple, but appearances internal to us. Here, "appearances" and "internal" are stolen concepts.

His argument, in essence, ran as follows: man is *limited* to a consciousness of a specific nature, which perceives by specific means and no others, therefore, his consciousness is not valid; man is blind, because he has eyes — deaf, because he has ears — deluded, because he has a mind — and the things he perceives do not exist, *because* he perceives them. [FNI, 32]

Kant does not shy away from but embraces the consequence: a thoroughgoing, blatant primacy of consciousness:

Hitherto it has been assumed that all our knowledge must conform to objects.... [We may] have more success in the tasks of metaphysics, if we suppose that objects must conform to our knowledge. [KANT 1958, B XVI]

When the *how* is turned into the *what*, process becomes everything, and substantive content becomes irrelevant or impossible. This *formalism*, which infects every aspect of modern culture, is another consequence of Kant's destructive legacy.

Consider how widely formalism reigns. It rules foreign policy (which consists in diplomacy and "talks" while ignoring the *nature* of the regimes involved), in painting (where the *object* has disappeared, leaving only formal relationships among color patches), in ethics (where "sincere intentions" and "compassionate" attitudes count, but results do not), in economics (where the leading journals appear as though they were journals of mathematics, filled with equations relating to the economists' own constructs, not to actual production and trade), in education (where "progressive" educators hold that "students need to learn not a body of knowledge but 'how-to' skills" [211]), and in constitutional law (where "due process" has become "substantive," while what is actually substantive — individual rights — is ignored).

Kant's conversion of the means of cognition into a barrier to cognition has corrupted even the field of logic, turning it into something purely formal, into the avowedly arbitrary manipulation of avowedly meaningless

---

211 E. D. Hirsch, Jr., in an article deploring the formalism: "Students would be better off gaining knowledge by studying real subject matters in a sensible, cumulative sequence. Instead, elementary schools are dominated by content-indifferent exercises ... on the erroneous assumption that reading comprehension is a formal skill akin to typing." [HIRSCH, 2012]

"inscriptions and utterances," as it is put, rather than being the method of proceeding from truth to truth. Kant was well aware of this implication: "[L]ogic . . . is justified in abstracting . . . from all objects of knowledge and their differences, leaving the understanding nothing to deal with save itself and its form." [KANT, 1958, B IX]

Or, as Wittgenstein more succinctly put the same doctrine, "all propositions of logic say the same thing, to wit nothing." [WITTGENSTEIN, 2011, 53]

In fact, logic is the means of staying in contact with perceptual reality and of using the unit-economy provided by concepts to extend our grasp of the world ever further. Logic is not severed from content; it is the means of expanding that content, in accordance with the metaphysically given *identity* of man's consciousness.

Rand identified the root of all Kantian systems: their "attempts to regard *identity* as the *disqualifying* element of consciousness." [ITOE, 80] Objectivism proceeds from exactly the opposite premise: the identity of consciousness is its means of operation, which enables it to grasp reality.

Of those means, I would select three facts as the essentials:

1. Perception provides data that are metaphysically given and inerrant.
2. A concept integrates that data by measurement-omission.
3. Conceptual integration provides unit-economy ("the crow epistemology").

Thus, Rand was able to show how (to modify her wording) identity is the qualifying element of consciousness — i.e., its enabler.

In addition, Rand identified the fact that man's volition, his free will, is not a blind, disruptive factor independent of reason but is precisely one's power to use reason — i.e., to initiate a process of focused thought, oversee it, subject it to the canons of logic, and thus attain objectivity.

This radically new understanding of volition allowed her to integrate volition with the identity of both the knower and the known: consciousness has a determinate means of knowing a determinate world; man's choice is to use those means or not.

> . . . man exists and his mind exists. Both are part of nature, both possess a specific identity. The attribute of volition does not contradict the fact of identity, just as the existence of living organisms does not contradict the existence of inanimate matter. . . . [M]an is able to initiate and direct his mental action only in accordance with the nature (the *identity*) of his consciousness.

His volition is limited to his cognitive processes; he has the power to identify (and to conceive of rearranging) the elements of reality, but not the power to alter them. He has the power to use his cognitive faculty as its nature requires, but not the power to alter it nor to escape the consequences of its misuse. [PWNI, 26]

Both the world and consciousness have identity; the facts of reality are firm and absolute; the methods of cognition a given man adopts are a matter of his choice, but there is a *right* choice: the one that accords with the requirements of cognition that are set by the identity of his cognitive equipment.

Conceptual knowledge is not automatic. Nor is it infallible. Even when a man chooses the right method and takes into account all the facts he knows, he can yet be mistaken. Logic is a necessary condition of knowing, but not a sufficient one. It is not illogical to conclude that the stick half-submerged in water is bent, but the fact remains that the stick is not bent. The senses didn't err, but the intellect *did*. The fact that such occasions are rare is not the point. The point is whether or not one can accept the fact that even a fully logical, rational process can reach a mistaken conclusion — a fact that does not negate or call into question the knowledge that one does possess.

The majority of philosophers have not been willing or able to accept the fact that there is no immunity from error. They have assumed that only the infallible can be certain, believing that without a metaphysical guarantee against error, there can be no certainty.

Some men, upon discovering that they can be wrong, pretend that they can gain infallibility by relying on supposed revelations or following rote rules (e.g., Rationalistic deduction). This is intrinsicism. Others respond by retreating into a world of "appearance" or "seeming" or "true for you, not for me." This is subjectivism, which is best captured by an epistemological paraphrase of Dostoyevsky: Since God is dead, everything is uncertain.

Both sides assume that only an infallible, divinely guaranteed certainty would be valid. They differ only as to whether or not that infallibility can be obtained. Both sides long for the epistemic safety they felt as children, the sense that parents and teachers were infallible authorities. Though having matured enough to realize the contrary, they have not matured enough to take a first-hand look at the epistemic situation, define rational standards for themselves, and take responsibility for their own thought and judgment. Instead, they continue to long for an automatic guarantee — a guarantee from another consciousness. They do not welcome the responsibility of choice, but rebel against it, feeling "a stranger and afraid in a world I never made," as Housman's poem puts it.[212] In this regard, Rand's description of the logical positivist applies to all those who long for automatic certainty:

> Like a spoiled, disillusioned child, who had expected predigested capsules of automatic knowledge, a logical positivist stamps his foot at reality and cries that context, integration, mental effort and first-hand inquiry are too much to expect of him, that he rejects so demanding a method of cognition, and that he will manufacture his own "constructs" from now on. (This amounts, in effect, to the declaration: "Since the intrinsic has failed us, the subjective is our only alternative.") [ITOE, 67–68]

Choice and the responsibility it brings are not to be denied. Nor do they threaten rationality. In fact, our fundamental and all-pervading choice is precisely whether to be rational or irrational. Choice is our power to free ourselves from merely reactive response. Our volition gives us the ability to make an unbiased assessment of the facts, to be self-critical and objective. Man's ability to focus his mind and set it to the task of knowing and living in reality is what makes conceptual knowledge and rational certainty possible.

Rational certainty, as opposed to the mystics' desire for automatic immunity to error, is not only possible, in regard to fundamentals it is normal — at least for a rational man. But the standard of certainty is not intrinsic. Nor is it subjective. Epistemic standards cannot demand omniscience, but they do demand doing what is possible: non-contradictory integration into the sum of one's knowledge. As I noted in discussing the need for logic:

> The issue is not: "What would one conclude if one were omniscient?" but: "what is the proper conclusion to draw given all the facts available now?" Epistemic standards are prospective, not retrospective. [CH 6, 204.]

The alternative is not commandments vs. whims, dogmatism vs. skepticism, or standards without choice (intrinsicism) vs. choice without standards (subjectivism). The proper alternative to all such dichotomies is: the choice to apply rational standards.

---

212 Surprisingly, Housman's poem opens with a vibrant assertion of proper independence. [A. E. Housman, "The Laws of God"]

SUMMARY

Knowledge, Rand writes, is "a mental grasp of a fact(s) of reality, reached either by perceptual observation or by a process of reason based on perceptual observation." [ITOE, 35] The method of reason is logic. Thus, conceptual knowledge is acquired by applying logic to perception, deriving ideas from perception and reducing them back to perception, integrating them into the full context.

I close by revisiting the inspiring passage in which Rand brings to life the meaning of a commitment to reason.

> It consists of a method of using one's consciousness, best designated by the term "conceptualizing." It is not a passive state of registering random impressions. It is an actively sustained process of identifying one's impressions in conceptual terms, of integrating every event and every observation into a conceptual context, of grasping relationships, differences, similarities in one's perceptual material and of abstracting them into new concepts, of drawing inferences, of making deductions, of reaching conclusions, of asking new questions and discovering new answers and expanding one's knowledge into an ever-growing sum. The faculty that directs this process, the faculty that works by means of concepts, is: *reason.* [VOS, 21–22]

And that's ... *how we know.*

BIBLIOGRAPHY

APHRODISAS, ALEXANDER OF, *Quaestiones* (1994), R. W. Sharples (trans.), Cornell University Press.

ARISTOTLE, *The Complete Works of Aristotle* (1984), J. Barnes (ed.), Bollingen Library Series, LXXI 2.

ARISTOTLE, *The Basic Works of Aristotle* (1941), R. McKeon (ed.), Random House.

AYER, A. J. (1954), *Philosophical Essays,* Macmillan.

BACH-Y-RITA, P., ET AL. (1969), Vision Substitution by Tactile Image Projection, *Nature,* 221.

BAYER, BENJAMIN (2011), A Role for Abstractionism in a Direct Realist Foundationalism, *Synthese,* vol. 180, no. 3, 357–389.

BERGSON, HENRI (1946), *The Creative Mind,* The Philosophical Library.

BINSWANGER, HARRY (1981), The Possible Dream, *The Objectivist Forum,* vol. 2, nos. 1 & 2.

BINSWANGER, HARRY (1986), The Goal-Directedness of Living Action, *The Objectivist Forum,* vol. 7, no. 4.

BINSWANGER, HARRY (1989), *Consciousness as Identification* (audio), https://estore.aynrand.org

BINSWANGER, HARRY (1990), *The Biological Basis of Teleological Concepts,* The Ayn Rand Institute Press.

BINSWANGER, HARRY (1991), Volition as Cognitive Self-Regulation, *Organizational Behavior and Human Decision Processing*, vol. 50, no. 2, 154–178.

BINSWANGER, HARRY (1999), *Free Will* (audio), https://estore.aynrand.org

BLANSHARD, BRAND (1939), *The Nature of Thought*, George Allen & Unwin Ltd.

BOYER, CARL (1968), *A History of Mathematics*, John Wiley & Sons.

BRANDOM, ROBERT (2000), Response, in *Rorty and His Critics*, Blackwell.

CHALMERS, DAVID (1997), *The Conscious Mind*, Oxford University Press.

DE WULF, MAURICE (1959), *The System of Thomas Aquinas*, Dover.

DESCARTES, RENÉ, *Rules for the Direction of the Mind*, in Haldane & Ross (eds.) *Philosophic Works of Descartes* (1955), Dover.

DESCARTES, RENÉ, *Meditations on First Philosophy*, in *Essential Works of Descartes* (1961), L. Blair (trans.), Bantam Books.

DEWEY, JOHN (2008), *The Logic of Inquiry*, Searching Press.

DOBZHANSKY, THEODOSIUS (1967), The Road Traversed and the Road Ahead, in I. W. Knobloch (ed.), *Readings in Biological Science*, pp. 441–466, Meredith.

DOBZHANSKY, THEODOSIUS (1970), *Genetics of the Evolutionary Process*, Columbia University Press.

EFRON, ROBERT (1966), What is Perception? *Boston Studies in the Philosophy of Science*, vol. 4, 1969, 137–173, Springer.

FREUD, SIGMUND (1960), *The Ego and the Id*, W. W. Norton.

GIBSON, J. J. (1950), *The Perception of the Visual World*, Houghton Mifflin.

GIBSON, J. J. (1986), *The Ecological Approach to Visual Perception*, Lawrence Erlbaum Associates.

GÖDEL, KURT (1992), *On Formally Undecidable Propositions of Principia Mathematica and Related Systems*, Dover.

GOODMAN, NELSON (1955), *Fact, Fiction, and Forecast*, Bobbs-Merrill.

HARRIMAN, DAVID (2010), *The Logical Leap*, New American Library.

HARRIS, SAM (2012), Free Will, *The National Post* (Toronto), July 31, 2012, A15.

HAWKINS, J. & BLAKESLEE, S. (2005), *On Intelligence*, St. Martin's Griffin.

HEIDEGGER, MARTIN (1929), What Is Metaphysics? [Inaugural lecture to the combined faculties], University of Freiburg.

HELD, R. & HEIN, A. (1963), Movement-Produced Stimulation in the
    Development of Visually Guided Behavior, *Journal of Comparative
    and Physiological Psychology*, vol. 56, no. 5, 872.
HIRSCH, E. D. JR. (2012), Vocabulary Declines with Unspeakable Results,
    The Wall Street Journal, Dec. 12, 2012, A 15.
HITLER, ADOLF (1928),*Volkische Beobachter,* in C. Cohen (ed.),
    Communism, Fascism, and Democracy (1962),
    University of Michigan Press.
HUME, DAVID (1961), *A Treatise of Human Nature*, Dolphin Books.
INNOCENT III (1966), On the Misery of Man, in B. Murchland,
    Two Views of Man, Frederick Ungar.
JAMES, WILLIAM (1890), *Principles of Psychology*, Henry Holt & Co.
JONAS, HANS (1966), *The Phenomenon of Life*, Harper & Row.
KALISH, DONALD (1966), quoted in: What (If Anything) to Expect
    from Today's Philosophers, *Time Magazine*, Jan. 7, 1966.
KANT, IMMANUEL (1958), *Critique of Pure Reason,*The Modern Library.
KANT, IMMANUEL (1949), On a Supposed Right to Lie from Altruistic
    Motives, L. W. Beck (transl.) in *Immanuel Kant: Critique of Practical
    Reason and Other Writings in Moral Philosophy,* University
    of Chicago Press.
KLINE, MORRIS (1980), *Mathematics: The Loss of Certainty,*
    Oxford University Press.
KNAPP, ROBERT (forthcoming), *Mathematics is About the World.*
KUHN, THOMAS (1970), *The Structure of Scientific Revolutions,*
    2nd ed., University of Chicago Press.
KUNZE, A. & MORONEY, J. (eds.) (1999), *Glossary of Objectivist
    Definitions*, Second Renaissance Books.
LAKATOS, I. & MUSGRAVE, A. (eds.) (1965), *Criticism and the Growth
    of Knowledge*, Cambridge University Press.
LENNOX, JAMES G. (ed.), (2000), *Aristotle's Philosophy of Biology,*
    Cambridge University Press.
LENNOX, JAMES G. (1981), The Anti-Philosophy of Science,
    The Objectivist Forum, vol. 2, no. 3.
LEROY, CHARLES G. (1870), *The Intelligence and Perfectibility of Animals
    from a Philosophic Point of View,* Chapman and Hall.
LOCKE, JOHN (1959), *An Essay Concerning Human Understanding*, Dover.
McDERMOTT, TERRY (2011), *101 Theory Drive*, Pantheon Books.

MILL, J. S. (1950), *A System of Logic*, Hafner.

MILL, J. S. (1957), *Utilitarianism*, Bobbs-Merrill.

MILLER, GEORGE A. (1956), The Magical Number Seven, Plus or Minus Two: Some Limits on Our Capacity for Processing Information, *The Psychological Review*, vol. 63, 81–97.

MONTESSORI, MARIA (1912), *The Montessori Method*, Transaction.

NAGEL, ERNEST (1944), Logic without Ontology, in Y. H. Krikorian (ed.), *Naturalism and the Human Spirit*, Columbia University Press.

NOË, ALVA (2004), *Action in Perception*, MIT Press.

PARKER, F. H. (1953), Realistic Epistemology, in John Wild (ed.), *The Return to Reason*, pp. 153–159, Henry Regnery Co.

PATON, H. J. (1970), *Kant's Metaphysics of Experience*, vol. I, George Allen and Unwin.

PEIKOFF, LEONARD (1976), *The Philosophy of Objectivism*, Lecture series, https://estore.aynrand.org

PEIKOFF, LEONARD (1988), Fact and Value. *The Intellectual Activist*, www.aynrand.org

PEIKOFF, LEONARD (1991), *Objectivism: The Philosophy of Ayn Rand*, Meridian.

PEIKOFF, LEONARD (2013), *Objective Communication*, NAL Trade.

PIERSON, L. & TROUT, M. (2005), *What Is Consciousness For?* Cogprints (preprint), www.cogprints.org/4482.

PLATO, *Meno* (Guthrie, transl.), in Hamilton & Cairns (eds.), *The Collected Dialogues of Plato* (1961), Bollingen Series LXXI, Pantheon Books.

PLATO, *Phaedo* (Tredennick, transl.), in Hamilton & Cairns (eds.), *The Collected Dialogues of Plato* (1961), Bollingen Series LXXI, Pantheon Books.

PLATO, *Republic*, F. M. Cornford (transl.), *The Republic of Plato* (1945), Oxford University Press.

QUINE, W. V. O. (1953a), On What There Is, *From a Logical Point of View*, Harper Torchbooks.

QUINE, W. V. O. (1953b), Two Dogmas of Empiricism, *From a Logical Point of View*, Harper Torchbooks.

RAND, AYN (1957), *Atlas Shrugged*, New American Library.

RAND, AYN (1961), *For the New Intellectual*, Signet.

RAND, AYN (1964), *The Virtue of Selfishness*, Signet.

RAND, AYN (1966), Our Cultural Value-Deprivation,
in *The Voice of Reason* (1990) L. Peikoff (ed.), Meridian.

RAND, AYN (1967), *Capitalism: The Unknown Ideal*, Signet.

RAND, AYN (1971), *The Romantic Manifesto*, Signet.

RAND, AYN (1982), *Philosophy: Who Needs It*, Signet.

RAND, AYN (1990), *Introduction to Objectivist Epistemology*,
expanded 2nd edition, H. Binswanger (ed.), Meridian.

RAND, AYN (1990), *The Voice of Reason*, L. Peikoff (ed.), Meridian.

RAND, AYN (1997), *Journals of Ayn Rand*, D. Harriman (ed.), Dutton.

RAND, AYN (1999), The Comprachicos, in Peter Schwartz (ed.),
Return of the Primitive, Meridian.

RANDALL, JOHN H., JR. (1940), *The Making of the Modern Mind*,
Riverside Press.

RIGGS, L. A. & RATLIFF, F., The effects of counteracting the normal
movements of the eye, *Journal of the Optical Society of America*,
vol. 42, 872–873.

RORTY, RICHARD (1986), From Logic to Language to Play, *Proceedings
and Addresses of the American Philosophical Association*, vol. 59, no. 5.

RUBY, LIONEL (2000), *Logic: An Introduction*, Paper Tiger.

SALMIERI, GREGORY (2006), *Objectivist Epistemology in Outline*,
Ayn Rand Institute Summer Conference (audio)
https://estore.aynrand.org

SALMIERI, GREGORY (2013), *Conceptualization and Justification*, in
A. Gotthelf & J. G. Lennox (eds.), *Concepts and Their Role in Knowledge:
Reflections on Objectivist Epistemology*, Ayn Rand Society Philosophic
Studies Series, University of Pittsburgh Press.

SARNAT, H. B. (1985), The brain of the planarian as the ancestor
of the human brain, *The Canadian Journal of Neurological Sciences*,
vol. 12, no. 4.

SARNAT, H. B. (2002), When does a ganglion become a brain? *Seminars in
Pediatric Neurology*, vol. 9, no. 4.

SCHWARTZ, J. & BEGLEY, S. (2003), *The Mind and the Brain:
Neuroplasticity and the Power of Mental Force*, Harper Perennial.

SIMPSON, GEORGE G. (1964), *This View of Life*, Harcourt, Brace & World.

SPINOZA, BARUCH (1949), *Ethics*, Hafner.

STACE, W. T. (1955), *The Philosophy of Hegel*, Dover.

STALIN, JOSEF (1924), *The Foundations of Leninism*, in C. Cohen (1962), *Communism, Fascism, and Democracy* (1962), University of Michigan.

TALLIS, RAYMOND (2011), *Aping Mankind*, Acumen.

WATSON, JOHN B. (1970), *Behaviorism*, W. W. Norton.

WINDELBAND, WILHELM (1958), *A History of Western Philosophy*, Harper Torchbooks.

WITTGENSTEIN, LUDWIG (1958), *The Blue and Brown Books*, Harper Torchbooks.

WITTGENSTEIN, LUDWIG (2011), *Tractatus Logico-Philosophicus*, Empire Books.

INDEX

Prepared by Allison T. Kunze

Printed in Great Britain
by Amazon

48591091R00235